The Mitchell Beazley Atlas of World

Wildlife

The Atlas of World
Wildlife

with a foreword by Sir Julian Huxley FRS

Mitchell Beazley

Consultant editor
Sir Julian Huxley MA, DSc, FRS

The Mitchell Beazley Atlas of World Wildlife has been produced in consultation with the Zoological Society of London and with contributions from leading zoologists throughout the world.

Editor Martyn Bramwell
Text Editor Victor Stevenson
Assistant editor David Black
Researcher Brendon Stewart
Art editor Sheilagh Noble
Designer Marion Neville
Assistant designer Susan Casebourne
Picture researcher Kate Parish

The Mitchell Beazley Atlas of World Wildlife
© Mitchell Beazley Ltd., 1973

Reprinted in new format 1980

ISBN 0 85533 261 1

Relief maps on pages 21, 41, 61, 87, 105, 119, 135
© Rand McNally & Company 1973.

Printed in the Netherlands

Gwynne Vevers M.B.E., D.Phil., F.L.S., F.I.Biol.
Assistant Director of Science, The London Zoo; Secretary to the Publications Committee, Zoological Society of London.
Prof. A. G. Bannikov
Academy of Veterinary Sciences, Moscow
Iain Bishop O.B.E., M.Sc.
Leader of the Royal Society/Royal Geographical Society Expedition to Central Brazil, 1967–1969.
Nigel Bonner B.Sc., M.I.Biol.
Head of Seals Research Division, Institute for Marine Environmental Research, Plymouth.
Prof. A. J. Cain D.Phil., M.A.
Professor of Zoology, University of Liverpool.
Nicole Duplaix-Hall M.Sc., B.Sc., F.L.S.
Editor, International Zoo Yearbook.
John M. Edington Ph.D., B.Sc.
Senior Lecturer in Zoology, University College, Cardiff.
M. Ann Edington Ph.D., M.Sc., B.Sc.
Post-doctoral Fellow in Zoology, University College, Cardiff.
Martin Holdgate Ph.D., M.A., F.I.Biol.
Formerly Chief Biologist, British Antarctic Survey.
Alan Longhurst D.Sc., Ph.D.
Deputy Director, Institute for Marine Environmental Research, Plymouth.

Ian MacPhail
Former Director-General, The World Wildlife Fund.
T. C. Marples Ph.D., B.Sc.
Lecturer in Zoology, Australian National University, Canberra.
Richard Marshall M.A.
R. D. Martin Ph.D., B.Sc.
Lecturer in Physical Anthropology, University College, London.
John Oates B.Sc.
New York Zoological Society and Rockefeller University, New York.
John Pernetta B.Sc.
Animal Behaviour Research Group, University of Oxford.
John Phillipson Ph.D., M.A., B.Sc., F.I.Biol.
Reader in Animal Ecology, University of Oxford.
Noel Simon
Formerly Head of Operations Intelligence Unit, International Union for the Conservation of Nature, Morges, Switzerland.
Bernard Stonehouse D.Phil., M.A., B.Sc., M.Inst.Biol.
Deputy Chairman and Senior Lecturer, School of Environmental Science, University of Bradford.
Nicolaas A. M. Verbeek Ph.D., M.Sc., B.Sc.
Animal Behaviour Research Group, University of Oxford.
Georg Zappler M.A.
Formerly of the American Museum of Natural History.

Santa Cruz Is. A small coral island in the Galápagos group.

I have been closely involved with wild animals and plants – and their conservation – for over sixty years, and was delighted when the Editors of the *Atlas of World Wildlife* first spoke to me of their project. I have followed their endeavour with deep interest and expectation, and find that their vast and complex operation has indeed succeeded in providing a splendid background for understanding the diversity of wildlife, its evolutionary history, its multiple functions and objectives, and, alas, the dangers that today increasingly threaten its healthy continuance.

The Atlas paints a vivid picture of Evolution's general course; illustrating the way in which some organisms persist over millions of years while others die out, to be replaced by new forms.

The Atlas demonstrates the evolutionary process whereby animals and plants have become generally more efficient in their ability to survive. On the other hand, many species and even major groups have become extinct. How are we to save the survivors? The Atlas deals clearly and lucidly with this important problem. It also explains ecology–the study of interrelations between organisms and their environments. This fast-growing science – now a priority in many countries – is made clear and memorable by excellent maps, photographs and diagrams.

I myself have learnt much from the Atlas, gaining especially a better comprehension of world ecology from its rational and objective treatment. I know of no other book which makes so clear and so scientific an exposition of life and matter in our world, or their relationships with man.

The reader will find many strange and interesting details about earth's wildlife. For instance, how a creature with a third eye on top of its head (the tuatara) has survived for over fifty million years – though only on an isolated Australian island. He will also learn much about the extraordinary feats of mimicry, when a resting animal escapes notice by resembling its background, or even some inedible object—such as a twig. The section on colouring devices is equally fascinating. Animals flaunting gaudy colours, thus announcing their nauseous or even poisonous taste to would-be predators; and flowers displaying sham insect-wings in order to seduce flies into pollinating them.

There is not a page in this remarkable work where the inquisitive reader will not find a treasure to ponder over and to remember, whether it be from the seashore, the steppes, the tropical forest, or the high mountains. I would strongly recommend its study to all who are concerned with the future of wildlife and unspoilt scenery; with refuges from the bustle of life; indeed with the future of man as a species. I hope that all will read, enjoy and inwardly digest what the Atlas has to say on these fascinating and vital topics.

Each one of us carries a share of the responsibility to keep alive the fascinating and wonderful miracles of life on this planet. We can best do this by knowing as much about them as we can. I am grateful to the many able and learned collaborators in this book for their invaluable contributions to this knowledge, and I hope that the Atlas will find many appreciative readers who care for the beauty and variety of our world and who will cooperate in the effort to save that magnificent but fragile beauty and variety.

Julian Huxley

Consultant Editor
Sir Julian Huxley, MA, DSc, FRS

The Living Earth

The World Before Man

To our stolid medieval forefathers the Earth was a pattern of unchanging continents and oceans, its wildlife unaltered since the fifth day of Creation. Modern man has discovered that, like his own restless nature, the face of the Earth is shifting and changing, and animals and plants have evolved and indeed are still evolving at rates measurable in his own lifetime.

The Earth consolidated over four and a half thousand million years ago, and the vapours surrounding it cooled and condensed. Some of the oldest rocks – nearly four thousand million years old by radio-isotope dating – were deposited as sediments, showing that water was present in quantity, and cycles of weathering and erosion were already carving the rocks of the primordial land. The oceans deepened and acquired an increasing concentration of soluble materials from earth and atmosphere. Gradually there developed the rich broth of inorganic molecules in which life was spawned. The first traces of life – humped or branching masses of chalk or silica, believed to have been formed by primitive plants – occur in Precambrian rocks two to three thousand million years old in Canada and the northern United States. The earliest traces of animals are much younger, dating from early Cambrian rocks of Australia approximately 600 million years old.

Five hundred million years ago, at the end of the Cambrian period, the oceans teemed with a variety of simple floating plants, which supported a mixed fauna of primitive sponges, worms, shelled brachiopods and molluscs, trilobites and crustaceans, and echinoderms related to sea urchins and starfish. As yet there were no vertebrates, though prechordate ancestors may already have been recognizable among the larvae of invertebrates in the plankton of the ocean surface. Almost certainly there were present the elements of ecological organization which are linked in every modern ecosystem.

The first traces of land animals and land plants appear in Silurian rocks some 400 million years old. Unshaded by vegetation and wide open to the elements, the Silurian landscape cannot have seemed hospitable to its first hesitant colonizers. But the 50 million years of the Devonian period saw the invasion, evolution and spread of plant life.

Protolepidodendron · Cyclostigma

1 Dipterus
2 Pterichthys
3 Drepanaspis
4 Pteraspis
5 Ichthyostega

Barrandeina · Psilophyton · Zosterophyllum · Sphaenophyllum

The Age of Fishes
Until the mid-Palaeozoic era (500 million years ago) there was neither oxygen nor ozone in the Earth's atmosphere. Then strong-stemmed plants advanced across the landscape, softening the environment for the pioneers breaking away from the rich Devonian fish stock – the lungfish and primitive amphibians which began the colonization of the landmass.

−400 MY
DEVONIAN
CARBONIFEROUS
−350 MY
−270 MY
PERMIAN
−225 MY
TRIASSIC
−180 MY
JURASSIC

The mammals take over
Forty to 50 million years ago flowering plants had overtaken all other forms of vegetation to clothe the land surface of the Earth. The reptiles were no longer dominant; the world was now ruled by mammals, warm-blooded offshoots of reptilian stock. Most modern animals have clearly recognizable Oligocene ancestors.

Sequoia

1 Indricotherium
2 Diatryma
3 Brontotherium
4 Uintatherium
5 Hyracotherium
6 Moeritherium
7 Andrewsarchus
8 Arsinoitherium

Ribbon of life *below*
Over the past 600 million years the planet Earth has been populated by a remarkable and ever-changing succession of life forms. The major divisions of this span of time, the geological periods, are shown to scale in the diagram, amplified by reconstructions of three of the most significant Ages of evolution.

−600 MY

CAMBRIAN

ORDOVICIAN

−440 MY

SILURIAN

Williamsonia

1 *Pterodactylus*
2 *Rhamphorhynchus*
3 *Diplodocus*
4 *Plesiosaurus*
5 *Peloneustes*
6 *Archaeopteryx*
7 *Antrodemus*
8 *Oligokyphus*
9 *Stegosaurus*

Conifer

Cycads

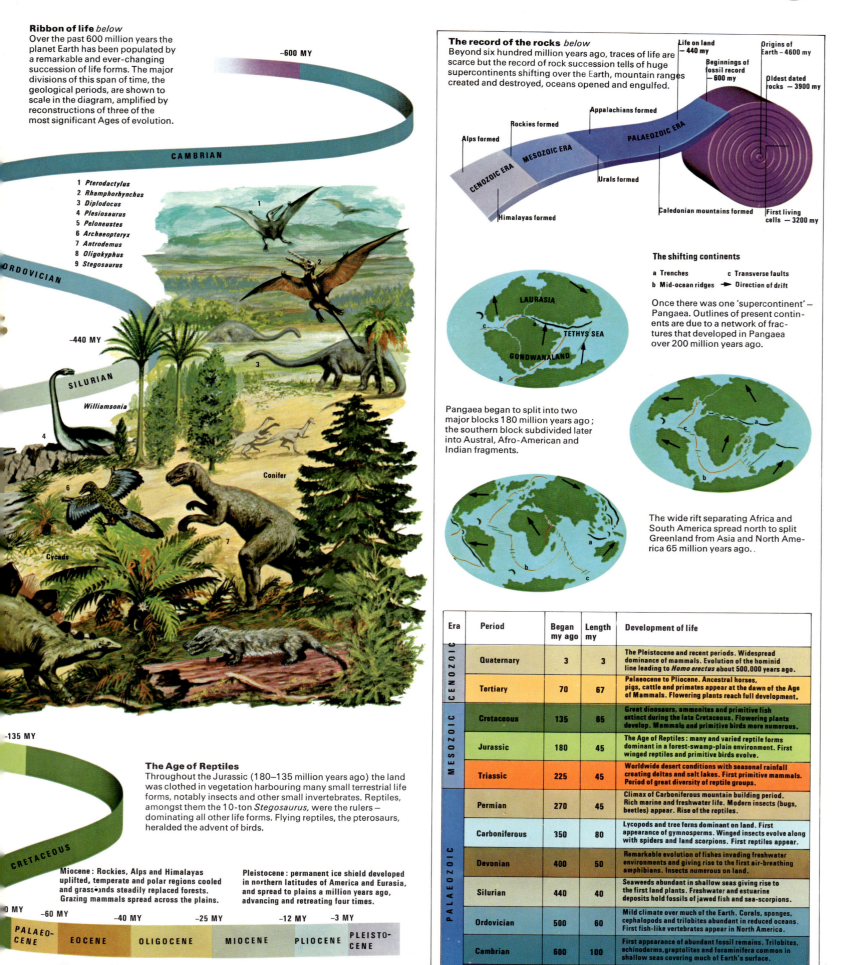

−135 MY

The Age of Reptiles
Throughout the Jurassic (180–135 million years ago) the land was clothed in vegetation harbouring many small terrestrial life forms, notably insects and other small invertebrates. Reptiles, amongst them the 10-ton *Stegosaurus*, were the rulers – dominating all other life forms. Flying reptiles, the pterosaurs, heralded the advent of birds.

CRETACEOUS

Miocene : Rockies, Alps and Himalayas uplifted, temperate and polar regions cooled and grasslands steadily replaced forests. Grazing mammals spread across the plains.

Pleistocene : permanent ice shield developed in northern latitudes of America and Eurasia, and spread to plains a million years ago, advancing and retreating four times.

−60 MY   −40 MY   −25 MY   −12 MY   −3 MY

| PALAEO-CENE | EOCENE | OLIGOCENE | MIOCENE | PLIOCENE | PLEISTO-CENE |

Pliocene : world continued to cool, tropical plants and animals retreated to lower latitudes. Camels, horses, antelopes, mastodons lived on northern plains of America and Asia.

Recent : with final retreat of ice sheets just over ten thousand years ago, man evolved from hunter-gatherer to settler-farmer, building his homes in the fertile regions.

The record of the rocks *below*
Beyond six hundred million years ago, traces of life are scarce but the record of rock succession tells of huge supercontinents shifting over the Earth, mountain ranges created and destroyed, oceans opened and engulfed.

Life on land – 440 my
Beginnings of fossil record — 600 my
Origins of Earth – 4600 my
Oldest dated rocks – 3900 my

Alps formed
Rockies formed
Appalachians formed

CENOZOIC ERA   MESOZOIC ERA   PALAEOZOIC ERA

Himalayas formed
Urals formed
Caledonian mountains formed
First living cells — 3200 my

The shifting continents

a Trenches
b Mid-ocean ridges
c Transverse faults
→ Direction of drift

Once there was one 'supercontinent' – Pangaea. Outlines of present continents are due to a network of fractures that developed in Pangaea over 200 million years ago.

LAURASIA
TETHYS SEA
GONDWANALAND

Pangaea began to split into two major blocks 180 million years ago ; the southern block subdivided later into Austral, Afro-American and Indian fragments.

The wide rift separating Africa and South America spread north to split Greenland from Asia and North America 65 million years ago. .

Era	Period	Began my ago	Length my	Development of life
CENOZOIC	Quaternary	3	3	The Pleistocene and recent periods. Widespread dominance of mammals. Evolution of the hominid line leading to *Homo erectus* about 500,000 years ago.
CENOZOIC	Tertiary	70	67	Palaeocene to Pliocene. Ancestral horses, pigs, cattle and primates appear at the dawn of the Age of Mammals. Flowering plants reach full development.
MESOZOIC	Cretaceous	135	65	Great dinosaurs, ammonites and primitive fish extinct during the late Cretaceous. Flowering plants develop. Mammals and primitive birds more numerous.
MESOZOIC	Jurassic	180	45	The Age of Reptiles : many and varied reptile forms dominant in a forest-swamp-plain environment. First winged reptiles and primitive birds evolve.
MESOZOIC	Triassic	225	45	Worldwide desert conditions with seasonal rainfall creating deltas and salt lakes. First primitive mammals. Period of great diversity of reptile groups.
PALAEOZOIC	Permian	270	45	Climax of Carboniferous mountain building period. Rich marine and freshwater life. Modern insects (bugs, beetles) appear. Rise of the reptiles.
PALAEOZOIC	Carboniferous	350	80	Lycopods and tree ferns dominant on land. First appearance of gymnosperms. Winged insects evolve along with spiders and land scorpions. First reptiles appear.
PALAEOZOIC	Devonian	400	50	Remarkable evolution of fishes invading freshwater environments and giving rise to the first air-breathing amphibians. Insects numerous on land.
PALAEOZOIC	Silurian	440	40	Seaweeds abundant in shallow seas giving rise to the first land plants. Freshwater and estuarine deposits hold fossils of jawed fish and sea-scorpions.
PALAEOZOIC	Ordovician	500	60	Mild climate over much of the Earth. Corals, sponges, cephalopods and trilobites abundant in reduced oceans. First fish-like vertebrates appear in North America.
PALAEOZOIC	Cambrian	600	100	First appearance of abundant fossil remains. Trilobites, echinoderms, graptolites and foraminifera common in shallow seas covering much of Earth's surface.
PALAEOZOIC	Pre-Cambrian	4600	4000	Evidence of primitive invertebrates – bacteria, sponges and worms. Earliest traces of life are algae and bacteria dated at over 3,000 million years old.

The Evolution of Life

To the naturalist, animals and plants are remarkable for the diversity of shape and form distinguishing species from species and race from race. Biochemists, however, are struck by the uniformity of living creatures. At a chemical level, whale and pine tree, bird and diatom use similar molecules as building bricks, process them in similar ways and are faced with similar problems of waste disposal.

We do not know how life began, but there is a strong supposition – backed by experimental evidence – that the methane, hydrogen, ammonia and water of Earth's primitive atmosphere were stimulated by electrical discharges to produce amino acids, the complex molecules on which life chemistry is based. From this level of organization to the simplest known form of life is a far step, but by no means an impossible one.

The first living organisms must have fed on the organic molecules surrounding them in the ocean, breaking them down to obtain their chemical energy without the help of oxygen. Perhaps more than a thousand million years later came the important chlorophyll pigments, which enable their possessors to create food substances from water and carbon dioxide using the energy of sunlight. So the first plants appeared, the 'primary producers' or fixers of solar energy on which all other life forms are dependent. The first predatory animals, capable of engulfing algae and bacteria, may have evolved at this time but, having no teeth, shells or other hard parts, have left no fossil record of their presence.

How evolution came about is difficult to demonstrate; the process of 'natural selection', to which Charles Darwin and Alfred Wallace drew attention over a century ago, is seldom seen in action though its effects can often be inferred. An astonishingly simple mechanism, natural selection relies on the ability of successful organisms to reproduce lavishly, with small but important variations between individuals. Variations arise both from the mixing of parental qualities and from aberrations (mutations) in the chromosomes which carry instructions for accurate reduplication.

In species well adapted to a stable environment, most mutations are unfavourable, their effects disappearing quickly from the population. Some recurring mutations may be disadvantageous to several generations, but come into favour when circumstances change and the standard pattern is no longer the best. In fluctuating environments, variety and experiment are at a premium; here natural selection confers its only prize – survival – on populations which have kept their options open.

Insect overlords *above*
The small and varied invertebrates dominate the living world. The insects are the largest group with over 700,000 known species.

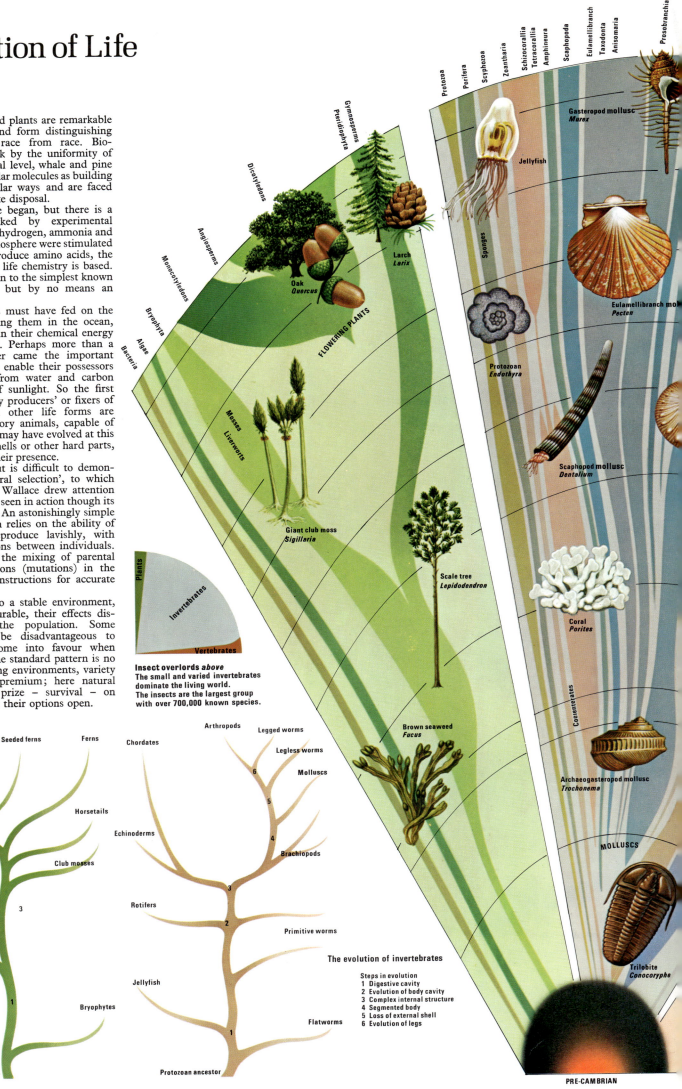

The evolution of plants

Steps in evolution
1 Primitive vascular system
2 Evolution of roots
3 Evolution of leaves
4 Evolution of cone seeds
5 Evolution of frond seeds
6 Evolution of flowers

The evolution of invertebrates

Steps in evolution
1 Digestive cavity
2 Evolution of body cavity
3 Complex internal structure
4 Segmented body
5 Loss of external shell
6 Evolution of legs

PRE-CAMBRIAN

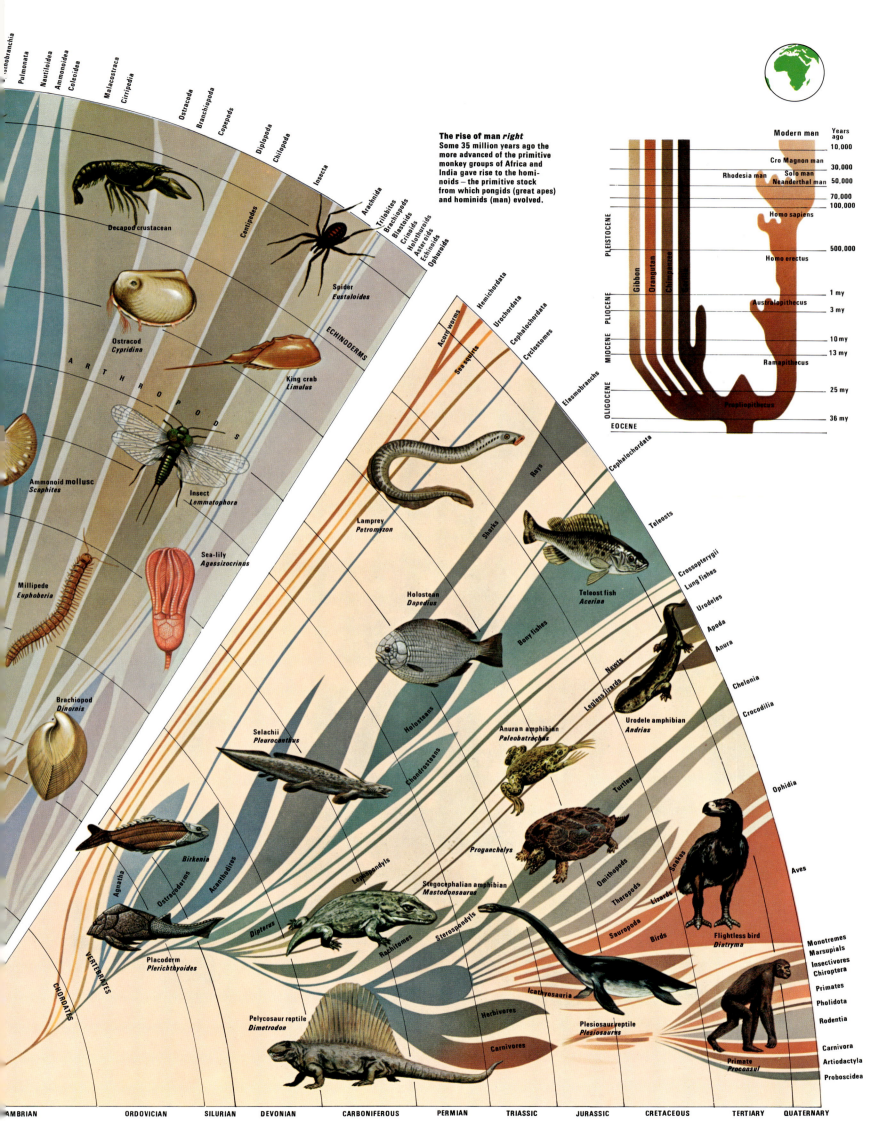

Pulmonata
Nautiloidea
Ammonoidea
Coleoidea
Malacostraca
Cirripedia
Ostracoda
Branchiopoda
Copepods
Diplopoda
Chilopoda
Insecta
Arachnida
Trilobites
Brachiopods
Blastoids
Crinoids
Holothuroids
Asteroids
Echinoids
Ophuroids

Decapod crustacean

Ostracod
Cypridina

Centipedes

Spider
Eustaloides

ECHINODERMS

King crab
Limulus

A R T H R O P O D S

Ammonoid mollusc
Scaphites

Insect
Lemmatophora

Sea-lily
Agassizocrinus

Millipede
Euphoberia

Brachiopod
Dinornis

The rise of man *right*
Some 35 million years ago the
more advanced of the primitive
monkey groups of Africa and
India gave rise to the homi-
noids — the primitive stock
from which pongids (great apes)
and hominids (man) evolved.

Acorn worms
Hemichordata
Urachordata
Cephalochordata
Cyclostomes

Sea squirts

Elasmobranchs

Rays

Sharks

Lamprey
Petromyzon

Teleosts

Cephalochordata

Crossopterygii
Lung fishes

Teleost fish
Acerina

Urodeles

Apoda

Anura

Holostean
Dapedius

Bony fishes

Newts

Legless lizards

Chelonia

Crocodilia

Urodele amphibian
Andrias

Anuran amphibian
Paleobatrachus

Holosteans

Selachii
Pleuracanthus

Chondrosteans

Ophidia

Turtles

Proganchelys

Lepospondyls

Stegocephalian amphibian
Mastodonsaurus

Ornithopods

Theropods

Lizards

Snakes

Aves

Birkenia

Acanthodids

Rhachitomes

Sterospondyls

Sauropoda

Birds

Flightless bird
Diatryma

Agnatha

Ostracoderms

Dipterus

Icathyosauria

Herbivores

Plesiosaur reptile
Plesiosaurus

Monotremes
Marsupials
Insectivores
Chiroptera
Primates
Pholidota
Rodentia

Placoderm
Plerichthyoides

VERTEBRATES

CHORDATES

Pelycosaur reptile
Dimetrodon

Carnivores

Primate
Proconsul

Carnivora
Artiodactyla
Proboscidea

Modern man | Years ago
Cro Magnon man | 10,000
Rhodesia man | Solo man | Neanderthal man | 30,000 | 50,000
Homo sapiens | 70,000 | 100,000
Homo erectus | 500,000
Australopithecus | 1 my
Ramapithecus | 3 my | 10 my | 13 my
Propliopithecus | 25 my
| 36 my

Gibbon
Orangutan
Chimpanzee

PLEISTOCENE
PLIOCENE
MIOCENE
OLIGOCENE
EOCENE

AMBRIAN | ORDOVICIAN | SILURIAN | DEVONIAN | CARBONIFEROUS | PERMIAN | TRIASSIC | JURASSIC | CRETACEOUS | TERTIARY | QUATERNARY

Zoogeography: The Realms of Nature

The distinguished early Victorian ornithologist P. L. Sclater first divided the world into six faunal regions, each with its own characteristic assembly of birds. Alfred Wallace, a widely travelled naturalist (and co-discoverer of natural selection), found that many other animals fitted readily into Sclater's scheme. The six original regions – Palaearctic, Nearctic, Neotropical, Ethiopian, Oriental (or Indian) and Australian – are still valid today, but one more is sometimes added to them – the Antarctic continent, unknown in Sclater's time.

Many animal groups seem to have originated in the warm central landmass of Arctogea (Palearctic, Nearctic, Ethiopian and Oriental regions), spreading from there towards the peripheral regions of southern Africa, Australia and the Americas. This is especially true of the mammals, which appear to have spread outwards in waves, each wave representing a new evolutionary development, and to some extent overtaking and replacing the last. The marsupials, an early pattern of mammals which produce their young only a few days after conception and rear them – firmly attached to a teat – in a pouch on the body wall, spread across the world between 60 and 80 million years ago. Fossil remains are found in Europe, and marsupials are still plentiful in Australia and South America. Later came a second wave of more advanced mammals – the placentals, which keep their young longer inside the mother's body and feed the developing embryo through a placenta attached to the wall of the uterus. Placentals, marginally more successful, replaced marsupials wherever the two competed.

Continental movement during the early Tertiary isolated Australia and South America from Arctogea, and in these two outposts marsupials continued to flourish and diversify. Later South America was invaded by placental mammals from North America, but Australia remained almost entirely free of placentals until the arrival of man.

The Nearctic or 'New North' Realm
This realm includes North America down to the highlands of Mexico ; many of its mammals (including deer and sheep) entered across the Bering land bridge. Others, (among them horses and camels) went the other way.

Pronghorn antelope
Antilocarpa americana

Beaver
Castor canadensis

Striped skunk
Mephitis mephitis

The Palaearctic or 'Old North' Realm
The Palaearctic is a vast realm extending from Britain to Japan, and from Spitzbergen to Saudi Arabia and Africa north of the Sahara. Many of its animals spread to peripheral Ethiopian, Oriental and Nearctic realms.

Mouflon
Ovis musimon

Edible dormouse
Glis glis

Dunnock
Prunella modularis

Saiga
Saiga tatarica

The Neotropical or 'New Tropical' Realm
Linked with the Nearctic by the isthmus of Central America the Neotropical reaches down to Cape Horn. Its fauna includes marsupials, sloths, armadillos and forest monkeys with prehensile tails.

Toco toucan
Ramphastos toco

Springbuck
Antidorcas marsupialis

Bald uakari
Cacajo calvus

Giant anteater
Myrmecophaga tridactyla

Cardinal
Richmondena cardinalis

ORIENTAL

AUSTRALASIAN

PALAEARCTIC

IOPIA

The Australasian Realm
The islands of Celebes and New Guinea mark the northernmost limits of the Australasian Realm, which includes New Zealand. Long isolated from the rest of the world, the realm has developed a distinctive fauna.

Red kangaroo
Macropus rufus

Koala
Phascolarctos cinereus

Tuatara
Sphenodon punctatus

Kiwi
Apteryx australis

White-handed gibbon
Hylobates lar

The Oriental Realm
Bounded on the north and west by the Himalayas, the Oriental Realm includes India and Ceylon, Malaysia, Indonesia and the Philippines, and is separated from Australia by the arbitary Wallace's and Weber's Lines.

Peacock
Pavo cristatus

Tiger
Panthera tigris

The Ethiopian Realm
Apart from a strip of northwest Africa which falls in the Palaearctic, the Ethiopian Realm covers all Africa, part of Arabia, and Madagascar. Its animals include African elephants, gorillas and chimpanzees, and many species of antelope.

African elephant
Loxodonta africana

Burchell's zebra
Equus burchelli

Aardvark
Orycteropus afer

Eastern highland gorilla
Gorilla gorilla berengei

15

Ecology: The Dynamic Equilibrium

As engines need to be fed with oil, gasoline, coal or other energy-containing fuels, so plants and animals need ready sources of energy to keep them going. Green plants make their own foods by photosynthesis. Using cheap and plentiful components (carbon dioxide and water), they synthesize sugars which hold, in their chemical bonds, energy derived from sunlight. This energy can be released and used to build more complex chemical compounds which the plant needs for its skeleton, replacement tissues, seeds and spores. Animals cannot make their own foods. Instead they steal energy from plants and from each other; they can live only at the expense of other living organisms.

To ecologists (who study living creatures in relation to their environment), green plants are 'producers' or 'fixers' of energy, animals are 'consumers', and organisms which feed on products of decay are 'decomposers'. Producers, consumers and decomposers living together in particular environments come to rely on each other and adapt to each others' peculiarities; they form closed or partly-closed systems which the ecologist calls *ecosystems*. Complex ecosystems may include many thousands of species, all interrelating to one degree or another with each other. Interactions include feeding and providing food, but plants and animals also provide shelter or protection, nesting material, homes and other amenities for each other.

Some of the relationships within a simple ecosystem can be shown by diagrams, for example

food-chains, which help to stress the common theme of interdependence between producers, several levels of consumers, and decomposers found in all ecosystems. However, in real life food-chains are usually cross-linked with each other to form food-webs, which quickly become too complex to be shown as diagrams. Generally speaking, the older the ecosystem, the more species it is likely to contain.

New environments (such as a newly formed pond, a field recently devastated by fire, a glacier bed from which the ice has retreated) attract at first only the hardy species of plants which can survive without shelter and the few animals capable of living among them. These early settlers modify the environment, by adding humus and nutrients to the soil, give shelter from sun and wind, and make it more hospitable to other creatures. As more organisms move in, more opportunities (niches) become available for others. Some of the world's most complex ecosystems are to be found in the tropics, where productivity is high, and conditions have been stable for many millions of years. Some of the simplest ecosystems occur in polar regions, where there is less energy available, and few organisms have had time to adapt to the new environments exposed after the retreat of the ice sheets. But however simple or complex an ecosystem, all the organisms within it are producers, consumers or decomposers, and all depend ultimately on the ability of green plants to fix the energy of sunlight. This is one of the unifying concepts underlying wildlife studies.

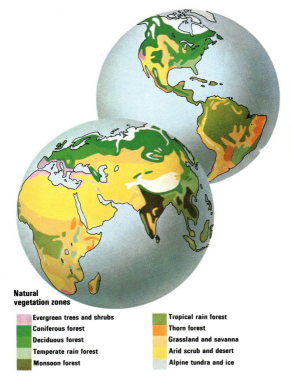

Natural vegetation zones

- Evergreen trees and shrubs
- Coniferous forest
- Deciduous forest
- Temperate rain forest
- Monsoon forest
- Tropical rain forest
- Thorn forest
- Grassland and savanna
- Arid scrub and desert
- Alpine tundra and ice

Mountain and tundra

The montane biome or plant and animal community (above and below) is found in cold, temperate and tropical regions. Species are few, and finely balanced as in an Arctic ecological system to which the high montane regions of temperate and tropical regions are similar. The richest of all biomes in plant and animal species is the tropical forest (right and below right). Larger animals are few and secretive, but small forms proliferate.

Tropical forest

Grassland

The most visually rewarding of all the biomes in the realm of nature is the savanna (above and below). Here the herb vegetation dominates with clumps of trees and bushes supporting the largest members, in the largest groups, of mammals, including herbivores, predators and scavengers.

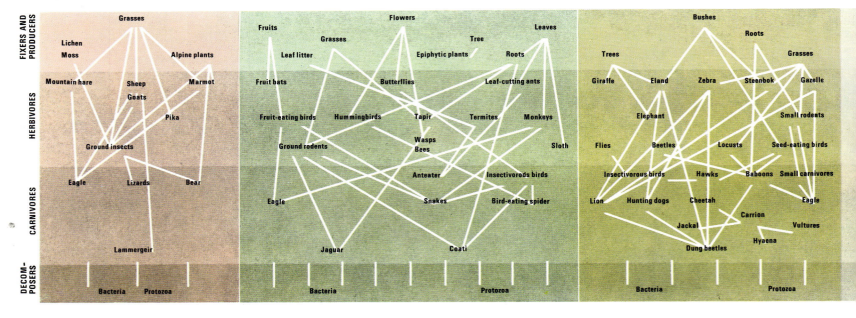

FIXERS AND PRODUCERS / HERBIVORES / CARNIVORES / DECOMPOSERS

Mountain and tundra web: Grasses, Lichen, Moss, Alpine plants, Mountain hare, Sheep, Goats, Marmot, Pika, Ground insects, Eagle, Lizards, Bear, Lammergeir, Bacteria, Protozoa

Tropical forest web: Fruits, Flowers, Grasses, Tree, Leaves, Leaf litter, Epiphytic plants, Roots, Fruit bats, Butterflies, Leaf-cutting ants, Fruit-eating birds, Hummingbirds, Tapir, Termites, Monkeys, Ground rodents, Wasps, Bees, Sloth, Anteater, Insectivorous birds, Eagle, Snakes, Bird-eating spider, Jaguar, Coati, Bacteria, Protozoa

Grassland web: Bushes, Roots, Trees, Grasses, Giraffe, Eland, Zebra, Steenbok, Gazelle, Elephant, Small rodents, Flies, Beetles, Locusts, Seed-eating birds, Insectivorous birds, Hawks, Baboons, Small carnivores, Lion, Hunting dogs, Cheetah, Eagle, Jackal, Carrion, Vultures, Dung beetles, Hyaena, Bacteria, Protozoa

The individual
The basic unit of ecology is the individual plant or animal. Many individuals, like the arctic hare, are genetically distinct from others of their kind; others, like the grass plant, reproduce vegetatively and form part of a 'clone' of identical individuals.

The population
A population is an interbreeding group of individuals, isolated wholly or partly from other populations of the same species. The arctic hare of northern Greenland may thus differ from that of Siberia.

An ecosystem evolves
Many of the world's seemingly stable ecosystems are changing as we watch. A shallow glacial tarn (right) is transformed to a forest in a time span of a few thousand years. First living creatures to colonize it are wind-blown spores of algae. Larvae of flying insects and water fleas feed on the algae and their debris accumulates on the bottom. Bacteria and unicells recycle the nutrient salts and small animals and plants enter the system. Surrounding sediments fill the tarn, marsh plants spread inward and land plants replace them as the ground consolidates.

The ecosystem
The ecosystem is an assembly of animals and plants, interacting within an environment. Ecosystems can be simple (such as unicellular algae on a tree trunk, browsing insects and predators); or complex (thousands of plants and animals interacting in a tropical rain forest).

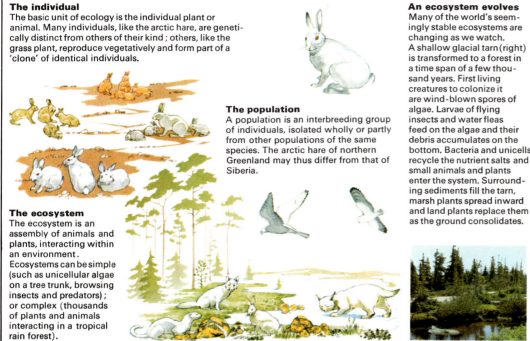

Lodgepole pine · Sedges · Reed · Water lily · Pondweed · Grass · Sediment

Lodgepole pine · Monkshood · Blueberry · Wild orchid · Labrador tea · Willow · Sediment

Lodgepole pine · Willow · Monkshood · Wild orchid · Wild lily · Red fir · Sediment

Desert

The desert and tundra offer the harshest conditions to plant and animal communities whose numbers are, therefore, that much fewer. Both are most often found in conditions of recent climatic change, to which neither plants nor animals, in any number, have been able to adapt. The desert biome is shown (above and below). The temperate forest biome (right and below right) is one of the most complex, containing hundreds of plant and animal species.

Temperate forest

Oceanic

The life forms of the ocean are far greater in number than those that exist on land, ranging from the largest of living creatures, the blue whale, to the great pastures of microscopic plankton.

The stable communities
Animals and plants the world over form themselves into stable, recognizable communities which ecologists call biomes. On land there are three kinds of forest biome (coniferous, deciduous and tropical), two kinds of grassland (temperate and savanna), two intermediate biomes (chaparral and open woodland) and two severely restricted by climate or soil (tundra and desert). In the ocean, four communities or biomes are recognized — surface/water, coral reef, mud/sand and rock/bottom. Biomes of tropical and temperate forest and grasslands are by far the most complex, containing many hundreds of species; desert and tundra biomes are simpler, containing few species with fewer links of dependency between them. This difference of complexity is due in part to the relative harshness of the environment, in part to its newness. Desert and tundra occur where climate is harsh and the soil unyielding, often in a new environment. Forests and grasslands grow in stable environments where conditions have altered only slightly over several millions of years.

Interlinking food webs
Whether simple or complex, all communities of plants and animals are organized along similar economic lines. Plants are 'fixers' of solar energy, the mainspring of all life. Energy, locked away in chemical bonds, passes from plants to herbivores and thence to carnivores. Interlinking food webs (shown in panel at the foot of this page) are an expression, perhaps over-simplified, of these relationships.

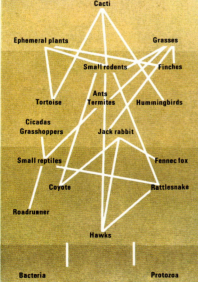
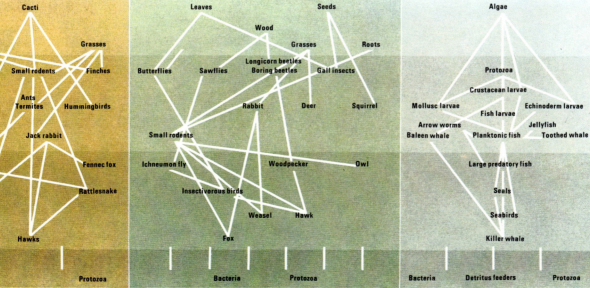

Desert: Cacti · Ephemeral plants · Grasses · Small rodents · Finches · Tortoise · Ants · Termites · Hummingbirds · Cicadas · Grasshoppers · Jack rabbit · Small reptiles · Fennec fox · Coyote · Rattlesnake · Roadrunner · Hawks · Bacteria · Protozoa

Temperate forest: Leaves · Seeds · Wood · Grasses · Roots · Butterflies · Sawflies · Longicorn beetles · Boring beetles · Gall insects · Rabbit · Deer · Squirrel · Small rodents · Ichneumon fly · Woodpecker · Owl · Insectivorous birds · Weasel · Hawk · Fox · Bacteria · Protozoa

Oceanic: Algae · Protozoa · Crustacean larvae · Mollusc larvae · Fish larvae · Echinoderm larvae · Arrow worms · Jellyfish · Baleen whale · Planktonic fish · Toothed whale · Large predatory fish · Seals · Seabirds · Killer whale · Bacteria · Detritus feeders · Protozoa

North America
THE NEARCTIC REALM

North America

The first Europeans to colonize the North American continent had little comprehension of the true nature of the land they had settled. The ancient grandeur of its topography and wildlife were perhaps hidden by an immeasurable potential for the creation of a new society, based on an improved image of the one the settlers had left behind. In such an image there was little concern for environment and conservation; these were concepts that had still to come. They arrived too late to save some species that had proliferated in earlier times and are not altogether effective in holding back the demise of others. But the North Americans were the first to introduce the idea of reserves, or national parks, to protect regions of singular value for posterity, and their prophets of conservation are among the most influential. The continent is large enough still to hold surprises for the naturalist fortunate enough to observe them at close hand, from the alpine regions of the Rockies and the misty forests of the Pacific seaboard to the swamplands and bayous of the southeast and Florida, almost touching the Tropic of Cancer. North of the 49th parallel there are still vast expanses where man is still less common than some of the larger animals he hunts and south, across the Rio Grande, the northern areas of the ancient bridge to South America retain much of their age-old faunal flavour. All this is North America, a continent where man has done his worst, and is still doing his best, for the landscape and the animals he shares it with.

Immature mule deer, Grand Canyon, Arizona, U.S.A.

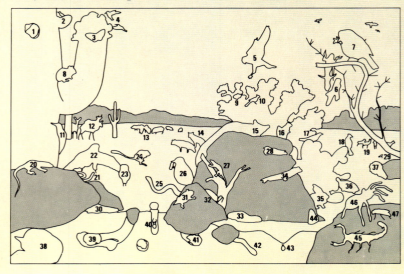

Key to panorama

1 Elf owl	17 Cactus wren	33 Diamond-back rattlesnake
2 Black-chinned hummingbird	18 Ashy-throated flycatcher	34 Chuckawalla
3 Swallowtail butterfly	19 Pronghorn	35 Jack rabbit
4 Costa's hummingbird	20 Collared lizard	36 Desert tortoise
5 American kestrel	21 King snake	37 Skunk
6 Grasshopper	22 Red-tailed hawk	38 Kit fox
7 Loggerhead shrike	23 Burrowing owl	39 Kangaroo rat
8 Pack rat	24 Kangaroo rat	40 Trapdoor spider
9 White footed mouse	25 Sidewinder	41 Pocket mouse
10 Pyrrhuloxia	26 Road runner	42 Bull snake
11 Gila woodpecker	27 Desert spiny lizard	43 Ant lion
12 Mule deer	28 Poorwill	44 Monarch butterfly
13 Peccaries	29 Gambel's quail	45 Desert scorpion
14 Coyote	30 Gila monster	46 Tarantula
15 Cacomistle	31 Horned lizard	47 Tarantula hawk wasp
16 Yuma antelope squirrel	32 Grasshopper mouse	

LOW
HIGH
LOW 1000
1000
1004
HIGH
1004
1008
1012
1016
HIGH
1012
1016
1016

1008
1016
1020
1012
1024
HIGH
LOW
LOW
1008
1012
1016

HIGH
1016
1012
1008

Rainfall
in   cm
40   100
30   75
20   50
10   25
5   12.5

Isobars
Prevailing winds

Beaufort
Sea

POINT BARROW
BROOKS RANGE
Barrow

Viscount Melville Sound
BANKS
ISLAND
VICTORIA
ISLAND
SOMERSET
ISLAND
PRINCE
OF
WALES
ISLAND
KING
WILLIAM
ISLAND
MELVILLE
PENINSULA
Gulf
of
Boothia
MAGNETIC POLE
Cambridge
Bay
Repulse Bay

STATES

MACKENZIE MOUNTAINS
Great Bear
Lake
Norman
Wells
Port
Radium
Yellowknife
Great Slave
Lake
Reindeer
Lake
Lake Athabasca
Churchill

SOUTHAMPTON
ISLAND
COATS
ISLAND
MANSEL
ISLAND

Hudson
Bay

UNGAVA
PENINSULA

HORN
MOUNTAINS
HAY
Fort Nelson
CARIBOU
MOUNTAINS
Dawson
Creek
Pine
Point
Uranium
City

CANADA

York
Factory
Nelson
Hayes
Fort George
Moosonee
James
Bay
Albany
BELCHER
ISLANDS

Ungava Bay
George

OTISH
MOUNTAINS
L. Mistassini

NEWFOUNDLAND
St. John's

QUEEN
CHARLOTTE
ISLANDS

ROCKY

Edmonton
Saskatoon
Calgary
Red Deer
Regina
Saskatchewan
Lake
Winnipegosis
Lake
Manitoba
Lake
Winnipeg
Winnipeg
Lake of
the Woods

Thunder Bay

AMERICA
NORTH

Timmins
L. Nipigon
LAURENTIAN HIGHLANDS
Saint Lawrence
Québec
MONTREAL
Saint John
Halifax
PRINCE
EDWARD
ISLAND
CAPE BRETON
Strait

VANCOUVER
ISLAND
Vancouver
Victoria
Seattle
CAPE FLATTERY
Spokane
COAST
Columbia
Portland

Missouri
Fort Peck
Reservoir
Great
Falls
BLUE
MTS
Bismarck
Fargo
BLACK
HILLS
Pierre
Lake Oahe
Reservoir
North Platte
Lake Francis
Case

Duluth
Lake Superior
Sault Sainte Marie
Sudbury
Georgian
Bay
Ottawa
TORONTO
Buffalo
L. Huron
Lansing
DETROIT
Lake Michigan
Milwaukee
CHICAGO
CLEVELAND
Pittsburgh

Albany
BOSTON
Providence
Hartford
NEW YORK
LONG ISLAND
PHILADELPHIA
Baltimore
WASHINGTON
Richmond
Norfolk
Chesapeake Bay
Portland
CAPE COD
GEORGES BANK

APPALACHIAN

MOUNTAINS

CAPE MENDOCINO
Reno
GREAT
BASIN
Sacramento
SAN FRANCISCO
SIERRA
RANGES
Mt Whitney
4421
Las Vegas
Lake Mead
Humphreys Peak
3851
Salt Lake City
Denver
Pikes Peak
4300
UNITED
Cheyenne
North Platte
Platte
Omaha
Des
Moines
Madison
Saint Paul
Minneapolis
Kansas
City
ST. LOUIS
Missouri
STATES
Indianapolis
Cincinnati
Ohio
Louisville
Charleston
Mount
Mitchell
2037
GREAT
PLAINS
Wichita
Ozark
Lake
OZARK PLATEAU
Nashville
Chattanooga
Charlotte
Columbia
Raleigh
CAPE FEAR
CAPE LOOKOUT

LOS ANGELES
San Diego
Phoenix
Santa Fe
Albuquerque
Gila
Oklahoma
City
Red
Little
Rock
Memphis
Arkansas
Birmingham
Atlanta
Charleston
Savannah

Colorado
El Paso
EDWARDS
PLATEAU
Dallas
Fort Worth
Shreveport
Jackson
Montgomery
Mobile
Jacksonville
BLAKE
TERRACE
CAPE KENNEDY

ISLA DE
GUADALUPE
(MEXICO)
PUNTA EUGENIA
BAJA CALIFORNIA
Hermosillo
Chihuahua
SIERRA
MADRE
Rio Grande
Laredo
Brownsville
Matamoros
San Antonio
Houston
New Orleans
GULF OF
Lake
Okeechobee
Tampa
Miami
Straits of Florida
CAPE SABLE
GRAND
BAHAMA
GREAT
ABACO
ELEUTHERA
CAT
ISLAND

CABO SAN LUCAS
La Paz
Golfo de
California
Torreón
Monterrey
Mazatlán
Tampico
MEXICO
Bahía de
Campeche
Veracruz
Campeche
YUCATAN
PENINSULA
ISLA DE
COZUMEL
Yucatan Channel
CUBA
La Habana
Havana
Santiago de Cuba
CAYMAN
ISLANDS
(U.K.)
JAMAICA
Kingston
GREATER
ANTILLES
HAITI
Port-au-
Prince
DOMINICAN
REPUBLIC
Santo
Domingo
PUERTO RICO
San Juan

Guadalajara
Lago de Chapala
SIERRA MADRE OCCIDENTAL
CIUDAD DE MÉXICO
MEXICO CITY
Puebla
SIERRA MADRE DEL SUR
Acapulco
Oaxaca
Golfo de
Tehuantepec
BRITISH HONDURAS
Belize
Villahermosa
Gulf of Honduras
GUATEMALA
Guatemala
San Salvador
EL SALVADOR
HONDURAS
Tegucigalpa
NICARAGUA
Lago de
Nicaragua
Bluefields
Managua
COSTA RICA
San José
CANAL
ZONE
Colón
PANAMA
Gulf of
Panama
Volcán de

W   E   S   T

CARIBBEAN

SEA

NETHERLANDS
ANTILLES
ARUBA CURAÇAO BONAIRE
CARACAS
Barranquilla
Cartagena
Maracaibo
Golfo de Venezuela
Barquisimeto
SIERRA NEVADA
Cúcuta
San Cristóbal
CORDILLERA ORIENTAL
LLANOS
Medellín
Manizales
BOGOTÁ
CORDILLERA OCCIDENTAL
Buenaventura
Cali
COLOMBIA

GULF OF

MEXICO

Natural vegetation zones
Tundra
Coniferous forest
Mediterranean
Tropical rain forest
Mixed forest
Semi-deciduous forest
Deciduous forest
Xerophytic forest
Tall grasses
Short-grass savanna
Desert scrub
Barren land

Montane and Boreal Forest

The boreal forest, as it is called, forms a broad belt up to 500 miles (800km) wide, south of the tundra in Canada and Alaska, dipping into the contiguous United States around Lake Superior and in the mountains of New England and New York.

It is a land of low relief, having been scoured by glacial sheets four times during the Ice Ages, with many lakes and slow streams and extensive boggy areas covered with sphagnum moss and called muskegs. The relatively infertile, acid soil is pale and sandy, beneath a layer of slowly decaying litter and humus. The climate is cold and moist with precipitation ranging from 15 to 30 inches (38–76cm) per year, and long, snowy winters, with as much as 200 inches (508cm) of snow in parts of Quebec.

Only the tundra has flower plants adapted to such extreme conditions. Trees are generally small, seldom over 50 feet (15m), but mostly they form a dense cover. The most characteristic dominant tree is the white spruce, commonly associated with balsam fir east of the Rockies. Tamarack and black spruce are also common. In drier areas, exposed to frequent fires, the jack pine takes over. The three species of broadleaf trees that occur in some abundance throughout are the paper birch, quaking aspen and balsam poplar.

The lynx, and to a lesser degree the wolverine, are widespread predators, and packs of timber wolves still roam the northwestern woods. Other carnivores include two rare members of the weasel tribe, the porcupine-hunting fisher and the arboreal marten, which chiefly preys on red squirrels or chickadees. But all the meat-eaters utilize the ubiquitous snowshoe hare. The northern flying squirrel, much more catholic in its taste than its cone-eating red cousin, includes the eggs and nestling of the numerous warblers, juncos and crossbills that breed here. Hawk-owls and boreal owls are endemic flying predators on bog lemmings, chipmunks, red-backed voles, and the insectivorous jumping mice. Moose and the non-migratory woodland caribou occur throughout, with whitetail deer browsing in lumbered and burned-over areas.

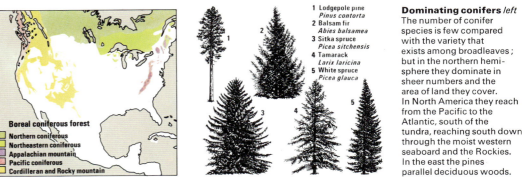

Boreal coniferous forest
- Northern coniferous
- Northeastern coniferous
- Appalachian mountain
- Pacific coniferous
- Cordilleran and Rocky mountain

1 Lodgepole pine *Pinus contorta*
2 Balsam fir *Abies balsamea*
3 Sitka spruce *Picea sitchensis*
4 Tamarack *Larix laricina*
5 White spruce *Picea glauca*

Dominating conifers *left*
The number of conifer species is few compared with the variety that exists among broadleaves; but in the northern hemisphere they dominate in sheer numbers and the area of land they cover. In North America they reach from the Pacific to the Atlantic, south of the tundra, reaching south down through the moist western seaboard and the Rockies. In the east the pines parallel deciduous woods.

Labrador tea *above*
Ledum groenlandicum is found in boggy habitats in the cooler regions of North America.

Bog community
The plant community of boggy country shown here extends from pioneer, shallow-rooted plants – hardy, and well adapted to wet conditions – to a climax community

1 Sphagnum moss
2 Sedge peat
3 Sphagnum peat
4 Woody peat
5 Humus layer
6 False bottom
7 Parent rock
8 Altered rock

Water lily *Nuphar variegatum*
Sedge *Carex rostra*
Sweet gale *Myrica gale*
Leather leaf *Chamaedaphne calyculata*
Labrador tea *Ledum palustre*
Spruce *Picea mariana*
Fir *Abies balsamea*
Birch *Betula papyrifera*
Young spruce *Picea mariana*

Mink and wolf
An agile, catholic hunter the eastern mink *Mustela vison* (left) swims to catch fish, enters burrows to seek reptiles and climbs trees to raid nests of eggs and nestlings. (Below) a diurnal hunter, the wolf *Canis lupus* usually pursues its quarry in family packs.

Tree strippers
With the onset of winter the summer vegetation on which the herbivores have lived becomes unobtainable, and animals which do not hibernate raid the exposed cover – the trees – for food. The American porcupine *Erethizon dorsatum* (centre, above and below) spends long periods in the same tree, stripping the branches of bark before moving on to another tree. The moose *Alces alces* (above and left) feeds on the tree bark as well, and often denudes a tree so much that the tree dies the following spring. The porcupine is found south to Mexico, in conifer regions.

Moose *Alces alces*

Porcupine *Erethizon dorsatum*

Cones and cone seed eaters

The fruits of most conifers are enclosed in woody cones (only yews and junipers have fleshy berries). Cone seeds are naked between the scales, which shut after fertilization. Pollination occurs in spring when male flowers shed pollen, some of which fertilize the seeds of the same tree. The seeds are a primary source of food for a number of arboreal mammals and some, like chipmunks and squirrels, hoard a stock of cones to tide them over the winter.

Douglas fir

Pinyon pine

Eastern white pine

Engelman spruce

Ponderosa pine

Red squirrel

Spruce mouse

Golden chipmunk

Grey Squirrel

Spruce grouse *above*
The spruce grouse *Canachites canadensis* displays elaborately during the breeding season.

Red squirrel *right*
Pine cones, toadstools, birds eggs and nestlings are the diets of the red squirrel *Tamiasciurus hudsonicus*.

Great horned owl *above*
Silent predator of the pine forests the great horned owl *Bubo virginianus* hunts down small mammals.

Sitka spruce, hemlock

Hemlock, Douglas fir red cedar

Douglas fir, redwood, cypress

Three-tier forests
The rich, moist forests of the north Pacific seaboard are a three-tier growth of giant firs overshadowing smaller conifers with a tangle of bushes and ferns in the understory. They are nourished by constant warm rains and mists from the Pacific Ocean.

Altitude thou.feet
12
11
10
9
8
7
6
5
4
3
2
1

White bark pine
Western white pine
Mountain hemlock
Jeffrey pine
Lodgepole pine
Red fir
Juniper
Pinyon pine
Redwood
White fir
Sugar pine
Incense cedar
Ponderosa pine
Rainfall
Pine

Sierra Nevada tree zonation

A cross-section through the Sierra Nevada of California reveals a series of botanical zones demarcated by rainfall and altitude. These factors define the principal tree species, which in turn have a native fauna : some of the mammals are illustrated (below).

Sierra Nevada

40
30
20
10
Rainfall inches

20
inches
35
50
35
30
25

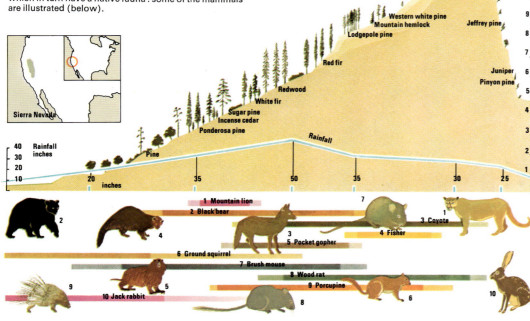

1 Mountain lion
2 Black bear
3 Coyote
4 Fisher
5 Pocket gopher
6 Ground squirrel
7 Brush mouse
8 Wood rat
9 Porcupine
10 Jack rabbit

Bristle-cone pine
Pinus aristata

Tallest – and oldest
The western forests of North America boast two of the most unique trees to be found anywhere ; the giant redwood (*Sequoia washingtonia* above), a genus that may grow to a height of 350ft (106m) ; and the bristlecone pine *Pinus aristata* (left), probably the oldest of living things. Bristle-cones of the White Mountains, California, are thought to have been alive for 8,000 years.

The Broadleaf Woodlands

Covering almost the entire eastern half of the United States from the Great Lakes to the southern coastal plains, from the eastern seaboard west beyond the Mississippi River, there once lay the great continuous, deciduous forest which so impressed the first European settlers of North America.

Most of this virgin forest has now been destroyed, but in some places the forest is in recovery, especially in New England, and in the Great Smoky Mountains of North Carolina and Tennessee there are still relatively undisturbed, virgin stands.

From Georgia to southern New England there was once a long fringe of oak-chestnut forest. The destruction of the American chestnut since 1900 by an introduced blight (a fungus) has changed much of the region to a solid oak, or oak-hickory community.

In the southern Appalachians, many of the trees are tall and stately, some well over 100 feet (30m) in height. The forest is organized into eight layers: the soil basement, forest floor, low herbs, high herbs, shrubs, low trees, tall trees whose crowns form the canopy, and finally the air above. Basswood, beech, buckeye, hickory, magnolia, maple, oak and tulip trees are the most abundant of the 130 species of trees found there. A number of low, flowering herbs such as spring beauty, anemone, hepatica, trillium and violet bloom in the early spring before the trees have leafed out.

During the summer the canopy forms an almost continuous cover, and very little sunlight reaches the ground. The annual shedding of leaves by the dominant hardwoods brings striking changes in light conditions and shelter for animals, and the forest is littered with a dense leaf layer in stages of decay.

At one time the whitetail deer and the wild turkey were important throughout the whole region. Both were once almost wiped out. Now the deer is common again in state forests and preserves, but the wild turkey is still a relatively rare bird, despite conservation efforts.

Two large predators, the timber wolf and the mountain lion, have been almost totally eliminated, but the black bear can still be found in isolated areas. Bobcats, grey and red fox, raccoons, long-tailed weasels, skunks and short-tailed shrews are the predominant hunters. Fox and grey squirrels, eastern chipmunks, white-footed mice and pine voles are the most populous of the plant and seed-eating mammals.

Back in circulation *above* The whitetail deer *Odocoileus virginianus* is now recovering in numbers from near-extinction.

Native squirrel *below* A plaguey import into Europe the grey squirrel *Sciurus carolinensis* is at home in American forests.

Turtle and skunk
Woodland ponds and streams are the home of the common box turtle *Terrapene carolinensis* (left). It hibernates during winter and has an omnivorous diet. The skunk *Mephitis mephitis* (below) hunts along the forest edge, controlling populations of small animals.

A tree returns to the soil
After perhaps centuries of growth, a tree falls and there begins a slow process by which its constituents are returned to the soil from which they came. Weathering will help, but many small creatures, some of them microscopic, are mostly responsible. Insects bore in, to prepare the way for fungi, bacteria and other insects. Tissues shrink and more space is provided for the invaders. The number of years to complete the breakdown will vary, but eventually all energy is released into the ecosystem.

Colours of autumn

How colours change
With the approach of autumn the tree slows up and ceases production of chlorophyll, the 'green' pigment. Now the other pigments—carotin (yellow) and anthocyanin (red)—shade the leaves, but without chlorophyll, sugar production stops and the leaf breaks away from the main stem (right).

Bud
Leaf stalk
Vascular tissue
Protective layer
Separation layer

Red maple *Acer rubrum*

Sugar maple *Acer sacharinum*

The centipede *Geophilus varians* lives underneath bark. The female lays a cluster of eggs and curls round them until they hatch.

Brontes dubius (right) and *Silvanus planatus* are small, flattened cucujid beetles that live under loosened bark.

The larva of the longicorn beetle *Xylotrechus colonus* bores into the sapwood. The adult is a nectar feeder.

The sawfly *Tremex columba* lays its eggs deep in the wood. Its larva is parasitized by the ichneumon *Megarhyssa*.

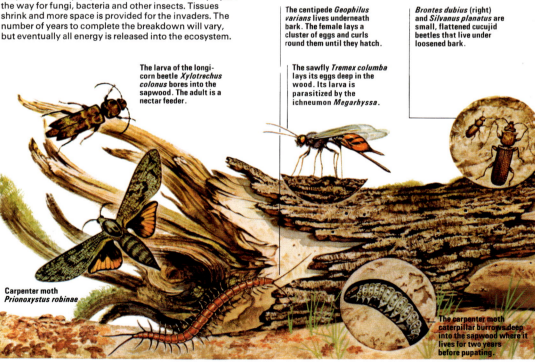

Carpenter moth *Prionoxystus robinae*

The carpenter moth caterpillar burrows deep into the sapwood where it lives for two years before pupating.

Apartment block
By nesting at different levels within the same tree and seeking out the foods to which they are individually partial a number of bird species are able to live in harmony. Birds shown are summer visitors.

Scarlet tanager
Piranga olivacea

Redstart
Setophaga ruticilla

Red-eyed vireo
Vireo olivaceus

Eastern wood peewee
Contopus virens

Yellow warbler
Dendroica petechia

Black and white warbler
Mniotilta varia

Ovenbird
Seiurus aurocapillus

Kentucky warbler
Opornis formosus

Confusion of colours *left*
The colour of the screech owl *Otus asio*, found in many of the woodlands of North America, varies from one locality to another. In damp forests, it tends to be darker than in drier areas. Some subspecies are 'dichromatic' — some birds are reddish, others grey.

Woodland birds
Sparrow-sized woodpecker *Dendrocopus pubescens* is a common bird of North American deciduous woodlands (right). The size and gaudy markings of the blue jay *Cyanocitta cristata* (below) should make it obvious — it is a clever, secretive bird.

Contrasting techniques
To supplement its insect diet and to lay in food stores for when insects are scarce the acorn woodpecker drills holes in trees and inserts a store of acorns and berries. The yellow-bellied sapsucker drills holes around tree trunks, particularly maple, and feeds on the sap. The red-headed woodpecker 'hawks' for insects.

Yellow-bellied sapsucker
Sphyrapicus varius

Acorn woodpecker
Melanerpes formicivorus

Red-headed woodpecker
Melanerpes erythrocephalus

Fungi *right and below*
The inert, forbidding appearance of woodland fungi obscures an interesting plant form which contributes to the forest ecosystem by breaking down dead matter. Fungi differ fundamentally from green plants in their lack of chlorophyll. Without it they are unable to photosynthesize their own organic food and must live on rotting matter, or as parasites on living tree trunks and branches.

Pest and control 1
Minute insects control the destinies of forest trees, sometimes infesting them mortally. The bark beetles *Hylurgopinus rufipes* (right) bore into elms and their larvae eat the fabric of their home (centre). The larvae of a wasp *Spathius* sp. act as a control, feeding on the beetle larvae (far right).

Pest and control 2
The parasitic fungus *Pleurotus ulmarius* (right) is found commonly on the trunks of elms. In time it infects the entire tree, causing a hollow centre. Cross-section of the fungus (centre). A natural control on the fungus is provided by a beetle, *Bilitotherus bifurcatus* which feeds on the fruiting fungus (far right).

The tenebrionid beetle *Alobates pennsylvanica* burrows into the outer sapwood after it has been softened by white rot.

The beetles *Uloma punculata* (left) and *Dioedis punctatus* attack rotten sapwood and heart wood.

The end of the decay process often marks the start of new growth. Acorns germinate in the rich leaf litter.

The slimy salamander *Plethodon glutinosus* hides among rotten wood by day and hunts small insects at night.

The carabid beetle *Tachyta nana* is an active hunter. At night it searches among decaying wood for small insects, snails and worms.

The termite *Reticulitermes lucifugus* attacks rotten timber. The genus lacks the large queen typical of tropical species.

The longicorn beetle *Ramalium atomarium* is 3 cm long. The larva bores into the shaded underside of the log.

Lost Range of the Bison

Before the coming of the Europeans the great mid-continental prairies and high plains formed a seemingly endless landscape of waving grass, bordered only by earth and sky. The grassland sea extended from the edge of the deciduous forest of what is now Pennsylvania and Ohio to the Rocky Mountains, and southward from the Mackenzie River in Canada to the Gulf of Mexico. Other similar grasslands existed in the arid climate of northern New Mexico, Arizona and southwestern Texas, and extended into Mexico. East of the Cascade Mountains in Oregon and Washington the Palouse bunchgrass prairies were once joined to the grass-carpeted great valley of California. Together, these grasslands made up the prairie formation, the most extensive natural vegetation on the North American continent.

The dominant large mammals – the bison and the pronghorn – which contributed so much to the physiognomy of the prairies by their presence, were hunted almost to extinction in the 19th century. Both are now protected and the pronghorn has made a phenomenal recovery.

West from the Mississippi River, the elevation of the land gradually rises in an almost imperceptible slope that gains about 3,000 feet (914 metres) before it reaches the Rocky Mountains, the source of the sediments which have been washed down to underlie the sloping grassland region. The closer to the rain shadow of the Rockies, the less the annual precipitation and there is a drop of more than half the amount of rainfall of 40 inches (100 cm) on the eastern border.

As a result, the grassland falls into two main subdivisions, with a transition zone between. A tall grass prairie extends from Ohio to eastern Oklahoma where native grasses – big and little bluestem, Indian grass and prairie cord grass – once grew high enough to conceal a man on horseback. The semiarid high plains east of the Rockies are short-grass country, mostly of sod-forming blue grama and buffalo grass. The zone in between these extremes is the mixed-grass prairie of medium-sized grasses.

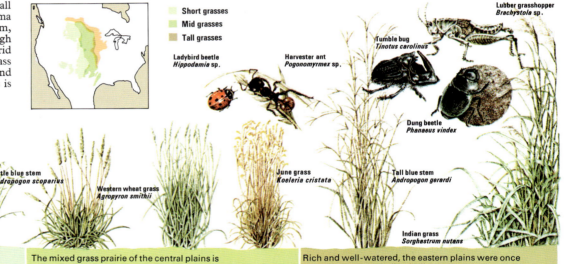

Short grasses
Mid grasses
Tall grasses

Ladybird beetle *Hippodamia* sp.

Harvester ant *Pogonomyrmex* sp.

Tumble bug *Tinotus carolinus*

Lubber grasshopper *Brachystola* sp.

Dung beetle *Phanaeus vindex*

Buffalo grass *Buchloe dactyloides*

Blue grama *Bouteloua gracilis*

Little blue stem *Andropogon scoparius*

Western wheat grass *Agropyron smithii*

June grass *Koeleria cristata*

Tall blue stem *Andropogon gerardi*

Indian grass *Sorghastrum nutans*

On the high, western plains where rainfall is least the ground is clad in a hardy, close-growing cover of blue grama and buffalo grass.

The mixed grass prairie of the central plains is composed of medium-sized grasses including june grass, western wheat grass and little blue stem.

Rich and well-watered, the eastern plains were once clad in grasses, including Indian grass, tall enough to conceal a man. These plains are now the 'corn belt'.

Prairie fowl
The development of agriculture has reduced the once infinite numbers of prairie grouse to isolation in remnant populations, but their 'booming grounds' still dot what remains of the virgin grasslands.

Courtship rituals
Spring mornings on the prairie echo to the booming of the courting prairie grouse. The male sage grouse *Centrocercus urophasianus* (left) prepares to display, puffing out his breast feathers and inflating air sacs on his neck. His display will be countered by another bird in an effort to outdo his territorial statements. (Above) two sharp-tailed grouse, *Pedioecetes* sp., strut together in a mating ritual.

The winner
The display contest draws to a close and one bird has successfully demonstrated his territorial rights; a female has been attracted (above). Eggs are laid in the thick grass and after hatching out the young follow their mother, feeding on the small insects and seeds she collects for them. The prairie fowl are so similar in nature and behaviour that they interbreed easily. (Left) greater prairie chicken *Tympanuchus americanus*.

Speedy burrower *above*
The bulky American badger *Taxidea taxus* swims and climbs efficiently and burrows rapidly to escape danger, or to hunt for one of its favourite prey – now diminished in numbers – the prairie dog *Cynomys ludovicianus.*

Parasitic beetle
The blister beetle *Tricrania sanguinipennis* gains all the benefits from its relationship with the solitary bee *Coletes thoracicus.*

1 Adult blister beetle lays its eggs beneath a stone (above) or around the base of grasses— but always near a nest of bees.

2 Beetle larvae are taken into the bees' nest, a ground structure where there is an ample supply of food (below).

3 Beetle larvae hatch out and move around. Eventually some of them attach to the body of a passing solitary bee (below).

4 The beetle larvae now devour both the food store and the eggs of the bee, before emerging as adults (right).

Successful coyote *left*
As other mammals have diminished in its habitat the coyote *Canis latrans* has successfully held its ground in many parts of the Great Plains. It can move at speeds up to 40 mph (64 kph) and – smaller and more solitary than the wolf – conceals itself easily from the hunter. A scavenger which will take carrion where it can, the coyote hunts down jackrabbits, rabbits and rodents. It has been known to have an unexplained hunting relationship with an unlikely partner – the burrowing badger of the prairies. Young are born in a den made by the mother.

Pronghorn and bison
Cropping their way across the prairies, great herds of pronghorns and bison once controlled the vegetational growth of the grassland until their numbers were decimated by the 19th-century hunters. Now both are protected, and the pronghorn has made a great recovery.

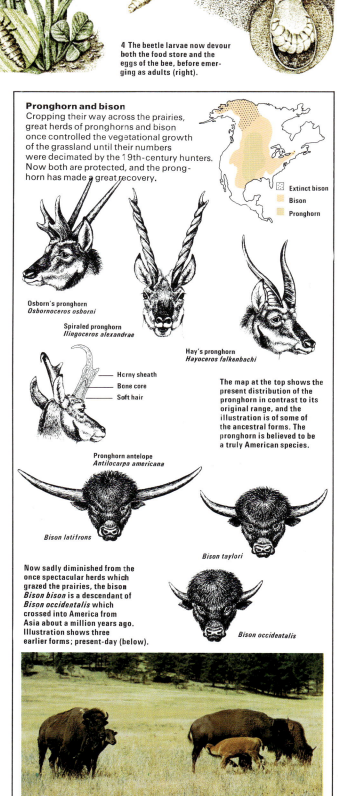

Extinct bison
Bison
Pronghorn

Osborn's pronghorn
Osbornoceros osborni

Spiraled pronghorn
Ilingoceros alexandrae

Hay's pronghorn
Hayoceros falkenbachi

Horny sheath
Bone core
Soft hair

The map at the top shows the present distribution of the pronghorn in contrast to its original range, and the illustration is of some of the ancestral forms. The pronghorn is believed to be a truly American species.

Pronghorn antelope
Antilocarpa americana

Bison latifrons

Bison taylori

Bison occidentalis

Colonial squirrel *right*
The prairie dog – no dog but a burrowing squirrel – once lived in vast underground 'cities', one of which was estimated to contain 400 million animals. Preyed on by coyotes, foxes, badgers, large hawks and eagles, the prairie dog has been systematically reduced by man, whose crops and grazing pasture for domestic animals were an attractive food source. There are five species.

Now sadly diminished from the once spectacular herds which grazed the prairies, the bison *Bison bison* is a descendant of *Bison occidentalis* which crossed into America from Asia about a million years ago. Illustration shows three earlier forms; present-day (below).

Prairie falcon
Falco mexicanus

Prairie falcon *Falco mexicanus* and black-footed ferret *Mustela nigripes* are hunters of prairie dog and jackrabbit.

Black-footed ferret
Mustela nigripes

Gregarious rodent *left*
The small white-footed mouse *Peromyscus leucopus* is a gregarious rodent, staying with its family and often interbreeding : mother with offspring, brother with sister. They provide food for most of the larger predators of the prairie lands.

Well-equipped jackrabbit *above*
The ubiquitous jackrabbit *Lepus* sp. is misnamed ; it is not a rabbit, but a hare, well adapted to the grasslands but equally so to cold, snow-covered forest terrain.

27

Death Valley and the Dry lands

The biggest of the North American deserts lies in the uplands of the Great Basin, 4,000 feet (940 metres) above sea level. It stretches from the Rockies in the east to the rain barrier of the Sierras in the west. Few cacti grow in this scrubland of sagebrush, and the principal animals are packrats, coyotes, bobcats, buzzards and several species of hawk and owl.

In the southwest, the Great Basin Desert merges with the Mojave via Death Valley, where an air temperature of 134°F has been recorded, the hottest-ever in North America. Death Valley is also lower than anywhere else on the continent: 276 feet (82 metres) below sea level. As little as two inches of rain a year falls on this grim arena of wind-sculptured rock, shifting sand dunes and lifeless salt flats, yet even here (except on the salt beds) more than 600 varieties of plant manage to grow. Over 100 species of birds and nearly 40 species of mammals have been seen.

Beyond Death Valley, the Mojave Desert is characterized by the Joshua tree and the creosote bush. 10,000 years ago mammoths and a type of camel wandered here, but today the desert is the province of sidewinder rattlesnakes, kangaroo rats, desert tortoises, cicadas, cactus wrens, and, in the rainy season, of royal lupines and golden gilea flowers. Farther still to the south, encircling the Gulf of California, are the subdivisions of the Sonoran Desert, 120,000 square miles (311,000km²) in all. The dominant plants here are the giant cacti, cardons and seguaros, growing up to 50 feet (15.2 meters) tall and weighing up to ten tons – of which nine tons may be water. The seguaros in particular provide homes for a great variety of animals, ranging from moth larvae to woodpeckers, from snakes to the sparrow-sized elf owl. Mesquite and palo verde trees are common.

East of the Sonoran Desert, between the east and west Sierra Madre, lies the Chihuahuan Desert. Crossed by north-south mountain ranges, some of which have mesquite grasslands on their upper slopes, the Chihuahuan desert includes a large part of the Mexican plateau, reaching a height of 6,000 feet (1,828 metres) in the south. Opuntia and barrel cacti grow here, and the spiny, crimson-flowered ocotillo shrub. Tarantula spiders, scorpions, lizards and antelope jackrabbits are common. To the north of the Chihuahuan Desert lies the Painted Desert, whose name comes from its abundance of vivid red, yellow, orange and brown sandstones.

The community centre
Mammoths and ancient camel forms once roamed what are now the desert areas of America's southwest. The giants have long since vanished but an active life is still to be found there. The yucca or Joshua trees provide community centres (right and below) for a variety of small creatures like Scott's oriole, which nests among the leaves. Insects around the roots attract small animals – and they tempt the night snake.

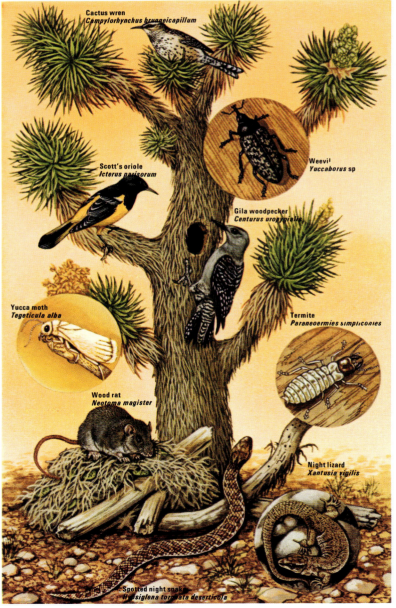

Cactus wren
Campylorhynchus brunneicapillum

Weevil
Yuccaborus sp

Scott's oriole
Icterus parisorum

Gila woodpecker
Centurus uropygialis

Yucca moth
Tegeticula alba

Termite
Paraneoermies simpliconies

Wood rat
Neotoma magister

Night lizard
Xantusia vigilis

Spotted night snake
Hypsiglena torquata deserticola

The yucca moth
Larvae of the yucca moth feed only on the developing seeds of the plant, pollinating the flowers in the process.

Spanish dagger *below*
Another form of yucca, the Spanish dagger, is shown in flower. Yuccas are members of the lily family and are common throughout the southwestern desert areas of the United States. They are found in Central America and the southern continent.

Female moth takes the pollen from the plant's anther (a), rolls it into a ball and takes it to the stigma of another plant (b). One or two eggs are laid (c), and the larvae feed on the seeds (d).

Mature larva falls to the ground, pupates for a year then returns to the surface, using small hooks on its back (e). The adult form then takes wing.

Horned lizard
Changes in light and heat intensity cause a rearrangement of pigment cells in the desert horned lizard *Phrynosoma* sp. (above) changing its colour to blend with its background. The white sand and sparse vegetation of New Mexico desert (right).

The hibernating bird
The nightjar *Phalaenoptilus nuttallii* (right) adjusts to the intense cold of the desert winter by hibernating. Its body temperature drops sharply from 100 °F to 60 °F and its respiration is virtually arrested in a stupor which may last three months. The dramatic geological forms of Monument Valley (below) rise up from the Utah Desert.

Poor-will
Phalaenoptilus nuttallii

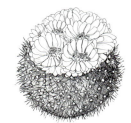

Common cacti
Opuntia sp. (above left) and *Ferocactus acanthodes* are two common cacti of the American deserts. Opuntia, or prickly pear, forms large, tree-like plants and *Ferocactus* may reach a height of 12 feet (3.7m) Some cacti are only pebble-sized. *Parodia* (left) is a South American species which has entered the northern continent.

Desert hunters
Widespread throughout the deserts of the Americas the burrowing owl *Speotyto cunicularia* (above) shares the burrows of desert animals and like them lives in colonies. The kit fox *Vulpes velox* (right), a smaller relative of the red fox, has acute hearing. Moving swiftly over short distances it runs down its quarry, of which the favourite is the kangaroo rat. Other food includes lizards, and an odd bird or rabbit.

Survivors in a hostile habitat
A lake almost as large as Lake Michigan today once covered much of the Great Basin Desert (Utah's Great Salt Lake is a remnant). To the west, another great lake, Lahontan, exists only in vestiges – the home of the strange, relict pupfish.

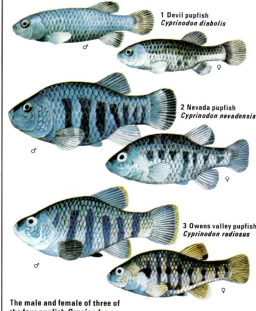

1 Devil pupfish
Cyprinodon diabolis

2 Nevada pupfish
Cyprinodon nevadensis

3 Owens valley pupfish
Cyprinodon radiosus

A 108°F Night feeding
B 108°F Day
C 110°F

The fatal heat of the desert pool centres force the pupfish to the marginally cooler ledges to survive. During the heat of the day some swim down to deep niches. Location of lakes (below).

The rattler *left*
The ominous rattle of the rattlesnake *Crotalus* sp. is made up of loose, interlocking rings of hard skin left after the snake has moulted. The rattler is one of the more venomous reptiles of the many with which the desert abounds; a number are quite harmless.

A hard case *below*
When the land tortoise *Gopherus* sp. retracts its hard-scaled limbs and neck it presents an almost insoluble problem to any would-be predator.

Desert tortoise
Gopherus sp.

Cottontail *left*
The cottontail rabbit has a widespread distribution in North America but there are a number of races, each to its area. The desert cottontail *Sylvilagus floridanus* relies on its agility to avoid predators. It needs little free water, gaining it from the plants it eats.

The male and female of three of the four pupfish *Cyprinodon* sp. are illustrated (above). They are relics of an aquatic fauna which lived in the great lakes once covering much of the south-western desert areas. There are 20 populations, living in the tiny aquatic 'islands' in the desert. (Right) the Lahontan cutthroat trout, Pyramid Lake, Nev.

Lahontan cutthroat trout
Salmo clarki henshawi

29

Appalachians and Rockies

The three principal mountain ranges of North America are the Appalachians, the Rockies and those of the Pacific Rim.

The Appalachians, thrust up some 200–230 million years ago, are by far the oldest. They stretch from the stumpy hillocks of Labrador to Georgia, via the lake-spattered, glacier-worn mountains of New England, the Adirondacks where some of the oldest rock on Earth can be seen in the extension of the Canadian shield, and the higher, unglaciated peaks of the Blue Ridge and Great Smoky mountains.

On the west coast, the ranges of the Pacific Rim, some 15 million years old, are the continent's youngest. They begin with the 1,600-mile-long (2,580km) volcanic chain of the Aleutian islands, continue on the mainland with the deeply folded crags of South Alaska, where elk, bear and mountain sheep roam, and swing south into the Kamloops of British Columbia and the Cascade ranges of Washington, Oregon and California.

Flanking these western ranges, from southern Alaska to the Washington Olympics, is a unique strip of lush temperate rain forest where hummingbirds can be found from late spring to autumn. Some of the mightiest trees in the world, the Douglas firs, grow here, and farther south the ancient redwoods and sequoias are all sustained by warm mists that drift inland from the Pacific – warm even this far north because of the Japan current.

The Rocky Mountains are North America's continental divide, and in Colorado their snows and glaciers give rise to six great rivers, the Missouri, Snake, Colorado, Arkansas, Platte and Rio Grande. The Rockies were formed about 70 million years ago, at roughly the same time as the dinosaurs died out, and in the same upheaval that produced the Andes and Himalayas. They stretch from Brooks Range in Alaska, the province of wolves and caribou, and end in Mexico's Sierra Madre Oriental, whose valleys are choked with tropical vegetation and alive with parrots. Like Brooks Range the mountains of the Sierra Madre Oriental have hardly been explored.

American bighorns *above* Bighorn sheep *Ovis canadensis* roam the Rockies.

Bears of North America *right* There are several species of brown bear *Ursus* and single species of black *Euarctos* and polar bears *Thalarctos maritimus*.

Alaskan grizzly 2.5 m
Ursus arctos horribilis

Kodiak bear 2.8 m
Ursus arctos middendorffi

Old World brown bear 2 m
Ursus arctos

American black bear 1.8 m
Euarctos americanus

Descriptive colours for bears—grizzly, blue, cinnamon and white – may mislead: black and brown bears can give birth to any or all of these variations.

Fire-forged symmetry *left* Montane ponderosa forests are characterized by their evenly spaced trees of a similar age, a natural symmetry created by the devastation of fire. The pines, *Pinus ponderosa* cover the ground with a flammable carpet of branches and needles which periodically bursts into flame. Some trees are destroyed but new seedlings develop in the ash layer. Once the new trees produce a litter of needles, small fires destroy the youngest seedlings but not the established adolescents. A new, evenly-spaced forest of trees is created – until, once more, enough litter is formed for a new fire.

Berry seekers
A grizzly mother and her cub forage on the mountainside for berries (above). Bears are omnivorous, eating fruits, berries, honey, insects and small mammals, but they are happy with a vegetable diet. The kodiak bear *Ursus middendorffi* (left) demonstrates its dexterity as a fisherman, hooking salmon from a river. It may grow to a height of more than 12 feet (3.7m). The black bear *Euarctos americanus* (far left).

Beaver remakes the landscape
A natural engineer, the beaver *Castor canadensis* reshapes the landscape around its lodges. Streams are dammed and ponds created, young trees are felled and canals dug to float the logs to the worksite.

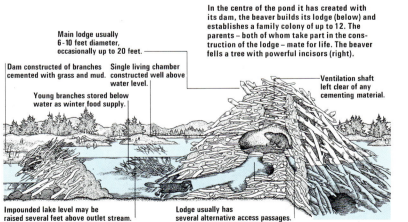

In the centre of the pond it has created with its dam, the beaver builds its lodge (below) and establishes a family colony of up to 12. The parents – both of whom take part in the construction of the lodge – mate for life. The beaver fells a tree with powerful incisors (right).

Main lodge usually 6-10 feet diameter, occasionally up to 20 feet.

Dam constructed of branches cemented with grass and mud.

Single living chamber constructed well above water level.

Young branches stored below water as winter food supply.

Ventilation shaft left clear of any cementing material.

Impounded lake level may be raised several feet above outlet stream.

Lodge usually has several alternative access passages.

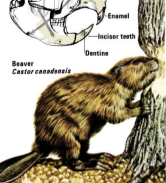

Muscles

Enamel

Incisor teeth

Dentine

Beaver *Castor canadensis*

Appalachian spectacle
With the coming of autumn many thousands of birds migrate along the line of the Appalachians. 15 different hawk species (some are shown here) have been seen on passage, taking advantage of the updraughts created by the mountain range.

Marsh hawk
Circus cyaneus
3.7ft 113cm

Rough-legged buzzard
Buteo lagopus
4.75ft 142cm

Sharp-shinned hawk
Accipiter striatus ♂
2ft 61cm

Red-shouldered hawk
Buteo lineatus
3.1ft 96cm

KITTATINNY MTS

New York

Red-tailed hawk
Buteo jamaicensis
4.2ft 129cm

Osprey
Pandion haliaetus
5.5ft 165cm

Washington

Golden eagle
Aquila chrysaetos
6.5ft 198cm

NOVEMBER

OCTOBER

SEPTEMBER

Broad-winged hawk
Buteo platypterus
2.8ft 86cm

Turkey vulture
Cathartes aura
6ft 182cm

Bald eagle
Haliaeetus leucocephalus
7ft 214cm

APPALACHIANS

Rams in conflict
Bighorn rams of the Rockies butt heads in a rutting season conflict. The animals lurch dizzily after their collision.

American bighorn
Ovis canadensis

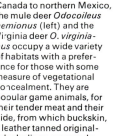

Hunting cats
The sharp-eyed lynx *Lynx canadensis* (above) and the mountain lion, or cougar *Felis concolor* (right) are montane predators. The leopard-size cougar hunts down deer and other herbivores, dragging carcasses three times its own weight over long distances.

Buckskin on the hoof
Widespread in western America, from southern Canada to northern Mexico, the mule deer *Odocoileus hemionus* (left) and the Virginia deer *O. virginianus* occupy a wide variety of habitats with a preference for those with some measure of vegetational concealment. They are popular game animals, for their tender meat and their hide, from which buckskin, a leather tanned originally by Indians, was made.

Underwater insectivore
Thrush-like in size and wren-like in form, the North American dipper *Cinclus mexicanus* walks in and out of racing torrents, seeking aquatic insects on the stream bed. Their feathers are waterproofed by an oil secretion; there is a flap over the nostrils to keep out water.

Catsmeat *above*
The hoary marmot *Marmota caligata* is the prey of cougar, lynx and eagle.

Dipper hunting under water for insects and larvae.

Agile climbers *above*
The mountain goat *Oreamnos americanus* can find rocky footholds where none apparently exist.

Small horns *right*
Agile bighorn ewes (see bighorn butting contest (above) have small horns compared with the male's.

Still Waters and Salmon Torrents

Landscape owes much of its appearance to the paths carved out by water moving across the land. In turn, each river system has been moulded by the condition of the land through which it flows – the climate, rock structure, and even vegetation.

Rivers are often described as young, mature or in their old age, referring to the stage of development they have reached. A good example is the Mississippi River, with its youthful headwater in Minnesota and its mature middle section between St Anthony Falls and south of Tennessee, where it is joined by the Missouri and Ohio Rivers. There it begins its long meandering 'old age' course to the Gulf of Mexico across a broad flood plain. Not all rivers possess these three stages. Most Maine rivers, rushing towards the Atlantic, lack the meandering stage, while some others (along the Gulf, for example) are in old age practically throughout their whole course.

Different kinds of running water provide variations in habitat. Fast-flowing streams require different adaptations for living than do quiet pools, and animals in these reaches have mechanisms to prevent them being washed downstream. The sculpin, a fish used to fast-running water, brace oversized forefins against the upstream sides of stones and the highly streamlined trout swims against the current with ease.

As the river approaches the ocean and the water becomes more salty, the aquatic insect population is replaced by crustaceans such as crabs and shrimps. Killifish, croakers, flounders and striped bass are common estuarine fishes.

Ponds and lakes are intermediary storage pools of quiet water and all are destined to grow shallower and smaller as sediments and organic debris fill them in and they become vegetation-covered land. The pond, in contrast to the lake (a sheet of open water), is generally defined as a quiet body of water so shallow that rooted plants grow completely across it. This aquatic vegetation provides food and shelter for many kinds of frogs, birds such as herons and ducks, and aquatic mammals. Bottom plants are scarce towards the centre and only a few snails, freshwater clams and mayfly larvae live there.

Water lily *above*
Surface leaves of the water lily absorb light energy: underwater leaves are thin.

Tongue bait *right*
The purple gallinule uses its long tongue as a bait to catch fish.

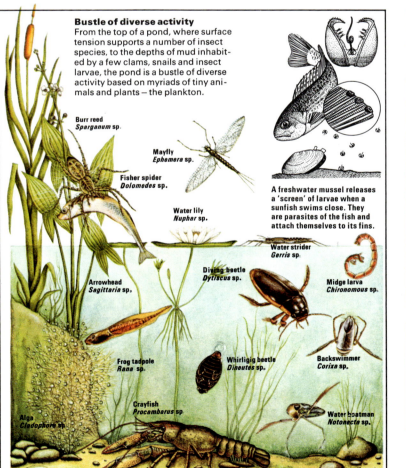

Bustle of diverse activity
From the top of a pond, where surface tension supports a number of insect species, to the depths of mud inhabited by a few clams, snails and insect larvae, the pond is a bustle of diverse activity based on myriads of tiny animals and plants – the plankton.

Burr reed
Sparganum sp.

Mayfly
Ephemera sp.

Fisher spider
Dolomedes sp.

Water lily
Nuphar sp.

A freshwater mussel releases a 'screen' of larvae when a sunfish swims close. They are parasites of the fish and attach themselves to its fins.

Water strider
Gerris sp.

Arrowhead
Sagittaria sp.

Diving beetle
Dytiscus sp.

Midge larva
Chironomous sp.

Frog tadpole
Rana sp.

Whirligig beetle
Dineutes sp.

Backswimmer
Corixa sp.

Alga
Cladophora sp.

Crayfish
Procambarus sp

Water boatman
Notonecta sp.

Turtles
The alligator snapping turtle (above) also uses a process on its forked tongue for bait. (Left) painted turtle.

Bright markings
The bronze frog *Rana clamitans* (above) is common in ponds; the northern diamond back turtle *Malachemys* sp. swims in coast streams.

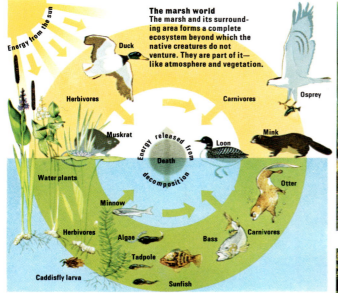

The marsh world
The marsh and its surrounding area forms a complete ecosystem beyond which the native creatures do not venture. They are part of it—like atmosphere and vegetation.

Energy from the sun

Duck

Herbivores

Carnivores

Osprey

Muskrat

Loon

Mink

Death

Energy released from decomposition

Water plants

Otter

Minnow

Herbivores

Algae

Carnivores

Tadpole

Bass

Caddisfly larva

Sunfish

Sunfish and muskrat
Weedy water is the home of the common sunfish *Lepomis gibbosus* (above). The largest of the voles is the muskrat *Ondatra zibethicus* (left) which lurks among the water plants in summer and builds an above-water lodge in the winter.

They outswim fish
A neat, effective diver the pied-billed grebe *Podilymbus podiceps* (left) hunts small fish beneath the water's surface. A mammal perfectly adapted to an aquatic life the otter *Lutra canadensis* (right) can outswim most fish and grabs small waterbirds.

Relict freshwater fish *below*
The slightly grotesque appearance of the fishes hints at an undisturbed evolution. Neither sturgeon nor paddlefish has developed a swim bladder since their origins in the Cretaceous. Garpike, bowfin evolved in the Permian.

Shovel-nosed sturgeon
Scaphirhynchus platorynchus
Mississippi basin

Bowfin
Amia calva
Great Lakes to Gulf of Mexico

Alligator gar
Lepisosteus tristoechus
Southern United States

Paddlefish
Polyodon spathula
Mississippi basin

Wood duck and kingfisher
The wood duck *Aix sponsa* (right) is found in wooded swamps.
The belted kingfisher *Megaceryle* sp. (below).

Belted kingfisher
Megaceryle alcyon

The quiet miracle of the salmon
The life of the salmon *Onchorhynchus* sp. is a quiet miracle of survival and determination. The egg, one of 5,000 born to the mother, hatches out in a mountain rill and drifts to the river-mouth. It is now a much-threatened 'fingerling' and has to adjust its metabolism to sea water and sea foods. Four years later, fattened at sea into a strongly-built carnivore, it heads unerringly back to the stream where it hatched, now adjusting from salt water to fresh. Overcoming every obstacle man and nature can put in its way, it reaches its native pool and breeds. Then, it heads back for the sea—but, exhausted, never makes it.

Lamprey attack salmon with horny rasping teeth

Young lamprey move downstream to the sea

Lamprey migrate upstream to spawn

Lamprey larvae live in burrows in stream bed

The lamprey threat
A sea of spawning salmon in an Alaskan river (right). To reach this, the climax of their lives, they have survived many predators, among them the lamprey *Petromyzon* (left) which attaches itself to the young salmon and, using a sucker, drains away the life of its host.

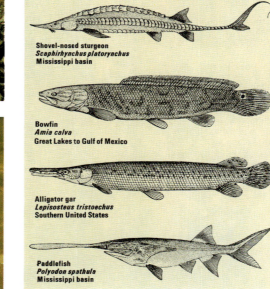

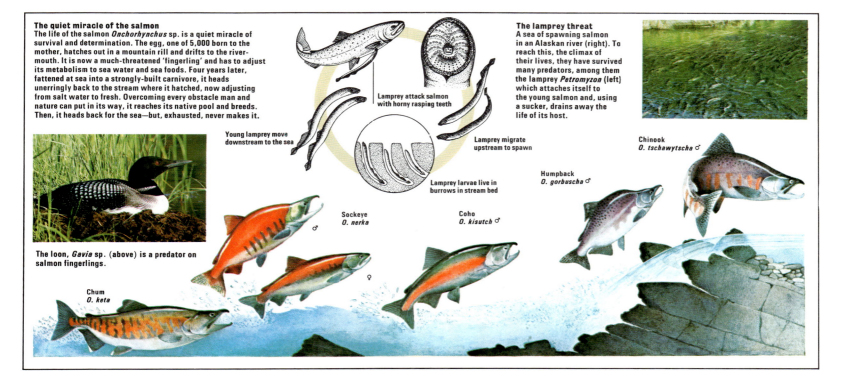

Chinook
O. tschawytscha ♂

Humpback
O. gorbuscha ♂

Sockeye
O. nerka ♂

Coho
O. kisutch ♂

The loon, *Gavia* sp. (above) is a predator on salmon fingerlings.

Chum
O. keta

Pines, Bayous and Everglades

The low-lying southeastern states were at one time densely forested, forming the bottommost tier of the great eastern temperate deciduous forest. The area is part of the coastal plain which has been gradually rising above sea level for the last 70 million years. The southern portion, about 100 miles (165 km) wide along the Atlantic, extends from Virginia through the Carolinas, into the Gulf states as far as eastern Texas, and loops up the Mississippi Valley to southern Illinois. Not counting the tip of the Florida peninsula, a distinct tropical realm, this area of some 200,000 square miles (518,000 km²) can be divided into three zones.

Along the northern margin, in the more upland, better-drained soils, what is left of the deciduous forest is dominated by post oak, hickory and holly. Next, there is a broad zone of pinelands composed chiefly of slash, long-leaf and loblolly pines whose continued dominion depends on repeated fires which have occurred for ages past and continue to occur. Closer to the coast, in fairly moist lowland but not swampy sites, the characteristic hardwood trees which replace the pines are sweet bay (an evergreen magnolia) and several species of live or evergreen oak, usually festooned with Spanish moss.

In areas flooded for longer periods, there are extensive swamps of pond and bald cypress with 'knees' growing up from root systems to buttress straight trunks. The swollen bases of black gum trees, or water tupelo, frequently share the soggy soil. On the outer fringes of the coastal plain, the stalks of the broad fan-shaped dwarf palmetto dot many acres of dry soil.

Two species of New World crocodilians, the American alligator throughout the swamps and the American crocodile only along the tip of Florida, are characteristic. The southern and oak toads, the pig and the carpenter frog, the pine-woods barking and squirrel tree frog are restricted to this region. Several aquatic salamanders such as the 'congo eel' or amphiuma and the dwarf siren are found nowhere else. The area holds a record number of poisonous snakes, in addition to many harmless southern species.

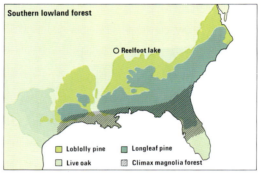

Southern lowland forest

○ Reelfoot lake

Loblolly pine   Longleaf pine

Live oak   Climax magnolia forest

The delta *left*
The bottomlands of the Mississippi and Red Rivers form one of the great delta regions of the world. The whole of the delta – part grassland, part riverine forest – is sinking as the weight of the river-deposited material causes the underlying layers to compress and sag. As it sinks, the delta grows seaward and old river mouths can be identified by the arcs of shallow water which are found offshore.

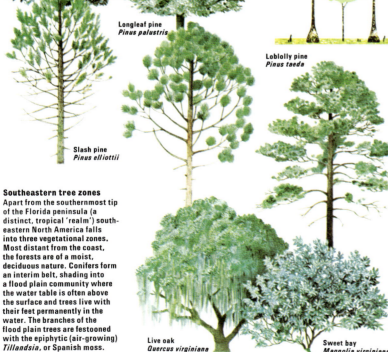

Holly
Ilex opaca

Overcup oak
Quercus lyrata

Longleaf pine
Pinus palustris

Loblolly pine
Pinus taeda

Slash pine
Pinus elliottii

Southeastern tree zones
Apart from the southernmost tip of the Florida peninsula (a distinct, tropical 'realm') southeastern North America falls into three vegetational zones. Most distant from the coast, the forests are of a moist, deciduous nature. Conifers form an interim belt, shading into a flood plain community where the water table is often above the surface and trees live with their feet permanently in the water. The branches of the flood plain trees are festooned with the epiphytic (air-growing) *Tillandsia*, or Spanish moss.

Live oak
Quercus virginiana

Sweet bay
Magnolia virginiana

'Cranetown,' a nesting colony of spear-fishing birds in the center of a flooded cypress grove, each species to its niche.

Common egret   Double-crested cormorant   Anhinga

Black-crowned night heron

Great blue heron

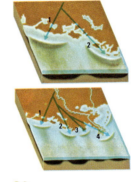

Tiny heron
Flooded swamplands provide paradise for long-legged, dart-beaked birds like the little green heron *Butorides* sp. (below).

Fishing birds
The little blue heron *Hydranassa caerulea* (above) female associates more often with other males than with her mate. The egret *Egretta alba* (below) is a world-wide species. Snake bird *Anhinga anhinga* (right) dries its wings like a cormorant after diving.

Anhinga
Anhinga anhinga

The Florida Everglades extending from Lake Okeechobee south comprise over 7,000 acres, the southern portion of which constitutes a national park. The region is essentially a river, although it is covered by coarse sedges, grasses and rushes, as it serves as a drainage outlet from the lake to the gulf. This sea of grass contains patches of open water and is spotted by scattered islands of trees called hummocks. Along the coast, mangroves form dense almost impenetrable thickets. The deeper sloughs, ponds and drainage courses hold water all year.

Here we find garfish, alligators, otters, ducks and grebes and a fantastic variety of wading birds, including egrets and herons, ibises and spoonbills. It is in the hummocks, however, that the greatest variety of tropical plant and animal life can be found. In addition to several palms, there are tropical trees such as gumbo-limbo, mahogany, joewood, pond apple, strangler fig and coco-plum. Most hummocks support rare ferns and orchids as well as a great variety of air plants or epiphytes, many with beautiful flowers. During the spring migration, warblers and other songbirds stop to rest and feed; some, like the spectacular painted bunting, remain to nest. Zebra butterflies and other insects swarm and delicately patterned tree-snails crawl along branches.

Swamp denizens
The terrapin *Pseudemys* sp. (above) lives in Florida wetlands. The alligator *A. mississippiensis* (right) has a widespread distribution in southern swamplands.

Everglade insect hunters
Insectivores of the insect-rich Everglades are the golden Orb spider (left) and the southern leopard frog (below).

Vegetation of southern Florida

	Mangrove
	Pine forest
	Wet prairie
	Marsh
	Tropical forest
	Cypress

The swamplands of Florida

Vegetational variety of the Everglades
Fringed with red, black and white mangrove communities, the Everglades are dominated by a climax community of southern cypress, with red maple, water tupelo and other trees. There are islands of grass called hummocks, merging with freshwater marshes of grass, sedge and rushes.

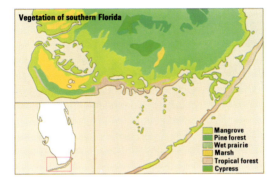

1 Everglade kite	10 Eastern fox squirrel
Rostrhamus sociabilis	*Sciurus niger*
2 Pileated woodpecker	11 Snail
Phloeocoastes pileatus	*Isognomon melina alata*
3 Prothonotary warbler	12 Green treefrog
Protonotaria citrea	*Hyla cinerea*
4 Rough green snake	13 Green anolis
Opheodrys aestivus	*Anolis carolinensis*
5 Limpkin	14 Zebra butterfly
Aramus guarauna	*Heliconius charitonius*
6 Raccoon	15 Purple gallinule
Procyon lotor	*Porphyrula martinica*
7 Flamingo	16 Snail
Phoenicopterus ruber	*Pomocea flagellata*
8 Mississippi alligator	17 Swamp rabbit
Alligator mississippiensis	*Sylvilagus* sp.
9 Roseate spoonbill	18 Oxeye tarpon
Ajaia ajaja	*Megalops cyprinoides*
	19 Cottonmouth moccasin
	Ancistrodon piscivorus

Life between the Tides

The coastline of North America is nearly 100,000 miles (160,000 km) long. It stretches from the frozen north to the coral islands of the Florida cays and the baked desert shores of the Gulf of California. To the west, off the coast of Alaska, Little Diomede Island lies close to the edge of Asia, and the full swell of the Pacific surf beats upon the coast. In the south, the Caribbean Sea heats under a tropical sun and spills into the Atlantic between Florida and Bimini Island at the rate of six thousand million tons a second, a jet of warm water that hugs the east coast as far as Cape Hatteras and then moves northeast across the Atlantic. From the north, the cold Labrador current surges south to the Grand Banks before being turned north again and warmed by the Gulf Stream.

The animals that live at the edge of these tides are, like all coastal animals, the sums of a variety of delicate responses to the factors of temperature, degree of exposure to the surf, tidal range, and the physical makeup of the coast – whether it be principally rock, sand, mud, or some combination of them.

The Pacific coast, north of Baja California, is predominantly rocky, and since it faces thousands of miles of open sea, with few islands or submarine ridges to break the force of the waves, wave shock here is probably greater than anywhere else in the northern hemisphere; though there are, of course, innumerable protected inlets, and in one of the biggest, Puget Sound near Vancouver, the waters are as waveless as a lake.

To the south, in the Gulf of California, sweltering summer temperatures force animals farther down the beach than they would normally be found. Along the other Gulf Coast, the Gulf of Mexico, the warm, modest tides of the Caribbean do little to disturb the endless sandy beaches and sandspits – which further shelter an 'inland waterway' and coastal region that sustains a greater variety of bird life than can be found anywhere else on the continent.

From Long Island, as far as the mouth of the St John River in Canada, the coastline grows progressively rockier and the water colder, and the shore life bears many resemblances to that of northern Europe.

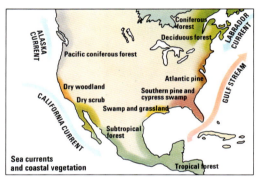

Sea currents and coastal vegetation

The protective cloak of seaweed
Dense 'forests' of kelp – giant seaweed, or algae – modify and subdue the stronger waves and currents and thus allow many animals to develop in relatively calm water.

Seaweeds of coastal California
1 *Calliarthon* sp.
2 *Egregia* sp.
3 *Laminaria* sp.
4 *Dictyoneurum* sp.
5 *Cystoseira* sp.
6 *Macrocystis* sp.
7 *Nereocystis* sp.
8 *Pterygophora* sp.
9 *Costaria* sp.

9.8 ft 3 m
19.6 ft 6 m
29.5 ft 9 m
39.3 ft 12 m

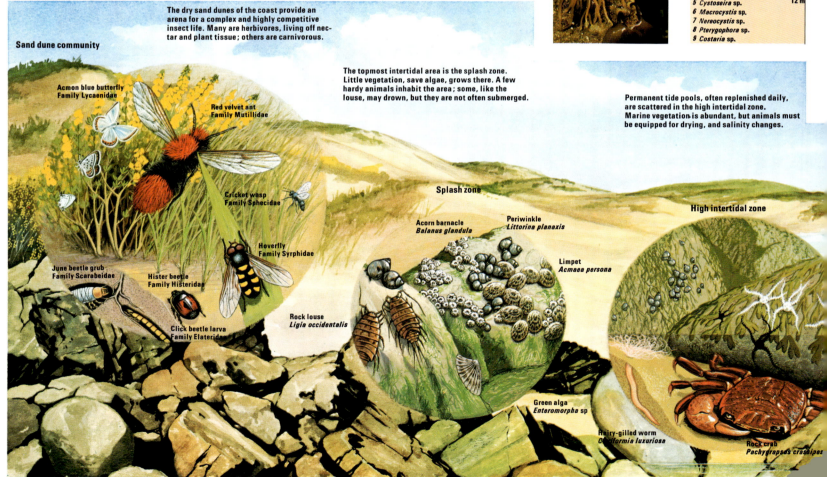

Sand dune community

The dry sand dunes of the coast provide an arena for a complex and highly competitive insect life. Many are herbivores, living off nectar and plant tissue; others are carnivorous.

Acmon blue butterfly
Family Lycaenidae

Red velvet ant
Family Mutillidae

Cricket wasp
Family Sphecidae

Hoverfly
Family Syrphidae

June beetle grub
Family Scarabeidae

Hister beetle
Family Histeridae

Click beetle larva
Family Elateridae

The topmost intertidal area is the splash zone. Little vegetation, save algae, grows there. A few hardy animals inhabit the area; some, like the louse, may drown, but they are not often submerged.

Permanent tide pools, often replenished daily, are scattered in the high intertidal zone. Marine vegetation is abundant, but animals must be equipped for drying, and salinity changes.

Splash zone

High intertidal zone

Acorn barnacle
Balanus glandula

Periwinkle
Littorina planaxis

Limpet
Acmaea persona

Rock louse
Ligia occidentalis

Green alga
Enteromorpha sp

Hairy-gilled worm
Cirriformia luxuriosa

Rock crab
Pachygrapsus crassipes

A popular nesting place

The birds illustrated here are cliff-nesting species. Severe and unwelcoming, the rock face nevertheless provides a series of nesting niches for a variety of species without competition – however different their other forms of behaviour may be. The rock face is so popular that birds often overpopulate them.

California murre
Uria aalge

Brandt's cormorant
Phalacrocorax penicillatus

Bank swallow
Riparia riparia

Cassin's auklet
Ptychoramphus aleutica

Tufted puffin
Lunda cirrhata

Baird's cormorant
Phalacrocorax pelagicus

Western gull
Larus occidentalis

Pigeon guillemot
Cepphus columba

Ashy petrel
Oceanodroma homochroa

Protection in numbers

A huge breeding colony is an effective deterrent against predation. Vigorous territorial behaviour is customary, keeping birds alive to the threat of crows, ravens, gulls and other predators. Colonial nesting birds often breed simultaneously, hatching their chicks at the same time. This confines predation to a short interval, when the whole colony is prepared. The nesters (above) are kittiwakes.

Stunning bird *below*

Widespread on the west coast of the Americas, the brown pelican *Pelecanus occidentalis* dives steeply into the water, striking it with its chest, its head and wings held back. The shock of the impact is thought to stun fish several feet below the surface.

Friendly neighbours *left*

Murres *Uria aalge* and kittiwakes *Rissa* sp. nest close together on precipitous cliffs.

Beached giants *right*

Huddled together on a Pacific beach a herd of walruses *Odobenus rosmarus* may number 100. At breeding time their tusks – extended canine teeth – are used in territorial fights; when feeding they are useful for grubbing crabs and molluscs from the sea bed (below).

Plant and animal life abounds in the middle intertidal area. Uncovered by the tides but constantly wetted by the waves the animals are adapted to keep themselves in place.

Sea plants are large in the low intertidal area and a multitude of animals hidden in and around them are rarely uncovered, except during freakishly low waters.

Low intertidal zone

Sea cucumber
Stichopus californicus

Brown seaweed
Laminaria sp.

Middle intertidal zone

Nudibranch
Triopha carpenteri

Starfish
Sphaeriodiscus placenta

Brittlestar
Ophiopholis pugetana

Sea lettuce
Ulva sp.

Sponge
Halciona permollis

Abalone
Haliotis rufescens

Purple shore crab
Hemigrapsus nudus

Sponge
Leucosolenia eleanor

Sea urchin
Strongylocentrotus franciscanus

Sea anemone
Epiactis prolifera

Secure against the tides

To stay in place as the tides move about them shelled animals use a number of techniques (below). The mussel secures itself with threads, the acorn barnacle uses a cement adhesive, and the limpet applies a muscular foot.

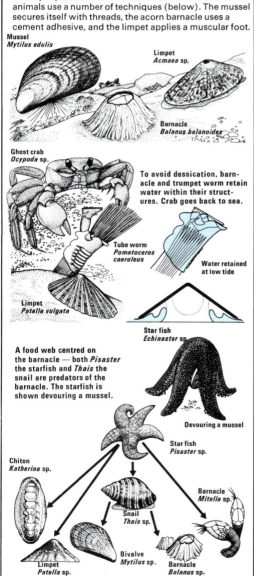

Mussel
Mytilus edulis

Limpet
Acmaea sp.

Barnacle
Balanus balanoides

Ghost crab
Ocypoda sp.

To avoid dessication, barnacle and trumpet worm retain water within their structures. Crab goes back to sea.

Tube worm
Pomatoceros caeruleus

Water retained at low tide

Limpet
Patella vulgata

Star fish
Echinaster sp.

A food web centred on the barnacle — both *Pisaster* the starfish and *Thais* the snail are predators of the barnacle. The starfish is shown devouring a mussel.

Devouring a mussel

Star fish
Pisaster sp.

Chiton
Katherina sp.

Snail
Thais sp.

Barnacle
Mitella sp.

Limpet
Patella sp.

Bivalve
Mytilus sp.

Barnacle
Balanus sp.

Central and South America
THE NEOTROPICAL REALM

Central and South America

The connexion between South America and the rest of the world has never been more than tenuous and — for much of the history of life on Earth — non-existent. It is an isolation that has given to the continent a flora and fauna characteristically its own, but owing some influence to the northern continent and, through it, to the great landmass of Eurasia. It is a continent of superlative geography. A mountain spine, the mighty Andes, reaches for thousands of miles from the northern hemisphere almost to touch Antarctica with a rocky finger. It has a river, the Amazon, much greater in almost every sense than any other in the world and a forest of unparalleled size and unbridled luxuriance. Its coastal waters teem with marine life, and offshore there are islands, the Galapagos, harbouring species which caused traditional theories of evolution to be revised. The great glories are, however, the river and the forest, the *Hylaea amazonica*, which clothes the basin of the Amazon and its tributaries, 17 of which are more than 1,000 miles (1,600 km) long. In this great forest, vegetation and river are largely indivisible. Most life forms must either climb or swim, unless they are birds or fish. The result is a lavish avian fauna and countless, many-hued fish, with a small but exceedingly diverse animal life that will climb, if need be, or take to the water with ease. The highlands of the Andes support a fauna uniquely adapted to its rarified air and deserts as barren as any in the world fringe the Pacific margins.

Buttressed roots in mangrove swamp, Amazon basin, South America

Key to panorama

1 Swifts	24 Tayra	47 Red-billed scythebill
2 Hyacinthine macaw	25 Vine snake	48 Crimson topaz hummingbirds
3 Ornate hawk eagle	26 Yellow-headed Amazon parrot	49 Geoffrey's marmoset
4 Harpy eagle	27 Blue-headed parrot	50 Grey four-eyed opossum
5 Blue and yellow macaws	28 Lettered aracari	51 Pygmy anteater
6 Geoffrey's spider monkey	29 Paradise tanager	52 Morpho butterfly
7 Boa constrictor	30 Swallow tanager	53 Gould's manakin
8 White crested guan	31 Blue-necked tanager	54 White-eared tufted marmoset
9 Red howler monkey	32 Kinkajou	55 Tree frog
10 Squirrel monkey	33 White-tailed trogan	56 Long-billed star-throat hummingbird
11 Cock of the rock	34 Emerald tree boa	57 Fork-tailed wood nymph
12 Black spider monkey	35 Blue-grey tanager	58 Heliconid butterfly
13 Chestnut woodpecker	36 Cotton-headed tamarins	59 Forest bat
14 Tree porcupine	37 Common iguana	60 Fisherman bats
15 Ornate umbrella bird	38 Black-capped capuchin	61 Beryl-spangled tanager
16 Wooly monkey	39 Tamandua	62 Bird-eating spider
17 Monk saki	40 Sulphur-breasted toucan	63 Tree frog
18 Coatimundi	41 Two-toed sloth	64 Tree hopper
19 Red uakari	42 Margay	65 Tree frog
20 Great razor-billed curassaw	43 Window pane butterfly	66 Parasol ant
21 Toco toucans	44 Squirrel monkey	67 Katydid
22 Scarlet macaws	45 Blue morpho butterfly	68 Mouse opossum
23 False vampire bat	46 Ruby topaz hummingbird	69 Vampire bat

Land Bridge to a Continent

Rich in mammal species (nearly 600), South America has few large herbivores in comparison with African fauna. The greatest number of species is found in two groups, the bats (140) and the rodents (340). Many bizarre species have evolved in the southern continent with anteaters and armadillos contrasting with the more familiar rats, squirrels, cats and foxes. Marsupials have survived, as in Australia, and the fossil record shows that many extinct endemic groups flourished in the past.

Although the fossil record is not complete the outlines of the development of the complex and varied fauna can be traced through the main stages. The ancient fauna of unknown origin in pretertiary times but containing some groups widely distributed across the world (marsupials and notoungulates) became isolated when South America was separated by sea barriers from the rest of the world. This ancient fauna continued to evolve during the period of isolation until a connection was re-established with North America during the late Oligocene. During the period of isolation three groups of mammals succeeded in reaching the island from elsewhere (caviomorph rodents, monkeys, and, much later, procyonids). Finally the land connection, tenuous at first, with North America allowed a complex exchange of fauna in both directions. Although the number of families of mammals moving north almost equalled the number moving south one of the latter families (Cricetidae-rodents) proved almost explosively successful in South America and now dominates the modern fauna in numbers of species.

During the Pleistocene, as in other parts of the world, a great part of the mammal fauna became extinct, particularly the larger herbivores and associated fauna, including sabre-toothed tigers. In South America this was a period of volcanic activity, glaciation and consequent climatic instability linked to major fluctuations in habitat distribution. Some authors point out that it was also the period during which man reached the continent. No clear picture of the cause of Pleistocene extinctions has yet been established by science.

Ancient inhabitants
Various groups of animals have occupied South America for differing lengths of time. The longer a group has existed there the more differentiated it has become from relatives living elsewhere. This feature is particularly noticeable in the Edentates – sloths, anteaters – which are peculiar to South America and seem to have no link with any other group. Early Palaeocene groups of the subcontinent include marsupials, notoungulates, condylarths, liptolerns, pyrotheres and astrapotheres. Little is known about the origin of these animals.

The great highway *right*
Mammalian migrations between the two Americas have been reconstructed from present-day evidence and from fossil remains. The narrow Central American isthmus has acted as a land bridge and important filter region for animal movements from north and south.

	South to north temperate
	1 Megatherium
	2 Mylodon
	3 Armadillo
	4 Didelphis
	5 Porcupine
	6 Glyptodon
	South to north tropical
	7 Cebid monkey
	8 Agouti
	9 Toxodon
	10 Sloth
	11 Paca
	12 Anteater

■ Temperate regions
■ Tropical regions
● Extinct species
○ Extant species

● Macrauchenia *left*
A quaint-visaged ungulate *Macrauchenia* survived the first waves of invading animals from the north, then became extinct. Its bones were found and identified by Darwin during his South American travels.

○ Opossum *right*
The North American opossum *Didelphis marsupialis virginiana* is a member of one of the earliest groups of pouched animals and the closest of all living animals to its ancestors.

● Giant sloth *left*
Huge animals have vanished from the Americas but in the Pleistocene era the giant sloth *Megatherium*—it was larger than the elephant—ranged from the south to North America before it became extinct.

○ Armadillo *left*
The nine-banded armadillo is a living member of the oldest South American group, the Edentata. During the past 100 years it has spread north to the state of Kansas in the United States.

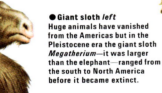

● Pyrotherium *right*
One of the curious herbivores that have vanished from South America and the world the *Pyrotherium* echoes the hippo and the elephant in appearance. It was an ungulate or grazing animal.

	North to south temperate
	13 Fox
	14 Horse
	15 Tapir
	16 Smilodon
	17 Spectacled bear
	18 Peccary
	19 Llama
	20 Cricetid rodent
	North to south tropical
	21 Shrew
	22 Heteromyid rodent
	23 Squirrel

Island-hopping 'waifs'

The monkeys of South America are quite clearly distinct from those of the old world – and yet are clearly related, suggesting a more recent entry into South America than the Edentates. The second faunal stratum, the native rodents (the South American histricomorphs) and the primates dates from the early Oligocene. Both groups are described as 'waifs', that is to say, they do not appear to have followed the land bridge but may have entered South America by a series of island hops. The monkeys display a parallel but independent development to their African cousins.

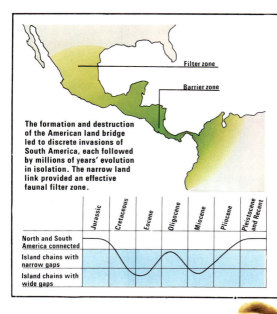

The formation and destruction of the American land bridge led to discrete invasions of South America, each followed by millions of years' evolution in isolation. The narrow land link provided an effective faunal filter zone.

Filter zone

Barrier zone

	Jurassic	Cretaceous	Eocene	Oligocene	Miocene	Pliocene	Pleistocene and Recent
North and South America connected							
Island chains with narrow gaps							
Island chains with wide gaps							

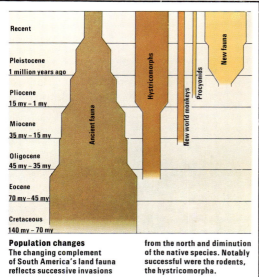

Recent

Pleistocene
1 million years ago

Pliocene
15 my – 1 my

Miocene
35 my – 15 my

Oligocene
45 my – 35 my

Eocene
70 my – 45 my

Cretaceous
140 my – 70 my

Ancient fauna
Hystricomorphs
New world monkeys
Procyonids
New fauna

Population changes

The changing complement of South America's land fauna reflects successive invasions from the north and diminution of the native species. Notably successful were the rodents, the hystricomorpha.

● **Rodents** *left*
Rodents were—and are—the most successful of all South American mammal groups. An early form, *Prodolichotis*, was the ancestor of *Dolichotis* the mara of the pampas (illustrated on page 53).

● **Primitive capybara** *right*
Protohydrochoerus found in the Upper Pliocene and Pleistocene of South America, was one of the ancestral forms of the modern capybara. It was one of the many species to disappear in the Pleistocene

○ **Coatimundi** *below*
A late arrival from the north the coatimundi *Nasua nasua* established itself successfully in South America. It is a relative of the North American raccoon and the South American crab-eating raccoon.

○ **Capybara** *right*
The largest of living rodents the capybara is descended from animals which with monkeys arrived in South America while it was still isolated from the north. It is both aquatic and terrestrial.

The latecomers

The third broad animal invasion was a staggered process. By the late Miocene a few northern forms had arrived, small carnivores related to the raccoon. In the early Pliocene some South American animals like the giant sloth had reached North America. This was the beginning of a large intermigration which reached its peak in Pleistocene times. Fifteen North American families moved south and seven South American families moved north. Where there was a battle for habitat, the north proved stronger and ousted its southern competitors.

○ **Tapir** *below*
The three South American species of tapir arrived from the north in Cenozoic times. They have relatives in Malaysia, supporting evidence that Asia and America were joined in recent times.

● **Vanished herbivore** *right*
The camel-like *Titanotylopus* was one of the many ungulate herbivores constituting the bulk of all early South American fauna. It died out at some time in the Pleistocene era.

● **Sabre-tooth** *below*
Smilodon, the fierce marsupial sabre-toothed tiger migrated from the north to South America and then, in Pleistocene times, vanished from the world for all time. It evolved in parallel with the mammal sabre-tooth tiger.

○ **Tayra** *above*
An active predator, the tayra *T. barbara senilis* is, like the coatimundi, bears, squirrels and rabbits a late immigrant from the north of the continent, during the Miocene era. It is now widespread.

The Island Invaders

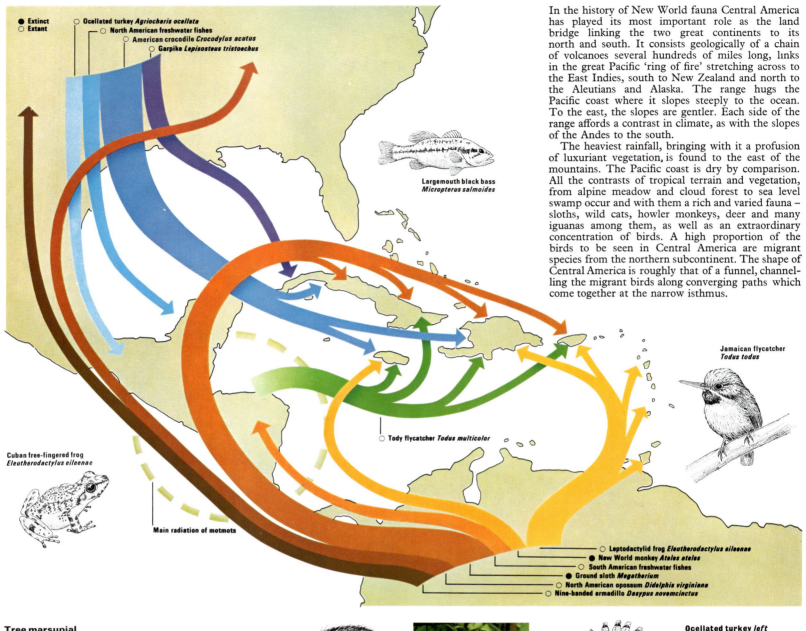

- ● Extinct
- ○ Extant
- ○ Ocellated turkey *Agriocharis ocellata*
- ○ North American freshwater fishes
- ○ American crocodile *Crocodylus acutus*
- ○ Garpike *Lepisosteus tristoechus*

Largemouth black bass
Micropterus salmoides

Jamaican flycatcher
Todus todus

○ Tody flycatcher *Todus multicolor*

Cuban free-fingered frog
Eleutherodactylus eileenae

Main radiation of motmots

- ○ Leptodactylid frog *Eleutherodactylus eileenae*
- ● New World monkey *Ateles ateles*
- ○ South American freshwater fishes
- ● Ground sloth *Megatherium*
- ○ North American opossum *Didelphis virginiana*
- ○ Nine-banded armadillo *Dasypus novemcinctus*

In the history of New World fauna Central America has played its most important role as the land bridge linking the two great continents to its north and south. It consists geologically of a chain of volcanoes several hundreds of miles long, links in the great Pacific 'ring of fire' stretching across to the East Indies, south to New Zealand and north to the Aleutians and Alaska. The range hugs the Pacific coast where it slopes steeply to the ocean. To the east, the slopes are gentler. Each side of the range affords a contrast in climate, as with the slopes of the Andes to the south.

The heaviest rainfall, bringing with it a profusion of luxuriant vegetation, is found to the east of the mountains. The Pacific coast is dry by comparison. All the contrasts of tropical terrain and vegetation, from alpine meadow and cloud forest to sea level swamp occur and with them a rich and varied fauna – sloths, wild cats, howler monkeys, deer and many iguanas among them, as well as an extraordinary concentration of birds. A high proportion of the birds to be seen in Central America are migrant species from the northern subcontinent. The shape of Central America is roughly that of a funnel, channelling the migrant birds along converging paths which come together at the narrow isthmus.

Tree marsupial
The grey four-eyed opossum *Philander opossum* is a nesting marsupial found from Mexico south to Argentina. It gains its name from the white eye spots over its actual eyes. In pictures its mouse-like appearance is deceptive for its head and body are about 10in (26cm) long.

Grey four-eyed opossum
Philander opossum

Distant relatives
The tenrec *T. ecaudatus* (top) of Madagascar and solenodon *S. paradoxus* of Hispaniola, live far apart but may have come from the same ancestral stock (Deltatheridium). They share a marked similarity in dental formations. Both are insectivorous animals.

Sacred quetzal *above*
To the civilizations of the Maya and the Inca the quetzal *Pharomachrus mocinno* was a sacred bird, the god of the air. Its tail feathers were used for ceremonies but it was never killed. The red-tailed guan (right) shares its rain forest habitat.

Ocellated turkey *left*
Similar to its close relative, the common turkey of the United States—but smaller, and with a blue head—the ocellated turkey *Agriocharis ocellata* is found in the Yucatán peninsula, Belize, and in Guatemala. The common wild turkey is the ancestor of the domestic bird which was imported into Europe by the Conquistadores.

Fast climber *right*
Sportive and intelligent the coati *Nasua nasua solitaria* frequents the forests of Central and South America. It is a relative of the raccoon, and a terrestrial carnivore with the ability to race up and down tree trunks at great speed, aided by its largely prehensile tail.

A mighty range of submarine mountains, with its peaks and topmost slopes protruding through the surface of the ocean, form the islands of the Antilles. Some are mere specks in an azure sea: others, like Cuba, Hispaniola, Puerto Rico and Jamaica, are sizeable. All are truly oceanic, and the fauna of the islands reflects this isolation.

Invasions of the kind that populate adjoining land masses are not possible where seas are as deep as those of the Caribbean and the larger animals which occur throughout the continental mainland have never appeared in the Antilles. Birds have never had the same inhibitions about overseas travel, and avian forms kindred to those of the mainland occur frequently. Small forms such as the anoline lizard (on this page) have rafted in to establish flourishing colonies throughout the island necklace.

These small-scale invasions have probably been assisted by the tempestuous winds and hurricanes which seasonally scour the coasts and islands, ripping debris from shorelines to act as 'landing craft' for the colonizers. Winds have also been responsible for the arrival of Old World species in the Antilles. Herons banded in France have been captured there and Old World egrets, by the same means, have become well established.

Primitive reptile
The rhinoceros iguana *Cyclura cornuta* (below) of Hispaniola is one of the most primitive members of its family and is distantly related to the ground iguanas of the Galapagos. The drawing (left) shows the mechanism for operating the iguana's throat-fan for display purposes.

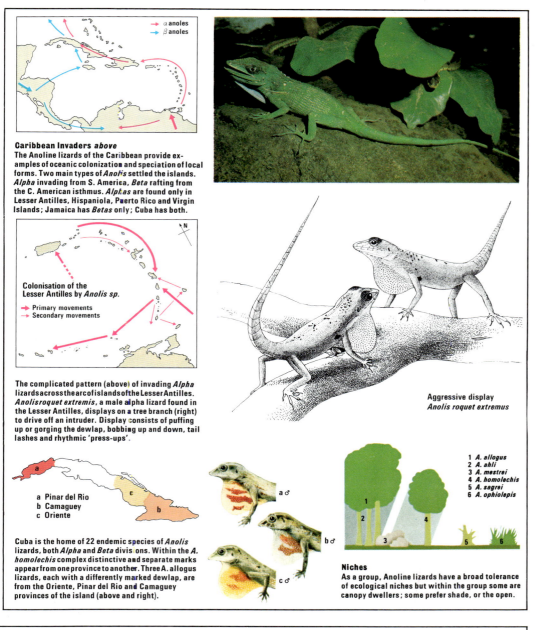

Caribbean Invaders *above*
The Anoline lizards of the Caribbean provide examples of oceanic colonization and speciation of local forms. Two main types of *Anolis* settled the islands. *Alpha* invading from S. America, *Beta* rafting from the C. American isthmus. *Alphas* are found only in Lesser Antilles, Hispaniola, Puerto Rico and Virgin Islands; Jamaica has *Betas* only; Cuba has both.

Colonisation of the Lesser Antilles by *Anolis sp.*
→ Primary movements
→ Secondary movements

The complicated pattern (above) of invading *Alpha* lizards across the arc of islands of the Lesser Antilles. *Anolis roquet extremis*, a male alpha lizard found in the Lesser Antilles, displays on a tree branch (right) to drive off an intruder. Display consists of puffing up or gorging the dewlap, bobbing up and down, tail lashes and rhythmic 'press-ups'.

Aggressive display
Anolis roquet extremus

a Pinar del Rio
b Camaguey
c Oriente

Cuba is the home of 22 endemic species of *Anolis* lizards, both *Alpha* and *Beta* divisions. Within the *A. homolechis* complex distinctive and separate marks appear from one province to another. Three A. allogus lizards, each with a differently marked dewlap, are from the Oriente, Pinar del Rio and Camaguey provinces of the island (above and right).

1 *A. allogus*
2 *A. ahli*
3 *A. mestrei*
4 *A. homolechis*
5 *A. sagrei*
6 *A. ophiolepis*

Niches
As a group, Anoline lizards have a broad tolerance of ecological niches but within the group some are canopy dwellers; some prefer shade, or the open.

Parrots and parakeets

West Indian birds derive principally from Central America. Remote riverine forest such as that shown (above) is the normal habit of the two genera of parrots and parakeets. *Amazona* and *Aratinga* which are now native to the islands of the Antilles.

Local residents
In the West Indies you can tell where you are by the parrots. Except for *A. leucocephala* all are endemic to particular Antillean islands.

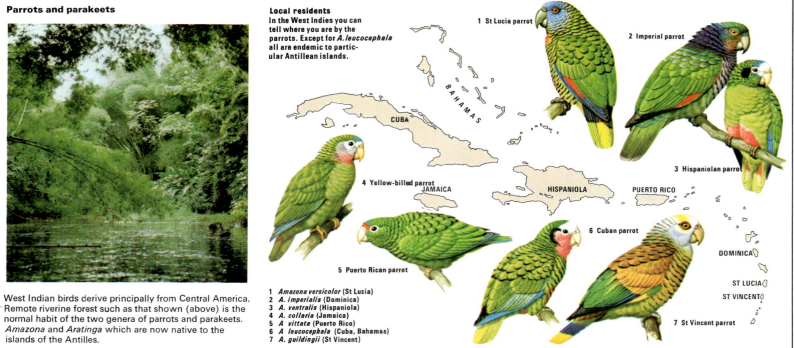

1 St Lucia parrot
2 Imperial parrot
3 Hispaniolan parrot
4 Yellow-billed parrot
5 Puerto Rican parrot
6 Cuban parrot
7 St Vincent parrot

1 *Amazona versicolor* (St Lucia)
2 *A. imperialis* (Dominica)
3 *A. ventralis* (Hispaniola)
4 *A. collaria* (Jamaica)
5 *A vittata* (Puerto Rico)
6 *A leucocephala* (Cuba, Bahamas)
7 *A. guildingii* (St Vincent)

Aquatic Life of the Amazon

The immensity of the Amazonian river system almost defies comprehension. Eighteen per cent of the freshwater flowing into the oceans of the world floods through the outlets of the Amazon at an average rate of $7\frac{1}{2}$ million cubic feet (212,380m³) a second. Apart from the main river, 17 of its tributaries exceed 1,000 miles (1,609km) in length.

The asymmetrical river basin covers some $2\frac{3}{4}$ million square miles (7 million km²) about one third of which lies to the north and two-thirds to the south of the main river. Two thousand miles from the sea the land in the centre of the basin is only 500 feet (152.4m) above sea level, giving the vast basin a minimal slope from the deep hinterland to the sea. The result is that most of the waters, except for occasional rapids, move only sluggishly throughout their great length.

The rainfall and wet seasons in the different regions of Amazonia occur at different seasons, each contributing to the smoothing of variations in the flow of the main river. Melting ice from the Andes also feeds the system which has been described as 'more like a penetration sea than a river network.'

The erosion of the Andes provides the greater part of the nutrients for the Amazon biota. The main southwestern tributaries and the main river carry heavy sedimental load which gives them a yellowish-white appearance while the waters from the River Negro are black, dyed by the decaying humus of the forest. This water is extremely poor in nutrients but is unequalled in its purity.

The wide flood plain of the lower Amazon – a complex of lakes, creeks, flooded forest and marshland, fluctuating water levels and unstable banks – includes fully aquatic, seasonally flooded and marginal habitats supporting diverse fauna. Contrasting roles are played by the swift carnivorous Amazon dolphins and the gentle, vegetarian manatees. Fish have radiated to fill the great variety of niches provided for them; air breathing lungfish, electric fish, 'four-eyed' anableps, carnivorous giants such as the arapaima, the voracious piranha and a huge variety of other forms abound.

Along the sandbanks turtles haul out to lay their eggs, caimans bask in the sun and the amphibious capybara feeds on the lush marginal vegetation, hunted by the jaguar and anaconda.

Since the vivid accounts of Amazonian wild life given by Bates and Wallace and others of the last century the caiman and turtles have become less common; jaguar and otter are declining in numbers as human influence and efficient hunting inexorably take their toll of this unique fauna.

The black and white rivers
The numberless tributaries of the Amazon drain widely differing ecological divisions of the rain forest (right). As a result the Amazon possesses a variety of faunal conditions most marked where the white waters of the alluvial zones meet the clear 'black' waters from harder terrains (above). They do not blend for many miles.

■ Central Amazon: poor sedimentary soil
■ Andean foreland: rich alluvium
□ Amazon border districts
■ Carboniferous strips
■ Surrounding highlands
⊢———⊣ 200 miles

Breeding for survival
The intricate mating ritual of the Surinam toad in an 'aquabatic' Immelmann turn (below) forces eggs into the skin of the female's back. More young survive their helpless early days when bred in this manner. Frog spawn is a much sought-after delicacy for fishes. These methods of breeding by-pass this hazard.

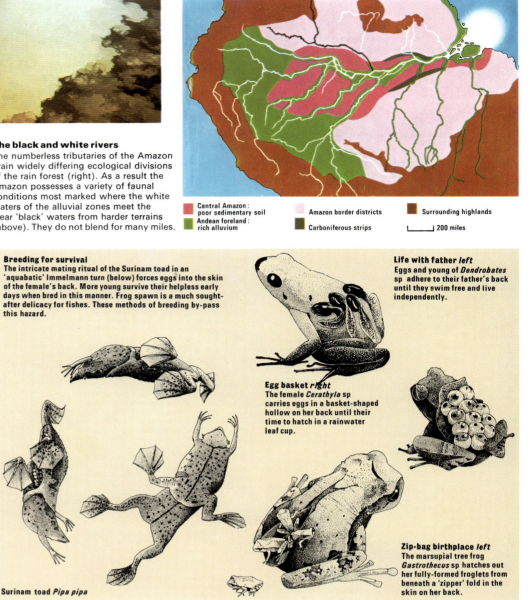

Life with father *left*
Eggs and young of *Dendrobates* sp adhere to their father's back until they swim free and live independently.

Egg basket *right*
The female *Cerathyla* sp carries eggs in a basket-shaped hollow on her back until their time to hatch in a rainwater leaf cup.

Zip-bag birthplace *left*
The marsupial tree frog *Gastrothecus* sp hatches out her fully-formed froglets from beneath a 'zipper' fold in the skin on her back.

Surinam toad *Pipa pipa*

The giant aquarium *right*
The remarkable diversity of the Amazon waters – rapid in some places, sluggish elsewhere, clear in parts, opaque with debris in others – breeds an unequalled variety of fish life. One of the largest families, the characids, displays a wide range of hues and habits, from the neon tetra *Hyphessobrycon innesi* to the savage piranha *Serrasalmus* spp. which, in a school, has been known to strip the flesh from a 100lb (45kg) capybara in under a minute. The hatchet fish *Carnegiella* spp. are true 'fliers' in pursuit of air-borne insects. The electric gymnotids (centre) are nocturnal feeders and include the knifefish *Gymnotus carapo* and the electric eel *Electrophorus electricus* which stuns its victims with a shock of up to 600 volts. The arapaima is the largest freshwater fish in the world – about 200lb (90kg).

Symphysodon discus
Anostomus anostomus
Leporinus fasciatus
Boulengerella lateristriga
Hyphessobrycon innesi
Carnegiella strigata
Metynnis schreitmuelleri
Serrasalmus nattereri
Prochilodus insignis
Electrophorus electricus
Gymnotus carapo
Gymnorhamphichthys hypostoms
Oxydoras niger
Ancistrus cirr

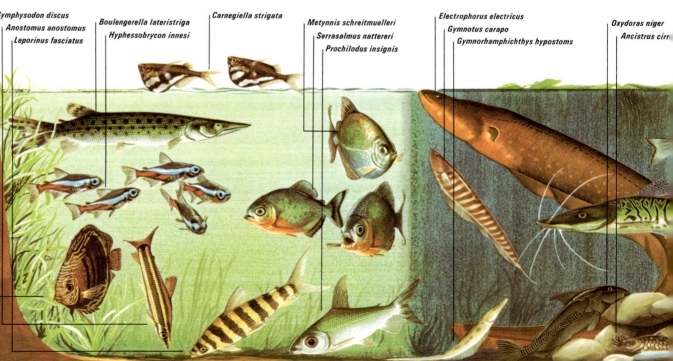

Home from the sea
Gallery (water's edge) forest and rafts of giant lilies provide a moist and luxuriant home for the terecay turtle *Podocnemis unifilis* (right), and a tempting habitat for the manatee and the Amazon dolphin, marine creatures which have become established in fresh water. Contrasting jaws of the fish-eating dolphin and vegetarian manatee are shown (below).

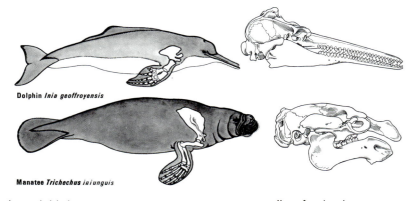

Dolphin *Inia geoffroyensis*

Manatee *Trichechus iniunguis*

Future in doubt
Hunters seeking the valuable pelt of the giant otter of Amazonia have reduced its numbers to the point of extinction over much of its range. A similar fate has befallen the spectacled caiman, for its hide, and the red-headed turtle, for its delicious eggs and meat.

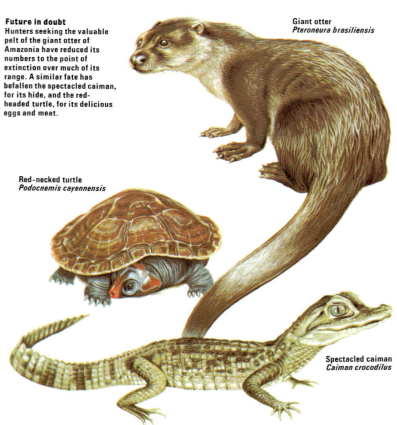

Giant otter
Pteroneura brasiliensis

Red-necked turtle
Podocnemis cayennensis

Spectacled caiman
Caiman crocodilus

Peaceful rodents *right*
The largest living rodents – they are well over 3ft (1m) long – Capybaras *Hydrochoerus hydrochoerus* are quiet and intelligent animals that rarely fight among themselves or even in self-defence against their enemies. Ashore, they run like horses and are hunted by man and by jaguars. When they take to the water where they spend much of their time, they become the prey of the caiman.

enipterus nigripinnis
udoplatystoma fasciatum

Young *Arapaima gigas*
Arapaima gigas
Osteoglossum bicirrhosum

Corydoras myersi

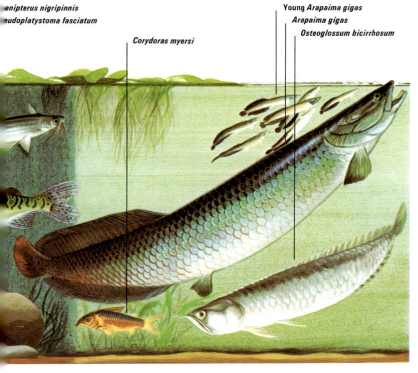

Distant relatives *left*
The arapaima and arawana fishes of the Amazon basin are two of the five surviving species of a family originating in Cretacean times (60-120 million years ago). Their relatives are *Clupisudis niloticus* and *Pantodon buchholtzi* in Africa and *Scleropages leichhardti* of Malay-Australian waters. The arapaima closely resembles *Clupisudis* while the arawana's nearest relative is *Scleropages*.

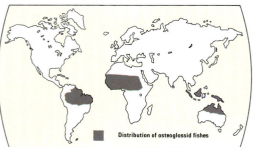

Distribution of osteoglossid fishes

Poles apart
South American gymnotid fish and African mormyrids share an ability to navigate and locate objects by electrical impulses. All adopt a stiff-spined posture as in *Gymnarchus niloticus* (right) to keep the electrical field effective. Contrasting electric fish are shown (below)—an African mormyrid and South American electric ray.

Marcusenius longianalis (Africa)

Narcine brasiliensis (Brazil coast)

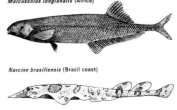

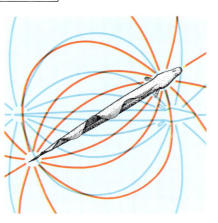

The Crowded Canopy

The Amazonian rain forest, the *hylaea amazonica*, is the largest in the world, covering some 1.6 million square miles (2.5 million km²) in Brazil alone. More than 4,000 species of trees are found in ragged confusion, interlaced with lianas and festooned by parasitic and epiphytic plants. Up to 80 species of plant have been found living on a single tree – and more than 400 trees of 87 different species have been found within an area of less than three acres (.8ha). An eminent naturalist has described the forest accurately as 'An undisciplined army composed of rigid giants and quivering dwarfs.'

Variations in soil, terrain and water level determine the distribution of the major types of forest and within each type many different layers or strata can be identified. Emergent trees may reach an average height of 150 feet (50m) with some exceptional examples twice as tall. The main canopy spreads at 75-100 feet (25-30m) and layers of smaller trees and shrubs below the canopy provide further arboreal habitats. The forest is thus a three-dimensional mosaic of niches varying in height, shade and the availability of food.

The fauna, too, is stratified and distributed in a complex manner to take advantage of many different ecological situations. Examples of special adaptations to arboreal life such as prehensile tails, opposable digits, enlarged claws and binocular vision (see diagram below) can be seen in various groups. The fauna, particularly in the upper storeys of the forest is characterized by many brightly coloured birds and relatively small mammals. Some, like the sloth, show an extreme specialization for life in a particular forest niche but – markedly among the more terrestrial species – the ability to live with floodwaters is vital. Even the sloth, almost an extension of the tree where it hangs motionless, can swim if the need arises.

The unlimited wealth of species to be found in the Amazonian rain forest is in marked contrast to the actual number of animals to be seen there. Populations are not large and, because of the almost opaque density of luxuriant vegetation, they are difficult to observe in the countless hiding places available.

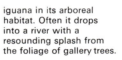

Leaping lizard *above*
Flattened sides and a long tail to give it stability in its leaps and clawed feet to grip branches aid the iguana in its arboreal habitat. Often it drops into a river with a resounding splash from the foliage of gallery trees.

Trapeze artists *left*
Unlike their African cousins South American monkeys use their prehensile tails for stability and locomotion. The spider monkey *Ateles* sp with elongated limbs and tail is the most acrobatic species of all, covering 30ft (9-10m) in its leaps.

A life in suspense *below*
The funereal sloth *Bradypus tridactylus* lives a life suspended beneath the high branches. Even its fur grows in an opposite direction, from the belly to the spine. Its grip on the branch is difficult to free, even when the animal is dead.

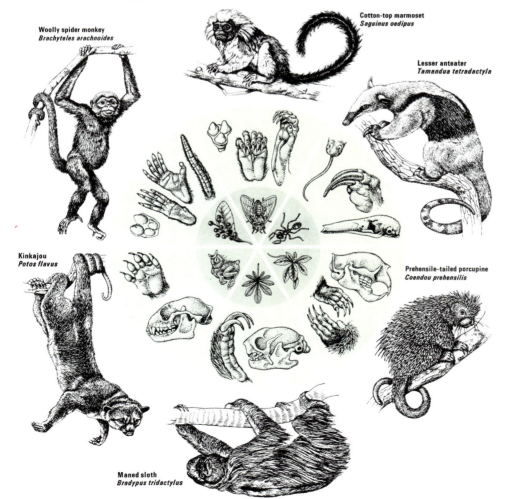

Woolly spider monkey
Brachyteles arachnoides

Cotton-top marmoset
Saguinus oedipus

Lesser anteater
Tamandua tetradactyla

Kinkajou
Potos flavus

Prehensile-tailed porcupine
Coendou prehensilis

Maned sloth
Bradypus tridactylus

The forest and forest life
Light penetrates through the forest canopy (above). The 'carousel' diagram describes some of the ways in which forest creatures with an arboreal habitat have become adapted not only for purposes of locomotion, but also for feeding. The highly developed limbs and hands and prehensile tails are matched by jaws – or tongues – enabling them to forage for the special foods to which they have become accustomed. These adaptations, of course, limit their behavior, often making them clumsy movers when not in the trees.

For bird key see page 205

Colouring

The Amazon forest is the home of the raucous, huge-billed toucan (2) whose distinctive colouring – like that of the macaws (3), parrots (4), jacamars (5), puffbirds (6) and humming birds (7) – does not isolate it against its background but helps it to blend with the luminous, light-dappled foliage of the higher forest strata. There are few threats to the inhabitants of the higher levels of the forest, the principal one coming from the harpy eagle (8) which preys on small mammals as well as birds.

Sedentary

The splendour of South American bird life has no equal in any other continent. The 52 species shown here represent only a fraction of those known to exist in the Amazon rain forest. More than 450 species were counted in one valley area alone. The heat, moisture and profusion of evergreen vegetation provides a permanently well-stocked larder, encouraging the birds to adopt a sedentary habit. They have short, broad wings to manoeuvre easily among the trees and which are not required to carry them any distance – an adaptation contrasting with the slender, pointed wings of the migratory species like the visiting chimney swifts from north America, shown (1).

Nesting

Hollow trees are favourite nesting places for many forest species but there are many genera of woodpeckers and woodcreepers (9) drilling into the plentiful timber. Ovenbirds, which build distinctive nests in the pampas, adopt the woodcreeper's habit in the rain forest. Huge bag nests are built by oropendolas (10) to keep nestlings safe from snakes. Strangest of all Amazonian birds, the hoatzin (11) has baffled classification. When very young its nestlings have two well-developed claws at the end of each wing, helping them to cling to branches like quadrupeds. The claws disappear when they are three weeks old.

Mimicry: A Talent for Deception

Part of every animal's environment consists of a threat to its existence. It survives because its whole being – its structure and form (morphology), its appearance and behavior – is attuned to an ever-present danger. It may be equipped to stand and fight, or to lurk motionless and camouflaged; on the other hand it may escape by its speed and agility. It will suffer some casualties (its predators may share the same abilities, or possess counterbalancing talents) for its losses are part of the critical equilibrium existing between all forms of life in a habitat; but it will survive as a species.

One of the most subtle and effective forms of defence against the predator is found among species that are most prone to devastation, the insects. Their ranks are decimated, particularly by birds, but they survive, partly because of their numbers but also because decimation means that generations follow each other swiftly and the benefits of natural selection are soon evident. The bird predator soon learns which insects are distasteful or poisonous because those insects have evolved 'warning' configurations and colours.

The talent of one insect to advertise itself as repugnant has produced in others the even more remarkable phenomenon of mimicry in which the edible impersonates the inedible with such success that it shares its security from attack.

Mimetic behavior, or advantageous resemblance, is known in plants as well as animals and examples are found throughout the world, but tropical America and its insects provide many of the most striking examples that have been observed. In his travels through the rain forests of Amazonia in the 1850s the Victorian naturalist Henry Bates first noticed the marked similarities which appeared to exist between utterly different species of butterflies – the one immune from predation by birds, the other of an edible family. The development and use by one, the mimic, of the 'warning' colours of the other, the model, came to be known as Batesian mimicry.

Later observations showed that there also existed a resemblance between widely separated insects, each of which was distasteful. The resemblance enabled them to share the pressure of predation, a mimicry known as Müllerian, after a German zoologist who defined the phenomenon.

Mimicry does not begin and end with the adoption of false colours nor is it limited to the victims predation, for some aggressive or parasitic species may use their resemblance to a victim to take advantage of it, like the fly which uses its resemblance to a bee to parasitise its nest.

Fooling the predator *below right*
Impersonating the inedible, aping the dangerous and startling or confusing the opposition are among the few defences on which many insects depend to survive in a world of predators. This is the world of the 'model' and the 'mimic'.

Two heads better than one
The butterfly *Thecla togarna* has a dummy head at its rear to confuse the predator. It turns rapidly on landing so that its dummy head points in the previous direction of its flight. The bird strikes to allow for the butterfly's forward movement—but strikes in the wrong direction and misses.

Thecla togarna

Gold marked warning syntomid moth

Orange and black leaf hopper

Aphantochilus rodgersii

Cephalotes atratus

The forms of mimicry

Parallel mimicry
Members of different animal groups such as beetles, bugs, and moths often have identical warning coloration.

Protective mimicry
The edible (green) mimics the distasteful (orange) within the same family for protection. This is Batesian mimicry. The harmless of one family mimics the harmful of another family.

Warning coloration
Basis of most visible mimicry is the 'warning' coloration; reds and oranges predominate since they impinge more sharply on the predator's vision than any other colour

Predatory mimicry
One harmful species mimics another of the same order for the purpose of predation.

Mertensian mimicry
Poisonous and non-poisonous mimic an intermediate, or mildly poisonous snake and each gains protection from predators. This is Mertensian mimicry.

Mullerian mimicry
Mimicry exists between separate species, all of which are distasteful. All provide a few victims to predation, but 'share the load'. This is Mullerian mimicry.

Orange banded long horned beetle

Orange banded warning lycid beetle

Danger - keep away
The vivid warning colours of the orange banded lycid beetle provide a sharp reminder to birds that it is inedible. The coloration of the lycid has been adopted by a number of edible insects illustrated here—the longicorn beetle, the leaf hopper and the syntomid moths. It is thought that bright oranges and reds impinge more sharply on a bird's eye than on a man's.

Ant-spider
Structural and behavioural mimicry is evident in some species of spider which impersonate—and often live with—ants by scuttling with an antlike movement and holding out their front legs to resemble the ants' antennae.

Arrow-poison frog
The warning colours of the poisonous tree frog (Dendrobatidae) mean just what they say. Even a tiny amount of the toxin secreted by the frog is lethal to man and is used by primitive South American Indians to tip their arrowheads.

Coral snakes
The venomous, the mildly venomous and the harmless share an almost identical livery among the 75 species of South American coral snake. Protection from attack is gained by the fact that predators cannot tell the difference. The poisonous *Micrurus* spp. of Venezuela alone are shown below.
1

Model middleman
A mildly poisonous coral snake *Oxyrhopus* sp.—which gives a predator an unpleasant experience to warn it off all snakes like itself—provides the 'model' mimicked by the near-identical, poisonous *Micrurus* sp. and the similar but quite harmless *Simophis* sp., a 'false' coral: in Brazil.
2

Simophis rhinostoma

Oxyrhopus trigeminus

Micrurus frontalis

Aggressive mimicry
Climbing on the back of the soft-shelled lycid (distasteful) beetle *Lycus loripes*, the longicorn *Elytroleptus ignitus* eats into it and absorbs the repellent body fluid of its victim. The edible longicorn thus tastes repulsive for a period of time.

Euglossa cordata

Volucella obesa

Elytroleptus ignitus

Lycus loripes

Eulema fallax

Mallophora tibialis

Orange banded warning syntomid moth

Startling
Eyespots on the hind wings of the Io moth *Automeris io*, concealed beneath the dull forewings of the moth are 'flashed' when it is alarmed. As the predator is startled, the moth makes its escape.

Bogus wasp
Taking advantage of the remarkable resemblance between the two insects, the robber fly *Mallophora tibialis* lays its eggs in the nest of the bumblebee *Eulaema* sp. and parasitises it. Fly/bee/wasp mimicry is one of the commoner forms of this behaviour.

Two defences
When the striking leaflike camouflage of the bush cricket *Tanusia brullaei* (right) fails in its purpose it uses its alarm display (below) to startle the predator, often a bird, and thus gain time to make its escape. Insects are food for many species have subtle survival techniques.

Mechanitis doryssus

A talent for deception
In the butterfly — a synonym for gaudy fecklessness — one of nature's most subtle forms of defence first revealed itself — a startling resemblance between an inedible family and members of an edible one, giving protection from predation to the latter. In the diagram (far right) models (inedible) from three countries are shown with their mimic (edible) species (*Dismorphia*).

GUATEMALA
1 *Melinaea imitator*
2 *Mechanitis doryssus*
3 *Ceratinia dionaea*
4 *Heliconius ismenius*
5 *Dismorphia praxinae*

COLOMBIA
1 *Melinaea idea*
2 *Mechanitis macrinus*

3 *Ceratinia philetaera*
4 *Heliconius anderida*
5 *Dismorphia beroe*

VENEZUELA
1 *Melinaea imitata*
2 *Mechanitis veritabilis*
3 *Ceratinia fraterna*
4 *Heliconius metabilis*
5 *Dismorphia astynomides*

COLOMBIA

VENEZUELA

GUATEMALA

Chaco, Pampas and Steppe

Southward from the forests of Amazonia and the Brazilian highlands and east of the Andes to the Atlantic seaboard, the grasslands of South America reach into the chilly latitudes of Patagonia.

Transitional zones of deciduous forest, scrub and swamp to the north and west separate the pampas or grassland proper from the ecological zones of Andean mountain and Amazonian rain forest. Such an area is the little-known Chaco, a lowland alluvial plain parched for part of the year, but inundated by flood water when the rains come.

The Chaco is a mixture of soils brought down by rivers from the Andes and presents a jigsaw of dry patches interspersed with swamps known as esteros. Quebracho, or axebreaker, trees and fanleaf palms stud an area which, although not well endowed with native species of plants and animals, has undergone some invasion by those of surrounding habitats.

Among the most interesting indigenous species of the Chaco is the maned wolf *Chrysocyon brachyurus*, one of the largest of its family and which is as tall as it is long. The tatu, or giant armadillo *Priodontes giganteus* is more numerous in the Chaco than elsewhere. The marshy expanses of the Pantanal, astride the Paraguay river, are a paradise for waterbirds.

The pampas, an ocean of grassland uninterrupted by trees other than a few alien species introduced by man, are the creation of the forces of erosion. The archaic geological structures which once formed the region have long since vanished beneath compacted layers of soil weathered from the Andes and carried by rivers and streams towards the Atlantic.

The grassy plains cover an area in excess of 300,000 square miles (500,000km²). Towards the Andes in the west a hot, dry climate has produced an arid steppeland covered with tufts of prairie grass and a few xerophitic (drought-resistant) bushes. To the east a moister climate is created by winds from the Atlantic seaboard and the landscape has been considerably modified by man, his cattle and trees.

In recent times the open habitat of the pampas has never been more than poorly stocked with large mammal species. The odd guanaco *Lama guanacoe*, once described as 'A careless mixture of parts intended for other beasts and turned down as below standard', is the best known; the only other herbivore of any size is the pampas deer, its number now reduced to danger point by the extension of ranching and agriculture across its natural habitat, and by overhunting. On the other hand, rodents abound, among them the viscacha, the mara and the tucutuco, members of a family whose explosive success has established them as its most successful group.

The guanaco remains the most typical animal of the Patagonian steppe where, south of the Rio Colorado, the alluvium of the pampas is replaced by stony, windswept plateau. Sheldgeese, particularly the Magellan goose, breed prolifically in the inhospitable lands at the end of the continent.

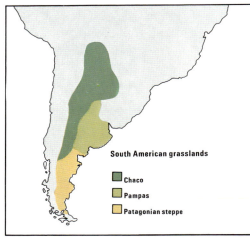

South American grasslands

- Chaco
- Pampas
- Patagonian steppe

The Chaco *above*
Forming a transitional zone between the great rain forest of Amazonia and the plains of the pampas, the Chaco has a sparse native fauna which is complemented by visiting species from the different zones which adjoin it.

Once protected pest *right*
The sole survivor of five earlier species the coypu or nutria *Myocastor coypu* is a native of the streams of South America where, for a time, it was protected. Bred in captivity for its pelt it became a pest where it escaped from fur farms in the US and Europe.

Fox – and foxlike wolf
The grey fox of the pampas *Dusicyon gymnocercus* (left) will 'freeze' if surprised and will remain motionless even if struck by a man with a whip. The foxlike maned wolf *Chrysocyon brachyurus* is wary and nocturnal. It has stilt-like legs which enable it to run down its quarry, pacas, agoutis and small reptiles.

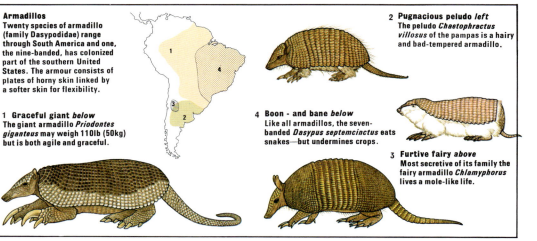

Armadillos
Twenty species of armadillo (family Dasypodidae) range through South America and one, the nine-banded, has colonized part of the southern United States. The armour consists of plates of horny skin linked by a softer skin for flexibility.

1 Graceful giant *below*
The giant armadillo *Priodontes giganteus* may weigh 110lb (50kg) but is both agile and graceful.

2 Pugnacious peludo *left*
The peludo *Chaetophractus villosus* of the pampas is a hairy and bad-tempered armadillo.

4 Boon - and bane *below*
Like all armadillos, the seven-banded *Dasypus septemcinctus* eats snakes—but undermines crops.

3 Furtive fairy *above*
Most secretive of its family the fairy armadillo *Chlamyphorus* lives a mole-like life.

Flightless rheas

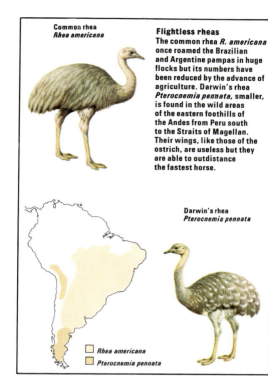

Common rhea
Rhea americana

The common rhea *R. americana* once roamed the Brazilian and Argentine pampas in huge flocks but its numbers have been reduced by the advance of agriculture. Darwin's rhea *Pterocnemia pennata*, smaller, is found in the wild areas of the eastern foothills of the Andes from Peru south to the Straits of Magellan. Their wings, like those of the ostrich, are useless but they are able to outdistance the fastest horse.

Darwin's rhea
Pterocnemia pennata

☐ *Rhea americana*
☐ *Pterocnemia pennata*

The baker bird *right*
The rufous ovenbird *Furnarius rufus* builds a domed nest of mud and straw on posts and bare branches — often in and around human settlements — south from southern Brazil to Argentina. Because of its oven-shaped nest, South Americans call it el hornero, the baker. The nothura (below) is one of 45 known species of tinamou, a shy, partridge-like bird found only in South America. It takes to the air with reluctance.

Chaco residents
Scarlet-headed blackbird *Amblyramphus holosericeus* (above) and red-breasted cacique (right) are two Chaco residents which, in winter, are joined by migrants from the northern hemisphere. As a builder of complicated nests the cacique rivals the forest oropendola.

Pampas dwellers

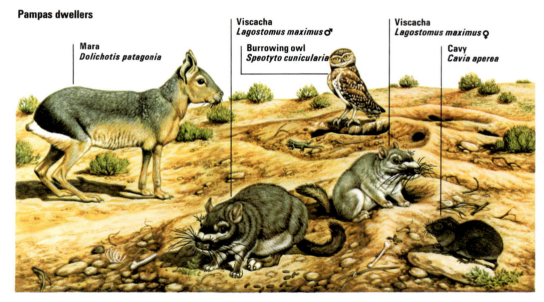

Mara
Dolichotis patagonia

Viscacha
Lagostomus maximus ♂

Burrowing owl
Speotyto cunicularia

Viscacha
Lagostomus maximus ♀

Cavy
Cavia aperea

Long tongue *above*
The tongue of the great anteater *Myrmecophaga tridactyla* can extend to 24ins (60cm), over half its body length. It is coated with a sticky saliva to which termites, ants and other insects adhere. It uses its huge nails for digging and protects them by walking on its knuckles.

Odiferous deer *below*
One of South America's few remaining herbivores of any size the pampas deer *Blastoceros campestris* was once widespread but is now rare. Glands on the rear hooves of the male emit an odour that can be detected more than a mile (1.5km) away. It has insignificant antlers.

Pampas township
The plains viscacha *Lagostomus maximus* builds labyrinthine underground homes in which generations of animals may live. Earth brought up by the viscachas as they extend and elaborate the viscachera—their underground township—forms mounds on the surface, which they have stripped bare of its grass cover. The lack of cover helps the viscacha to observe an approaching predator. The pampas fox will often share the viscachera with its occupants in amity until young viscachas provide it with easy meat in the spring. The mara or Patagonian hare and the burrowing owl, *Speotyto cunicularia*, are other pampas inhabitants which lodge with the viscacha. The illustration also shows the pampas guinea pig *Cavia aperea*, a surface dweller.

End of a continent *left*
Tussock grass and bushes clothe huge areas of Argentine Patagonia, where it is possible to travel hundreds of miles without seeing a tree. Endless winds blow and rain is rare. A flower from the end of the world, *Leucenia hanii* (below) is a native of stark Tierra del Fuego.

Patagonian weasel
Lyncodon patagonicus

Andes: The Lofty Wilderness

The distribution of plants and animals is largely determined by physical factors such as temperature and humidity, and the biota thus tends to be divided into zones across the land, each zone having characteristic fauna and flora – and the zonal limits are more or less complied with, depending upon the degree of specialization of the particular organism. Such zones are condensed by the effects of altitude on climate in mountain ranges.

The Andes show a clear zonation into four major levels – tropical, subtropical, south temperate and paramo. The distribution of these zones is affected by latitude and exposure. Subdivisions such as arid tropical and wet tropical are superimposed on the main plan.

As a general rule there is a diminution in diversity of species from tropical forest to paramo habitats. Monkeys, for example, do not extend into the south temperate forest and the numbers of species of ants and mosquitos are greatly reduced.

The northern part of the uppermost zone, usually at about 12,000 feet (3,600m), possesses remarkably green plains (paramo) in which grass grows all the year round; rainfall is high, though snow is not common, at least below 15,000 feet (4,570m). The mammal fauna is rich and includes the spectacled bear, tapir and deer. The vicuña is native to this region and has been much exploited. Strong, positive efforts have now been made to conserve this species and to manage it as a continuing resource.

A characteristic of all the creatures of the high plateaux is that they have developed both physiological adaptations related to the altitude and ecological adaptations to the climate that has been produced by the altitude. The hearts of the animals of the high Andean plateaux are – like those of the human dwellers – considerably enlarged. Other physiological functions are also modified to allow life in which the metabolism of other creatures not similarly adapted would be thrown completely off balance. Paradoxically, many migratory birds unused to the height appear to fly with ease.

Barrier between extremes
The cordilleras of the Andes form a barrier between extremes of climate and vegetation. The Pacific coast is one of the world's driest regions. To the east lies the great rain forest of the Amazon basin, as humid as the Pacific coast is dry. Between the east and west cordilleras lies the altiplano, the high plains of puna grass.

Coastal desert
Loma
Dry scrub
Evergreen scrub
Puna, dry thorn

Puna, moist
Mixed forest
Cloud forest
Montane rain forest
Rain forest

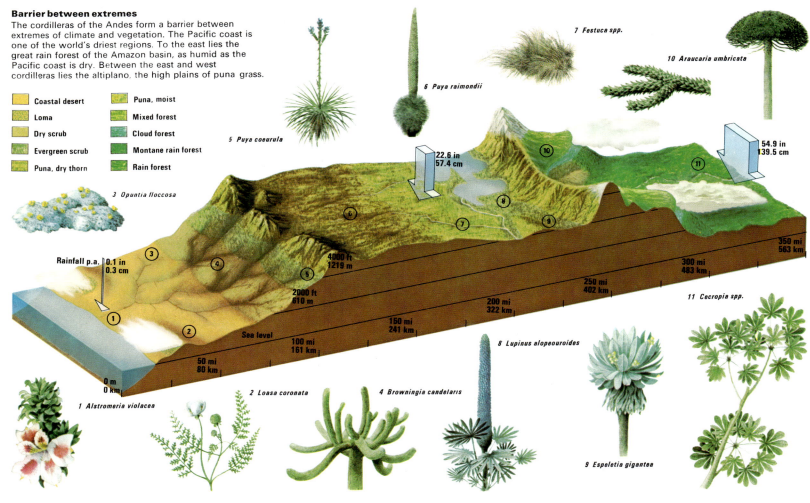

3 Opuntia floccosa

Rainfall p.a. 0.1 in 0.3 cm

7 Festuca spp.

10 Araucaria umbricata

6 Puya raimondii

5 Puya coeurula

22.6 in 57.4 cm

54.9 in 139.5 cm

4000 ft 1219 m

2000 ft 610 m

Sea level

350 mi 563 km
300 mi 483 km
250 mi 402 km
200 mi 322 km
150 mi 241 km
100 mi 161 km
50 mi 80 km
0 m 0 km

11 Cecropia spp.

8 Lupinus alopeouroides

2 Loasa coronata

4 Browningia candelaris

9 Espeletia gigantea

1 Alstromeria violacea

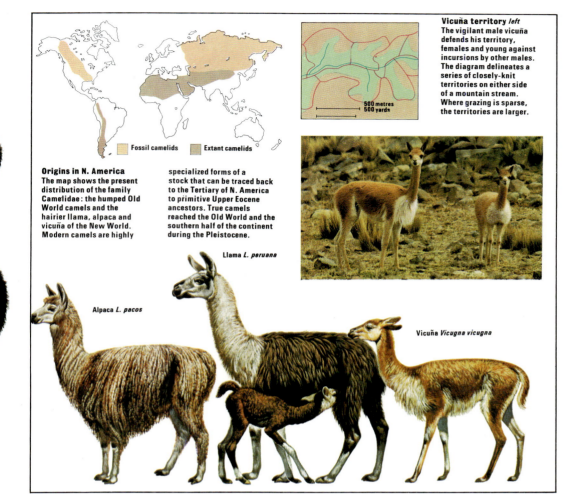

Origins in N. America

The map shows the present distribution of the family Camelidae: the humped Old World camels and the hairier llama, alpaca and vicuña of the New World. Modern camels are highly specialized forms of a stock that can be traced back to the Tertiary of N. America to primitive Upper Eocene ancestors. True camels reached the Old World and the southern half of the continent during the Pleistocene.

Fossil camelids   Extant camelids

Alpaca *L. pacos*

Llama *L. peruana*

Vicuña *Vicugna vicugna*

Vicuña territory *left*

The vigilant male vicuña defends his territory, females and young against incursions by other males. The diagram delineates a series of closely-knit territories on either side of a mountain stream. Where grazing is sparse, the territories are larger.

500 metres
500 yards

Change of spectacles *above*

A wide variation often exists from animal to animal within a species although they may look superficially the same. A strongly marked example of this intra-specific variation is shown by the Andean spectacled bear *Tremarctus ornatus* in which the facial markings, including the white 'spectacles', change from one animal to the next. *T. ornatus* is the only South American bear, an adept climber which will ascend a 100ft (30m) palm, tear off the branches and descend to the ground to eat the leaves.

High living *left*

The treeless and barren upper slopes of the Bolivian Andes in the neighborhood of Mount Chacaltya, 16,300ft (5,000m) harbour many small birds which, by behavioural rather than physiological adaptation, have been able to flourish in a hostile habitat. Some species of finch huddle together in hundreds beneath rocks and fissures to counteract heat loss during the icy chill of the night. A number of species, including *Geositta* and *Upucerthia* (known as mineros, or miners, among the natives) from their burrowing habits.

Political ducks

Endemic to the tumbling streams of the Andes cordilleras, the torrent ducks *Merganetta armata* are found from Colombia to southern Chile. The coloration of the sub-species varies almost exactly with the political boundaries of the western seaboard.

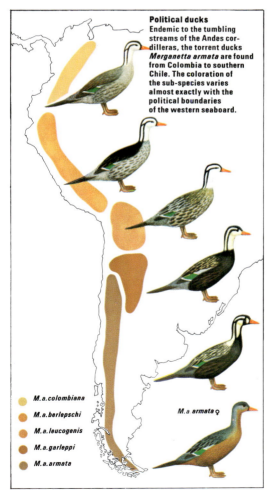

M.a.colombiana
M.a.berlepschi
M.a.leucogenis
M.a.garleppi
M.a.armata

M.a. armata ♀

Deep shelters

Among the spiny leaves of the puya—on which many birds impale themselves and die—the sierra finch *Phrygilus gayi* builds its nest (right). The Andean flicker *Colaptes rupicola* bores tunnels (below); the diuca finch *D.speculifera* huddles with scores of its kind beneath the rocks.

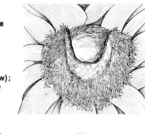

Pick and shovel bird *above*

A skilful underground architect, the ground tyrant *Muscisaxicola* sp. hollows out a burrow up to three feet (1m) in length, and an incubating chamber, using its beak as a pickaxe and claws to clear away earth.

Teeming Ocean and Barren Land

Off the west coast of South America lies one of the ocean's richest nutrient sources. The cold Peruvian, or Humboldt, current from the Antarctic added to the nutrient-rich upwelling water from the Pacific deeps provides ideal conditions for the development of plankton. In particular, vast swarms of zooplankton support anchovy fisheries and dense colonies of sea birds – cormorants, gulls, pelicans and boobies.

The birds further concentrate the nutrients in guano islands built up by hundreds of years' accumulation of the excrement of the colonies. These deposits are sources of agricultural fertilizers, being rich in nitrates and phosphates.

Occasionally, about once every seven years, a warm current called 'El Nino' – The Child – because it occurs around the time of the Nativity, has a drastic effect on the system. Warm water from the north pushes down to the Peruvian coast. Rain falls on normally arid coasts, the rich plankton disappears and is replaced by 'red tide' organisms. The seabirds scatter and many die, but the colonies begin to reform the following year.

The cold currents also allow the penguins to reach as far north as the Galápagos Islands, and enable seals to join in the exploitation of the riches from the deep waters. There are similar upwellings and nutrient concentrations to be found off the coast of south-west Africa (the Benguella current) and off the shores of south-west Asia, but none produce the treasures that, in a unique ecological cycle, bring so many benefits to man either as fisheries or in fertilizer.

The Chincha Islands, lying off the Peruvian coast, were once covered to depths of tens of feet by guano. Old sailors believed it was the droppings of giant primeval animals.

2000 feet
600 metres

Contrast of styles *left*
Fishing in flocks, the cormorant 'torpedoes' in pursuit of the anchovies. The pelican plummets vertically, air sacs in its skin helping it to bob quickly to the surface.

Priceless bird *right*
The Peruvian cormorant *Phalacrocorax bougainvilli* has been described as the most valuable bird in the world. It is the most important contributor to guano stocks.

Endemic tern *above*
The inca tern *Larosterna inca* is endemic to the waters of the cold Humboldt current.

Source of life *below*
The Humboldt current is reinforced by nutrient-rich upwellings from the Pacific Ocean.

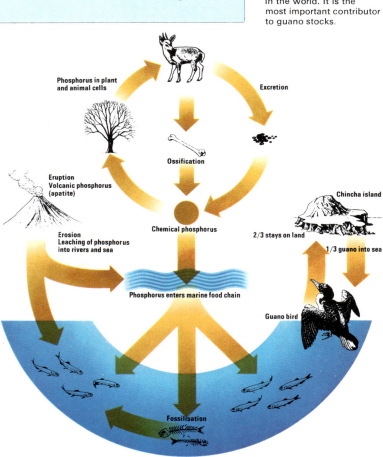

Phosphorus in plant and animal cells

Excretion

Ossification

Eruption
Volcanic phosphorus (apatite)

Erosion
Leaching of phosphorus into rivers and sea

Chemical phosphorus

Chincha island

2/3 stays on land

1/3 guano into sea

Phosphorus enters marine food chain

Guano bird

Fossilisation

The Guano cycle *left*
Guano, one of the most valuable nitrogenous fertilizers known to man, is the end product of a remarkable ecological cycle (left). Terrestrial rock sediments, animal decomposition and vegetable detritus are carried by the rivers to the sea, enriching the depths with phosphates. Alive with phyto- and zooplankton, the coastal waters support vast shoals of anchovies, the staple diet of the guanay, or Peruvian cormorant, boobies, pelicans and terns. The nests and roosting sites of these fishing birds, on islands and rocky promontories, are coated with their droppings—the guano fertilizer. The nesting sites are now a closely guarded source of wealth for Peru; guarded most of all from man whose greed once wiped them out.

The Guano producers

1 Cormorant 85%
2 Booby 10%
3 Pelican 5%

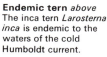

Symbolic of the Andes the great condor, largest of the long-flight birds, soars on out-stretched pinions. Like the eagle it nests on high, rocky ledges, soaring down over the plains in search of carrion.

Between the Pacific Ocean and the Andes on the western side of South America a desert stretches for some 2,000 miles (3,200km) from Arica to Caldena, through Chile and Peru.

The desert owes its existence to the influence of the cold Humboldt or Peruvian current, together with the upwelling of cold water along the coast from the depths of the Pacific. The current cools the prevailing winds, reducing their moisture content. On reaching the warm land the winds are heated, increasing their water-carrying capacity and thus further drying out the moisture in the air. The coastal desert thus created is one of the richest in mineral deposits.

A variety of xerophitic (drought-resisting) cacti and mesquite are the dominant plant life in this arid zone except where the occasional stream supports a deciduous gallery forest. Lizards are common. Toads shelter during the day and feed on insects at dusk. Oven birds, cactus wrens and fly-catchers are among the fairly large number of bird species represented, although densities are low and tend to be aggregated in areas of shelter and water. Mammals are mostly confined to the few areas where water is available and the fauna is reduced to a few small rodents, tucotuco, a few species of marsupials and the occasional fox.

The effect of the Humboldt current reaches inland until it breaks on the rising slopes of the Andean western cordilleras, producing the strange pattern of heat and humidity described by the diagram on this page. Warmth and moisture increase with altitude and, as a result, vegetation becomes lusher.

A world turned upside down *left*
A dense shroud of cloud and mist wraps hundreds of miles of Peruvian coastline for much of the year, bringing with it a strange inversion of atmospheric and biological values. Temperatures are higher above the cloud than they are below. Vegetation, thin to non-existent at low altitudes, becomes richer at higher levels, its density increasing with that of the fog cover which condenses on the plants. The condensation drips from the vegetation to provide water in what is otherwise an almost completely rainless landscape.

Food for gulls
Marine food in abundance attracts countless seabirds to the otherwise barren beaches of the South American Pacific coast, among them the grey gull *Larus modestus* which feeds exclusively on the shellfish *Emerita analoga.*

Metres	20.0°C plus			
800		Rare		Open colonies of fog plants
		Common		Dense colonies of fog plants with trees
600		Sustained		
		Frequent		Open colonies of fog plants
400		Common		
200				Lichen/algae
17.0°C		Rare		Desert
0				

Roaring bulls
The sealion *Otaria byronia* breeds in colonies of many hundreds at a time. It is distributed widely along South American coasts.

Water is absorbed by the leaves of the coast dune plant *Tillandsia* spp. (above) Fog-green Loma vegetation (left).

Exotic lizards
The lizard *Callopistes*, small gecko *Phyllodactylus* and the three iguanas are members of a group that has had its greatest success in the New World. Iguanas are only found there, apart from two relic genera in Madagascar and one in the Fiji islands.

Fatal meeting
Emerging from the depths of the Pacific and edging northwards along the South American coast, the cool Humboldt current swings northwest, away from the land mass towards the Galapagos Islands when it encounters the warm Nino equatorial current from the Gulf of Panama. Every seven years the pattern takes a fatal twist. The warm waters are pressed south-wards by monsoon winds and overlie the nutrient-rich Humboldt waters. Plankton is wiped out, fishes starve, seabirds are scattered to the winds and perish in millions.

② *Phyllodactylus inaequalis*
Tropidurus peruvianus tarapacensis
Tropidurus peruvianus quadrivittatus
Tropidurus peruvianus araucanus
Callopistes maculatus manni

Timid dragon *above*
Largest and best-known of South America's iguanas, *Iguana iguana* reaches a length of 6ft (1.8m). Dragon-like in appearance it is in fact quite timid.

Africa
THE ETHIOPIAN REALM

Africa

The richest of all continents in the exuberance and variety of its wildlife, Africa forms an entire zoogeographical realm, the Ethiopian, excluding a narrow coastal strip to the northwest which falls in the Palaearctic. The dominant vegetational cover of the continent's heartland is the tropical rain forest, a green world of even temperature and humidity stretching from the Gulf of Guinea in the west to the highlands and Great Rift Valley (a huge fracture in the surface of the earth) in East Africa. Evidence suggests that this great forest was once even greater before it was supplanted, to its north and south, by grassy savanna – the plains and open skies which provide the backdrop for the world's great herds, the stalking cats which prey upon them, and the ravenous dogs and vultures performing their unpleasant but biologically necessary scavenging tasks. The savanna is the tourists' Africa; to the zoologist, it is one of a series of environments harbouring plant and animal communities each uniquely adapted to its niche. The deserts which lie, north and south, beyond the savanna – the Sahara, the Kalahari, and the Namib – contain life forms endowed with features which enable them to survive where man cannot. The fauna of African lakes ranges from the threatened crocodile basking along the shores to the spectacular flocks of flamingos wading happily in the searingly alkaline waters of the shallow lakes. Alpine highlands, rivers and swamps complete the rich tapestry of the continent where man himself may have originated.

Savanna near Mt. Kilimanjaro, Tanzania, East Africa

Key to panorama

1 Weaver birds	16 Vervet monkey	31 African buffalo	46 Elephant shrew
2 Auger buzzard	17 White rhinoceros	32 Bat-eared fox	47 Four-striped mouse
3 African wild cat	18 Wildebeest	33 Rock hyrax	48 Spring hare
4 Red-billed hornbill	19 Common waterbuck	34 Warthog	49 Citrus swallowtail
5 Blue glossy starling	20 Ostrich	35 Steinbok	50 Flap-necked chameleon
6 Superb glossy starling	21 Elephant	36 Impala	51 Large-striped swordtail
7 Purple glossy starling	22 Klipspringer	37 Preying mantis	52 Broad-bordered acraea
8 Angola kingfisher	23 Anubis baboon	38 Greater kudu	53 Grimm's duiker
9 Leopard and gazelle	24 Burchell's zebra	39 Gerenuk	54 Dwarf mongoose
10 Carmine bee eater	25 Topi	40 Cape eland	55 Oxpecker
11 Boomslang	26 Red lechwe	41 Zorilla	56 Ground hornbill
12 Nubian woodpecker	27 Kori bustard	42 Yellow-billed hornbill	57 Striped ground squirrel
13 Lilac-breasted roller	28 Kob	43 Oribi (female)	58 Lesser bushbaby
14 Hoopoe	29 Thomson's gazelle	44 Oribi (male)	59 African python
15 Scops owl	30 Kenyan giraffe	45 Two-striped field mouse	60 Kirk's dik-dik

Savanna Herbivores

The degree of biological productivity generated by Africa's perennial grasslands is displayed in the seemingly infinite numbers and variety of wild animals which they support. The open grasslands are the backdrop against which the world's supreme wildlife spectacle unfolds.

The sward is a mixture of palatable grasses and herbs, of which red oat grass *Themeda triandra* is frequently predominant. The pristine grass, knee-high, resembles a standing crop of rust-coloured grain, tolerant of light grazing but disappearing quickly under intensive grazing.

The animals are mainly grass eaters. Some browse as well as graze but the broad base of the ecological structure is founded upon grass. The most abundant species are wildebeest, zebra, hartebeest and Thomson's gazelle which normally live in scattered troops, but at the time of the calving and grazing migrations assemble in massed herds filling the plain from horizon to horizon with trekking animals.

Numbers fluctuate from year to year according to climatic circumstances. In a drought year the lactating mothers are short of milk and few calves are reared. The heavy losses caused by drought and disease are, however, matched by remarkable powers of recovery. A year of good grazing ensures a large crop of healthy calves and numbers build up quickly.

Less numerous species include grazers such as the topi, oribi and warthog (which also roots in the ground for bulbs and tubers); partial grazers like the elephant, buffalo, Grant's gazelle, impala and steenbok; and, where a suitable habitat occurs, browsing animals such as the eland, the black rhinoceros and the giraffe.

All the major African predators – lion, leopard, cheetah and wild dog – are to be found on the grasslands of East Africa, as well as many of the smaller predators such as the serval, the bat-eared fox, civet, ratel and banded mongoose. Many scavengers, chiefly the hyena and jackal and several species of vultures, are in constant attendance upon the predators, squabbling among themselves for the leftovers from the kill.

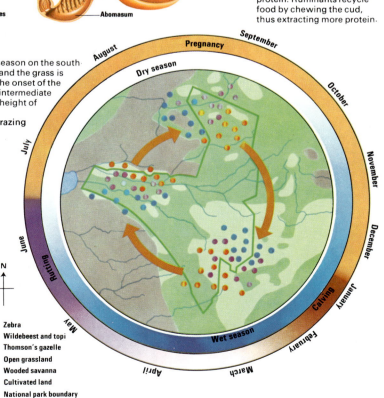

Serengeti *left*
A national park, Serengeti supports more than half a million wild animals, most of them grazing ungulates. Buffalo, zebra, wildebeest, topi and Thomson's gazelle feed together; far from competing each species grazes in a manner beneficial to the next.

Herbivore stomachs *left*
The relatively simple stomach of the non-ruminant zebra processes more food in a given time than that of the ruminant antelope but is less efficient in extracting protein. Ruminants recycle food by chewing the cud, thus extracting more protein.

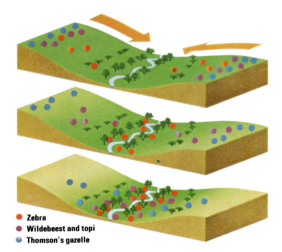

• Zebra
• Wildebeest and topi
• Thomson's gazelle

Grazing succession *above*
The undulations of the Serengeti plain influence the local movement of grazing animals. In the wet season when grass is plentiful, mixed groups graze on raised areas, moving to the long grass in damp hollows as the season progresses. First to descend are the larger animals (zebra, buffalo) followed by the wildebeest, topi and Thomson's gazelle. Larger ungulates break down the long grass by feeding and trampling, enabling the smaller animals to find their food among the lower herb layers and seeds.

Seasonal migration *right*
The Serengeti herds spend the wet season on the south-eastern plains where rainfall is least and the grass is shortest. In a dramatic migration at the onset of the dry season they move to a region of intermediate rainfall and grass in the west. At the height of the dry season they are found in the alluvial pastures of the north. The grazing succession still applies with zebras feeding first, and gazelles last.

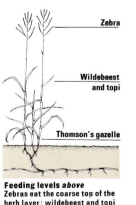

Zebra

Wildebeest and topi

Thomson's gazelle

Feeding levels *above*
Zebras eat the coarse top of the herb layer; wildebeest and topi the leafy centre; gazelles the high protein seeds and young shoots at ground level.

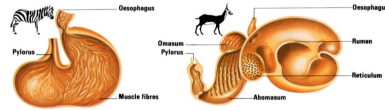

• Zebra
• Wildebeest and topi
• Thomson's gazelle
  Open grassland
  Wooded savanna
  Cultivated land
— National park boundary

Total exploitation – but no competition

'No two distinct species can occupy exactly the same environment and make the same demands on it' is a basic truth of nature which ensures that a habitat such as the savanna teems with wildlife and yet is never overstocked. Each species exploits a different category of plant food and puts the vegetation to a thorough but not excessive use. The manner in which the grazing animals such as zebra, buffalo and antelope share the low vegetation (see opposite) is echoed in the vertical feeding patterns of the larger game (right). There is, however, no rigid demarcation of feeding levels, for both the giraffe and the elephant, for example, will browse on the lower vegetation where it is easily found. While the gerenuk and dikdik are essentially browsing animals the steenbok will both browse and graze. The vervet monkey, shown high in the branches, forages among the trees of the open savanna but will descend to the ground to supplement its diet of leaves and young shoots with bulbs, roots and eggs and young of ground nesting birds.

1 Springbuck
2 Eland
3 Kudu
4 Giraffe
5 Warthog
6 White rhinoceros
7 Elephant
8 Vervet monkey
9 Gerenuk
10 Steenbok
11 Kirk's dik dik

In addition to its freakish neck, the giraffe, *Giraffa camelopardalis* possesses a long, prehensile upper lip and an extensible tongue with which it collects leaves and twigs, particularly of leguminosae, its principal diet. 20 feet (6m) from the ground.

Almost as dexterous as a primate's hand the trunk of an elephant *Loxodonta africana* permits it to feed on leaves and shoots beyond the reach of all but the giraffe. The elephant is a destructive feeder and will uproot a tree to gather a few leaves out of its reach.

The Cape eland *Taurotragus oryx* stands almost six feet at the shoulder. Its size enables it to browse on bushes and trees, using its heavy horns to collect twigs by twisting and breaking them. Eland will also use hooves to dig for bulbs and tubers.

The black rhinoceros *Diceros bicornis* rarely grazes : it has a hooklike prehensile upper lip which it uses to feed on bark, twigs and leaves. The larger, more placid white rhino *Ceratotherium simum* has a broad, square muzzle for grazing.

Meeting place *above*
Impala *Aepyceros melampus* at a waterhole with warthog *Phacochoerus aethiopicus* and a solitary wildebeest *Connochaetes taurinus.*

Trekkers *above*
Springbuck *Antidorcas marsupialis* once migrated in herds of hundreds of thousands in water-seeking treks across the veld.

Water lovers *right*
The nyala *Tragelaphus angasi* is rarely found far from water. (Below) Buffalo *Syncerus caffer* migrating across the Serengeti plain.

Ritual fights *below*
Male hartebeest *Alcelaphus buselaphus* lock horns. Ritual fights are common among antelopes, but are rarely fierce and do little damage.

Heaviest flier *above*
An inhabitant of the savanna the kori bustard *Choriotis kori* is the heaviest of flying birds. It weighs up to 50 lb (22.6 kg). It flies well but reluctantly.

Hunters of the Plains

Savanna is a blanket description for a number of different types of vegetation. Broadly, it describes open grasslands with varying combinations and densities of mainly deciduous trees and shrubs intersected by occasional fingers of riverine forest and thicket along watercourses.

Where it links with the desert at its extremes north and south of the Equator, African savanna is a semi-arid zone of bushland defined as 'Sudan' savanna. Within it there are subsidiary zones of scant grasses and xerophitic shrubs close to the desert where rainfall is least and grasslands with a higher proportion of trees where rainfall is higher. In the north, Sudan savanna reaches from east to west across the continent from northern Senegal to the Horn of Africa. Its southern counterpart is the bushveld which emerges from the Kalahari basin and stretches from Angola to Mozambique and from Zambia to the Transvaal.

The northern bushlands are the home of the scimitar-horned oryx *Oryx tao*. Once, herds of 1,000 animals were often seen, but the species is disappearing as a result of uncontrolled hunting and the introduction of domestic livestock. Gazelles of the northern zone include the long-legged dama gazelle *Gazella dama*, Dorcas gazelle *G. dorcas* and red-fronted gazelle *G. rufifrons*. Common herbivores of the southern bushveld include the tsessebe, hartebeest, eland, impala wildebeest, springbuck and greater kudu. Large mammals include elephant, black rhinoceros, giraffe, zebra, gerenuk and dikdik.

The great 'raft' of herbivores in the savanna regions supports a pyramid of predation – a pattern of life, which, although fierce and uncompromising, poses no threat to the species that are preyed upon. At the apex of the pyramid are the big cats. The lesser carnivores, small predators and scavengers form the intermediate levels above the herbivore base.

Predators do not know the meaning of overkill and strike only of necessity. The numbers of prey allow for this and, as the grass available imposes limits on the numbers of herbivores, so their numbers in turn impose limits on the numbers of carnivores.

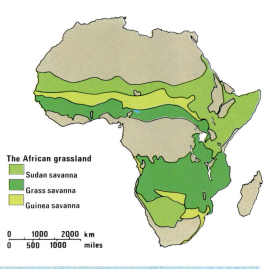

The African grassland

Sudan savanna

Grass savanna

Guinea savanna

0 1000 2000 km
0 500 1000 miles

The killer dogs *above and right*
The big cats are not the only primary predators of the savanna. A threat even to lions, the hunting dogs *Lycaon pictus* exhaust their prey by attacking as a team. Here, a zebra has been pursued and brought to a standstill by the snapping jaws of the dogs which will devour the prey within minutes of bringing it down. The dogs attack characteristically from the rear, unlike the cat's leap to the neck and throat. The range of the hunting dog is remarkable; it is found from savanna country to the summit of Mount Kilimanjaro, 19,340ft (5,595m).

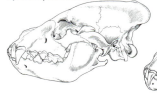
Spotted hyena *Crocuta crocuta*

Cheetah *Acinonyx jubatus*

Jaw development *left*
The jaw structures of a dog (hyena) and cat (leopard). The jaw of the hyena is longer for seizing and ripping at the flesh of its victim. And has massive molars for bone crushing. The short faced cat has highly developed teeth at the front for the killing grab at the neck or throat of its quarry.

Tree larder *left*
The leopard *Panthera pardus* preys on birds and small mammals, springing on its quarry from a tree. The branch provides a larder where the kill is beyond the reach of scavengers. The leopard is a friend of man for it kills crop-destroying baboons.

Lightning cat *right*
Timid and threatened with extermination for its skin the cheetah *Acinonyx jubatus* is a creature of the open plain where its incredible speed (up to 75mph, 120kmh) over short distances enables it to run its victim down. Its kill here is a warthog.

Death of a wildebeest

The wildebeest's size makes it a frequent quarry of the lion which, like other predators such as the leopard and the cheetah, chooses its prey among animals of a size similar to itself. But the death and disintegration of a carcass has a host of contributors whose functions seem to overlap and yet, because of their physiological features, feed quite distinctively.

Lion Cheetah
Hunting dog

Of the lion family, the lioness is generally the killer. The male then feeds first and if hungry may eat 75lb (34kg) of meat. A kill of average size will provide meat for a pride of lions, the liver providing them with Vitamin A which lions, like other cats, cannot produce. The wildebeest will provide food for a couple of days.

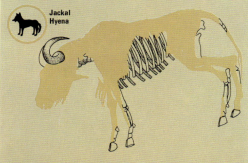

Jackal
Hyena

The scavengers arrive. Hyenas will contest the remains of a kill with the primary predator and, in groups, will drive away a feeding lion which loathes the hyena enough to kill it, given the chance. The smaller jackal darts in and out, snatching what it can from the remains of the feast.

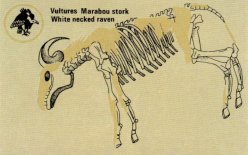

Vultures Marabou stork
White necked raven

Vultures are often first to see a kill but observe it patiently until the more aggressive scavengers have withdrawn. Several types of vulture may feed on a carcass without competing and will be joined at the feast by the evil looking marabou stork and white-necked raven.

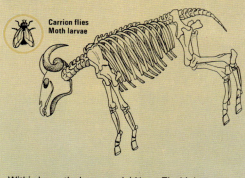

Carrion flies
Moth larvae

Within hours the bones are laid bare. The higher orders of predator and scavenger have gone. Carrion flies and beetles, complete the gruesome task.

The bone cracker *above*
The spotted hyena *Crocuta crocuta*, with jackals at a wildebeest carcass, feeds on carrion but is itself a predator which will attack in packs. It has powerful jaws to crack and swallow the largest bones after the meat has been taken.

Ugly but practical

The naked and unattractive heads and necks of the white headed and white backed vultures are hygienic adaptations enabling them to delve cleanly into the carcass of a dead animal. The Egyptian vulture is feathered and eats scraps flung aside.

White headed vulture
Trigonoceps occipitalis

Egyptian vulture
Neophron percnopterus

White backed vulture
Gyps africanus

The carcass spotters *above*
A group of vultures including the white backed *Pseudogyps africanus* and griffon *Gyps ruppellii* squabble over the remains of a wildebeest. Vultures planing down from the sky provide a bearing to the kill for other scavengers such as the hyena and jackal.

Thanatophilus micans

Sarcophaga haemorrhoidalis

The last rites *left*
Least in status but ever present in the hierarchy of scavengers are the flesh flies *Sarcophaga* sp. and the carrion beetles *Thanatophilus micans* which attend the rotting carcass of the animal long after the vultures, storks and kites have gone.

Total utilization *above*
Horns of a gnu are eaten away by the larvae of the horn boring moth, a close relative of the clothes moth.

Less than 36 hours after its death, all that the hyenas, jackals and vultures have left of an elephant weighing several tons (right).

Community Life on the Savanna

A pattern of communal living exists among almost all the animals of the savanna. Few creatures are hermits, least of all in the open, grassy plains where species proliferate as they do in few other places on earth. Predators, the hunters, and herbivores, the hunted, form collective groups to fulfil their need to survive. Woodland and forest species tend to be far less social.

The savanna's vast herds of antelope are aggregations drawn together for feeding or migratory purposes (see pp 62,63) rather than communities, but patterns of social behaviour exist within these aggregations. Grant's gazelle establishes stable family territories defended by the male, but the impala forms small breeding herds with no distinct territory. The Uganda kob *Adenota kob* establishes a unique breeding ground in which each mature male occupies and defends a small, circular territory to which the female comes for mating. There are often 40 or 50 such territories, tightly packed within a small area, with the central ones the most hotly contested.

Many orders of predator adopt a social or communal pattern of existence, particularly in hunting, although its impact on the game herds is hardly social. The fierce and snapping wild dogs *Lycaon pictus* work as a highly effective team in bringing their quarry to bay (pp 64, 65) but they work in an equally cooperative manner in defense of territory surrounding their burrows and young. As a contrast in kindred species, the black rhinoceros *Diceros bicornis* is a sour-tempered and solitary animal whereas the gentler, grazing white rhinoceros *Ceratotherium simum* is gregarious, living in small family parties and often in larger groups.

The examples of communal life described on these pages – the subterranean termites, terrestrial elephants and avian weaver birds – have been among the most closely observed. In the case of the elephant this is probably due to the fact that it has drawn the interest of man throughout – and probably before – recorded time. Its sheer size and eccentric shape, its adaptable intelligence and its recognizable code of behaviour towards its fellows have proved an irresistible source of study to man. At the other end of the scale, the ants and termites provide an illustration of tens of thousands of creatures acting as a corporate unit. Alone, a driver ant *Megaponera foetens* is almost meaningless, except beneath a microscope; on safari it becomes a relentless threat to everything in its path. Even an elephant has been driven mad and killed itself when ants have succeeded in penetrating its trunk. One termite is a vulnerable speck; a colony will construct an air conditioned city more adequate to its needs than any town planner can achieve.

The matriarchal society
Elephant communities have a well defined structure of group units in which the female is dominant. A family or sub-clan is an individual cow and her young of both sexes. Several families make up a clan at the head of which stands the matriarch, an older female distinguished by her greater size and 'awareness'. In this matriarchal society the male spends his time in male company – a sire bull with sub-adults, some distance from the clan. Another sub-group is made up of a senile cow and attendants. Some senile 'loners' lose the herd instinct completely.

Key to herd structure

- Mature bull
- Immature bull
- Mature cow
- Immature cow
- Young

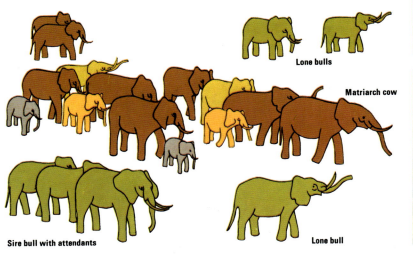

Lone bulls

Matriarch cow

Sire bull with attendants

Lone bull

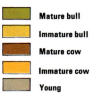

A death in the herd *left*
A cow elephant lies dying. Her clan has gathered round trying to help her back on her feet, force-feeding her with herbs and grass. To no avail. Despairingly, a bull elephant makes several attempts to mount her in a strange and wonderful gesture of defiance of death. The photographs illustrate the remarkable bond which has been seen to exist within the elephant clans and family units. An elephant injured by a falling tree or in a fight will be helped to its feet by others and propped by them on the march and they are difficult to drive away from a mortally wounded clan member. They have been observed to 'hang around' the carcass of a dead elephant for at least two hours and, if not disturbed, may wait until nightfall when they tear out branches and uproot grass which they drop on and around the dead animal.

Communal architecture 1 ; weaver bird colonies

The scattered trees of the savanna and a gregarious nature encourage flocks of weaver birds to make their homes together. The weaver birds build complex and ingenious nests, sometimes in dozens in the same thornbush or tree. The red-billed quelea *Quelea quelea* is by far the most numerous. Its gregarious way of life extends to feeding ; wheeling, locust-like flocks descend on cropland during the dry season, with disastrous results for the farmer. Control of the quelea has become a major concern in countries where crop raising is vital to the economy.

Acacia community *right*
A typical weaver bird community in Tanzanian savanna. These nests are well spaced. Some weaver species sling their nests beneath that of a 'protector' such as a stork or eagle as a means of defence against nest robbers like the boomslang snake.

Urban bird *left*
The vitelline masked weaver *Ploceus vitelinus* is one of the 96 species of Ploceinae or typical weavers. The masked weaver builds its nest at the end of a branch which has been stripped bare of leaves. It is a friendly bird, nesting in urban areas of southern Africa.

Building the nest *left*
Step-by-step construction of a quelea nest. The foundations are a ring of knotted leaf strands from which the walls and roof are extended to form the egg chamber. The quelea completes the nest by weaving the aperture for front entrance.

Communal architecture 2 ; the termites

The termite mound encloses a sealed world. Its iron hard crust is much more than a defence against predators ; the termite is a soft bodied insect living on a restricted diet of cellulose (wood, leaves, humus) and can exist only in a stable atmosphere with regulated temperature and humidity. The walls of the mound enclose a 'micro-climate' and protect the nest from fatal atmospheric changes. The crust of the mound, when granulated, is used by villagers as an effective 'cement' for floors.

Richest in termites
Macrotermes bellicosus is distributed widely across the equatorial region of Africa (left). There are 12 genera of fungus-growing termites, ten of which are found in the Ethiopian, or African, region, the richest of all regions in its number of termite families.
Left Distribution of *M.bellicosus*

The nest of the fungus growing termite *Macrotermes bellicosus* (shown right) has been developed over the years by its occupants to a height of eight feet (2.5m). The work began when a mating pair nested in a tiny hole after flight. This is now the royal chamber occupied by the gross and flaccid queen. Around it generations of workers have constructed a network of fungus gardens, attics storing vegetable foods, airshafts and passages to the outside world which are opened and closed by soldier termites escorting the foraging worker termites.
Smaller soldiers within the termitarium fill an administrative function, marshalling, guiding and controlling the hectic traffic of workers tending the queen.

Nest
Outer wall of termitarium

Wall of the nest

Air space within the nest

Chimneys help to control the micro-climate of the nest

Fungus *Eutermitomyces letestui* growing from the mound. The fungus is cultivated by the termites for food

Termite tower *above*
A termitarium in Tanzania. The 'tower' and its neighbouring mounds house a colony of upwards of 20 years' standing. Few animals can damage it.

Raiders *below*
Safari ants *Megaponera foetens* return from a raid on a termite nest. Some carry as many as 15 termites in their jaws. They are ruthless raiders.

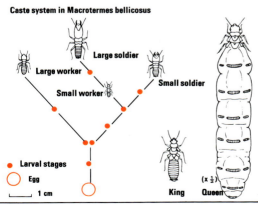

Caste system in Macrotermes bellicosus

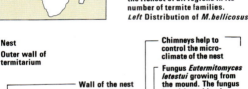
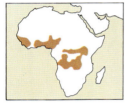

Large soldier

Large worker

Small soldier

Small worker

● **Larval stages**

● **Egg**

├─┤ **1 cm**

King   **Queen**   (x ½)

An impregnable fortress to many predators the termite mound may fall to the powerful claws of the aardvark and pangolin.

Copularium or royal chamber around which the nest has grown

Base pillars supporting the nest

Fungus gardens of decayed vegetable matter brought in by foragers

Primates: The Shy Nomads

Although the primates of Africa and Asia are closely related the only genera common to both continents are *Papio* and *Macaca*. The range of the hamadryas baboon *Papio hamadryas*, regarded as sacred by the ancient Egyptians, reaches across the Red Sea into southwestern Arabia. The Barbary ape *Macaca sylvana*, which inhabits Morocco and Algeria, is the only African representative of this Asian genus – and edges into Europe, on the Rock of Gibraltar.

The African primates range from the archaic prosimians, such as the lemurs and bushbabies, to the great apes. Of the four species of great apes — orang utan, chimpanzee, pigmy chimpanzee and gorilla – all except the orang utan live in Africa.

Most of them inhabit the forests and savanna regions south of the Sahara. The great majority are forest dwellers but some species such as the baboons and the patas monkey *Erythrocebus patas* have abandoned arboreal living (though they still sleep in trees) and have adapted themselves to a life on the ground. They inhabit both woodland and grassland savannas and even subdesert environments.

Within the rain forest the various species of primates have adapted themselves to widely differing ecological niches which, broadly speaking, are based on the system of vertical stratification; the larger species tend to be terrestrial or live close to the ground while the smaller species are more arboreal.

The forest canopy comprises a latticework of small branches and foliage. This topmost stratum is warmer by day than the interior of the forest, is highly productive in edible fruits, flowers, leaves and insect fauna and lies beyond the reach of most predators. It thus forms an extremely attractive primate habitat. But although food is plentiful most of it grows at the extremities of wide-spreading branches which cannot support the weight of large animals and thus calls for food gathering techniques, locomotion and behavioural patterns of a very different order from those required at lower levels.

These complex ecological interrelationships are as yet little studied or understood. With one or two notable exceptions, few comprehensive field studies of the primates have been undertaken. The current status and ecological requirements of most species are therefore imperfectly known. The study of such shy and highly mobile animals living in the upper strata of dense forest clearly presents formidable problems. But it is essential that methods of assessing the status of wild primate populations should be developed if their future is to be assured.

The African primates are a diminishing asset with nominal protection afforded to only a few species. The spread of settlement and cultivation into the forested areas destroyed or degraded much of the natural habitat on which they are dependent for existence, and the widespread use to which they have been put for bio-medical research purposes is an additional drain on their numbers.

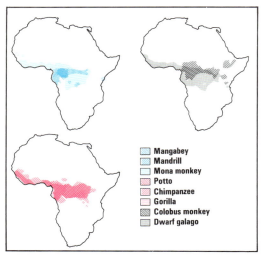

	Mangabey
	Mandrill
	Mona monkey
	Potto
	Chimpanzee
	Gorilla
	Colobus monkey
	Dwarf galago

Equatorial primate distribution
The range and limits of the species of primate illustrated on this page are almost all found within the boundaries of Africa's tropical forests which straddle the Equator from the Atlantic in the west to the Great Rift Valley in the east.

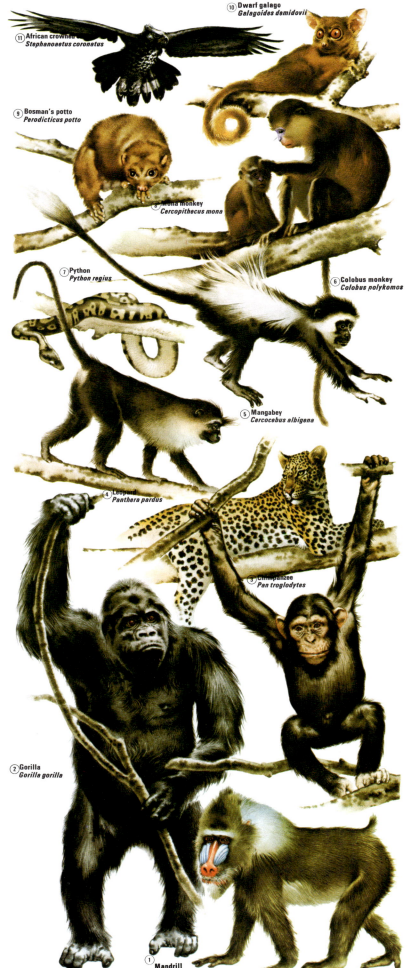

11 African crowned
Stephanoaetus coronatus

10 Dwarf galago
Galagoides demidovii

9 Bosman's potto
Perodicticus potto

Mona monkey
Cercopithecus mona

7 Python
Python regius

6 Colobus monkey
Colobus polykomos

5 Mangabey
Cercocebus albigena

4 Leopard
Panthera pardus

Chimpanzee
Pan troglodytes

2 Gorilla
Gorilla gorilla

1 Mandrill
Mandrillus sphinx

Multi-storey habitat
The African rain forest is a stable world of even temperature and humidity. Most of the trees are of evergreen species which provide a permanent canopy, a continuous layer of tree crowns of approximately even height. Emergent, or exceptionally tall, trees push their way through the canopy, while in clearings where a dead tree has fallen and sunlight is reaching the forest floor, a secondary growth of young trees and shrubs is established. Through this 'multi-storey' habitat moves the African monkey, largely nomadic in its search for fruit, insects and vegetation which the forest provides in abundance. Its predators are few. At canopy level, the crowned eagle; among the branches, the python; and, in the lower storeys of the forest, the leopard takes its toll.

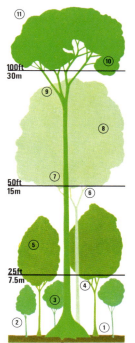

High in the tree cover are the archaic prosimians, represented by the nocturnal and slow moving potto and the lively galago, known popularly as the bushbaby.

The mona monkey is found throughout the rain forest of central and west Africa and is typical of the guenons. Colobus monkeys rarely descend to the ground and whole families have been known to starve to death in a tree rather than descend and cross open ground. They are prodigious leapers, using their tails as airbrakes. African monkeys are far more agile than their prehensile tailed South American relatives. An exception is the mangabey which is slower than either the colobus or the guenon. The gorilla and the chimpanzee remain close to or at ground level.

Playing *above*
Baby chimps are a centre of attraction. They are often carried by other juveniles as well as by their mothers.

Grooming *right*
Grooming among chimpanzees begin when they are about ten months old. They may live to 40.

The big apes
The two African members of the ape family Pongidae, the gorilla and the chimpanzee are closely related to each other and differ from the monkeys in the length of their limbs (the arms particularly), the lack of tail and the greater size of the brain. Without the agility of monkeys they possess greater manipulative skills and are able to 'communicate' socially to a greater degree. The chimpanzee is smaller, more arboreal and more active than the leisurely gorilla. In the rain forest both species feed on vegetation but the chimpanzee is often carnivorous when it lives in a savanna area. It is known to kill and eat monkeys, young antelopes and birds. Of all animals, apes are closest to man and observers of their behaviour have seen clear pointers to the evolution of *Homo sapiens*.

The community behaviour and common postures of the gorilla suggest an ability to relax in a way which has been lost to the human.

Female at rest with young

Social grooming

Juveniles at play

Female and infant with dominant male

Nomad in its nest *above*
Nesting is a typical feature of chimpanzee behaviour. The nests are located high in the trees, from 15 to 120 feet (5-36m) and are made from branches that have either been bent or broken and then intertwined to form a platform. The cup is then lined with twigs. A day nest is often made during the rainy season when the normally nomadic chimpanzee spends the greater part of its time in trees and less time in search of its wide range of foods close to the forest floor. The chimpanzee has a flexible social organisation and may scatter to feed or remain in one area.

Gentle giant *right*
The fearsome 'wild man' appearance of the gorilla disguises the placid, non aggressive nature of the true herbivore. It is not as excitable as the chimpanzee but when displaying in the face of a threat will hoot and drum on its chest. This is largely bluff. Its mock charge at a human will almost always stop if the man holds his ground. Among some tribesmen it is a disgrace to be bitten by a gorilla since it is understood that only a coward is likely to be attacked. Gorillas travel quietly in tightly-knit groups, feeding on a completely vegetable diet as they go.

The noisiest and most expressive of animals, the chimpanzee indulges in a great variety of gestures and facial expressions.

The pout of curiosity or distaste might be one of scepticism or doubt in a human. The smile is an expression of pleasure.

When thoughtful or anxious the chimpanzee wears the least dramatic of its many expressions and what appears as outright

laughter, is the chimp's expression of annoyance or unhappiness. When it seems to laugh its feelings are probably the opposite.

Colours of the Rain Forest

A belt of rain forest centres around the Congo basin extends both north and south of the Equator from the west coast of Africa to the western arm of the Great Rift Valley. At one time it was more extensive as shown by the relict communities of typically west African species – for example, the Zanzibar and Tana River red colobus monkeys – which were isolated when climatic change induced the forest to retreat.

Equatorial rain forest is characterised by the great variety of tall trees, devoid of branches for the greater part of their height and with spreading crowns forming a luxuriant evergreen canopy at a height of more than 100 feet (30m) above the ground; some emergents are substantially taller.

Beneath the canopy, the understory – comprising the crowns of small trees and saplings of forest giants—provides a dense and more or less continuous layer of foliage and branches festooned with lianas, which forms a strong and extensive platform 30-100 feet (9-30m) above the ground.

At groundlevel the forest is relatively open for there are no grasses and few shrubs or herbs on the forest floor. Between the boles and buttresses of forest giants are scattered clumps of shrubs and bushes, in places dense, interspersed with occasional rotting trunks of fallen trees and other forest debris.

Pristine rain forest is botanically exceptionally rich both in tree species and biological productivity. This is reflected in the forest fauna. In the absence of grass the ungulates are primarily browsers. They include such species as the okapi, bongo, buffalo, bushbuck and numerous duikers. Elephants, bush pigs, giant forest hogs and small mammals are abundant. The predators include the leopard, golden cat and various civets.

Although substantial tracts of equatorial forest remain, much has been locally exploited. Commercialized logging and spreading cultivation have resulted in widespread fragmentation and in many areas the nature of the forest has been profoundly altered. Undisturbed primary forest is becoming increasingly scarce and with its diminution, the habitat for many secretive mammals is reduced.

Tree snake and moth
Two examples of the hues of the rain forest: echoing to perfection the colour of the vegetation, Blanding's tree snake (above) slithers in pursuit of its prey. (right) The oleander hawk moth *Daphnis neri*.

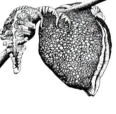

Threat display
One of the more exotic African mantises, *Pseudocreobotra wahlbergii* (left) uses its eye-like markings as an effective threat display to ward off its enemies. (below) The forest bee hawk moth *Cephanodes* sp.

Spongy capsules
The egg sac or ootheca of a praying mantis (above); eggs are laid in tough, spongy capsules for protection. A hapless lizard is seized in the raptorial and spiny front legs of a mantis (left). Another forest mantid form (right).

Camouflage *left*
Cryptic (or disruptive) coloring in forest animals is pronounced. Markings which would appear strident against any other background enable many species to exist in great numbers and yet remain elusive and difficult to observe. Many forest animals also have an adaptation of movement. The bongo and the banded duiker, for example, use a crouching run to take them through the low branches. Dimensions given for the chevrotain, okapi, duiker and bongo are heights at shoulder; for the genet, shrew and squirrel, head and body length.

Okapi 1.6m

Bongo 1.3m

Banded duiker
50cm

Water chevrotain   30cm

Forest genet
40-50cm

Chequered
elephant shrew
30cm

Four-striped squirrel
20cm

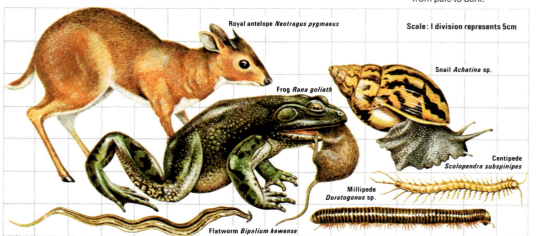

Accelerator muscle *left*
When it is fully extended a chameleon's tongue is as long as its body and tail. It is shot out in 1/25 sec by a remarkable accelerator muscle, pinning its insect prey on the mucus-adhesive and partly prehensile pad at the tip of its tongue.

Colour change *right*
Varying conditions of light are the most important factor in a chameleon's change of colour. If, in response to a nervous signal from the eye, the black melanophores (b) expand while the yellow (y) and red (r) melanophores remain contracted, the reptile turns from pale to dark.

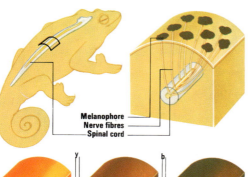

Melanophore
Nerve fibres
Spinal cord

Royal antelope *Neotragus pygmaeus*

Scale : l division represents 5cm

Snail *Achatina* sp.

Frog *Rana goliath*

Centipede
Scolopendra subspinipes

Millipede
Doratogonus sp.

Flatworm *Bipalium kewense*

Giants and dwarfs *left*
Forest conditions produce extremes of size. The six species shown are drawn to the same scale.

Colourful frog *above*
Sometimes known as sedge frogs, *Hyperolius* sp. come in a wide range of colour combinations.

Savage marchers *above*
Safari ants attack a millipede. On the march, these ants are voracious predators on any animal in their path.

Telltale marks *below*
White marks on a Gaboon adder *Bitis gabonica* reveal its presence among the forest floor leaves.

Forest bird fauna
Equatorial forest birds range from the garish, adept flyers like the hornbills and parrots of the canopy to the quieter birds of more subdued colour found in the lower stories and the forest floor. Of the former the parrot has a bullet-like flight across the roof of the forest and the hornbills escort monkeys on their travels.
Of the terrestrial birds the Congo peafowl is the only African species of peacock and was unknown until 1936. The strong feet and legs of the Angola pitta mark it as a bird which grubs in the humus of the forest floor for its food.

Gold Coast touraco
Turacus persa

Blue fairy flycatcher
Erannornis longicauda

Yellow-casqued hornbill
Ceratogymna elata

Grey parrot
Psittacus erithacus

Congo peafowl
Afropavo congensis

Angola pitta
Pitta angolensis

Forest robin
Stiphrornis erythrothorax

The Swamplands

Wetlands are more extensive in tropical than in temperate regions and are especially characteristic of Africa's inland waters. Nowhere is this better exemplified than in the upper Nile drainage area where immense papyrus-choked swamps occupy several thousand square miles of the southern Sudan and Uganda or, farther south, in the sand flats of the northern Kalahari where the Okovango flood plain extends for more than 7,000 square miles (18,000km²).

Few animals inhabit the dense interiors of the great swamps but a number of species living around the periphery have become adapted to the semi-aquatic way of life. The most prominent are the hippopotamus *Hippopotamus amphibius*, the sitatunga *Tragelaphus spekii*, lechwe *Kobus* spp. and other antelopes. Visitors to the swamps will include many animals at home in other habitats such as the elephant and buffalo.

Large numbers of fish-eating birds populate the swamps. Herons, egrets, ibises, storks and pelicans, among others, are abundant. The cry of the fish eagle fills the air and several species of kingfisher provide touches of exquisite colour. Faunal diversity is particularly evident among the fishes.

Because swamp waters are deficient in dissolved oxygen many swamp-dwelling organisms have evolved ingenious methods for satisfying their own requirements. A worm of the genus *Alma* obtains atmospheric oxygen through a special 'lung' in its tail extremity which it raises above the surface while its head is in the mud.

African swamps serve the important purpose of acting as gigantic natural reservoirs which collect and hold excess water during the rainy season and release it during the dry.

For wildlife the annual inundation provides dry season grazing for great numbers of plains game when savanna productivity is at its lowest. Desert ungulates are drawn from the Kalahari, for instance, to the grasslands fringing the Okovango delta, to feed with flood plain species such as the waterbuck, tsessebe and lechwe, and woodland species like the kudu, roan and sable antelopes. These dry season concentrations of herbivores are one of Africa's finest faunal sights.

Heavyweight of the swamps

The hippopotamus *H. amphibius* is the king of the African swamps and the key to much of the life to be found there. The movements and wallowing of this heavyweight (2,500-3,000lb, 1,000-1,300kg) stir the bottom mud, liberating nutrients to the benefit of other aquatic life. It feeds during the day on water cabbage *Pistia stratiotes* and its excrement helps feed the cabbage and other plants to the advantage of the water snail – and the open-bill stork which in turn feeds on snails. At dusk the hippopotamuses leave the swamps to graze on dry land.

The chain of life

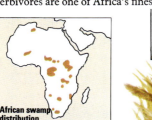

African swamp distribution

Papyrus swamps
Coarse and luxuriant, swamp vegetation is dominated by papyrus *Cyperus papyrus* which reaches heights of 25 feet (8m) or more. Water lilies and water cabbage float on the surface and in some swamp areas water hyacinths form rafts beneath which the stagnant waters are lethal to fish. An important contribution to the organic life of the swamp is made by *Alma* spp. the worm which abounds in papyrus swamps. They pass huge quantities of organic matter through their guts and the casts form layers inches deep upon the swamp bed.

Hippo grass
Vossia cuspidata

Matetite reed
Phragmites sp

Hammerhead stork *Scopus umbretta*

Hippopotamus *Hippopotamus amphibius*

Saddlebilled stork *Ephippiorhynchus senegalensis*

Sitatunga *Tragelaphus spekii*

Black crake *Limnocorax flavirostra*

Water cabbage *Pistia stratiotes*

Swamp worm *Alma emini*

Bichir *Polypterus* sp

Catfish *Malapterurus* sp

papyrus *Cyperus papyrus*

Malachite kingfisher
Corythornis cristata

erald snake
otaphopeltis hotamboeia

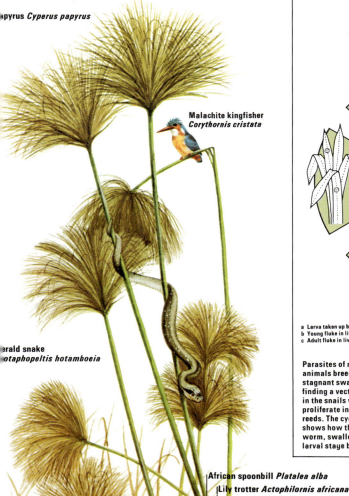

Parasite and hosts

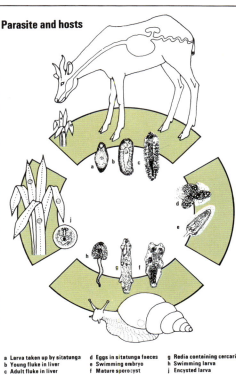

a Larva taken up by sitatunga
b Young fluke in liver
c Adult fluke in liver
d Eggs in sitatunga faeces
e Swimming embryo
f Mature sporocyst
g Redia containing cercaria
h Swimming larva
j Encysted larva

Parasites of man and animals breed in the stagnant swamps of Africa, finding a vector, or carrier, in the snails which proliferate in the mud and reeds. The cycle illustrated shows how the liverfluke worm, swallowed at the larval stage by a browsing sitatunga, matures and breeds in its liver. The eggs are returned to the water in its faeces, are taken up by the snail and released again as larva in a cyst, or membrane, to settle on a reed. Bilharzia, a disease once rampant among the people of Africa's wetlands, is transmitted similarly.

African spoonbill *Platalea alba*
Lily trotter *Actophilornis africana*
Water lily *Nymphaea* sp
Shoebill *Balaeniceps rex*

Squacco heron *Ardeola ralloides*
Marsh mongoose *Atilax paludinosus*
Snail *Biomphalaria sudanica*
Lungfish *Protopterus aethiopicus*

Spear fisherman *above*
Solitary and retiring, the goliath heron *Ardea goliath* haunts the swamps and pans of Africa, its spear-like bill the perfect weapon for fishing. It is one of the largest of herons. 4-5ft (120–150cm) in height.

Swamp adaptation *left*
The remarkable hooves of the sitatunga (top) splay widely from the pastern to support its weight on boggy ground and on the swamp bed but make its movements clumsier on land. The extended toes of the jacana or lily trotter (centre) take its weight over a wide area of surface vegetation. To breathe when the waters of the swamp dry out the aquatic snail *Biomphalaria sudanica* (left) has a lung and blood containing haemoglobin which acts as an oxygen reservoir.

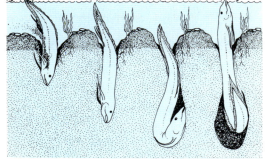

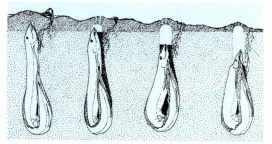

Swamp survivor 1 *above*
A relic species, the lungfish *Protopterus annectens*, survives the dry season in the swamps by burrowing into the mud. It curls up in a cocoon of mucus which hardens and protects the fish from dessication. The lid is sealed with a porous mud through which the lungfish breathes. When the rains return the lungfish breaks out and swims away.

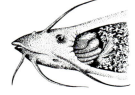

Swamp survivor 2 *left*
Breathing equipment to help the catfish live when the waters diminish takes the form of respiratory 'branches' and a gill cavity adapted to absorb atmospheric oxygen.

Lakes of the Great Rift

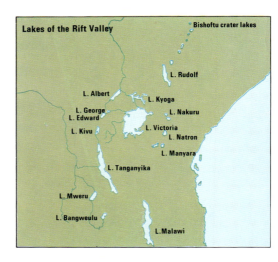

Lakes of the Rift Valley

Bishoftu crater lakes

L. Rudolf

L. Albert
L. Kyoga
L. George
L. Nakuru
L. Edward
L. Kivu
L. Victoria
L. Natron
L. Manyara
L. Tanganyika

L. Mweru

L. Bangweulu
L. Malawi

The largest and most remarkable fracture on the earth's surface runs for more than 4,000 miles (6,437 km) from the Jordan Valley to the Mozambique Channel. This Great Rift Valley follows the course of the Red Sea into Ethiopia and thence into the highlands of Kenya and Tanzania. A western arm runs from Uganda along the eastern extremity of the Congo through Malawi before submerging beneath the waters of the Indian Ocean into the deep trench separating Madagascar from the mainland of Africa.

The course of this great cleft is studded with a chain of spectacular lakes and there is widespread evidence of recent and continuing volcanic activity. The eastern branch of the Rift contains such lakes as Awash, Rudolf, Baringo, Hannington, Nakuru, Naivasha, Natron and Magadi. The western branch includes lakes Albert, Edward, George, Kivu, Tanganyika, Rukwa and high Malawi. In a shallow depression between the walls of the Rift but not regarded as part of its lake system in Lake Victoria.

Lake Tanganyika is one of the largest and deepest lakes in the world and shares with Lake Malawi a remarkable endemic cichlid (mouth breeding) fish fauna. Many of the lakes provide a home for the much maligned and over-hunted crocodile, whose value to the ecology of the lakes is greater than the value of the skin for which it is ruthlessly hunted.

The levels of many of the smaller lakes in the Rift Valley fluctuate to cycles of rainfall. As the level declines, those lakes that have no outlet become increasingly saline. This factor, in combination with high temperatures and constant sunlight creates perfect conditions for algae and diatoms which breed prodigiously and provide food for multitudes of lesser flamingos. Huge flocks of these magnificently coloured birds, numbered literally in millions, inhabit the Rift Valley lake system and provide a spectacle that is regarded as one of the wonders of the bird world.

Migrant corridor *above*
The lakes of the Great Rift Valley are the home of many species of bird, to be seen there throughout the year. They are joined, periodically, by many migrants from the north, using the Rift as a natural corridor to wintering grounds.

Teeming lakes *above*
Papyrus, rafts of lilies fringe the shallows of a Great Rift lake. The waters teem with life except (in a number of smaller lakes in the east) where the water has a high saline content. Even here, algae and crustaceans provide ample food for immense flamingo flocks.

Lily trotter *left*
The remarkable spreading feet of the african jacana *Actophilornis africana* or lily trotter have adapted it to walk with ease and confidence across floating vegetation. Graceful and not shy, the sharp spurs on its wings are formidable in fight. They are Old and New World birds.

Lake origins
The geological structure of the Great Rift has established three main types of lakes : Graben, lying in faults in the earth's surface and which are generally deep, like Lakes Malawi and Tanganyika ; volcanic where lava flows have barred drainage ; and tectonic, which were formed by a reversal of drainage patterns or by up-warping around a basin. Victoria is such a lake. The lakes are further classified by the degree to which their waters are stratified in temperature layers. Meromictic lakes are those which are deep and in which the water rarely if ever circulates. The depths are without oxygen or life, which is found in the layers closer to the surface. Polymictic lakes have little depth and are subject to constant mixing of surface water with lower levels. Between the two extremes lie the oligomictic lakes, where the water circulates at intervals during the year.

Lake Tanganyika
Depth max. 4823ft (1470m)
Graben/meromictic lake permanently stratified but top layers contain more species of fish than any other lake in the world, apart from L. Malawi formerly known as Lake Nyasa. Like L. Tanganyika, L. Malawi is also meromictic.

Bishoftu Crater Lake
Depth max. 285ft (87m)
Volcanic/oligomictic lake near Addis Ababa, Ethiopia, stratifies throughout summer; mixes sporadically in winter when surface water cools and sinks. Productive in plankton populations. Bishoftu Crater Lake is one of the few oligomictic lakes of Africa.

Lake Victoria
Depth max. 262ft (80m) (exceptional)
Tectonic/polymictic lake. Mixing of surface water with deeper layers is constant. With Lakes Tanganyika and Malawi has richer fish fauna than any other lake in the world. Most E. African lakes are polymictic. A freshwater jellyfish *Limnocnidu victoriae* is found there.

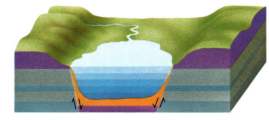

Flamingo pastures

The shallow Rift lakes provide unequalled aquatic pasture for immense numbers of flamingos. The most numerous species, the lesser flamingo *Phoeniconaias minor* has a deep-keeled bill lined with filtering laminae with which it extracts the minute blue-green algae, on which it feeds exclusively, from the lake's surface waters. In the course of a year a million flamingos on one lake will consume nearly 65,000 tons of algae. With its shallow-keeled bill the greater flamingo *Phoenicopterus antiquorum* feeds in a more catholic manner, on crustaceans, fish and the rich organic mud.

Flamingo diet

Algae and diatoms (tinted) in the surface water and crustaceans, rotifers and worms at deeper levels provide the major source of food.

Lesser flamingo — **Greater flamingo**

Deeply keeled upper mandible

Shallow keeled upper mandible

Large area of filter laminae

Filter laminae

Kaleidoscopic cichlid fish *above*

The adult male cichlid *Labeotropheus ffuellborni*, in full breeding colour, is one of the many endemic cichlid fish of Lake Malawi. Cichlids have a huge variety of colour and forms and within the *Labeotropheus* genus the colour may vary from dull brown to vibrant blue. The colour of the male may disappear suddenly if it is alarmed. *Labeotropheus* is a 'lipped' fish with a ventral mouth, eating algae which it scrapes from the surface of rocks with its grooved and spatulate teeth. Cichlids are perch-like, pugnacious fish.

Pink spectacular *above*
Widespread in much of the Old World and the New the flamingo is one of nature's most attractive birds and never more spectacular than where its greatest numbers are to be seen — in the alkaline lakes of the Great Rift Valley.

Deep lakes ritual *left*
Mating between mouth-brooding fish is a brief but elaborate encounter. 1 A male cichlid *Haplochromis burtoni* approaches the female. 2 He brings her into the breeding condition by flashing the set of dummy eggs on his anal fin. 3 the female lays her eggs and 4 almost immediately takes them into her mouth. Once spawning has taken place the male again spreads the anal fin. 5 The female attempts to take up these eggs, also; instead she takes up the sperm emitted by the male. This involved encounter between strangers ensures that all the eggs in the mouth of the female are fertilized.

Friends in a world of enemies *above*

The spur-wing plover and the water dikkop feed on ticks and insects lodged in the scaly but valuable hide of the Nile crocodile *Crocodilus niloticus*. More threatened than threatening, the crocodile has been reduced to the point of extermination in many parts of Africa. Poachers after its skin have been responsible for the major decline in its numbers; eggs and hatchlings are subject to savage predation by olive baboons, marabou storks and monitors by day and by honey badgers, white-tailed mongooses, and others at night.

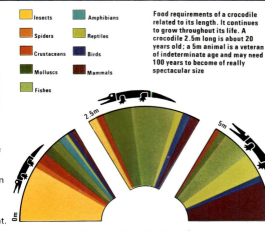

Insects	Amphibians
Spiders	Reptiles
Crustaceans	Birds
Molluscs	Mammals
Fishes	

Food requirements of a crocodile related to its length. It continues to grow throughout its life. A crocodile 2.5m long is about 20 years old; a 5m animal is a veteran of indeterminate age and may need 100 years to become of really spectacular size

2.5m

5m

0m

Sahara: The Struggle for Life

The northern half of the African continent is almost wholly desert, occupying a belt 1,250 miles (2,012 km) wide reaching from the Atlantic to the Red Sea and beyond the continent into Asia. It is both the largest and hottest desert on earth, where the monotony of the illimitable plain is relieved only occasionally by mountain massifs and the desert is waterless except for a rare rock pool or a small oasis nurtured by subterranean sources.

In only a few parts of the Sahara does the rainfall exceed four inches; in many places it is substantially less. Even this small amount is subject to a wide variation: much of the total may be the product of a single storm and be followed by a long period of rainlessness which in some parts of the desert may last for years. But rainfall is not the only source of precipitation. In places, dew yields more moisture than rain.

In physical terms the Sahara can be broadly divided into three principal types of terrain: *hamadas*, elevated plateaulands of rock and stone; *regs*, extensive areas of silt, gravel and stone, having a hard surface and laid down by past flood waters; and *ergs*, seas of sand dunes which are thought by many, mistakenly, to typify the Sahara.

All life in the Sahara, of whatever form, is activated by the unceasing struggle for water. Both animals and plants have devised a variety of ingenious methods of satisfying their water requirements: plants have developed extensive underground root systems for storing water and minimizing evaporation; reptiles conserve water (much of it deriving from their prey) more efficiently than warm-blooded animals and can tolerate greater heat; birds have both a naturally higher body temperature and the ability to regulate it in accordance with the temperature of the air, thus minimizing the loss of water through evaporation.

The metabolism of desert mammals permits them to go for long periods without water or to dispense with it altogether. The addax, in particular is so well adapted to its harsh enviroment that it can live even in the *ergs* in conditions that no other large mammal (except perhaps the slender-horned gazelle) could tolerate. The addax never drinks; it meets all its water requirements from the plant on which it feeds. It is the supreme example of perfect adaptation to an extremely arid enviroment. Its ability to convert scant desert vegetation into high quality protein sets it apart as a singularly productive animal under Saharan conditions and its potential economic value far exceeds that of any domestic animal in comparable circumstances. It is a much threatened animal and has decreased rapidly throughout its range, except in completely uninhabited areas.

Until a few years ago the harshness of terrain and climate was sufficient to discourage other than peripheral human interest in the Sahara. The interior of the desert formed, therefore, a vast natural sanctuary so remote that wildlife could live free from human intrusion. But the discovery of oil has broken down the invisible barriers that hitherto surrounded this fastness and no part of the desert, however distant or forbidding, is now secure for wildlife. The wealth deriving from oil has provided both the oil crews and the indigenous nomads with unprecedented mobility and killing power, with the result that many forms of desert animals are now imperiled, some to the point of extinction. In the barren expanses, any form of protective measure is impossible.

The Sahara
The world's largest desert, the Sahara, is made up of three principal types of terrain: *hamada*, rocky uplands and mountains as high as 11,000 feet (3,300m); *reg* vast areas of silt and gravel; and *erg*, the seas of wave-like sand dunes which, although regarded as typical of 'Beau Geste' country, form only one tenth of its area. Both *hamada* and *reg* are shown in the photograph (above) and the dunes of the *erg* fringe an oasis (below). The whole is characterized by its extremes of temperature and minimal rainfall.

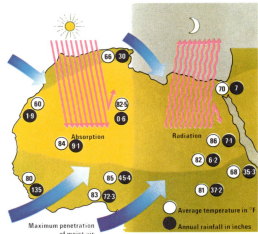

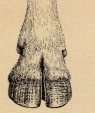

Average temperature in °F
Annual rainfall in inches

Maximum penetration of moist air

Day and night extremes
The desert's prevailing winds lose their moisture at sea. With no cloud to bar or diffuse the sunlight, 90pc of its heat is absorbed by the ground. At night the heat escapes upward, again without hindrance, and thus extremes of temperature are brought about every 24 hrs.

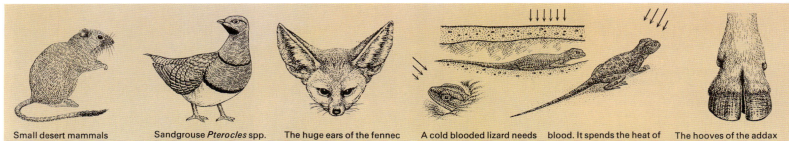

Small desert mammals have specially adapted kidneys to concentrate urine and so reduce their water loss.

Sandgrouse *Pterocles* spp. flies far to find water and soaks its breast feathers to take water back to its young.

The huge ears of the fennec *Fennecus zerda*, a tiny desert fox, act as radiators, dispersing its body heat.

A cold blooded lizard needs heat to become active. The head is protruded into early sunlight to warm its blood. It spends the heat of the day in shelter, emerging later to sun itself again, parallel to the sun's rays.

The hooves of the addax antelope *Addax nasomaculatus* are enlarged to help it walk on the soft sands.

A life without water

Survival in the desert requires an ability to conserve or apparently go without water, the principal requirement of all life forms. The addax, a heavily-built antelope shares with the tiny jerboa a subtle physiological mechanism enabling it to conserve and utilize what little moisture it can obtain from a dry diet. All the animals, insects and birds illustrated have made their home in the inhospitable heat and aridity of the world's greatest desert.

Lanner falcon *Falco biarmicus*

Locust hopper (swarming) *Schistocerca gregaria*

Jerboa *Jaculus* sp

Antlion *Myrmeleon* sp

Locust hopper (solitary)

Anacyclus radiatus

Fat sand rat *Psammomys obesus*

Cistanche lutea

Addax *Addax nasomaculatus*

Convolvulus tricolor

Fennec *Fennecus zerda*

Pintail sandgrouse *Pterocles alchata*

Long-eared desert hedgehog *Hemiechinus auritus aegyptiacus*

Skink *Scincus scincus*

Desert digger

A relative of the mouse, rat and squirrel, the jerboa, *Jaculus* spp. uses every part of its tough body, including its nostrils to build the burrows in which it establishes a comfortable ecoclimate. The temperature and humidity of the burrow relative to outside values are shown (below). These are maintained (right) by the use of internal and external seals in the burrows.

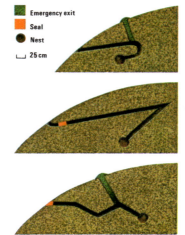

Emergency exit
Seal
Nest
25 cm

Minimum contact of the sidewinder *below*

The unique movement of the sidewinder snake is that of a helical coil in which only part of its trunk is in contact with the hot sand surface.

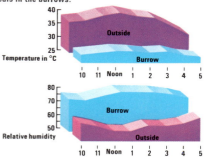

Start position
Head and forebody lifted across to new position
Main trunk 'loops' forward into new track
New track already vacated by forepart of body
Points of contact

Lateral locomotion *above*

The sidewinder snake *Cerastes* spp. and the parallel tracks made by its movements across the surface of the sand. Sidewinders are common to many desert regions.

Sand swimmer *left and below*

In the twinkling of an eye the toad-headed agamid *Phrynocephalus nejdensis* disappears beneath the loose sand by wriggling its body from side to side. Projecting eyelids protect its eyes from the pressure of sand and rows of fine scales like the eyelashes of a human flick away the windblown particles. Despite its physical adaptations *Phrynocephalus* does not live a subterranean life. It burrows only to escape the heat or its predators.

Change of clothing *right*

A scorpion of the family Buthidae moults its old skin which cracks and is shed, seven or eight times in the scorpion's life. The sting, killing a prey (below), varies from species to species. In a human the poison may induce a fever or temporary paralysis. In some species the venom is as toxic as that of a cobra.

Namib: The Hidden Desert

Ecologically unique and for years little known, the Namib Desert forms a narrow strip running the length of Namibia and reaches from the Atlantic coast to the edge of the subdesert plateau lying from 15 to 85 miles (24-137 km) inland. The northern part of the Namib is mainly gravel while the southern half is formed of a series of sand dunes which are among the largest known, some of them 1,000 feet (304km) high. Apparently sterile, the dunes carry a surprisingly diverse fauna and several hundred species of tenebrionid beetles, spiders, scorpions and other insects make their homes there. Many exhibit extraordinary resourcefulness in their methods of adaptation to the extreme environmental conditions in which they live. This rich invertebrate fauna sustains a variety of other forms of life, notably reptiles, among them several species of lizards, geckos, snakes and even a chameleon. The sparse vegetation includes the strange endemic *Welwitschia mirabilis*.

The mountainous region to the northwest of the Namib is well populated with wildlife including the mountain zebra which ranges the plateau fringing the Namib and into the desert, as far as the coast.

Apart from the Cunene river in the extreme north and the Orange River in the south there are no perennial rivers in the Namib. It is, however, traversed by several sand rivers which flow only briefly when rare rain storms bring them down in sudden, violent spate. The flood water quickly disappears but is retained beneath the surface as in some gigantic subterranean cistern, thus sustaining not only a narrow ribbon of lush, riverine vegetation but providing year-round water for animals that are not true desert dwellers.

Offshore the Benguela current exerts a powerful influence on the ecology of the Namib, generating a nightly fog which rolls inland for more than 20 miles (32km) and, through condensation, provides the normally rainless desert with sufficient moisture to support a scanty drought resistant vegetation.

Rich in gems

Notorious among mariners for the many wrecks on its fog-shrouded coast, its stony plains rich with gems, the Namib Desert has been revealed by scientists to be a distinct and remarkable ecological zone. The northernmost part, known as the Kaokoveld and eroded by the wind into fantastic shapes A where it faces the Atlantic, reaches into the Etosha pan where many species of wildlife gather in the vicinity of permanent water. Elephant, black rhinoceros are common and Hartmann's mountain zebra ranges from the hills across the desert as far as the coast.

Flash floods

Diamond-rich gravel plains between the coast and the hinterland plateau are slashed by rivers of sand. Beneath their surface the rare flash flood waters B are retained and sustain a riverine flora which provides year-round feeding for many species. Off the coast the cool, north flowing Benguela current E gives rise to a rich marine fauna, bringing penguins to feed in the same area as tropical flamingos. At Cape Cross there is Africa's only colony of breeding fur seals.

Unique fauna

The great sand dunes of the Namib are the home of much of its unique endemic fauna, catching and storing windborne detritus from the hinterland C. Rain seldom falls yet – because of the almost permanent fog D generated by the Benguela current – the air is more humid than anywhere on earth. There is seemingly no food yet the surface is crossed by the tracks of countless creatures, from tiny beetles to the solitary strand wolf.

Walking 'water' *above*
The 'Namib clown' dune cricket *Comicus* sp. has flowerlike feet to move across the sand. It is eagerly hunted by predators of a higher order because of the high moisture content which gives it a transparent appearance.

Darkling beetles *above*
Tenebrionid beetles *Stenocara eburnea* of the Namib gravel plains. Tenebrionids, or darkling beetles, are among the most numerous in arid areas and have a thick shell to reduce evaporation and so conserve moisture.

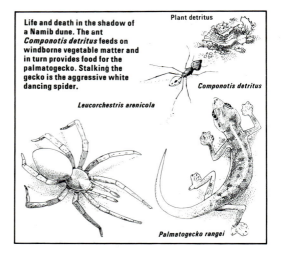

Life and death in the shadow of a Namib dune. The ant *Componotis detritus* feeds on windborne vegetable matter and in turn provides food for the palmatogecko. Stalking the gecko is the aggressive white dancing spider.

Plant detritus

Componotis detritus

Leucorchestris arenicola

Palmatogecko rangei

Kalahari and Namib *left*
The Kalahari desert covers the greater part of the territory of Botswana and west into the mandated territory of Botswana and west into Namibia. A highland strip separates it from the Namib Desert which reaches from Cape province to Angola. Blocks mark the main zones (below).

Namib
Kalahari
Orange River

1 Black-faced vulture
2 Klipspringer
3 Grass
4 Rock hare
5 Rock hyrax
6 Hartmann's zebra
7 Grass
8 Welwitschia
9 Courser
10 Naras gourd
11 Meerkeet
12 Cape fur seal
13 Brown hyena
14 Genet
15 Riverine vegetation
16 Pygmy falcon
17 Sociable weaver
18 Gemsbok
19 Springbuck
20 Gecko
21 Sidewinding adder
22 Golden mole
23 Pale chanting goshawk
24 Black oystercatcher
25 Namib plated lizard
26 Flamingo
27 Damara tern
28 Jackass penguin
29 Detritus
30 Sandgrouse
31 Gerbil
32 Fish

The Kalahari in Botswana and the Karroo in Cape Province form, with the Namib, the principal desert areas south of the African equatorial zone. Unlike the Namib, the only true desert of the three, the Kalahari is relatively well endowed with vegetation. It is an immense upland basin over 4,000 feet (1,219m) high, of mainly subdesert steppe and is the home of the diminutive bushmen who live almost symbiotically with the wild herds.

The sandy plains carry a fauna that is as rich and varied as anywhere in Africa. It is characterized by the gemsbok, the southernmost and largest representative of the oryxes, and by the lyre-horned springbuck, which bears a physical resemblance to the gazelles of eastern and northern Africa, and occupies a similar ecological niche.

Disease control fences which blocked the normal migratory routes of the wild herds on which the bushmen depend have caused a decline in their numbers. Many thousands of zebra, gemsbok, eland, wildebeest, hartebeest and springbuck have died on the wire. For most of the year the wild herds are widely dispersed across the Kalahari but at the height of the dry season there is a concentration in the vicinity of permanent water, principally on the Okovango Swamps and the Makarikari and Etosha Pans. The gemsbok *Oryx gazella* shown (left) is found throughout the desert areas of southwest Africa. It can stand long periods of drought.

The Karroo is a large inland plateau lying at an altitude of 3,000-5,000 ft. (914 - 1,524m) and covering much of Cape Province. Except for a short period immediately following the rains when the countryside becomes a veritable flower garden, the Karroo is a parched land of rock and stone where the once-abundant wild fauna has been almost entirely replaced by domestic herds.

Acanthosicyos horrida

Welwitschia mirabilis

Old home for bugs *above*
Striking plant bugs of the family Pyrrhocoridae found only on the cones of the female *Welwitschia mirabilis,* a plant unique to the Namib Desert. The welwitschia (a male plant is shown right) reproduces with difficulty but once established reaches a great old age. A few are known to have lived for 2,000 years, using their lateral roots to absorb the rare light rains and tap roots to find sub-surface moisture. The naras gourd *Acanthosicyos horrida* (shown above right) provides food for browsing animals like the gemsbok.

Niche for living *right*
A favorite ecological niche of the desert is found in rock fissures where the slightest amount of rain or fog precipitation runs into cracks protected from direct evaporation. *Commiphora saxicola* (below) is typical of the Namib vegetation.

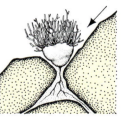

The dune dwellers
The apparently compact sand dune is a web of intergranular spaces and channels which maintain the process of oxygen circulation. In this veinous structure the sand dwellers make their lives, so specifically adapted to the dune element that they cannot live away from it any more than a fish can live away from water. They concentrate on the slip faces of the dunes where the sand is quasi-fluid and easy to sink into and where most of the life-forms of the desert dunes are to be found.

Diving *right*
At the first sign of trouble nearby a tenebrionid beetle dives headlong into the sand. It is one of many hundreds which will be found in a few square meters of dune beneath the 'smoking' crest or in patches forming quicksands.

Swimming *left*
The diurnal sand lizard *Meroles cuneirostris* moves from slip face to slip face of the dunes in its daily search for food. Like other dune dwellers it is adapted to swim with great ease into the loose surface of the sand.

Vanishing *right*
Almost indistinguishable from the sand on which it rests a member of the Sicariidae or spitting spiders performs its vanishing act when alarmed. Spitting spiders trap their victims in a spray of gluey mucus.

The Equatorial Highlands

The most spectacular of Africa's numerous massifs and mountain ranges are those which rise from the highlands of Ethiopia and East Africa. Of these, three areas flanking the Great Rift Valley are of surpassing interest; Kilimanjaro, 19,340 feet (5,595m), the continent's highest mountain; Mount Kenya, 17,058 feet (5,200m) and the Ruwenzori range, the fabled Mountains of the Moon, which reach a maximum height of 16,794 feet (5,117m).

Apart from their scenic splendour – their exceptional heights are enhanced by the level of the plains from which they rise – these are the only places in Africa having both permanent snowfields and glaciers.

The vegetational succession of all three areas is broadly similar. The grassland savannas of the open plains and foothills lying at about 4,000-5,000 feet (1,200-1,500m) give way to luxuriant high forest in which, in the moister localities, *Juniperus* (cedar) and *Podocarpus* are among the dominant components. On drier slopes the vegetation is less luxuriant.

At about 8,000 feet (2,400m) the rain forest merges into a well defined belt of mountain bamboo *Arundinaria alpina* forming a growth up to 40-50 feet (12-15m) in height and sufficiently dense to exclude the sun. The bamboo ends at about 10,000 feet (3,000m) and becomes sub-alpine moorland characterized by sedges and coarse tussock grasses interspersed with tree heaths *Phillippia* and *Erica*, their branches bearing long lichen tresses.

Although the moorlands mark the upper distributional limit for most of the fauna (certain specialised forms flourish at higher altitudes) the alpine flora continues upwards to a height of about 14,000 feet (4,000m). This equatorial alpine region is a world apart, dominated by such bizarre vegetation as giant groundsel *Senecio* growing 30 feet (9m) high and giant lobelia. It is carpeted with short alpine grasses, mosses and everlasting flowers, *Helichrysum*, in a setting of tarns, lakes and frozen waterfalls.

To the north there are the high plateaus and the precipitous escarpments of the Ethiopian highlands, which include some of the most dramatic mountain massifs in Africa.

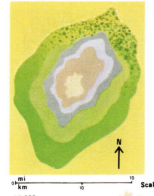

North-south zonation
A plan and section of Mt Kenya shows how zonation of vegetation on its slopes is not uniform. On drier northern slopes scrub replaces the more typical montane forest. Subalpine moorland also varies. While it forms continuous belt on neighboring Mt Kilimanjaro distribution is erratic on Mt Kenya; it forms a broad belt on the eastern side but on the west is found only by the sides of gullies and sheltered streams.

Scale
mi 0 ___ 10
km 0 ___ 10

16,000
14,000
12,000
10,000

Vertical scale in feet

AFRO-ALPINE ZONE
SUB-ALPINE MOORLAND ZONE
BAMBOO MONTANE FOREST ZONE
SAVANNA

17,000 ft — 5,800 m
14,000 ft — 4,800 m
11,000 ft — 3,800 m
10,000 ft — 3,300 m
8,500 ft — 2,700 m
6,800 ft — 2,100 m

Groove-toothed rat
Hyrax
Duiker
Leopard
Bushbuck
Mole rat
Blue monkey
Forest hog
Bushbaby
Elephant
Bongo
Buffalo
Tree hyrax
Rhinoceros

Afro-alpine
Beneath the perpetual snows of Africa's highest peaks – the nival region – a unique world of nightmarish plants makes up the Afro-alpine belt. Extremes of cold at night and complete isolation give life to arborescent, pillar-like plants such as the giant lobelia, *L. keniensis* and senecio *S. adnivalis*. The Afro-alpine belt represents the limits at which montane fauna is found; hyrax, groove-toothed rat *Otomys orestes* and duiker *Sylvicapra* sp. are the principal mammals.

Sub-alpine moorland
Tree heaths *Erica arborea* and *E. Philippia* dominate the ericaceous or moorland belt. Tussocky bogs of *Carex runssoroensis* are found in the wetter valleys. The wildlife of the zone is similar to that of the higher Afro-alpine region, but the leopard appears, to prey on hyrax, rat and duiker. Packs of wild dogs live in some moorland areas.

Bamboo/montane
A well-defined belt of bamboo *Arundinaria alpina* marks the upper limit of the montane forest of *Juniperus, Podocarpus,* camphor *Ocotea usumbarensis* and other trees supporting a rich variety of game. Montane forest is fairly open compared with lowland forest and abounds in elephant, black rhinoceros, buffalo, giant forest hog *Hylochoerus meinertzhageni,* guereza and guenon monkeys and the mountain gorilla *G. gorilla beringei.*

Sunbirds

Jewel-like sunbirds feed on lobelia growing at high altitudes. Like hummingbirds, they siphon nectar but prefer to perch rather than feed on the wing.

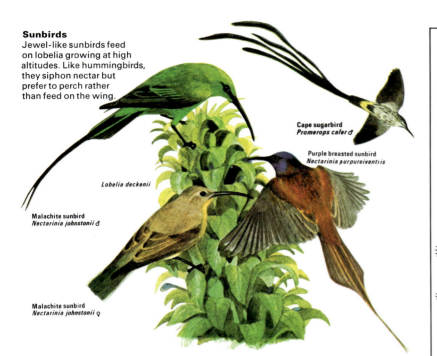

Cape sugarbird
Promerops cafer ♂

Purple breasted sunbird
Nectarinia purpureiventris

Lobelia deckenii

Malachite sunbird
Nectarinia johnstonii ♂

Malachite sunbird
Nectarinia johnstonii ♀

High level isolation *right*

Alpine zones are discontinuous, isolating species which cannot spread across surrounding terrain. Such is the toad *Bufo osgoodi*, found only in the Ethiopia highlands.

Vanishing species *left*

The walia ibex *Capra walie* once ranged throughout the Ethiopian highlands. Today this rare species is found only in two tiny, craggy areas of the Semien mountains.

Safety in heights *below*

A dominant male gelada baboon *Theropithecus gelada* marshals his troop in the safety of precipitous slopes of Ethiopia.

Air strike

Soaring on the upcurrents of air around the bare upper slopes of Africa's mountains, Verreaux's eagle *Aquila verreauxi* (right) follows the eagle's classical pattern of flight and strike. The planform of its soaring wings (below A) contrasts with the broad, rounded wings of the crowned hawk eagle (B) which weaves through the canopy of montane forest, dropping suddenly on its unwary quarry — a small antelope or monkey.

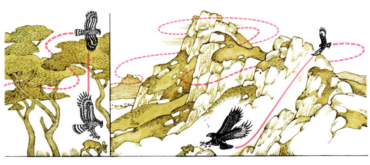

Weightlifter *left*

The thick legs and powerful claws of the crowned hawk eagle enable it to seize and lift a monkey or antelope weighing 20lb (9kg) and take off vertically through the tree cover. It is one of the most powerful birds of prey, and has an unusually attractive piping call.

Flight patterns *above*

The contrasting flight patterns of the crowned hawk eagle dropping suddenly on its prey, and that of a Verreaux's eagle, swooping from height on a rock hyrax. Verreaux's eagle's range may cover more than 250 sq. miles (650 sq km).

Flower of alarm

The unusual 'flower' of erectile hair on a gland on the spine of a hyrax, or rock dassie, 'blooms' when it is threatened.

Hooved hyrax *right*

The surrealistic landscape of Mount Kenya's Afro-alpine zone, studded with giant senecio and lobelia (above) is the home of the smallest of the hooved mammals, the hyrax, *Procavia capensis*. The hyrax climbs rocks with ease; its tiny hooves have semi-elastic, rubber-like pads to give it a grip on steep rocks. The elephant is its closest ungulate relative.

Madagascar:The Island Continent

Madagascar has been an isolated island for tens of millions of years. Only a fraction of the size of Africa, it has the same range of climatic conditions as the whole of its giant neighbour. Together, the climate and ancient isolation have made the island a natural laboratory for evolution, and a biologist's paradise.

The high central plateau of Madagascar is relatively cold and many species are isolated in the warmer coastal areas. The east coast is humid as it is met by trade winds from the east, but the remaining areas are drier. The northwest has moderately wet deciduous forest and there is a gradient down the west coast, leading to semidesert conditions in the extreme south.

Apart from a few late arrivals the animals and plants of Madagascar are mainly derived from ancestral forms which were carried away as the island drifted away, a giant Noah's ark, from Africa. As in Australia, the animals and plants are descendants of early stocks which were once widespread but have since largely disappeared from other areas. Nine-tenths of the animal and plant species occur nowhere else in the world.

All of Madagascar's mammals are unusual apart from a few which were introduced by the first human settlers between two and three thousand years ago. Until that time Madagascar had been free of human influence, but recent centuries have seen the rapid extinction of many large, bizarre animals such as the subfossil lemur *Megaladapis* and the enormous, ostrich-like *Aepyornis*.

The four main mammal groups, each derived from primitive ancestors, are lemurs, carnivores, rodents and tenrecs. Although some bird species have invaded Madagascar, many are peculiar to the island; only the most powerful fliers have managed to colonize the island without losing links with other continents. The island has notable absentees; there are no woodpeckers at all and it is possible that the peculiar aye-aye has evolved to fill their role.

Madagascar reptiles are striking and the island has three-quarters of all the world's chameleons, some of them extremely impressive. Whereas, in other areas, some chameleons give birth to live offspring, all the Madagascar species have retained the primitive egg-laying habit. The island has a number of large tortoises and a weird, camouflaged lizard *Uroplatus* which flattens itself against mottled tree bark to hide.

The plant life of the island is a botanist's delight. There are several entire plant families – like the strange, cactus-like Didiereaceae of southern Madagascar – which are unique to the island.

The last survivors
Through the forests of Madagascar, the ghosts walk – but in dwindling numbers. They are the last 20 species of lemur (the name is from the Latin, meaning 'spectre'). They are the survivors of a once abundant dynasty of primates; at least 14 species have become extinct in the last few hundred years.

Verreaux's sifaka
Propithecus verreauxi verreauxi

- ▦ Brown mouse lemur
- ▢ Grey mouse lemur
- ▨ Mongoose lemur
- ▧ Ring-tailed lemur
- ▤ Indri
  Aye aye

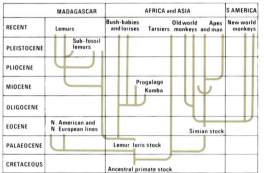

	MADAGASCAR	AFRICA and ASIA				S AMERICA
RECENT	Lemurs	Bush-babies and lorises	Tarsiers	Old world monkeys	Apes and man	New world monkeys
PLEISTOCENE	Sub-fossil lemurs					
PLIOCENE						
MIOCENE			Progalago Komba			
OLIGOCENE						
EOCENE	N. American and N. European lines			Simian stock		
PALAEOCENE		Lemur loris stock				
CRETACEOUS		Ancestral primate stock				

Leaping lemur *above*
Lemurs are primitive arboreal primates and one of them, the sifaka, *Propithecus sifaka* is able to leap tremendous distances from one tree to another. On the ground its walk is a bounding, bipedal gait.

Ring-tailed lemur
Lemur catta

Sportive lemur (brown race)
Lepilemur muste...

'Woodpecker' primate
The rare aye-aye *Daubentonia madagascariensis* is a lemur which occupies the niche common to woodpeckers (these are absent in Madagascar). Its incisor teeth are like those of a rodent and the aye-aye uses them to bite into branches and tree trunks for insect larvae.

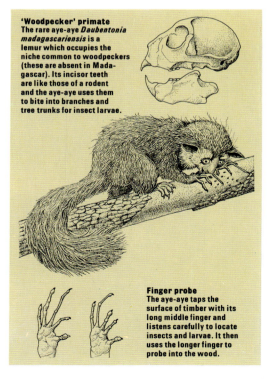

Finger probe
The aye-aye taps the surface of timber with its long middle finger and listens carefully to locate insects and larvae. It then uses the longer finger to probe into the wood.

One family, many niches
The isolation of Madagascar has enabled one family of insectivores, the tenrecs, to evolve a variety of species to fill a wide range of ecological niches which would otherwise have been occupied by a number of different creatures. The 'hedgehog' tenrec *Echinops telfairi*, has a heavily spined back, making it a formidable adversary. *Tenrec ecaudatus* is a large insectivore which burrows with strong front limbs in search of insects and worms. *Geogale avrita* hibernates during the winter months in its sandy burrows in both coastal regions of the island. *Orizorictes hova* has a way of life similar to that of a mole. It has large forefeet and claws, with the reduced eyes and ears of a subterranean animal. One of the family takes to the water. *Limnogale mergulus* is a strong swimmer even in fast-flowing rivers, feeding on shrimps and crayfish. *Fossa fossa*, a carnivore, preys on the tenrecs.

Tenrec family tree

Subfamily Tenrecinae   Subfamily Oryzorictinae

Tenrec   Hemicentetes   Setifer   Microgale   Geogale   Oryzorictes   Limnogale

Dasogale

Echinops

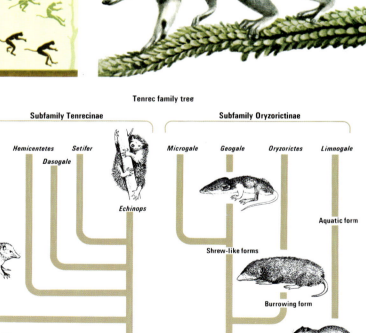

Aquatic form

Shrew-like forms

Burrowing form

Hedgehog-like forms

Fossa fossa

Family Tenrecidae

Lesser mouse lemur (grey race)
Microcebus murinus

Sportive lemur (grey race)
Lepilemur mustelinus

Ruffed lemur
Lemur variegatus

Indri
Indri indri

rk-crowned
arf lemur
ner furcifer

Lesser mouse lemur (brown race)
Microcebus murinus

Fat-tailed dwarf lemur
Cheirogaleus medius

Mongoose lemur
Lemur mongoz

Coquerel's sifaka
Propithecus v. coquereli

A continent in microcosm
The varied climates and
vegetational zones of Africa
are encapsulated in the
one island of Madagascar.
But the island boasts a
unique flora of its own.
Vegetational map *left*

● East coast rain forest
● Plateau forest
● Western deciduous forest
● Sambirano domain (rain forest)
● Semi-arid vegetation

Orchid and moth
The probiscus (tongue) of
the moth *Xanthopan morgani
predicta* (1) is 18 ins (45 cm)
long and is able to reach
the nectar at the bottom of
the flower of the orchid
Angraecum sesquipedale (2).
Aloe capitata (3) is one
of a variety of aloes
growing on the central
plateau. The baobab *Adansonia*
sp. (4) holds water like a
sponge. Water is found in
the leaf base on *Ravenala
madagascariensis* (5).

Cacti counterparts
Didiereaceae have evolved
in the semi-arid areas of
southwest Madagascar. They
have thick, succulent leaves
and resemble cacti of
other regions. *Alluaudia
procera* (6) and *Pachypodium
lamerei* (7) are tall and
sparingly branched.
Didierea trollii (8) sometimes grows as a sprawling
plant at ground level.

Colorful tortoise *below*
The striking carapace of
the land tortoise *Testudo
radiata* is seen only in
the far south of Madagascar,
an almost waterless region
where succulent plants
provide it with both shelter
and food. Each plate of its
carapace has a yellow
spot with radiating bands.

Two-gallon egg *above*
The elephant bird *Aepyornis*
became extinct on Madagascar
in historical times. Its egg,
larger than a football, had a
capacity of two gallons.

Madagascar egret *above*
The lacelike plumes worn
by the egret *Egretta
dimorpha* once caused it to
be hunted almost to
extinction. The egrets build
their nests of stick plat-
forms high in the trees,
feeding their young on
invertebrate succulents
fished from nearby rivers.

A wealth of reptiles *left*
Madagascar's wealth of
reptiles include the
majority of the world's
chameleons. Largest of the
chameleon species, *oustaleti*
(also called *globifer*) may
reach two feet (60cm) in
length. It seeks out insects,
small rodents, and often
birds and their eggs.

Europe
THE PALAEARCTIC REALM 1

Europe

The smallest of the continents with the exception of Australia, Europe is a series of peninsulas within peninsulas, and islands, giving it a coastline longer, in proportion to its size, than any other continent. It is only marginally larger than Canada, and the only continent (apart from Antarctica) that has no tropical lands. Its vegetational and climatic regions form slender bands ranging from the sub-tropical Mediterranean in the south through the broadleaf and coniferous belts to the Arctic tundra. It is faunally impoverished when compared with the other great continents, a fact partly due to the successful occupation of man and to a climatic history in which it has been largely covered by an ice sheet at least four times during the past million years. During the inter-glacial periods plants and animals moved in, only to be driven back with the advance of yet another ice sheet. Prehistoric man shared the land with many animals that have now vanished from Europe and may have hunted some to extinction, but the real diminution of wildlife has followed intensive agriculture and forest clearance. Yet there remains a fascinating flora and fauna on a smaller, less dramatic scale than that found in other continents, but which is none the less rewarding to the observer. The arrival and departure of migrant birds hint at other climes, and the ability of many small life forms to survive warily in competition with man is demonstrated even in those areas where intensive agriculture, and even industrialization, is found.

Short-eared owl nesting in heathland, Northern Europe

Key to panorama

1 Pied flycatcher	19 Fallow deer	37 Damsel fly
2 Tawny owl	20 Roe deer	38 Pond skater
3 Red squirrel	21 Red Fox	39 Grass snake
4 Great tit	22 Sand martin	40 Stag beetle
5 Marsh fritillary	23 Bank vole	41 White admiral
6 Kingfisher	24 Grey heron	42 Wood mouse
7 Oak eggar	25 Wood fritillary	43 Red admiral
8 Lesser spotted woodpecker	26 Rabbit	44 Large white caterpillar
9 Jay	27 Weasel	45 Water vole
10 Dragonfly	28 Badger	46 Common frog
11 Reed Warbler	29 Hedgehog	47 Water shrew
12 Tree wasp nest	30 Blackcap	48 Water boatman
13 Green woodpecker	31 Wood warbler	49 Smooth newt
14 Long-eared bat	32 Wood white	50 Stickleback
15 Treecreeper	33 Dormouse	51 Crayfish
16 Sparrowhawk	34 Dragonfly pupa	52 Bullhead
17 Woodpigeon	35 Pied wagtail	53 Water beetle
18 Magpie	36 Otter	54 Dragonfly larva

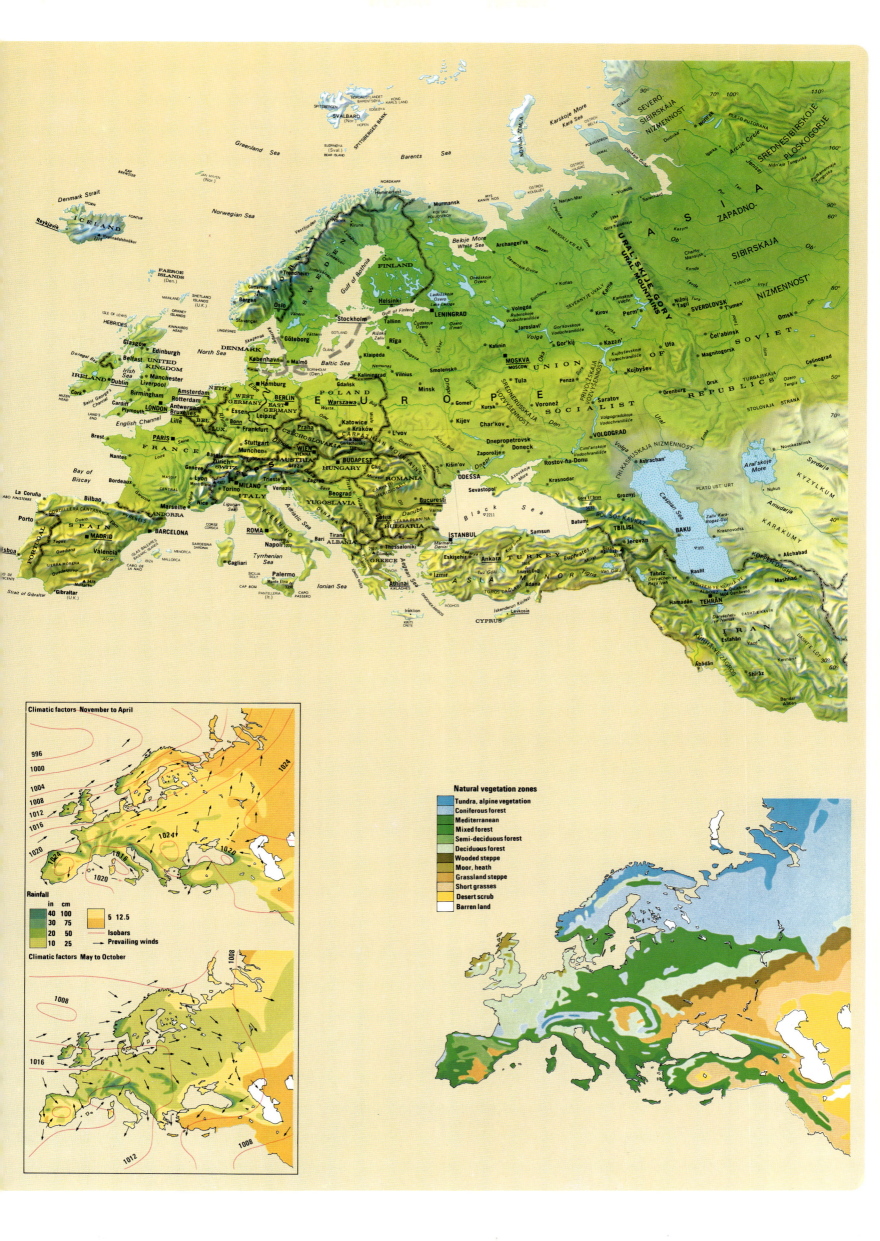

The Temperate Mixed Woodlands

The forests of Europe are of two main types, the boreal coniferous, or taiga, and the temperate deciduous. Their geographical distribution is governed primarily by climate although the nature of the underlying rock is of great importance.

The boreal forest extends from Norway across Sweden and Finland to Siberia, and has a severe climate. The deciduous forest lies immediately to the south, extending from the British Isles and northern Spain, across central Europe into Russia. The climate is fairly humid, with summer rainfall and moderately severe winters. In southern Europe, a Mediterranean type of climate does not support true forest and is characterized by a broad-sclerophyll scrubland, or maquis, but the higher montane areas have a climate similar to that of the boreal forest, and have stands of conifers. On many upland moors, new conifer forests have been created by man.

An interaction of climate, parent rock, plants and animals has produced the soil types typical of the mature forests. The typical soil of the boreal forest is podsol – a thick layer of needles, twigs and cones overlying black, partly decomposed organic material known as humus. The layers are thick because decomposition is slowed by low temperatures. The characteristic soil of the deciduous forest is brown; the litter layer is thin and overlies a mixture of well-decomposed organic material and mineral soil rich in plant nutrients. This type of soil is believed to result primarily from the burrowing activities of the earthworms which occur in large numbers in the woodland floor.

The coniferous trees of the boreal forest and the broad-leaved trees of the deciduous forest provide different kinds of food for plant-eating animals and in consequence the animals occurring in the two types of forest are quite characteristic – despite some overlap. Deciduous forest, having the greatest structural complexity, provides the greater variety of 'micro-habitats' in which different animal species can live and therefore shows the higher diversity of insects, birds and mammals seeking out their livelihoods within the ecosystem of the tree.

Woodland and forest life in Europe

The panorama to the left of the centrefold illustrates typical examples of the flora and fauna of Europe's broad-leaved forests and woodlands. Oak, ash, beech and chestnuts are among the common trees but they are dwindling in numbers in the face of modern pressures on land use. The conifer forests of the north (on the right hand page), although far fewer in species, cover much greater areas for they exist in habitats much less acceptable to man than the milder regions where the broadleaves grow.

1 Wild boar
  Sus scrofa
2 Green woodpecker
  Picus viridis
3 Great spotted woodpecker
  Dendrocopos major
4 Grey squirrel
  Sciurus carolinensis

European coniferous and broadleaved trees
Climate, geography and the soil types in which they grow (and to which they contribute) determine which trees are characteristic of what part of Europe. The contrasting shapes of conifer and broad-leaf indicate the kinds of weather each has to endure—or enjoy.

Norway spruce
Picea abies

Scots pine
Pinus silvestris

Silver birch
Betula pendula

Sycamore
Acer pseudoplatanus

Oak
Quercus petraea

Larch
Larix decidua

Beech
Fagus sylvatica

Horse chestnut
Aesculus hippocastanum

Tundra soils	Chernozems (black soils) temperate grassland
Podzols (northern forests)	Red soils (Mediterranean)
Brown earths (deciduous forests)	Chestnut soils (arid grasslands)
Grey forest soils (forest-steppe)	Mountain soils

Podzol
Humus
Organic mineral rich layer
Parent rock

Black soil
Thick organic layer
Loamy parent rock

Red soil
Thin humus
Iron-clay
Limestone

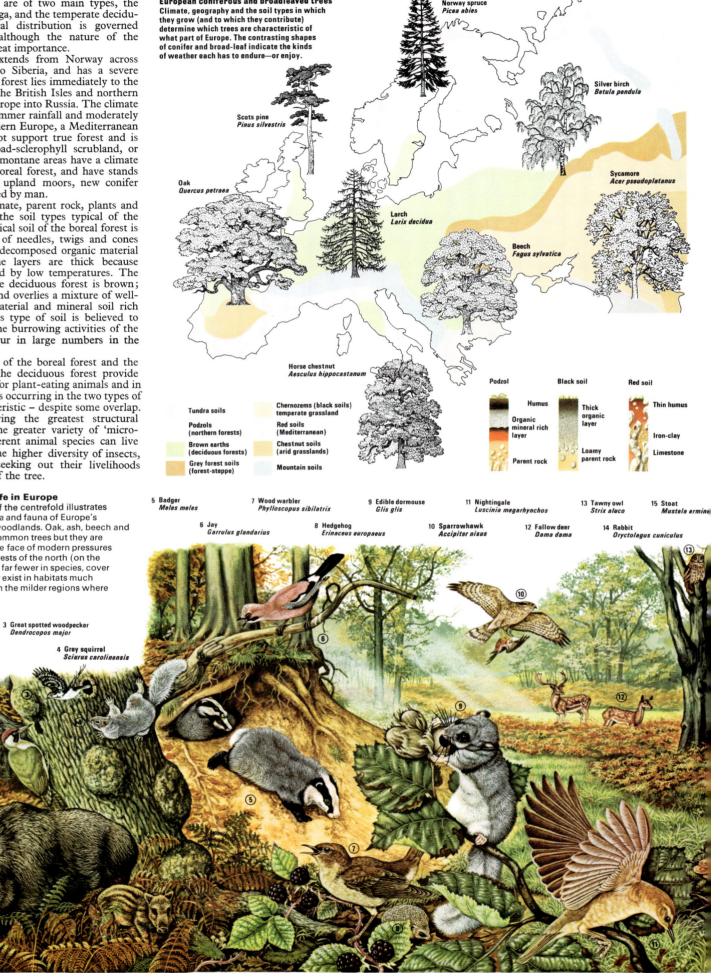

5 Badger
  Meles meles
6 Jay
  Garrulus glandarius
7 Wood warbler
  Phylloscopus sibilatrix
8 Hedgehog
  Erinaceus europaeus
9 Edible dormouse
  Glis glis
10 Sparrowhawk
  Accipiter nisus
11 Nightingale
  Luscinia megarhynchos
12 Fallow deer
  Dama dama
13 Tawny owl
  Strix aluco
14 Rabbit
  Oryctolagus cuniculus
15 Stoat
  Mustela erminea

Nocturnal animals

With its wide-opening mouth the nightjar *Caprimulgus europaeus* (left) catches insects on its nocturnal flights. The hedgehog *Erinaceus europaeus* (below) is also nocturnal, hunts mice worms and insects and will happily take on a snake baffled by its spines.

Soil and tree in mineral exchange

Through their spreading roots, trees draw on the vital food supplies in the earth. Some elements, such as magnesium and copper, are required only in minute traces; others are required in far greater quantities, among them potassium, calcium, nitrogen and phosphorus. Most of these minerals are dissolved in water in the earth and in this way are easily absorbed by the roots. The constant shedding of leaves and branches returns a portion of the original food to the soil. This 'fall-out' decays to liberate the minerals it contains.

Dusk hunters

Both the fox *Vulpes vulpes* (left) and the tawny owl *Strix aluco* (far left) are busy at twilight and at dawn. The fox enjoys a wide range of foods from insects to a young deer. It will raid domestic stock during harsh weather. The tawny owl spends its day hunched up in a tree, perhaps harried by smaller birds. It ranges at dusk through the woods and across adjoining land, seeking mice and small birds.

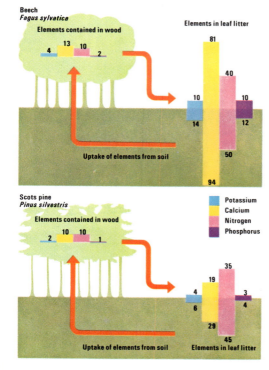

Beech
Fagus sylvatica
Elements contained in wood
Uptake of elements from soil
Elements in leaf litter

Scots pine
Pinus silvestris
Elements contained in wood
Uptake of elements from soil
Elements in leaf litter

- Potassium
- Calcium
- Nitrogen
- Phosphorus

17 Black woodpecker
Dryocopus martius

18 Wild cat
Felis sylvestris

19 Wood ant nest
Formica rufa

20 Capercaillie
Tetrao urogallus

21 Long-eared owl
Asio otus

22 Red deer
Cervus elaphus

23 Red squirrel
Sciurus vulgaris

24 Three-toed woodpecker
Picoides tridactylus

25 Pine marten
Martes martes

26 Crested tit
Parus cristatus

Red fox
Vulpes vulpes

The Tree: A World of its Own

The crown of a tree provides countless 'micro-habitats' where numerous herbivores, both vertebrate and invertebrate, inhabit the canopy and feed directly on the nutritious leaves and fruit. Larvae, such as those of the oak eggar moth, wander over the leaf surface and bite large pieces from it; others burrow into the softer parts and form tunnels.

Many small sawflies, gall wasps and mites lay their eggs on and in leaves. On hatching, the larvae begin to feed, and plants respond by producing additional tissue around the growing animals to form characteristic galls. In some areas over 50 species of gall-producing insects occur on oak alone. Other insects such as coccids and aphids have long, stylet-like mouth parts which are inserted into the plant so that cell contents, or the nutrient flow of material can be withdrawn by suction and capillarity. These herbivores form a rich food source for woodland predators such as insectivorous birds, wasps and spiders – and these in turn are eaten by larger predators.

The ground zone is occupied by characteristic litter dwellers. Some, like woodlice, millipedes and certain mites and springtails, feed directly on the dead plant material, and others are predators. Beneath the litter layer live the true soil animals, the nematodes, potworms and earthworms. The burrowing activities of the latter carry dead leaves and leaf fragments into the mineral soil and provide a food source for the plant feeders. These provide food for predatory invertebrates and often shrews, badgers and insectivorous birds.

All of these animals and more are key workers in the forest's economy for they are responsible for breaking down the plant and animal material into little pieces and preparing it for occupation by the millions of soil bacteria and fungi which contribute some 80 per cent of the soil's respiratory activity. The forests are complex ecosystems, their innumerable plants and animals all interacting to maintain a balanced economy. Any disruption of this structure, and round-the-clock activity, will put the forest into imbalance, often detrimentally.

Threat of the tree bark beetles
The activities of the diminutive bark beetle are capable of mutilating – and sometimes killing – a strong, well established forest tree. The female bores a vertical tunnel through the bark and along the line of the tree. Then, at right angles to the tunnel, she constructs a series of egg niches. The male follows, clearing away the dust and detritus. If the beetles attack the apical growths they destroy vital tissues, resulting in the deformation of the tree, if not its death.

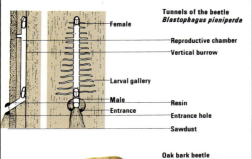

Tunnels of the beetle
Blastophagus pinniperda
- Female
- Reproductive chamber
- Vertical burrow
- Larval gallery
- Male
- Resin
- Entrance
- Entrance hole
- Sawdust

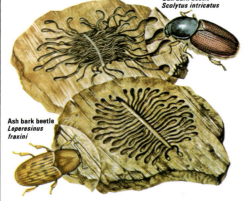

Oak bark beetle
Scolytus intricatus

Ash bark beetle
Leperesinus fraxini

Insect populations of the leaves
The fresh leaves and young twigs of the tree canopy provide both a home and a hunting ground. Profuse numbers of 'grazing' aphids serve as food for tiny predators like the ladybird *Coccinella decempuncta* and the lacewing *Drepanopteryx phalaenoides*. The cross spider *Araneus diadematus* will eat a variety of prey. The robber fly *Laphria ephippium* preys on the wing. Cross-section (right) the complex leaf 'factory'.

Aphids—prey to ladybird and lacewing
Ten-spot ladybird larva
Ten-spot ladybird *Coccinella decempunctata*
Robber fly *Laphria ephippium*
Dead-leaf lacewing larva
Dead-leaf lacewing *Drepanopteryx phalaenoides*
Cross spider *Araneus diadematus*

One-seed fruit *left*
Acorns of *Quercus coccifera* are representative of the one-seed fruit produced by oak trees. On some the acorns may take up to two years to mature. The cup structure is formed by a fusion of small leafy bracts. The lesser purple emperor butterfly *Apatura ilia* (below) is a widespread species throughout Europe. The lesser purple emperor is a woodland form and chooses certain trees on which its larvae feed.

The tree – a living entity
Each individual tree of the forest is a world of its own and, with the animals to which it gives food, shelter or hunting facilities, forms an entity of biological cohesion, or ecosystem. To survive it must comply with thermodynamic laws in which its energy intake is more or less balanced by its energy loss. The visible, if sometimes minute activity to be found in the tree, its branches and leaves has almost a 'mirror reflection' below the surface. The root system forms the 'branches' on and around which a supporting life of underground animals contribute to the tree's well being.

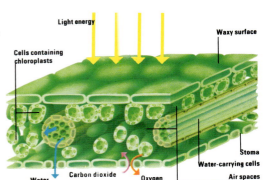

Light energy
Waxy surface
Cells containing chloroplasts
Water
Carbon dioxide
Oxygen
Stoma
Water-carrying cells
Air spaces

Canopy parasites
The oak tree canopy illustrated includes vignettes of some of the small life forms and the effects they have on the foliage supporting them and their larvae.

1 Nut weevil x 2
Curculio venosus
2 Oak apple x ⅓
(gall wasp *Biorhiza pallida*)
3 Kidney gall
(gall wasp *Trigonaspis megaptera*)
4 Cherry gall x ½
(gall wasp *Diplolepis quercus folii*)
5 Striped gall x ⅓
(gall wasp *Diplolepis longiventris*)
6 Gall wasp x 3
Biorhiza pallida
7 Cockchafer beetle
Melolontha melolontha
8 Moth larva
Acrobasis consociella
9 Green tortrix moth
Tortrix viridana
10 Weevil x 2¾
Phyllobius pyri
11 Greater stag beetle x ½
Lucanus cervus
12 Langhorn beetle x ½
Cerambyx cerdo
13 Tiger beetle larva x 1½
Cicindela campestris
14 Woodland snake millepede x 2
Cylindroiulus punctatus
15 Cockchafer beetle larva x ½
Melolontha melolontha
16 Skipjack beetle x 2
Ectirius aterrimus

Flying passengers

Itself part of a greater ecosystem, the bird is central to another. A variety of minute invertebrates lives on, or in, its body. Some are parasitic, living off the bird's blood; others, like the flatworm, in its abdomen. Some even occupy its muscles and eyes. Other small creatures use the bird merely as a means of transport and utilise the bird's nest as a staging post during migrations from one tree to another.

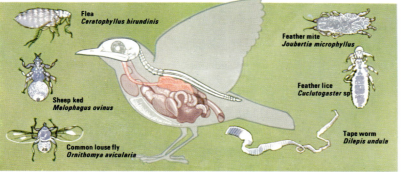

Flea
Ceratophyllus hirundinis

Feather mite
Joubertia microphyllus

Sheep ked
Melophagus ovinus

Feather lice
Cuclutogaster sp

Common louse fly
Ornithomya avicularia

Tape worm
Dilepis undula

The bird's nest provides a permanent home for a number of small invertebrates carried in by the builder or arriving independently.

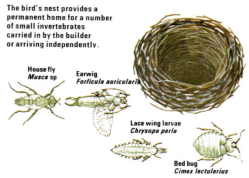

House fly
Musca sp

Earwig
Forficula auricularia

Lace wing larvae
Chrysopa perla

Bed bug
Cimex lectularius

4,000 species

The tiny creatures of the deciduous canopy form the great majority of woodland animals. 4,000 species have been recorded in a 60-acre (24ha) patch of European deciduous woodland.

Carpet moth *above*
On a lichen-covered branch the green carpet moth *Colostygia pectinataria* blends with its background.

Comb nest *above*
The wasp *Polistes gallicus* builds a comb nest with as many as 300 cells. The nest has no outer case.

Ceaseless search
Life for the parents of tit nestlings is a ceaseless pursuit of food for their greedy, squeaking brood. The tit (family *Paridae*) are the chickadees of North America. In Europe they have a widespread woodland range. Along the forest edges the wild strawberries *Fragaria vesca* (left) send out their runners, growing adventitious roots at intervals. At the rooting points leaves appear and a new plant is established.

Medullary rays   Heartwood

Annual growth rings   Phloem

Xylem   Bark

17 Wireworm x 1½
Denticollis linearis
18 Root gall x 2
Gall wasp x 4
Biorhiza pallida (form aptera)
19 Marsh worm x ½
Lumbricus rubellus
20 Pot worm x 2½
Mesenchytraeus setosus

Nourishment from rotting hosts
Fungi are 'non-green' plants; they lack chlorophyll, and are unable to manufacture their own food. They obtain nourishment from the rotting life on which they live by absorbing it with the aid of an enzyme secretion.

1 *Pleurotus ostreatus*
2 *Phallus impudicus*
3 *Amanita muscaria*
4 *Ramaria formosa*
5 *Daldinia concentrica*
6 *Peziza radiculata*

Fungus host and forms
The fungus *Ganoderma applanatum* (above) grows heavily and in clusters on the trunks of ash and beech trees. The section of the fungus *Daldinia concentrica* (right) shows the concentric layers of tissue. Mature spores are shed from the outer layer, or stroma, during the spring.

Relics of a Glacial Age

The history of European mountains is important to an understanding of their present ecology. All were centres of glacial activity during the Ice Ages while the surrounding lowlands – if not actually covered with ice – were subject to harsh winter conditions similar to those found in Scandinavia today.

As the ice sheets melted, those plants and animals preferring cold conditions either moved up the mountains, or to more northerly latitudes. Many of the plants and animals now associated with mountains are really subarctic organisms that have become stranded on the isolated mountain 'islands' far from the habitats where they commonly occur.

One important outcome of the island nature of upland areas is seen in the evolution and radiation of plants and animals. Movement between mountain ranges of organisms with poor dispersal mechanisms is restricted and consequently populations become isolated; differences arise and are maintained. A good example of this process may be seen in the apollo butterflies; each montane area supports a different race or species of the same, or closely related butterfly.

Because of the similarity exisiting between the high montane areas and more northerly latitudes, many birds occur in both situations either permanently or seasonally. The capercaillie lives both in Scandinavia and the mountains of southern Europe and birds such as the whimbrel migrate south to breed on moorlands and mountainsides.

Rocky cliffs and crags, fast torrent streams present habitats quite unlike those of the lowlands. They support various sheep and goat species adapted for rapid movement from rock to rock, supplying them with tussock grass on which to feed. The dipper and desman, an aquatic mole, forage on the bottom of fast mountain streams.

As a result of man's persecution, many of the predatory birds and mammals of Europe are now confined to mountain areas; lynx and wild cat, golden eagle and lammergeier vulture prey on young sheep and goats, hares, marmots and many other small animal bird prey species.

Where songthrush and vulture meet
The Pyrenees form a great, natural faunal barrier. They are wilder, less eroded than the sierras of Spain, less affected by glaciation than the Alps. The necrophiliac bearded vulture and the griffon vulture are found there, and the bullfinch and the songthrush reach their southerly limits.

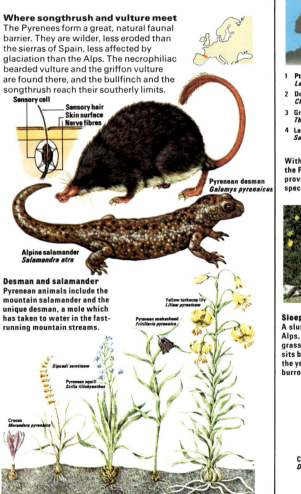

Sensory cell
Sensory hair
Skin surface
Nerve fibres

Pyrenean desman
Galemys pyrenaicus

Alpine salamander
Salamandra atra

Desman and salamander
Pyrenean animals include the mountain salamander and the unique desman, a mole which has taken to water in the fast-running mountain streams.

Dipcadi serotinum

Pyrenean squill
Scilla liliohyanthus

Crocus
Merendera pyrenaica

Yellow turkscap lily
Lilium pyrenaicum

Pyrenean snakeshead
Fritillaria pyrenaica

Last glaciation

Mountains

1 Ptarmigan
   Lagopus mutus
2 Dotterel
   Charadrius morinellus
3 Grayling
   Thymallus thymallus
4 Lake trout
   Salmo trutta lacustris

With the retreat of the Ice Ages the Pyrenees, Alps and Carpathians provided 'island' refuges for species isolated by the retreat.

Sleepy flower eater *above*
A slumberous creature found abundantly in the Alps, the marmot *Marmota marmota* eats grasses and other small herbaceous plants and sits back on its haunches. It spends more than half the year in hibernation at the base of a burrow ten feet (3m) deep.

Northern birds at home in the Alps
Jagged peaks and deep, U-shaped valleys creating their own climate, characterize the Alps, a youthful range as mountains go. Birds customarily found in more northern climes make their homes here.

Alpine chough
Pyrrhocorax graculus

Rock thrush
Monticola saxatilis

Citril finch
Serinus cintrinella

Wallcreeper
Tichodroma muraria

Edelweiss
Leontopodium alpinum

Apollo butterfly
Parnassus sp

Common pink
Dianthus plumarius

Yellow mountain anemone
Pulsatilla montana

Trumpet gentian
Gentiana kochiana

Where the Arctic reaches into Europe

Nearly 1,000 miles (1,600km) long, the mountainous spine of Scandinavia forms a climatic barrier between the moist Atlantic and the dry, eastern continent. Vast birch forests form the highest natural vegetation, huge, untouched areas containing unique plant and animal communities. The Scandinavian mountains form the southernmost subarctic and Arctic vegetation zones.

Bluethroat 14cm
Luscinia svecica♂

Wolverine 90 cm
Gulo gulo

Wood lemming 10cm
Myopus schisticolor

Scandinavian life *above*
The wolverine is the dominant carnivore of Scandinavia, the bluethroat the nightingale of the birch forests. The wood lemming is quiet, unquarrelsome.

Melancholy thistle
Cirsium heterophyllum

The wild flowers of the birch forests are notable for their great height. Species shown here are all more than five feet (1.5m) tall.

Great valerian
Valeriana sambucifolia

Angelica
Angelica archangelica

Northern monkshood
Aconitum septentrionale

King Charles's sceptre
Pedicularis sceptrum-carolinum

Wary whistler *right*
The wary mouflon *Ovis musimon,* a mountain sheep once found only in Corsica and Sardinia but now widespread in western Europe, whistles and hisses when alarmed. Its preferred habitat, typical of Corsica (below) is maquis (mountain scrub and thicket) and pine vegetation 3,000 feet (914m) above sea level.

Swedish Lapland
The barren, subarctic moorland of Swedish Lapland (below) provides nesting sites for waders like the whimbrel (above) and a hunting ground for the adder (left).

The Carpathians
No longer jagged like the Alps – of which they once formed part – the Carpathian mountains of east/central Europe have rounded contours clothed in green vegetation. The diagram (right) shows the difference in plant zonation found on the northern and southern limits of the range. The fauna is typically alpine, with some species originating in the east.

Tatra mountains	Bucegi mountains	
8000ft	2750m	Alpine vegetation
7620ft	2500m	
6715ft	2250m	Brush vegetation *Pinus mughus*
6100ft	2000m	
5470ft	1750m	Coniferous forest
4570ft	1500m	
3940ft	1250m	Beech or mixed forest
3050ft	1000m	

Mountain clouded yellow
Colias phicomone

Shepherd's fritillary
Boloria pales

Hungarian glider
Neptis rivularis

Mountain butterflies
The wealth of close-growing flowers carpeting alpine meadows attract many species of butterflies. The clouded yellow is found from the Pyrenees to the Carpathians, the fritillary from the Alps eastward to the Balkans.

Bird of prey
Swooping from height on its prey the lesser spotted eagle *Aquila pomarina* ranges eastward from the mountains of central Europe to the Caucasus.

Lesser spotted eagle
Aquila pomarina

European suslik
Citellus citellus

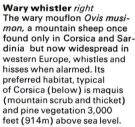

Prisoners of the Dark

Most of the world's cave structures, and the most important of those in Europe, are found in limestone sedimentary rocks where, over hundreds of thousands of years, forces of solution and corrosion have created labyrinths of passages, shafts and chambers. In places, immense caverns of an almost gothic splendour have been sculpted by the reaction of a mild acid solution – surface water seeping from the topsoil through the crevices – eating away at the limestone. Some networks run for scores of miles and caverns have been created large enough to contain a medieval cathedral.

As a habitat, caves were traditionally regarded as the home of primeval monsters and did in fact provide shelter and refuge for many species which are now extinct, like the huge cave bear. But these were not true cave species, for they used only the twilight thresholds. True cave, or cavernicolous, animals are regarded by zoologists as those that live within the dark zones. The overall cavernicolous habitat has a series of characteristics: a uniform, total darkness, uniform temperature, high humidity and limited supplies of food. Within these overall features there is a range of aquatic and terrestrial habitats available for colonization.

The inhabitants of this strange world form three groups: Troglobites, or those that live permanently in caves and are restricted to them; Troglophiles, which live successfully in caves although common in outside habitats; and Trogloxenes, which are more common outside and cannot complete their life cycles in caves.

Troglobites show marked adaptation to cave life and have a loss of pigmentation and eyes. The loss of sight is often compensated for by increased tactile sense and many invertebrates like *Aphaenops* sp. have greatly enlarged antennae. Some blind cave fish have been found to be far more sensitive to water vibrations than their related species in surface waters. Troglophiles include species of segmented worms, beetles, millipedes and other springtails. The best-known Trogloxenes are bats, which benefit from the large insect populations of the cave mouth.

Precipitate splendour
The splendour and extent of many limestone caves have proved an irresistible magnet to a breed of explorers, the speleologists — more commonly, spelunkers or potholers. The dramatic formations of stalactites and stalagmites are the results of the dripping of water over tens of thousands of years. Dissolved calcium carbonate precipitates and forms thin layers of lime on roof and floor, forming stalactites from the roof and stalagmites on floor.

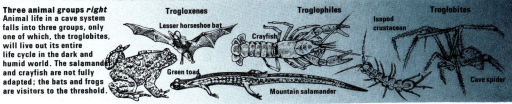

Three animal groups *right*
Animal life in a cave system falls into three groups, only one of which, the troglobites, will live out its entire life cycle in the dark and humid world. The salamander and crayfish are not fully adapted; the bats and frogs are visitors to the threshold.

Trogloxenes — Lesser horseshoe bat, Green toad, Mountain salamander
Troglophiles — Crayfish
Troglobites — Isopod crustacean, Cave spider

Major cave regions of Europe

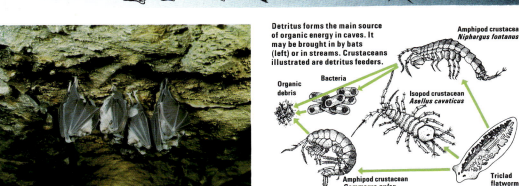

Detritus forms the main source of organic energy in caves. It may be brought in by bats (left) or in streams. Crustaceans illustrated are detritus feeders.

Amphipod crustacean *Niphargus fontanus*
Organic debris
Bacteria
Isopod crustacean *Asellus cavaticus*
Amphipod crustacean *Gammarus pulex*
Triclad flatworm

Caves are created by corrosion
Three stages in the creation of a limestone cave system are shown (below). Rain and surface water collect carbon dioxide and become a mild acid. Filtering between the bedding layers it eats away at the limestone, creating a network of shafts and chambers.

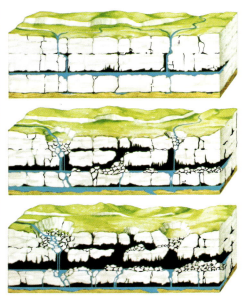

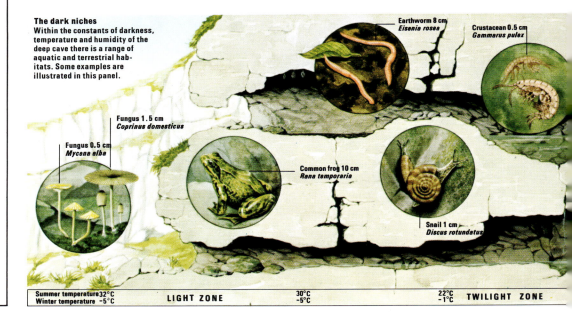

The dark niches
Within the constants of darkness, temperature and humidity of the deep cave there is a range of aquatic and terrestrial habitats. Some examples are illustrated in this panel.

Earthworm 8 cm *Eisenia rosea*
Crustacean 0.5 cm *Gammarus pulex*
Fungus 1.5 cm *Coprinus domesticus*
Fungus 0.5 cm *Mycena alba*
Common frog 10 cm *Rana temporaria*
Snail 1 cm *Discus rotundatus*

Summer temperature 32°C
Winter temperature −5°C
LIGHT ZONE
30°C
−5°C
22°C
−1°C
TWILIGHT ZONE

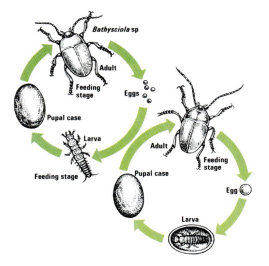

Contrasting life styles *left*
The beetles *Bathysciola* and *Speonomus* spp. are related but occupy different cave niches. *Bathysciola* lives in bat caves with ample food; *Speonomus* lives in food-scarce caves. *Bathysciola* larva and adult feed at larval stage, but the larva of *Speonomus* stays dormant.

Prisoner of the dark
Species of harvest men and crickets (above) are common cave dwellers. The centipede *Lithobius* sp., shown moulting (left), is one of the highly-adapted cave dwellers, total prisoners of their environment, unable to exist where there is any light.

New World caves *right*
More than 30,000 caves have been explored in the United States, some of them of staggering size and complexity. The concentration in the Appalachians, in the east of the continent, includes the Flint Ridge system in Kentucky, 73 miles (116km) long. The Carlsbad cavern in New Mexico has the largest 'cave room' in the world. It is 255 feet (76m) high and 1,800 feet (540m) long.

Major cave areas in the United States

Legend: Major cave areas ▪ Sea caves ● Limestone caves ▫ Sandstone caves ▪ Lava caves ★ Talus caves

The bat bird *left*
An echo-location system similar to a bat's is possessed by the oil bird *Steatornis caripensis*. Its natural radar enables it to fly easily and to nest in the total darkness of the Andean caves from which it emerges to feed on the seeds of oil palms. The body fat it acquires from this diet is highly prized by local Indians, who obtain from the oil birds bodies an oil used for light and heating.

American cave dwellers

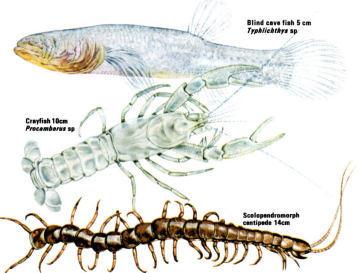

Blind cave fish 5 cm
Typhlichthys sp

Crayfish 10cm
Procambarus sp

Scolopendromorph centipede 14cm

Fading features *right*
At birth the cave proteus, a salamander, has characteristics of outer-world species. It has well-developed eyes and small black chromatophores — black pigments cells — on its upper surface. Over the months, the pigmentation fades away and the eyes and optic nerves degenerate. At 18 months, the proteus is completely white and also totally blind. It breeds at the larval stage.

Proteus anguinus
6 months
1 year
Adult

Distant affinities
The blind and colourless cave fish (above) is found in many underground rivers in North America. Like the fish, the crayfish is also colourless but survives without ill-effect. In North America it has evolved as a separate species to its surface relatives. The centipede of the class Scolopendromorpha differs little from its surface forms. True cavernicoles (some are shown right) represent an ancient fauna existing before the isolation of the continents. Crickets, beetles and salamanders from North America and Europe display affinities which help to substantiate evidence of old land links between the continents. Similarities have also been seen in cave forms in America and Japan.

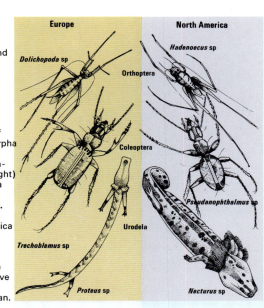

Europe | North America

Dolichopoda sp — *Hadenoecus* sp — Orthoptera
Trechoblemus sp — Coleoptera
Urodela — *Pseudanophthalmus* sp
Proteus sp — *Necturus* sp

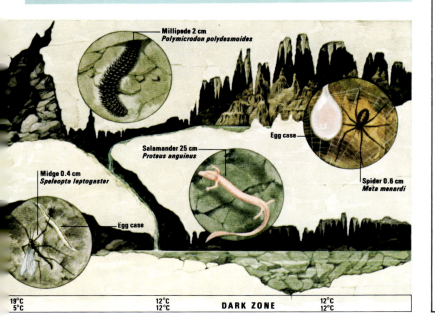

Millipede 2 cm
Polymicrodon polydesmoides

Egg case

Salamander 25 cm
Proteus anguinus

Spider 0.6 cm
Meta menardi

Midge 0.4 cm
Speleopta leptogaster

Egg case

19°C
5°C

12°C
12°C

DARK ZONE

12°C
12°C

The Life of the River

The character of a river changes down its length, and with the change of character there follows a change in the animal and plant life. The headwaters and side-tributaries typically run in deep-cut valleys. The bed is stony and the water cool, fast-flowing and well oxygenated. In these conditions, not enough silt is deposited to support the growth of water weeds and the main vegetation consists of a covering of moss on some of the stones.

The animals of the headwaters are well adapted to these conditions. Some reduce the risk of being washed away by clinging to the moss, others have flattened bodies and crouch close to the surface of the stones where the current flow is reduced. Some make use of the current to provide them with food. The net-spinning caddis larvae *Plectrocnemia* and *Hydropsyche* trap food organisms in their nets, and the blackfly larvae *Simulium* filter off smaller food particles using their mouth brushes.

Typical fish of the headwaters are trout and bullhead. The trout is a strong swimmer, streamlined in shape and able to negotiate the swift currents. It grows well at low temperatures, requires well-oxygenated waters and, for spawning, clean gravel uncontaminated by mud. It feeds by sight, taking invertebrate animals from the stream bed, as they drift down with the current – or as they emerge from the water as adult flies.

The lower reaches of a large river present a very different kind of habitat. The current is sluggish and silt forms a thick mud supporting a variety of water weeds and aquatic plants quite unlike the simple moss carpets of the headwaters. The mud is the home of *tubifex* worms and chironmid larvae (blood-worms), which can live in conditions of poor oxygen supply, a characteristic of the more sluggish waters.

Roach, bream and carp, all deep-bodied and poorer swimmers than the trout, are found here. They are adapted to live successfully in the higher temperatures and oxygen-sparse conditions. In the weeds, the pike lurks in wait for smaller fish.

The upper reaches
In the upper course of the river—the headwaters in higher country—the gradient is steep and the swift, turbulent flow slices a deep V-shaped channel.

Royal fern
Osmunda regalis

Marsh marigold
Caltha palustris

Water crowfoot
Ranunculus fluitans

Spring

Trout stream

Butterwort
Pinguicula vulgaris

Starry saxifrage
Saxifraga stellaris

Water aven
Geum rivale

Minnow reach

Flush

Club moss
Selaginella selaginoides

Marsh cinquefoil
Potentilla palustris

Insects and fish of the fast streams
The pyramid of life in the fast streams is based on the many small life forms and insect larvae which metamorphose into flies (below). The flies, which as larvae adopt 'netting' techniques to feed, provide food stocks for the bullhead *Cottus gobio* (left) and the best-known of all river fish, the agile, strong-swimming trout *Salmo trutta* (right).

Caddis fly
Plectrocnemia conspersa

May fly
Rhithrogena semicolorata

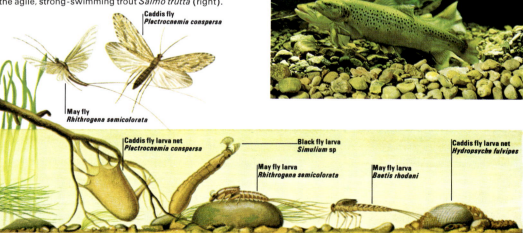

Caddis fly larva net
Plectrocnemia conspersa

Black fly larva
Simulium sp

Caddis fly larva net
Hydropsyche fulvipes

May fly larva
Rhithrogena semicolorata

May fly larva
Baetis rhodani

At home in water *above*
All snakes swim, their heads held high, moving through the water with undulating movements.

Edible frog *right*
Mostly aquatic, the edible frog *Rana esculenta* sometimes migrates overland from one pool to another.

Out of the water, into the air
The dragonfly undergoes a striking metamorphosis which transforms it from an aquatic larva into a winged adult. The larva crawls out of the water onto a stem and – becoming used to breathing air – splits its skin and the adult emerges and expands its wings.

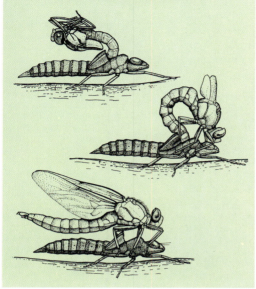

Skullcap
Scutellaria galericulata

Water violet
Hottonia palustris

Frogbit
Hydrocharis morsus-ranae

Flowering rush
Butomus umbellatus

Aquatic rodent *left*
The water vole – the single species *Arvicola amphibius* is found throughout Europe and is one of the larger rodents of the Old World. It nests, often in colonies, in holes constructed a little above water level and lined with grass. It has a vegetarian diet.

Towards the mouth
The firm banks now wide apart, the river flows sluggishly through its lower course, shedding its load of silt as it meanders across the plain.

Greater reedmace
Typha latifolia

Curled pondweed
Potamogeton crispus

Yellow loostrite
Lysimachia vulgaris

Lake

Soft rush
Juncus effusus

The middle reaches
The current now slows as it passes through the middle course. The channel is wider but the flow is still sufficient to transport silt, mud and pebbles.

Lady's smock
Cardamine pratensis

Water forget-me-not
Myosotis scorpioides

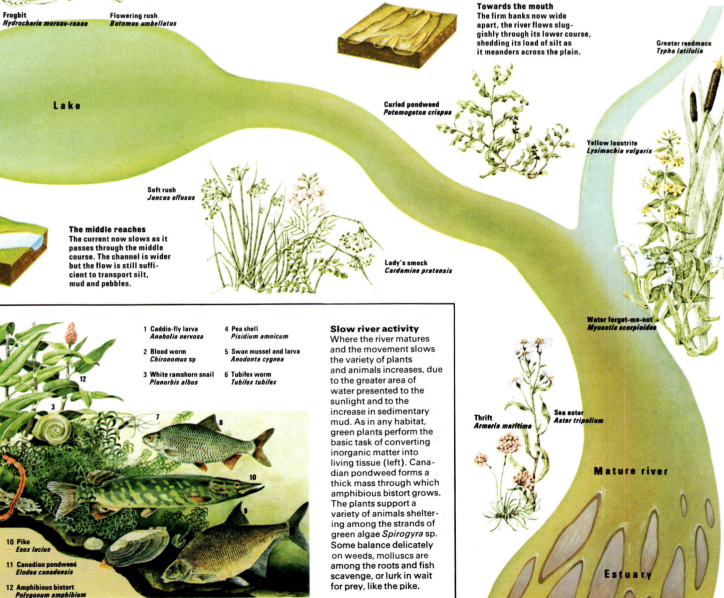

1 **Caddis-fly larva** *Anabolia nervosa*	4 **Pea shell** *Pisidium amnicum*
2 **Blood worm** *Chironomus* sp	5 **Swan mussel and larva** *Anodonta cygnea*
3 **White ramshorn snail** *Planorbis albus*	6 **Tubifex worm** *Tubifex tubifex*
7 *Hydra vulgaris*	10 **Pike** *Esox lucius*
8 **Roach** *Rutilus rutilus*	11 **Canadian pondweed** *Elodea canadensis*
9 **Bream** *Abramis brama*	12 **Amphibious bistort** *Polygonum amphibium*

Slow river activity
Where the river matures and the movement slows the variety of plants and animals increases, due to the greater area of water presented to the sunlight and to the increase in sedimentary mud. As in any habitat, green plants perform the basic task of converting inorganic matter into living tissue (left). Canadian pondweed forms a thick mass through which amphibious bistort grows. The plants support a variety of animals sheltering among the strands of green algae *Spirogyra* sp. Some balance delicately on weeds, molluscs are among the roots and fish scavenge, or lurk in wait for prey, like the pike.

Thrift
Armeria maritima

Sea aster
Aster tripolium

Mature river

Estuary

Marshland Sanctuaries

The glories of Europe's freshwater marshlands, estuaries and other wetlands are their bird populations. The ornithologist with the means to travel will not feel that he has seen all the continent has to offer unless he has visited the Coto Doñana in southwest Spain, the Camargue of France and the estuary of the Danube. Here are dramatic concentrations of the waterbirds and waders to which he is accustomed elsewhere in Europe, but also other attractive species whose homes and breeding grounds are more often to be found in other continents.

The intimate links that most of the wetlands have with rivers and the sea ensure the supply of minerals and large quantities of food materials, and are thus biologically rich in the plants and small animals forming the diet of water-feeding birds. The marshy nature of the terrain has the additional advantage that terrestrial predators find the going difficult, if not impossible. To these well-provided sanctuaries birds flock in their thousands.

The appearance of each species of bird is an indication of the form of food or feeding niche to which it is adapted. Beak shapes vary considerably from the dagger-like bill of the heron, for spearing fish, to the flattened type of the spoonbill, which sieves small organisms from the water.

Some mammals share the moist habitat with the birds, among them species of vole, small herbivores attracted to the vegetation. Where the going is preponderantly dry, the fox and stoat wreak havoc among the breeding colonies of birds. A hunter of the Coto Doñana is the Spanish lynx *Lynx pardellus*.

Nesting in the reeds
Securely woven into the swaying reeds of the marsh, the nests of the reed warbler *Acrocephalus scirpaceus*, sedge warbler A. *schoenobaenus*, bearded tit *Panurus biarmicus* and reed bunting *Emberiza schoeniclus* are well above the waterline. The reed warbler, feeding a nestling cuckoo, is one of the birds most often chosen to foster the cuckoo offspring.

Reed warbler
Acrocephalus scirpaceus

Cuckoo
Cuculus canorus

Sedge warbler
Acrocephalus schoenobaenus

Bearded tit
Panurus biarmicus ♂

Reed bunting
Emberiza schoeniclus ♂

European marshes, bogs and other wetlands

Brave mating display of a marsh bird, the ruff *Philomachus pugnax* (above). Nest and eggs of little bittern *Ixobrychus minutus* (left).

Marshland vegetation
The map (above) shows the main marshland areas of Europe, many of them coastal but others, in the heartland of the continent, in the neighborhood of rivers such as the Danube. Vegetation of the northern marshes is rich and varied and tempts many attractive creatures. Bullrushes and reedmace dominate with water dock and meadowsweet in the transition stage between water and firm land. Alder is a common marshland tree, in patches of firmer soil.

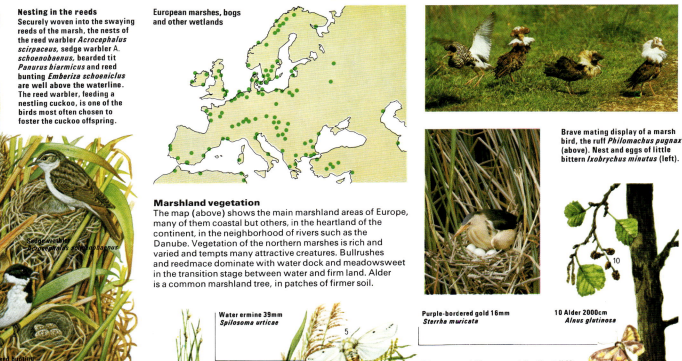

Water ermine 39mm
Spilosoma urticae

Purple-bordered gold 16mm
Sterrha muricata

10 Alder 2000cm
Alnus glutinosa

Brimstone moth 35mm
Opisthograptis luteolata

Swallowtail 82mm
Papilio machaon

Brown china-marks 20mm
Nymphula stagnata

Reed dagger 37mm
Simyra albovenosa

| 1 Yellow water lily 12cm *Nuphar lutea* | 2 Water soldier 5-20cm *Stratiotes aloides* | 3 Bulrush 100-300cm *Schoenoplectus lacustris* | 4 Great reedmace 250cm *Typha latifolia* | 5 Common reed 150-300cm *Phragmites communis* | 6 Great water dock 200cm *Rumex hydrolapathem* | 7 Meadow sweet 120cm *Filipendula ulmaria* | 8 Milk parsley 100cm *Peucedanum palustre* | 9 Common black sedge 7-70cm *Carex nigra* |

The Camargue *above*
The saline marshes of the Camargue have extensive, waterlogged meadows of the halophytic plant *Salicornia fruticosa*. The region now largely trapped in an encircling ring of urban and industrial development at the mouth of the Rhône in France, remains one of the last great refuges for aquatic wild life in western Europe. Flocks of greater flamingos are one of its spectacles ; (left) the avocet is commonplace.

Marshland waders
The marsh pools of the Camargue support large numbers of wading birds, each species feeding in a distinct zone. The black-winged stilt *Himantopus himantopus* chooses the shallows to hunt insects ; little egrets *Egretta garzetta* penetrate submerged vegetation ; the purple heron *Ardea* sp. fishes deeper waters.

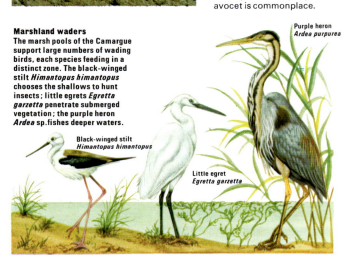

Purple heron
Ardea purpurea

Black-winged stilt
Himantopus himantopus

Little egret
Egretta garzetta

Weatnerman frog *below*
The normal colour of the tree frog *Hyla arbcrea* is green but in certain conditions – usually associated with climatic changes but sometimes with fright – it is able to change its appearance. On overcast, rainy days, it may take on a slate blue colouring.

Poisonous swamp snake *above*
An important predator of southern swamps, the Montpellier snake *Malpolon monspessulanus* is venomous, and lives off other reptiles. It grows to a length of six feet (2m) or more.

The Coto Donana
Like the Camargue and other important remaining marsh areas of southern Europe, the Coto Doñana in south-west Spain lies at the delta of a great river ; here, the Guadalquivir. It owes its remarkable wildlife population in part to a physical nature until now unappealing to man and its position as a natural stopover at the north end of a short overseas route to Africa. Facing the Atlantic, its consists of vast fields of sand drift and, behind them, extensive marshes, the Marismas, along the Guadalquivir. For much of the year – in the spring and autumn – the marshland is flooded and attracts the largest flocks of ducks and geese in Europe. During the summer months the Marismas is a parched heathland, as the photograph (below) shows.

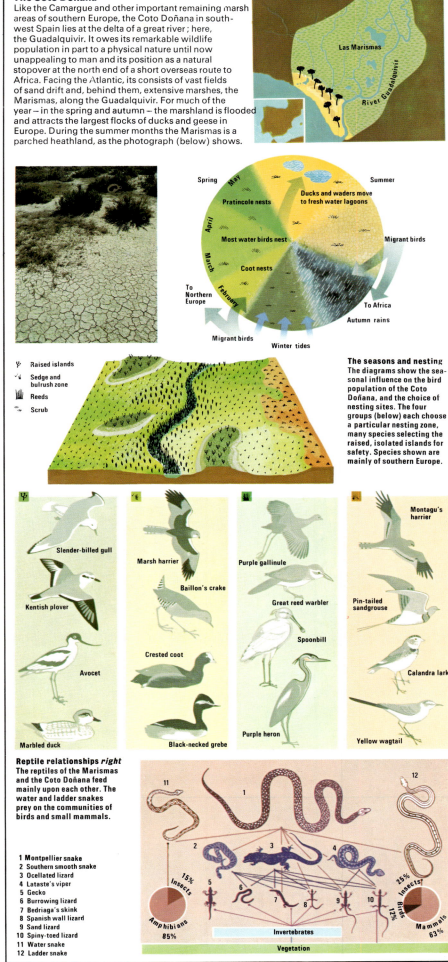

The seasons and nesting
The diagrams show the seasonal influence on the bird population of the Coto Doñana, and the choice of nesting sites. The four groups (below) each choose a particular nesting zone, many species selecting the raised, isolated islands for safety. Species shown are mainly of southern Europe.

Reptile relationships *right*
The reptiles of the Marismas and the Coto Doñana feed mainly upon each other. The water and ladder snakes prey on the communities of birds and small mammals.

1 Montpellier snake
2 Southern smooth snake
3 Ocellated lizard
4 Lataste's viper
5 Gecko
6 Burrowing lizard
7 Bedriaga's skink
8 Spanish wall lizard
9 Sand lizard
10 Spiny-toed lizard
11 Water snake
12 Ladder snake

Sand, Shingle and Rock

Judged by the standards of larger continents, Europe is almost all coastline and very little else. No part of the continent is more than 500 miles (800km) from the sea and most of it is far less. The coast reaches from well inside the Arctic Circle, down through the deeply etched margins of Norway and the British Isles, to Portugal. It includes the almost enclosed Baltic Sea and the northern shores of the Mediterranean (which, like the Baltic, is all but an inland sea) and all types of shore – the region bounded by high and low tides – are to be found.

The tide, or lack of it, plays a fundamental part in the structural and faunal nature of the coasts. It shapes the land – eroding this stretch, retreating from that – provides nutrients and acts as a dispersal agent for shoreline species of animals and vegetation. Those shores exposed to the high tides of the Atlantic Ocean compare favourably with those of the faunally poor fringes of the almost tideless Mediterranean.

The most fertile of all types of coast is the rocky shoreline, where the mark of the tide is strong and rockpools left by its retreat provide both permanent and temporary habitats. Such shorelines vary considerably in composition. Eroded limestone, shale and slate contain fissure crevices which serve as ideal niches. In contrast, the smooth basalt rocks of coastal Scandinavia offer little in the way of attachment for either plants or animals.

Long reaches of sandy shore are found around Europe's coasts. The most extensive are found in the Landes region of southwest France, Jutland in Denmark, and the North Sea coasts of the Low Countries. In appearance they are sterile and desolate, but in fact they harbour a number of interesting burrowing species. Where the sands are stable they are characterized by a large number of a relatively few species.

On sheltered shores, where the force of the tides is felt less strongly, fine organic material is deposited and sand gives place to mud. Habitats such as this are common around river estuaries and the animal species which are found there show a distinct tolerance to variations in salinity.

Feeding and surviving in sand

An abundant, highly specialized life is found on and in sandy shores. The medium is not entirely stable for the surface layers are sometimes churned by heavy seas, but – except at the highest shore levels – it retains water. The characteristic behaviour of its animal population is burrowing. The molluscs, crustaceans and worms which form the bulk of the population include suspension feeders which draw in and filter water; deposit feeders which collect organic matter settled on the surface; sand swallowers; and carnivores, including certain snails.

Tube dweller

The sand mason *Lanice conchilega* is commonly found on lower parts of shores, often close to weed-covered rocks which provide a source of edible detritus. At low tide the animal retreats into the base of a 10in. tube. Group of tube tops (below).

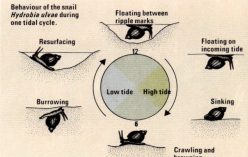

Behaviour of the snail *Hydrobia ulvae* during one tidal cycle.

Floating between ripple marks

Resurfacing

Floating on incoming tide

12

Low tide | High tide

Burrowing

Sinking

6

Crawling and browsing

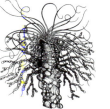

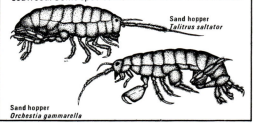

Beach birds

One of the commonest of northern seashore birds is the ringed plover *Charadrius hiaticula* (above). It is found mostly on sand and shingle beaches. The nest and eggs (left) are of the oystercatcher *Haematopus ostralegus*, another characteristic shore bird.

Food for the birds

A common food for shoreline birds, sandhoppers are rarely found on sand and even fewer hop. The species shown are frequently found on and under seaweed. Some species make their home in dead crabs.

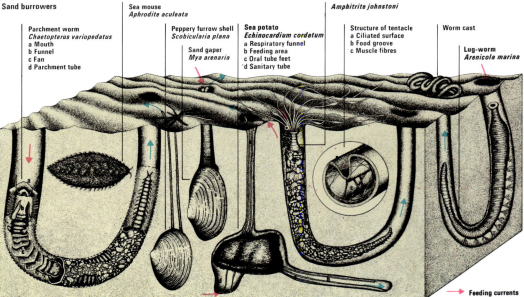

Sand hopper
Talitrus saltator

Sand hopper
Orchestia gammarella

Sand burrowers

Parchment worm
Chaetopterus variopedatus
a Mouth
b Funnel
c Fan
d Parchment tube

Sea mouse
Aphrodite aculeata

Peppery furrow shell
Scrobicularia plana

Sand gaper
Mya arenaria

Sea potato
Echinocardium cordatum
a Respiratory funnel
b Feeding area
c Oral tube feet
d Sanitary tube

Amphitrite johnstoni

Structure of tentacle
a Ciliated surface
b Food groove
c Muscle fibres

Worm cast

Lug-worm
Arenicola marina

→ Feeding currents

Shortage of living space in rich habitat

Contrasting with the limited habitat provided by sand rocky shores have a wealth of niches on and beneath the rocks and the seaweed which clothes them. Many animals have sucker-like discs to contend with the powerful advance and retreat of the tide. Living space in this rich habitat is at a premium and some species solve this problem like the acorn barnacles *Balanus balanoides*, encrusting the shell of the crab *Carcinus maenas* (below). Others (right) bore into the rock. All are adapted to avoid desiccation – drying out – when the tide retreats.

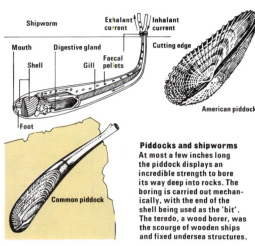

Shipworm
Exhalant current
Inhalant current
Mouth
Digestive gland
Cutting edge
Shell
Gill
Faecal pellets
Foot
American piddock

Common piddock

Piddocks and shipworms

At most a few inches long the piddock displays an incredible strength to bore its way deep into rocks. The boring is carried out mechanically, with the end of the shell being used as the 'bit'. The teredo, a wood borer, was the scourge of wooden ships and fixed undersea structures.

Jewel anemone *right*

In appearance and name the anemone suggests a marine flower – but is in fact an animal. The jewel anemone *Corynactis viridis* takes on its green colour from an alga which lives symbiotically with it. (Below) anemones and other creatures of the rock pool.

Beadlet anemone *Actinia equina*
Green seaweed *Cladophora arcta*
Springtail *Anurida maritima*
Sea-snail *Liparis liparis*
Sagartia elegans
Common prawn *Leander serratus*
Red seaweed *Lithophyllum incrustans*
Devonshire cup coral *Caryophyllia smithii*

Acorn barnacles *right*

Commonest of all animals of the rocky shore the acorn barnacle groups together in colonies, sometimes as many as 30,000 to a square metre. It uses its thoracic appendages as a means of catching food (below); other crustaceans use them for movement.

Mutual benefit *left*

The hermit crab *Eupagurus bernhardus* and anemone *Calliactis parasitica* strike up a mutually beneficial relationship. The crab is protected by the camouflage of the anemone, which in turn feeds on scraps of food left over by its host.

Seaweed a shelter for shore life

Seaweed is giant algae and an important component of shore life, but it is not confined to the shallows and the margins: some is found in deeper waters. The various species of this marine vegetation provide fodder for many browsing animals, but are probably more important as groves of shelter for a large number of invertebrates. The fronds provide attachment points for hydroids and sea squirts, among many others. The diagram (below) shows the shore zonation of the main green, brown and red groups of seaweeds.

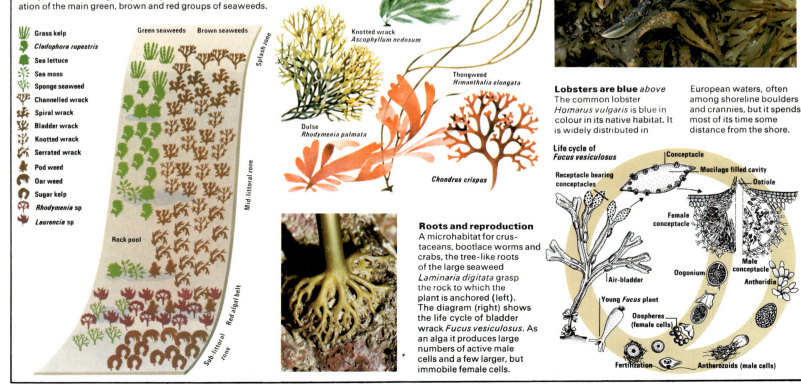

Grass kelp
Cladophora rupestris
Sea lettuce
Sea moss
Sponge seaweed
Channelled wrack
Spiral wrack
Bladder wrack
Knotted wrack
Serrated wrack
Pod weed
Oar weed
Sugar kelp
Rhodymenia sp
Laurencia sp

Green seaweeds
Brown seaweeds
Splash zone
Mid-littoral zone
Rock pool
Sub-littoral zone
Red algal belt

Sea lettuce *Ulva lactuca*
Cladophora rupestris
Knotted wrack *Ascophyllum nodosum*
Thongweed *Himanthalia elongata*
Dulse *Rhodymenia palmata*
Chondrus crispus

Lobsters are blue *above*

The common lobster *Homarus vulgaris* is blue in colour in its native habitat. It is widely distributed in European waters, often among shoreline boulders and crannies, but it spends most of its time some distance from the shore.

Life cycle of *Fucus vesiculosus*
Receptacle bearing conceptacles
Conceptacle
Mucilage filled cavity
Female conceptacle
Ostiole
Male conceptacle
Antheridia
Oogonium
Air-bladder
Young *Fucus* plant
Oospheres (female cells)
Fertilization
Antherozoids (male cells)

Roots and reproduction

A microhabitat for crustaceans, bootlace worms and crabs, the tree-like roots of the large seaweed *Laminaria digitata* grasp the rock to which the plant is anchored (left). The diagram (right) shows the life cycle of bladder wrack *Fucus vesiculosus*. As an alga it produces large numbers of active male cells and a few larger, but immobile female cells.

Northern Asia
THE PALAEARCTIC REALM 2

Northern Asia

Continent is barely adequate a term to describe Asia, the world's largest landmass. Europe, little more than a seafrayed appendage to it, is also a continent. Asia reaches out almost to touch the Americas; Africa, across the man-made ditch of the Suez Canal; and Australia, through the chain of islands of Indonesia. The following pages describe the northern and central regions of the continent – the great, horizontal bands of taiga, steppe and desert bounded to the north by the Arctic tundra and to the south by the soaring mountains of the Karakoram, Pamir and Himalaya. The seemingly endless expanses of conifer in the taiga form the greatest forest in the world, linking the Atlantic (through Scandinavia) with the northern margins of the Pacific. The deserts reach from China to join the Sahara with little interruption and the fertile steppes unroll across the Russian river basins into eastern Europe. The breathtaking scale of everything in Asia is exemplified by the great natural barrier of mountains to the south where any one of a hundred peaks is higher than any mountain in any other part of the world. Each of these unique regions is occupied by life forms peculiar to itself, albeit in diminishing traces like Przewalski's horse, the last of its species in the wild, or the Siberian and Caspian tigers, still holding on to life in a habitat from which their genus first emerged. Conservation authorities have had some notable success in saving indigenous herbivores such as the saiga antelope and the wild ass.

Pine trees damaged by moose, Siberia, U.S.S.R.

Key to panorama

1 Siberian jay	11 Common cranes	21 Wolves	31 Snowy owl
2 Pine marten	12 Wood-boring beetle	22 Eurasian ground squirrel	32 Blue hare
3 Great grey owl	13 Willow tit	23 Pupa of longhorn beetle	33 Ravens
4 Lynx	14 Siberian rubythroat	24 Pygmy shrew	34 Greenshank
5 Pine grosbeaks	15 Elk	25 Siberian weasel	35 Pika
6 Goshawk	16 Wolverine	26 Ichneumon wasp	36 Bramblings
7 Capercaillie	17 Boar	27 Siberian tit	37 Stoat
8 Eurasian flying squirrel	18 Willow grouse	28 Crossbill	38 Arctic fox
9 Northern bat	19 Brown bear	29 Pine weevil	39 Masked shrew
10 Black woodpecker	20 Reindeer	30 Nutcracker	40 Root voles

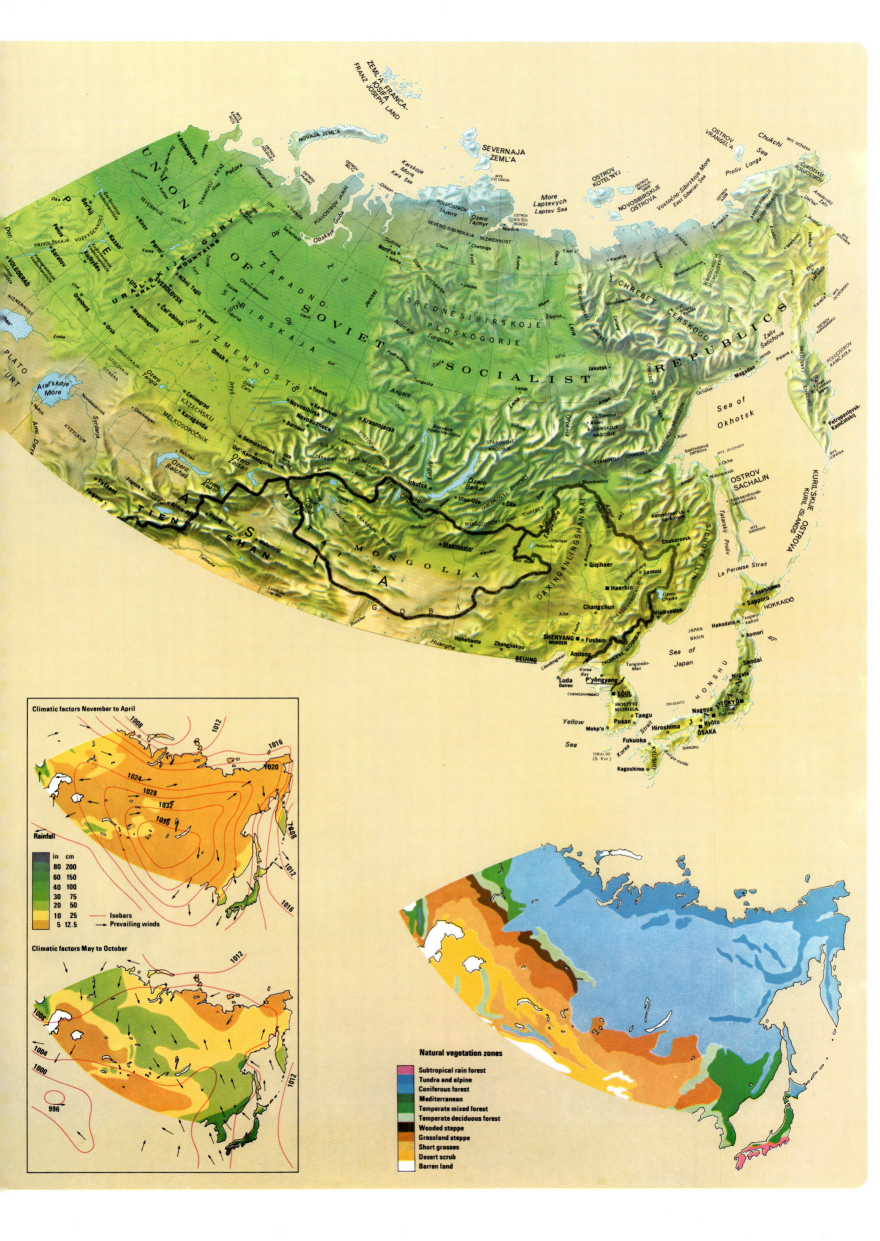

Taiga: The Siberian Wilderness

The taiga is a belt of predominantly coniferous forest extending across the entire Eurasian continent from Scandinavia to the Sea of Okhotsk. It is particularly broad to the east of the Yenisey River, where it reaches into Mongolia. Larch is the taiga's dominant tree species, but fir, spruce and other conifers are also characteristic, especially in the montane regions of the south and east.

Extensive fires are commonplace throughout northern Asia. The taiga is to a great extent the product of flash fires existing at varying stages of regeneration. The pioneer tree species on newly burned areas are predominantly deciduous, notably light-loving birches and aspens.

Although the taiga lies under snow for several months during the winter, relatively few animals emigrate: most of the small mammals and many birds have adapted themselves to living under snow. It is at this time of year that the seeds of coniferous trees are of supreme importance as the basic winter food for numerous animals; thus, either directly or indirectly, the yield of conifer seeds exerts a controlling influence over the numbers of wild animals that can be supported on the taiga.

The brown bear *Ursus arctos* and the elk *Alces alces* are the most widespread of the large taiga mammals. The southern regions are inhabited by the Altai wapiti *Cervus elaphus asiaticus*. The musk deer *Moschus moschiferus* is found only to the east of the Yenisey. Rodents are particularly abundant on the taiga: the red squirrel *Sciurus vulgaris* is a common arboreal form, and the Siberian chipmunk *Eutamias sibiricus* is particularly common on the forest fringes and on recently burned areas. Various predators, among them valuable fur-bearers such as the sable *Martes zibellina*, the Siberian weasel *Mustela sibirica*, and the wolverine *Gulo gulo*, feed mainly on the northern redbacked vole *Clethrionomys rutilus* and the large-toothed redbacked vole *C. rufocanus*. The dependence of the northern lynx *Felis lynx* on its principal prey species, the varying hare *Lepus timidus*, is equally close.

A number of bird species, including the two-barred crossbill *Loxia leucoptera*, the nutcracker *Nucifraga caryocatactes*, and several woodpeckers, have specialized in feeding on the seeds of larch, spruce and pine. But the most common and widespread birds of the taiga are members of the grouse family, the Tetraonidae. Members of this family eat pine needles, catkins, buds, berries and a limited amount of other plant food. Nevertheless, insectivorous birds are also quite common. Even in winter they feed on dormant insects inhabiting cracks and crannies among the bark and crowns of trees.

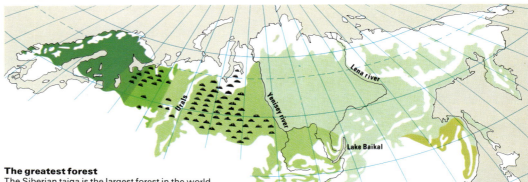

The greatest forest
The Siberian taiga is the largest forest in the world, covering an area more than one-third larger than the United States. A few species of conifer, with fringes of hardy broadleaves such as aspen, birch and alder, are the dominating vegetation. A natural 'divide', the Yenisey river, splits the taiga into two distinctive regions.

Pine, spruce
Pine, spruce, Siberian larch
Pine, spruce, Siberian fir
Siberian fir, stone-pine, eastern larch
Siberian larch, fir, spruce, silver fir
Manchu pine, oak, maple, elm
Marsh

The oldest lake in the world
The long-standing isolation of Lake Baikal – the oldest lake in the world, adjoining the southern edge of the taiga – has given it a fauna uniquely its own ; three-quarters of its animal life are found nowhere else. It covers nearly 12,000 square miles (31,000 km²).

Baikal contains ancestors of animals found in other Asiatic and North American fresh waters—a reminder that the continents were joined when the lake was formed in the Miocene.

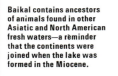

L.Windermere 12,000y L.Tanganyika 12my L.Baikal 25my

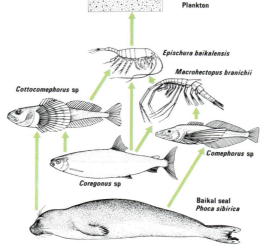

Plankton

Epischura baikalensis

Macrohectopus branichii

Cottocomephorus sp

Comephorus sp

Coregonus sp

Baikal seal *Phoca sibirica*

Isolated aquatic life
The baikal seal is the dominant predator of the great lake. Now adapted to a life in landlocked waters, the seal is closely related to the northern ocean species. It may have reached the lake at the time the glaciers retreated, by swimming up the River Lena from the Arctic Ocean. The fish on which the seal preys, and the crustaceans eaten by the fish, have taken on strange forms in isolation. A typical Baikal food chain, based on plankton, is shown (above).

Fish hawk and swan
A bird totally dependent on fish for its food, the osprey *Pandion haliaetus* hunts across Lake Baikal and other lakes of the taiga. It catches its prey by plunging from height into the water, and seizing the fish in its powerful claws. The whooper swan (right) is found in lakes locked in deep coniferous forest.

Four taiga hunters
Of the taiga owls shown here, the great grey owl and the hawk owl are native to the habitat. The eagle owl—largest of the species—ranges through Europe to Africa. Tengmalm's owl, which occupies dense spruce country, is the most pleasantly-voiced of owls.

Hawk owl
Surnia ulula

Eagle owl
Bubo bubo

Great grey owl
Strix nebulosa

Tengmalm's owl
Aegolius funereus

Conifer food *right*
Birds which feed wholly on conifer vegetation include the pine grosbeak which eats young needles, buds and seeds of all types of conifer, and species of crossbill which individually choose pine or spruce. The nutcracker and Siberian jay crack open cones with their strong bills, and capercaillie and hazel grouse pick up seeds from the ground. There are small mammal seed-eaters, too ; even the carnivorous sable supplements its diet in autumn with seeds. In years of seed shortage some species migrate over hundreds of miles for food.

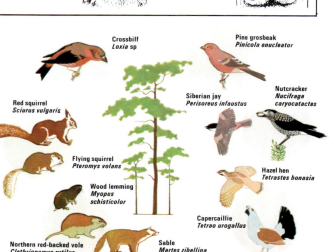

Crossbill
Loxia sp

Pine grosbeak
Pinicola enucleator

Red squirrel
Sciurus vulgaris

Siberian jay
Perisoreus infaustus

Nutcracker
Nucifraga caryocatactes

Flying squirrel
Pteromys volans

Hazel hen
Tetrastes bonasia

Wood lemming
Myopus schisticolor

Capercaillie
Tetrao urogallus

Northern red-backed vole
Clethrionomys rutilus

Sable
Martes zibellina

Taiga activity *right*
To the newcomer the taiga is a depressingly monotonous region in which visibility is limited by the endless conifer forests that hem him in. On closer acquaintance the forest comes to life, for conifers provide a rich habitat for bird and other forms of life. The summer swarms of flying insects which plague man are a prolific food source for birds ; in winter there is a store of dormant insects in the cracks and crannies of the tree bark. Among the more unlikely inhabitants of the taiga forest trees, the goldeneye and goosander ducks choose to nest in holes abandoned by the black woodpecker, where their young can hatch out in reasonable safety from predators like the squirrel.

Pine marten
Martes martes

Sable
Martes zibellina

Taiga carnivores *above*
The sleek pine marten *Martes martes* and the sable *Martes zibellina* are closely related predators. There are six Old World marten species.

Taiga herbivore *below*
The female elk *Alces alces* lacks the magnificent spread of antlers characteristic of the male. The elk is the Eurasian equivalent of moose.

Waxwing and jay
A companionable, berry-eating bird of the conifer forests is the waxwing *Bombycilla garrulus* (above). The Siberian jay *Perisoreus infaustus* (below) accompanies taiga travellers.

Ural owl
Strix uralensis

Flying squirrel
Pteromys volans

Siberian tit
Parus cinctus

Goosander
Mergus merganser ♂

Goldeneye
Bucephala clangula

Siberian rubythroat
Luscinia calliope

Red squirrel (black phase)
Sciurus vulgaris

Ground-squirrel
Eutamias sibiricus

Hazel hen
Tetrastes bonasia

The Windswept Heartland

An almost treeless corridor of grassland, bounded to the north by the endless forests of the taiga and to the south by arid deserts, the steppes reach out from the eastern lands of Europe, into the Orient. Through this corridor, provided with rich grazing for their mounts the medieval hordes of Tartary poured to occupy much of eastern Europe before withdrawing, centuries later, back across the steppes.

The rich herb cover of the steppes grows in the famous black earth, the chernozem, and the redder soils farther south. Like the American prairies and pampas, they have undergone considerable change in recent centuries. After the retreat of the last Ice Age they supported vast populations of grazing animals, some of which are now extinct, like the tarpan, a wild horse, and the bison, which has been re-bred in captivity. Other ungulates which survive include the saiga (an antelope once threatened with extermination but now breeding again in numbers), red and roe deer, and the goitered antelope.

These animals helped maintain the natural economy of the original steppe country by trampling the herb seeds into the ground, cropping the superfluous vegetation, fertilizing the soil with their droppings and clearing the spaces between the grass tussocks for new growth. Despite protective measures, the surviving animals tend now to thrive in the more arid regions of the steppe – where man finds it more difficult to make a living. Ground-nesting birds such as the steppe eagle have also suffered and the most numerous animals are now (as in similar regions of the world) the burrowing rodents.

The true steppe is a sea of grass, and one of singular beauty in the spring when the snows retreat and wild flowers, including tulips, irises and anemones, burst forth. Later in the year the dominant feather grass displays its plume-like seed-heads in a billowing ocean.

Across the steppelands, the great rivers of Russia wind. Natural corridors for migratory species, these rivers, including the Dnieper, Don, Volga and Ural are rich in a native river and marshland fauna of their own.

Giant bird *below*
One of the largest flying birds the great bustard *Otis tarda* never perches and flies reluctantly.

Ground-nesting eagle *right*
The steppe eagle *Aquila nipalensis orientalis* is another ground nester, but increasingly rare.

Narrow-leaved plants
There is no continuous sod in many parts of the steppes and most of the grasses grow in clusters. Narrow-leaved plants, well adapted to the climate, are predominant.

Black wormwood
Artemisia pauciflora

White wormwood
Artemisia maritima

The steppes are a mixture of flowering plants and grasses, in two main types of soil – the chernozem, the rich black soils of the cooler climes and the dry red soils of the south.

When the snows clear in the spring moss plants and algae appear, followed by a variety of wild flowers including common tulip, and blooming sage carpets the steppes in blue.

Stipa capillata

Magenta peony
Paeonia tenuifolia

Anemone
Anemone patens

Wild tulip
Tulipa schrenki

Sedge
Carex stenophylla

Bulbous blue grass
Poa bulbosa

Ranunculus polyrhizus

Crested hair grass
Koeleria cristata

Gagea
Gagea bulbifera

Steppe forest areas
The crested lark *Galerida cristata* (above) is a bird of steppe forest, which occurs (below) where the terrain undulates slightly to retain increased moisture.

The progression from steppe to wooded steppe.

Laburnum   Dwarf almond   Wild apple   Wild pear   Birch   Oak

The rare wild horse *left*
The last of the wild horses, Przewalski's horse *Equus przewalskii* roams, in its few remaining herds, through semidesert and upland country on either side of the Altai mountains of Mongolia. Sightings of them are rare, for — happily, for the remaining specimens — few men other than occasional nomads share their habitat. Their numbers and their range were once far greater, but the firearm, and competition from domestic stock for the limited water supplies caused their decline. They are distinguished from domestic forms by upright manes.

The saiga
The powdered horns of the saiga *Saiga tatarica* were once a prized nostrum for Chinese apothecaries. The species is now found, stringently protected, east from the Volga basin through Kazakhstan. The odd, downward-pointing nostrils and highly developed nasal tracts of the saiga may be an adaptation for moistening and warming inhaled, dusty air (below).

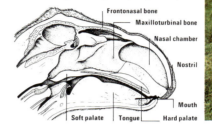

Frontonasal bone
Maxilloturbinal bone
Nasal chamber
Nostril
Mouth
Soft palate   Tongue   Hard palate

Migrant corridors
Arid Asia is crossed by a number of rivers and streams which provide natural corridors for animal movement. The common cobra and the Indian lapwing move northward, the rook south from cold regions.

Aral Sea

TURANIAN PLAIN

Syr Darya

Cobra
Naja naja

Tien Shan

Indian mynah
Acridotheres tristis

Rook
Corvus frugilegus

Amu Darya

PAMIR MOUNTAINS

Djout is a Russian word describing the mass death of animals caused by savage winter weather. The saiga is one of the few animals to survive these rigors in any numbers. Another ungulate, the goitered gazelle, loses 80 to 90 per cent of its numbers. Survival success of the saiga is helped by its varied diet (right).

Lichen
Weeds
Flowering plants
Wormwood
Shrubs
Salt plants
Goosefoot
Grasses

Spring   Summer   Autumn   Winter

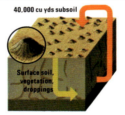

Prey for wolves
Young saigas are born in mid-spring, after a gestation period of five months. Twins (left) are common, triplets are not unusual. Although they are nursed for some months, young saigas nibble grass at four months. In this state they are easy prey for wolves.

Contributors to the economy
The herds of large herbivores grazing the grasslands of the steppes are vital to the region's natural economy and their importance is echoed by millions of rather less noticeable animals — mostly rodents — at and below ground level. This subterranean population of herbivores churns millions of tons of fresh soil to the surface. Their numbers are kept in check by a variety of carnivores, including polecats, wolves, snakes and eagles — a profusion of predators who are the reason for burrowing anyway, in a region where other forms of cover are limited.

Soil engineers *right*
The suslik — a marmot-like rodent of the steppes — is one of the architects of the surface. In an area of less than 400 square yards (334 square meters) there may be up to 12,000 of its burrow entrances, the mounds of earth equivalent to three cubic yards (2·3 cu. m.) shifted from the earth below.

40,000 cu yds subsoil

Surface soil, vegetation, droppings

Changing the plants *right*
Burrowing away beneath the surface, rodents often bring up soil types which are out of context with the surface. Where saline subsoils are brought up, halophytic plants take root. Where salt-free subsoil is brought to a highly saline surface, meadow grasses spring up where once they were unable to grow.

Salt vegetation   Meadow grasses

Brown earth   Brown earth

Saline subsoil   Carbonate subsoil

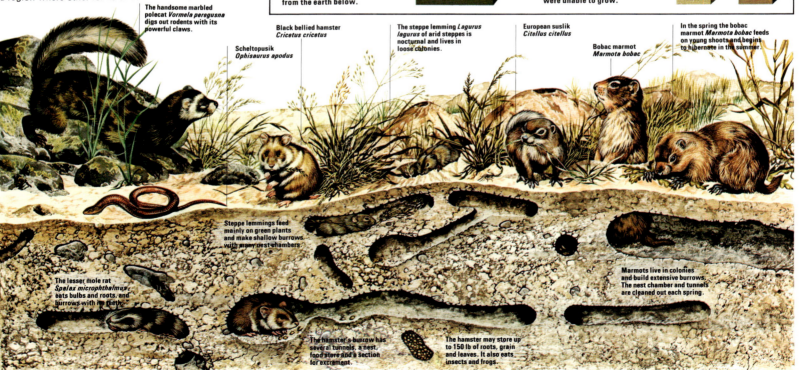

The handsome marbled polecat *Vormela peregusna* digs out rodents with its powerful claws.

Black bellied hamster
Cricetus cricetus

Scheltopusik
Ophisaurus apodus

The steppe lemming *Lagurus lagurus* of arid steppes is nocturnal and lives in loose colonies.

European suslik
Citellus citellus

Bobac marmot
Marmota bobac

In the spring the bobac marmot *Marmota bobac* feeds on young shoots and begins to hibernate in the summer.

Steppe lemmings feed mainly on green plants and make shallow burrows with many nest chambers.

The lesser mole rat *Spalax microphthalmus* eats bulbs and roots, and burrows with its teeth.

The hamster's burrow has several tunnels, a nest, food store and a section for excrement.

The hamster may store up to 150 lb of roots, grain and leaves. It also eats insects and frogs.

Marmots live in colonies and build extensive burrows. The nest chamber and tunnels are cleaned out each spring.

Kyzyl Kum to Alashan: the Cold Deserts

From the Caspian Sea and the plateau of Iran, and interrupted only by the mountains of the soaring Tien Shan range, the deserts of central Asia sweep across the continent to Mongolia and western China. Land-locked wildernesses of sand, clay plain and stone, they are seared by baking temperatures which fall as much as 70°F at night, during the summer; in winter, no barriers protect them from the icy air of the Arctic wastes to the north. Rain is brief, during the spring and autumn, and the summer months are almost dry.

To the east of the Tien Shan range and the Pamirs the Takla Makhan is the largest sand desert of northern Asia. Sweeping into Mongolia the Gobi Desert is a series of alluvial valleys filled with pebbles. Vegetation is short-lived after the spring rains, when the deserts are covered with ephemeral plants that sprout, bloom and seed in a short period. The most distinctive plants of the region are the saxoul shrubs – white saxoul *Halozylon persicum* of the sand deserts and black saxoul *H. aphyllum* of more saline soils. While *persicum* has small leaves *aphyllum* has none, and both plants 'breathe' through their branches, which fall off after the plant has fruited.

The severity of the climate and the scarcity of vegetation imposes stringent restrictions on wildlife and many herbivores such as the land tortoise are active only in the spring when they gorge themselves on vegetation. The rest of the year is spent in a burrow or similar shelter. Like desert animals throughout the world, many avoid the heat by nocturnal activity.

The fauna is a mixture of European, African and Oriental, with some distinct species. It includes the most northerly representative of the monitor lizards, the grey monitor, *Varanus griseus*, and the gecko *Crossobamon eversmanni*, which has extended pads on its feet to use as snowshoes. The lizards form an important link in the desert food chain, for most eat insects and in turn are eaten by snakes – including the lebetine viper – desert shrikes and hawks. The larger desert animals, including the two-humped Bactrian camel *Camelus bactrianus*, solve the problem of arid conditions by constantly searching for new pastures.

Jerboas: most prolific, least seen *right*
In the darkness of the desert night the most prolific species of the region, the jerboas *Dipodidae* emerge to feed on shoots, flowers and seeds, when available, as well as insects and larvae. There are 16 known species of jerboa in central Asia, and there may be more, for their nocturnal habits and incredible speed of movement render them difficult to observe. Each species is adapted to its chosen habitat; among others, the five-toed to clay/stone, the hairy-pawed to sand.

Entrance
Dry flowing and shifting sand
Moist loose sand
Burrow of brush-tailed jerboa
Moist compact sand

Humidity controls
The burrow of the jerboa (above) is sealed during the day to conserve humidity. The animal's skull (left) is adapted to retain humid air to check the dehydration of middle ear fluid. The photograph (below) shows typical jerboa country, with tamarisk in the foreground.

Cold deserts of northern Asia

Gobi desert
Inner Mongolia
Ordos desert
Alashan desert
Lake Balkhash
Aral Sea
Kyzyl Kum
Kary Kumy
Takla Makan desert
Tibet
Cold drying wind

Sand
Dunes
Clay
Mountain desert
Stone, loess, clay

The shifting barchans
The dominating desert regions of central Asia (map left) include areas of sand which, through overgrazing, have become unstable. Here the winds form barchans, or crescent-shaped dunes (below.)

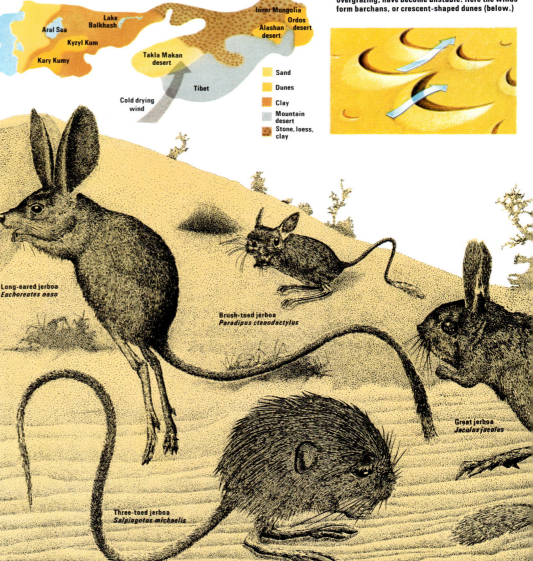

Long-eared jerboa
Euchoreutes naso

Brush-toed jerboa
Paradipus ctenodactylus

Three-toed jerboa
Salpingotus michaelis

Great jerboa
Jaculus jaculus

Desert species
The lebetine viper
Vipera lebetina (above) is
one of the largest of the
desert snakes. A migrant
species which winters farther south, the pallid
harrier *Circus macrourus*
is shown (left). The sand
grouse *Syrrhaptes tibetanus*
(below) is a plateau bird.

Agamid and monitor
Lizards are commonplace in the
Asian deserts. Two are shown here.

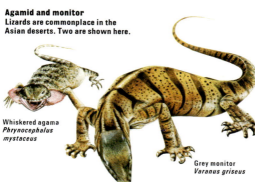

Whiskered agama
*Phrynocephalus
mystaceus*

Grey monitor
Varanus griseus

Sand grouse
Pterocles orientalis

Air-pocket

Thick skin

Underbelly heat shield *above*
The unique adaptation of the black-bellied
sand grouse to the heat of the desert is an
air chamber between underskin and its flesh.

Protected grazers
Tough protective measures
have saved the gazelle
Gazella subgutturosa
(above) and wild ass *Equus
hemionus* (left) from extinction. Vast herds of these, and
other ungulates—wild
sheep and horses—once
roamed the deserts.

Desert visitors
Many small insectivorous and herbivorous birds fly into the desert to
take advantage of ephemeral summer
activity. All are cryptically coloured

Stone curlew
Burhinus oedicnemus

Desert warbler
Sylvia nana

Desert lark
Ammomanes deserti

Fat-tailed jerboa
Salpingotus crassicauda

Four-toed jerboa
Allactaga tetradactylus

Speedy hedgehogs
Lighter in build and
faster movers than their
European cousins the
desert hedgehog *Paraechinus hypomelas* (right) and
the long-eared hedgehog
Hemiechinus sp. are two of
the more important insectivores of the desert.
They also seek birds' eggs.

Long sleep *above*
A long hibernation from
September until March
enables the marmot
Marmota caudata to survive
the rigours of the harsh
desert winter. Species of
marmot are of widespread
occurrence throughout the
cooler ranges of the
northern hemisphere.

111

A World in the Clouds

The highlands of central Asia are of particular interest and importance as they harbour a large number of endemic plants and animals. On the enormous elevated plateau encircled by the Tien Shan, the Pamirs, the Kunlun, the Tibetan Plateau and the Himalayas the number of arcto-alpine groups is proportionately lower than in the montane regions of Europe, and the number of endemic species higher.

The large-eared pika *Ochotona macrotis* and the high mountain vole *Alticola roylei* invariably live in rocky regions. These animals remain active throughout the year, establishing caches of hay in dry places beneath stones or in rock clefts for use during the critical winter period. Another common highland species, the alpine marmot *Marmota marmota baibacina*, prefers to spend the winter hibernating in the depths of its burrow. The large ungulates migrate to the snow-free southern slopes. The Siberian ibex *Capra ibex sibirica* favours the security afforded by the highest ridges: it is the principal prey of the snow leopard *Panthera uncia*, the most handsome of the big cats, which spends both winter and summer above the snow line, seldom descending to lower elevations.

The argali *Ovis ammon*, largest of all living sheep, favours the flatter, more arid plateau-lands. Marco Polo was the first European to describe the massive curved horns of the rams inhabiting the Pamirs. The largest animal of the cold deserts of Tibet, the wild yak *Bos grunniens mutus*, was first described only a century ago by the famous Russian naturalist explorer N. M. Przewalski. This once-common animal has in recent years undergone a rapid and perhaps irreversible decline. The small domesticated yak, on the other hand, remains common and widespread.

The highland birds include numerous carrion-eaters, exemplified by the lammergeier *Gypaetus barbatus*, the Himalayan griffon *Gyps himalayensis*, and the black vulture *Aegypius monachus*. Three species of the crow family (Corvidae) – the raven *Corvus corax*, the chough *Pyrrhocorax pyrrhocorax*, and the alpine chough *P. graculus* – are equally typical throughout the mountains of the southern Palaearctic

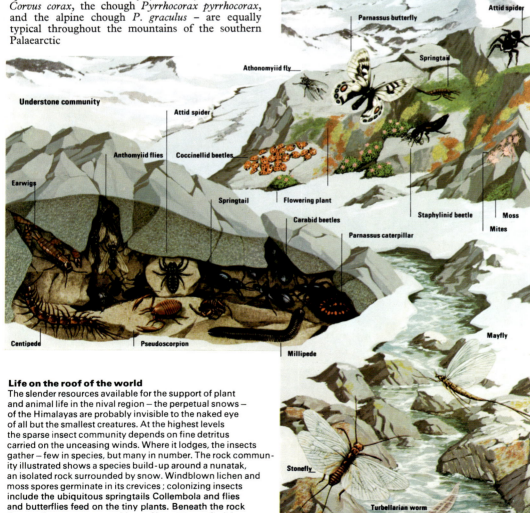

Rock Community

Parnassus butterfly

Athonomyiid fly

Attid spider

Springtail

Attid spider

Understone community

Anthomyiid flies

Coccinellid beetles

Earwigs

Springtail

Flowering plant

Carabid beetles

Staphylinid beetle

Moss

Mites

Parnassus caterpillar

Centipede

Pseudoscorpion

Millipede

Mayfly

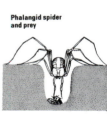

Stonefly

Turbellarian worm

Air Transport
Air currents rising from the Indian plains lift vast clouds of organic and inorganic dusts, spores, pollens and insects. Upper air currents carry them north and they settle on the Himalayan snows. These particles and the derelict, frozen insects are food for nival life.

Cold air

Upper air currents

Updraft of warm air from the Indian plain

Himalayas

Foothills

Hardy spider
A dead insect sinks into a hole made by its body heat in the snow. A scavenging Phalangid spider feeds on the corpse by lowering its body into the depression without coming into contact with the snow. Phalangids have been seen above 18,000 ft

Phalangid spider and prey

Isolation by glaciation *below*
During the Pleistocene, glaciers widened and deepened the valleys, breaking up the populations of cold-adapted insects. Each peak is now a centre for distinct species.

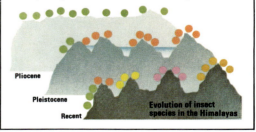

Pliocene

Pleistocene

Recent

Evolution of insect species in the Himalayas

Life on the roof of the world
The slender resources available for the support of plant and animal life in the nival region – the perpetual snows – of the Himalayas are probably invisible to the naked eye of all but the smallest creatures. At the highest levels the sparse insect community depends on fine detritus carried on the unceasing winds. Where it lodges, the insects gather – few in species, but many in number. The rock community illustrated shows a species build-up around a nunatak, an isolated rock surrounded by snow. Windblown lichen and moss spores germinate in its crevices; colonizing insects include the ubiquitous springtails Collembola and flies and butterflies feed on the tiny plants. Beneath the rock there gathers a mass assemblage of insect types, for it is a stable, protected habitat. In the streams and runnels of meltwater, stone flies, mayflies and flatworms are found.

Asian mountain habitat *above*
The species described on this page are residents of the great Asian mountain massif of which the Himalayas form the dominant southern section.

Snow leopard prey
The massively-horned Siberian ibex is a favourite prey of the rare and beautiful snow leopard.

Himalayan species
The carrion-eating Lammergeier vulture *Gypaetus barbatus* (above) feeds on bones which it swallows whole, or drops from height to break and extract the marrow with its hooked beak. *Rhododendron arboreum* (right) is one of 500 species of its kind found in the Himalayas. Most massive of the mountain mammals, the yak *Bos grunniens* (below) has been reduced to a few in number in its wild state.

Tahr and markhor
The Himalayan tahr *Hemitragus jemlahicus* (above) chooses the most inaccessible habitats ; the patriarchal animal (left) is a spiral-horned male markhor *Capra falconeri*.

Montane butterflies
The butterflies shown here are all Himalayan species; variations of the Parnassus are found in the European Alps. *Baltia* sp. occurs only in Turkestan.

Parnassus charltonus charltonus

Baltia shawii

Orchid
Dendrobium nobile

Bhutan glory
Armandia lidderdalei

Scale in thousand ft

Chiru antelope
Pantholops hodgsoni
18,000–20,000 ft

Yak
Bos grunniens
14,000–20,000 ft

Tibetan wild ass
Equus hemionus kiang
9,000–17,000 ft

Bharal
Pseudois nayaur
12,000–15,000 ft

Nayan
Ovis ammon hodgsoni
9,000–15,000 ft

Tibetan gazelle
Procapra picticaudata
9,000–12,000 ft

Shapu
Ovis orientalis
8,000–9,000 ft

Tibetan ungulates
The uplands, plateaus and steppes of Tibet are the home of the ungulates shown here. Some, like the wild yak, are dwindling in numbers ; others like the chiru, or Tibetan antelope, exist in large herds.

Montane mynah *above*
The Indian hill mynah *Gracula religiosa* travels in small flocks and feeds on montane fruits.

Migrant goose *right*
The bar-headed goose *Anser indicus* breeds in the Himalayas and winters on the plains of India.

The Far East and Japan

A distinct region covering more than a half a million square miles (800,000km²), eastern Asia includes the great river basins of Manchuria (the northeast province of China), and Korea. Offshore are the islands of Japan, Sakhalin and the Kurils. The climate is dominated by summer monsoons and cold Arctic winds during the winter. The monsoon winds reach far inland, producing the moist conditions necessary for the growth of lush vegetation, but the winter cold is far more severe than any encountered in southern Europe, which lies in the same latitudes.

The whole area demonstrates the reappearance of broadleaf forest, absent from the rest of northern Asia east of the Urals. Common woodland species like oak and hornbeam are once again manifest but now in species peculiar to the region; and there is a link also eastward to North America in similar species of conifers (an illustration on the opposite page shows Japan's rare umbrella pine, a relative of the American sequoia, or redwood).

As might be expected, the fauna includes types encountered at the other end of the Eurasian land mass, in Europe; often, the same species. Others demonstrate their links with more southerly forms. There are many relics, also – species that were once widespread but were later reduced to discontinuous 'patches' by climatic changes in prehistoric times, surviving only in favoured localities such as southern Europe, the Caucasus, Tien Shan, Manchuria and Japan. In addition to the Manchurian forms in the Amur province, some of the northerly Okhotsk forms have been preserved, including the Pacific salmon and the freshwater pearl mussel. Among the indigenous species of the region, none is more noble than the greatest of big cats, the Siberian tiger, of which little more than 100 remain.

The Siberian tiger hunts through the forested river basin of the region, seeking the huge wild boars, elks and roe deer which abound.

Off the northeast coast of Asia there lies a chain of islands, volcanic by nature, which form part of the 'ring of fire' stretching south to the islands of the east Indies. These are Sakhalin – separated only from the mainland by a strip of water four miles (6.4km) wide – the numerous islands of Japan and their northern neighbours, the Kurils.

Torn throughout its history by major earthquakes and inundated by cataclysmic flood tides, little of Japan is level ground. It is richly forested and its fauna reflects that of Manchuria. The Kurils to the north have a consistently foggy climate and Sakhalin is clad in taiga-like forest, echoing the cover of the nearby mainland.

Flora of eastern Asia
The flora of eastern Asia changes gradually from coniferous taiga to richer, mixed forest containing many endemic broadleaf species. Whereas the taiga has little undergrowth the far eastern forests have a canopy of tall trees (pine and elm illustrated here) with a middle layer of small trees and a thick undergrowth which includes fern and ginseng—a plant used as a cure-all by the Chinese.

Small-leaved elm
Ulmus pumila

Wild vine
Vitis amurensis

Fern
Dryopteris crassirhizoma

Korean pine
Pinus coraiensis

Cork
Phellodendrom amurense

Ginseng
Panax ginseng

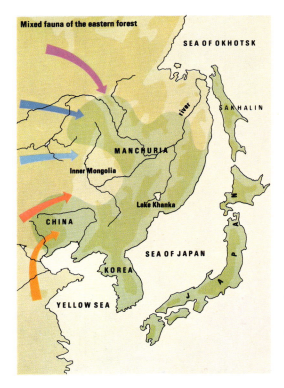

Mixed fauna of the eastern forest

SEA OF OKHOTSK

SAKHALIN

river

MANCHURIA

Inner Mongolia

Lake Khanka

CHINA

KOREA

SEA OF JAPAN

YELLOW SEA

Siberian
Temperate forest
Steppe
Himalayan
Tropical
Mixed forest
Mountains

Faunal invasion
The map (left) shows the invasion routes of species which moved into Mongolia and northern China when the Ice Ages came to an end and withdrew northward. Some tropical elements like the leopard, and many bird species, came north; Himalayan forms like the goral and the bear infiltrated through the mountains; the bustard followed the steppe corridor eastward, and the Siberian forms are those which were able to flourish in broadleaf forests. The omnivorous badger is a highly successful, worldwide animal in the mixed forests and the northern hemisphere.

Siberian ground squirrel
Eutamias sibiricus

Goral
Nemorhaedus goral

Himalayan bear
Selenarctos thibetanus

Leopard
Panthera pardus

Badger
Meles meles

Great bustard
Otis tarda

Greatest cat *right*
The Manchurian tiger *Panthera tigris altaica* is the rarest and the largest of all the great cats. It may grow up to 13 feet (4m) long and reach a weight of 715 lb. (325kg). About 120 are thought to remain in its habitat, in the forest basins between the rivers Amur and Ussuri. Fossil remains found in Siberia suggest that the tiger originated there and spread later to other parts of Asia.

Raccoon dog
Nyctereutes procyonoides

Mandarin duck
Aix galericulata

Korean grey hamster
Cricetulus triton

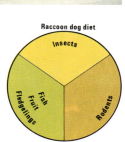

Raccoon dog diet

Insects

Fish Fruit Fledgelings

Rodents

Omnivorous success
The raccoon dog, the single species *Nyctereutes procyonoides* (left) once occurred in eastern Siberia, Manchuria, parts of China and the islands of Japan, where its numbers have now dwindled; it is hunted for its fur and meat. By way of compensation it has now spread, following the clearance of large areas of taiga, across Asia and into Europe where it is now known to occur in Germany. Its success is due to an omnivorous diet (diagram top). Mandarin duck and aggressive Korean hamster also shown.

War victim
Elsewhere in this book reference is made to animal species diminished or threatened by modern war. Among birds whose numbers have been reduced are Asiatic cranes, like the Japanese *Grus japonensis* (right). The Korean War was fought over the historic wintering grounds of the bird, reducing the flocks to a fragile remnant. Their greatest protection comes in eastern countries where they are held in religious esteem by Buddhists.

Cosmopolitans
The thrushes and their relatives the warblers are among the most cosmopolitan of species. (left) The Chinese bush warbler *Cettia diphone* and (right) the whitethroated rock thrush *Monticola gularis*.

Azure-winged magpie
Cyanopica cyanus

Far from its relatives
The azure-winged magpie (above) provides an illustration of the manner in which prehistoric climate changes wiped out species from most of their range, leaving them in widely-separated pockets (map right).

Rich forests of Japan
Unlike mainland Asia, Japan was spared the worst effects of the last Ice Age and this, with a moist climate ranging from cool to warm has given the islands a rich and varied plant life. The number of tree species occurring is 168 compared with 85 in Europe and—even in the densely populated country—forests still cover 60 per cent of the land area.

Hokkaido

Cone

Leaves

C. japonicum male flowers

Umbrella pine *Sciadopitys verticillata*

Honshu

C. japonicum female flowers

Japanese flowering cherry *Prunus serrulata*

Shikoku

Kyushu

Cercidiphyllum japonicum

Trochodendron araloides

Magnolia *Magnolia soulangeana*

Vocal monkey *left*
The intelligent and timid Japanese macaque *Macaca fuscata* is the northernmost of monkey species. About 50,000 are believed to live in Japan. The macaque group has a distinct hierarchy, with a dominant male as leader. *Fuscata* travels in social groups of anything between 30 and 200 animals, feeding on small animals and plants. It is a vocal species. More than 30 different cries having been recorded.

Variety of fishes
The waters of Japan are renowned for their wide variety of fishes, a mixture of tropical Indo-Pacific, and forms from more northern waters. The puffer fish Tetraodontidae is a delicacy called fugu among the Japanese. Northeast Asia is the distribution centre for carps.

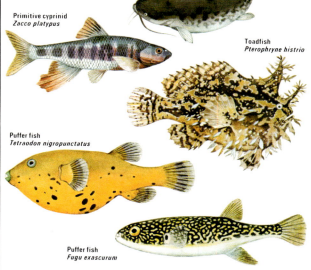

Catfish
Parasilurus asotus

Primitive cyprinid
Zacco platypus

Toadfish
Pterophryne histrio

Puffer fish
Tetraodon nigropunctatus

Puffer fish
Fugu exascurum

115

Southeast Asia
THE ORIENTAL REALM

Southeast Asia

The Himalayas, a young giant among mountain ranges, is a natural divide separating northern and central Asia from another, completely different world – the warm, moist south and southeast, a series of ocean-washed peninsulas dominated by a monsoon climate caused by regions of low pressure over Asia drawing in rain-laden winds from the Indian Ocean. The extreme southeast of the continent forming the islands east to Borneo and Java is the least stable region, a volcanic, fragmented tapestry of islands on a shallow shelf of submerged land. Rich in reminders of the spread and extinction – or threatened extinction – of species, the islands remain among the most rewarding, and intriguing, for naturalists as well as being among the most scenically beautiful. The wildlife of India, geologically a newcomer to the old Asian landmass, provides many illustrations of animal invasion when new, amiable habitats present themselves. And lost in the secret fastness of Szechwan, where the Himalayas tumble away into China, there is a faunal crossroads between north and south and a home for some of the rarest of the world's animals, including the giant panda and the gaudier forms of pheasant. The forests of southeast Asia are the home of one of man's closest relatives, the orangutan, the odd proboscis monkey and other primates whose survival depends on their ability to adjust to man and his ways. Races and species of two of the world's great beasts, the tiger and rhinoceros, cling to diminished habitats dotted across the region.

Mature tiger bathing, Sundarbans, West Bengal

Key to panorama

1 Siamang	20 Silver langurs	39 Binturong
2 Malayan colugo	21 Orang-utan	40 Mangrove snake
3 Flying lizard	22 Sumatran rhinoceros	41 Soldier crab
4 Stick insect	23 Malayan tapir	42 Yellow appias
5 Lesser-green broadbill	24 Banded linsang	43 Prothaeid butterfly
6 Horsfield's tarsier	25 Indian darter	44 Fiddler crabs
7 Green pit viper	26 Sumatran tiger	45 Soldier crab
8 Wreathed hornbill	27 Indian muntjac	46 Mudskipper
9 Leaf insect	28 Sun bear	47 Sword-tailed swallowtail
10 Orchid mantis	29 Jungle fowl	48 Swallowtail
11 Malayan colugo	30 Lesser adjutant stork	49 Atrophaneuran butterfly
12 Flying fox	31 Black-naped blue monarch	50 Mudskippers
13 Great hornbill	32 Fishing cat	51 Male fiddler crab
14 Lar gibbons	33 Malayan moon rat	52 White-breasted water hen
15 Brahminy kite	34 Crab-eating macaques	53 Blue-winged pitta
16 Flying foxes	35 Graphium butterfly	54 Female fiddler crab
17 Prevost's squirrel	36 Salt water crocodile	55 Reticulated python
18 Common tree shrew	37 Malayan small-clawed otter	56 Soldier crab
19 Yellow-crowned bulbul	38 Indian three-toed kingfisher	

Natural vegetation zones

- Mediterranean
- Coniferous forest
- Subtropical rain forest
- Tropical rain forest
- Temperate mixed forest
- Semi-deciduous forest
- Deciduous forest
- Tropical deciduous forest
- Locally wooded savanna
- Grassland steppe
- Short grasses
- Desert scrub
- Barren land

Climatic factors : November to April

HIGH

1036
1032
1028
1024
1020
1016
1012

Climatic factors : May to October

1004
1007
1000
996
LOW

200
150
100
75
50
25
12.5

80
60
40
30
20
10
5

— Isobars
→ Prevailing winds

India: Meeting of East and West

Separated from the land mass of northern Asia by the greatest range of mountains in the world, the Indian subcontinent forms a giant triangular pendant washed by the warm tropical seas of the Indian Ocean. Only two relatively narrow corridors provide passage-ways for land animals to and from the subcontinent; the desert between the foothills of the Hindu Kush and the Arabian sea to the west and the flood plains and delta of the Ganges-Brahmaputra river system to the east.

South of the great alluvial plains across which the Indus and the Ganges carry water from the melting snows of the Himalayas to the Indian Ocean, most of the Indian peninsula is a raised plateau, the Deccan, once covered by open woodland with lusher forest growing along its draining river valleys. It has a monsoon climate with a hot dry 'summer' from March to May, a wet season from June to October and a cooler, dry 'winter' from November to February. The diagram (below) shows how the west coast and the Ganges-Brahmaputra delta receive the brunt of the monsoon and it is in these areas that tropical rain forests occur.

In the perspective of the earth's history this pattern is of recent origin. Tens of millions of years ago India was not even part of Asia. It was an island-continent edging slowly northwards towards Asia across a lost ocean which also isolated Africa from Eurasia. All that remains of the vanished ocean, sometimes known as the Tethys, are the Mediterranean, Black and Caspian seas.

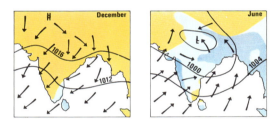

About 15 million years ago India moved up against the southern coast of Asia, the impact forcing a crumpling of the land mass into the towering Himalayas. At the same time, Africa closed with Europe and the Near East (the Alps and the mountains of the Caucasus are evidence of this other great 'merger') and the three land masses of Africa, Eurasia and India became fused together. There then began a great faunal interchange between the three.

West, to Africa, went civets and dogs, rhinos and giraffes and the ancestors of the African baboons and guenon monkeys. From Africa, the elephants moved east. Knowledge is sparse about India's unique contribution to these early interchanges since the tenuous corridor links may often have changed climatically. Certainly a desert barrier, crossable only by specially adapted animals, has existed between India and Africa for the last three thousand years.

Animals living today in the moist forest on the west coast of India are quite closely related to the forest animals of Malaya and Indo-China because there have been tropical forest connections between these areas in recent times. Other species, pushing eastward into India through the northwestern desert, such as the gazelle and jackal, are identical to species found in Africa and the Near East. The wild boar, an adaptable species, occurs throughout much of Eurasia, including India, and the tiger has spread south from chill Siberia, invading India from the east in quite recent times. The Asiatic lion, which arrived from the west, survives only in the forest of Gir reserve.

A subcontinent arrives
Modern evidence suggests that India once formed part of a great southern continent from which it became dis-engaged, moving north over a period of 200 million years. The other land masses, shown in their present form here, will also have undergone changes at the same time.

New species move in
The link-up between India and the land mass of Asia in the Tertiary brought about an invasion of species through corridors in the northwest and northeast and some displacement of the original fauna. The modern fauna of Rajasthan, 'endemic and invader' is shown (below).

Key:
- Arid corridor
- Deccan plateau
- River valleys
- Tropical forest
- Original colonization
- Arid advance
- Chinese influx
- Retreat of original species

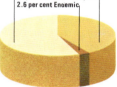

56.4 per cent Palearctic
41 per cent Indo-Malaysian
2.6 per cent Endemic

Fauna of the Indian deserts
The desert areas of the northwest Indian region are the eastern limits of a great arid zone reaching through Persia and Arabia and linking up with the greatest of all deserts, the Sahara. The fauna consists mainly of species which have migrated into it from the lands to the west – hence the presence of the hyena and jackal. The macaque monkey, the only genus of monkey common to both Africa and India, is limited in its range by the availability of water. The elegant Indian gazelle *Gazella dorcas* reaches into the Deccan and the Indian porcupine is widespread throughout the subcontinent.

1 Indian gazelle *Gazella gazella*
2 Small Indian mongoose *Herpestes auropunctatus*
3 Common mongoose *Herpestes edwardsi*
4 Indian porcupine *Hystrix indica*
5 Pale hedgehog *Paraechinus micropus*
6 Striped hyena *Hyaena hyaena*
7 Rhesus macaque *Macaca mulatta*
8 Jackal *Canis aureus*
9 Wild boar *Sus scrofa*
10 Gaur *Bos gaurus*
11 Sloth bear *Melursus ursinus*
12 Giant squirrel *Ratufa indica*
13 Nilgai *Boselaphus tragocamelus* ♂
14 Nilgai *B. tragocamelus* ♀
15 Common langur *Presbytis entellus*
16 Blackbuck *Antilope cervicapra* ♂

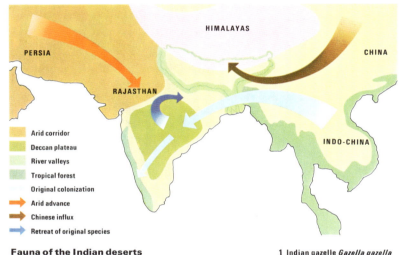

Widespread trotter *left*
The pheasant-tailed jacana *Hydrophasianus chirurgus*, the largest of all lily trotters, has a widespread distribution throughout the Indian subcontinent, from sea level to the high lakes of Kashmir. The yellow patch on its neck intensifies in colour during its nuptials.

Toddy drinker *below*
The palm civet *Paradoxurus hermaphroditus* is a member of one of the most ancient families inhabiting the Old World tropical forests and ranges from India into Burma and Malaya. It is called the toddy cat, for it raids plantation palms which are tapped for toddy.

Symbol of happiness
In a land of legend and simple belief the sarus crane *Grus antigone* is highly esteemed and protected. It mates for life and is the symbol of a happy marriage among the natives of India. The elaborate court-ship dance of the sarus crane is illustrated (below).

Courtship dance of the sarus crane

With a side-to-side sweeping movement the gavial, an Indian crocodile, catches its fish instead of snapping at its prey in the usual way.

Siamese crocodile *Crocodylus siamensis*

Gavial *Gavialus gangeticus*

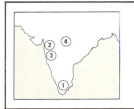  

Local colours
Common though difficult to see, the Indian giant squirrel *Ratufa indica* has a widespread distribution in India. Marked variations in colour have been observed and the locations where they occur, are shown (left).

The amiable deer *above*
Gentle and beautiful, the spotted deer *Axis axis* is endemic to India. The deer move in herds of ten to 30 containing two or three stags and wander into human settlements without fear. They are found throughout the Peninsula south of the foothills of the Himalayas, wherever jungle, grazing and water come together.

Deccan – home of the native animals
Open plain, scrubland and patches of deciduous jungle made up of stunted teak, bamboos and small trees provide the habitat for the fauna of the Deccan plateau, the home of most of India's native animals. Gaur, sambar, the sloth bear and wild dogs are found in the open deciduous hill forests, and in the open country the common fox, mongoose, Indian wolf, palm squirrels and hares are common. Where the region becomes moist and humid in the north, elephant, buffalo and swamp deer occur. The Indian elephant comes from the same stock as its African counterpart.

Naja naja   *Boiga trigonata*

Strikers
The jaw of the lethal cobra *Naja naja* contrasts with that of the less venomous *Boiga trigonata*. The cobra, like sea snakes, is front-fanged or proteroglyphid. The boiga is an opisthoglyph—its enlarged teeth are at the posterior end of the maxilla, and less deadly than the fangs of the cobra.

121

Szechwan: The Lost Horizon

To the east of the Tibetan plateau the ramparts of the Himalayas fall away in a series of mountain ranges which form the highlands of southwestern China and northern Burma. Older than the Himalayas and bathed in the diffuse light of a constantly cloudy sky, the mountains are clothed with broadleaved trees on their lower slopes. At higher altitudes, broadleaves mix with conifers until, towards the treeline where the forest becomes stunted, stands of bamboo and thickets of rhododendron break the conifers. Exposed outcrops of rocks are found at all levels. This is Szechwan, an ancient habitat ranging from the sub-tropical of the valleys to the alpine of the upper meadows which reach up to perpetually snowclad peaks, the world of the Lost Horizon.

The area stands at a great zoogeographical cross-roads. To the south are the subtropical and tropical forests of the Oriental region; to the west, the Tibetan plateau (a distinct subdivision of the Palaearctic region); to the east the lowlands of southern China are a great mixing zone between the Palaearctic to the north and the Orient to the south.

Although the western China highlands are in-habited by animals from all these areas, they also support their own unique fauna. The mountains may have been sheltered from invasion by northern forms during the Pleistocene ice ages, protected by the desert barrier in the continental heartland to the north. In this refuge, cold-climate mammals have survived which have disappeared from other parts of the world. Strange and primitive insectivores burrow through the soil and plunge in the cool streams. This is the home of the giant panda (perhaps a relative of the earliest raccoons) and of the weird goat-antelopes, primitive members of the family Bovidae.

Few zoologists have visited this remote area so that many of the animals are known only from a few museum skins and information on their ways of life is scanty. Many of the first specimens and informa-tion about the animals were gathered by a French missionary, Père Jean Pierre David, in the second half of the 19th Century. Père David is best-known today for the deer named after him, which he en-countered in the Imperial hunting park in Peking in 1865. He is also the man who made the giant panda and the golden snub-nosed monkey *Pygathrix (Rhinopithecus) roxellanae*, another Szechwan animal, known to the western world

Szechwan *left and below* East of Tibet and the young Himalayas, the old habitat of Szechwan is at a cross-roads between Palaearctic and Oriental regions. It is a home for the primitive and the rare, providing niches ranging in climate from the subtropical of the valleys to the snow-clad peaks.

4800 m — 14,200 ft	Snow
4200 m — 13,800 ft	Alpine vegetation
3900 m — 12,800 ft	Rhododendron scrub
3200 m — 10,500 ft	Conifer/Rhododendron forest
2000 m — 6,500 ft	Cloud forest (Bamboo)
1000 m — 3200 ft	Montane Rain forest
	Arid rocky ground

Lesser panda *above* Nocturnal, mild-mannered, the raccoon-like lesser panda *Ailurus fulgens* is at home in the high altitude bamboo forests of southeast Asia. The young stay in the family group for a year until able to forage alone.

Primitive shrews
The undisturbed fastnesses of the Szechwan mountains provide accommodation for several species of primitive insectivores —shrews which live a mole-like subterranean existence and others which are adept swimmers and fishermen. The single species *Anourosorex squamipes*, found from Szechwan south to Tonkin, has long claws with which it builds its own burrows: the web-footed water shrew *Nectogale elegans* occurs only in the southeastern Himalayan streams, where it catches small fish. *Chimarrogale himalayica* is also a fishing shrew.

1 hind-foot
Anourosorex squamipes

2 skull and hind-foot
Nectogale elegans

1 Mole shrew
Anourosorex squamipes

2 Web-footed water shrew
Nectogale elegans

3 Himalayan water shrew
Chimarrogale himalayica

Giant panda
A solitary way of life in the forests of west China makes the giant panda *Ailuropoda melanoleuca* seem rarer than it probably is. It is uniquely adapted to feed on bamboos, its principal diet—strong jaws and an accessory pseudo-thumb (shown above) on its forefoot to grasp the stems. The bear-like panda may be related to the real bears (*Ursidae*).

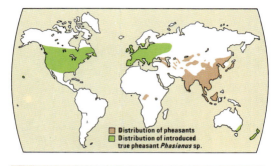

Dispersion of the true pheasant *left*
An ability to acclimatize and breed wherever it has been introduced has made the pheasant one of the world's best-known birds. The true pheasant *Phasianus colchicus* has a natural range from the Black Sea to Japan, and a world-wide 'introduced' range. Szechwan is the probable dispersion centre for the whole family
In their normal state pheasants may be found in a variety of habitats from equatorial lowland forest and dry plains to high mountain woods, plateaus and Asian steppe oases.

Koklass *Pucrasia macrolopha* A medium-sized pheasant found on steep, wooded slopes the koklass ranges throughout the Himalayas from Afghanistan to central China. There are ten forms.

Over 40 races of ring-necked pheasant are known. The white-necked form originates in the east, the dark-necked form (above) in western Asia.

Monal *Lophophorus lhuysi* Largest of the three monals L.lhuysi is limited to mountains of Szechwan on open meadows above forest zone. It roosts in scrub rhododendrons. Now rare.

Tragopan *T. temmincki* Most arboreal pheasant: *temmincki* only in W. China.

Lady Amherst's pheasant *Chrysolophus amherstiae* Gorgeously plumaged, and now more common in captivity than in the wild, *C.amherstiae* is, with *C.pictus* one of the two 'ruffed' pheasants.

Himalayan goat-antelopes
The takin *Budorcas Tibetanus*, serow *Capricornus crispus* and the goral *Naemorhedus griseus* are goat-antelopes and like the chamois, musk-ox and Rocky mountain goat occupy an evolutionary position between true antelopes and goats and sheep.
The takin, a clumsy, heavily built animal, lives in the steepest, most wooded slopes; the coarse-coated goral associates in small parties on upland meadows; the serow, widely distributed south to Sumatra, inhabits thickly wooded gorges.

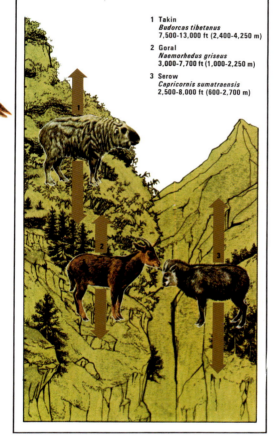

1 Takin
Budorcas tibetanus
7,500-13,000 ft (2,400-4,250 m)

2 Goral
Naemorhedus griseus
3,000-7,700 ft (1,000-2,250 m)

3 Serow
Capricornis sumatraensis
2,500-8,000 ft (600-2,700 m)

Pre-orbital gland *right*
All Cervidae, or deer, have pre-orbital or face glands consisting of sacs containing a strong smelling secretion beneath the eye. They open on to the surface by means of a slit-shaped cavity, most marked in Père David's deer and the muntjac *Muntiacus muntjak* (right).

Musk deer glands
Other deer glands

The musk deer
Unique among the Cervidae the musk deer *Moschus* sp. of eastern Asia mountains has a gland beneath the skin of its abdomen and on the underside of its tail. The gland beneath the stomach contains a valuable secretion from which the perfumery ingredient, musk, is obtained.

123

Life and Death in the Leaves

The rain forests of tropical southeast Asia form no continuous block like those in South America and Africa, though before agricultural man appeared much of Burma and southern Indo-China was clothed in tropical forest. From there, the forest reached down through the finger of the Malay peninsula and scattered itself across the thousands of islands of the East Indies archipelago, with concentrations on the great islands of Java, Sumatra and Borneo. Tropical forest plants and animals survive in many places over this wide, broken area but large stands of forest persist only in places such as Borneo, away from the centres of population, intensive agriculture and wars.

For plants, dispersal across water is not an intractable problem and there are similarities between the rain forests of the East Indies and those of Australasia. But Australia and New Guinea have only recently drifted to their present position east of Java and as yet there has been little faunal interchange across the gaps separating them from the Orient.

The floor of the ocean connecting the Malay peninsula with the islands of Sumatra, Java and Borneo and a host of smaller islands is less than 600 feet (200m) deep and during the ice ages the whole area must have formed a single (or much less broken) land mass. This area, termed Sundaland, today forms a distinct geographical and climatic subregion. Warm and humid, Sundaland has been a centre of evolution for tropical plants and animals of which some species occur only there. Borneo has more unique forms than other parts of the subregion.

The vegetable predators
Graceful and tempting the pitcher plant feeds on the insects which are drawn to it. The cup of leaves or pitcher has nectar on its slippery edges; the doomed insects tumble into a fluid containing a protein-digesting enzyme. In this way the plant obtains vital phosphorus and nitrogen from its victim but it also relies on normal food sources, as with all green plants, on its roots and on photosynthesis.

The lure
The flower-like lid of the plant secretes a nectar and acts as a lure to the unwary insects.

Misumenops spider
There are body snatchers, too; species of crab spider occupy the pitcher and reap a share of its victims.

Glandular area

Glandular cell wall X 7

Digestive fluid

Insect prey

On the scaffold
Above the digestive fluid in the plant, the crab spider constructs a scaffold of silk. It can also retreat for safety into the liquid which does not harm it.

The web
The crab spider constructs its 'scaffold' web in the upper part of the pitcher to catch the falling prey before they are lost in the digestive fluid in the 'basement'.

Fatal flowers
The gaping mouths of a cluster of pitcher plants *Nepenthes ampullaria* (above) into which some insects are tempted; others, like the cockroach, probably tumble in through sheer clumsiness. *Aristolochia* (right) is another death trap for insects, displaying its corolla to attract its victim. Insects are attracted by the sweet nectar around the lip of a pitcher plant (far right).

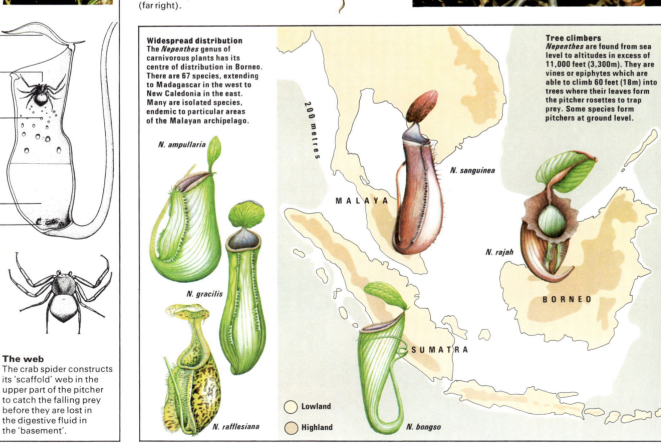

Widespread distribution
The *Nepenthes* genus of carnivorous plants has its centre of distribution in Borneo. There are 67 species, extending to Madagascar in the west to New Caledonia in the east. Many are isolated species, endemic to particular areas of the Malayan archipelago.

N. ampullaria

N. gracilis

N. rafflesiana

200 metres

MALAYA

N. sanguinea

N. rajah

BORNEO

SUMATRA

N. bongso

Lowland

Highland

Tree climbers
Nepenthes are found from sea level to altitudes in excess of 11,000 feet (3,300m). They are vines or epiphytes which are able to climb 60 feet (18m) into trees where their leaves form the pitcher rosettes to trap prey. Some species form pitchers at ground level.

The structure of the Sunda rain forest, and that in other parts of southeast Asia, is similar to that found in other parts of the world. Climbing plants abound with giant lianas reaching up into a canopy that may extend to 100 feet (30m) above the forest floor. Epiphytes festoon the branches of the forest trees, especially in mountain areas where clouds provide moist surroundings far above the water in the soil. The epiphytes obtain the nutrient minerals they require from rotting tree leaves and other material trapped on branches or, like the carnivorous pitcher plants, by digesting the mineral-rich bodies of insects.

Typical large trees of the rain forest have smooth, slender trunks and rounded crowns and, often, buttressed roots to prop them up. The buttresses are necessary because many tropical trees have very shallow rooting systems spreading out through the thin, nutrient-rich surface layers of the forest soil which overly the hard, leached soil beneath. These forests support extremely diverse numbers of species of both plants and animals, but the number of individuals in any one species is correspondingly small.

Small animals, which can exploit the arboreal vegetation more efficiently than large forms, abound in the rain forest. In particular, a huge variety of insect life is present, many of them of spectacular size and colouration. The mammalian fauna is also incredibly varied; in Malaya and Singapore there are more than five times the number of mammal species native to the British Isles.

Stink bug and moth
Leafy look of the stink bug *Pycanum* sp. (left) and the giant atlas moth (above).

Fungus forms *above*
The heat and moisture of the equatorial forest lands provide ideal breeding conditions for a variety of gaudy fungi.

Epiphytic ferns *right*
Fronds of epiphytic ferns provide a close-growing cover of vegetation for numberless tiny forest creatures in southeast Asia.

Weaving ants
Oecophylla smaragdina build their nests from leaves, the edges of which they draw together and seal.

Teamwork
Working as a team the ants first bridge the gap to draw the edges together in building a new nest or repairing a damaged one.

Larvae shuttles.
Finally, using their silk-producing larvae as shuttles, they glue the edges of the breach together.

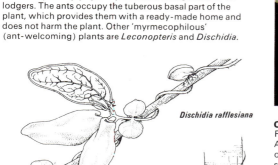

Accommodation available for ants *below*
The Malaysian epiphyte Myrmecodia welcomes ants as lodgers. The ants occupy the tuberous basal part of the plant, which provides them with a ready-made home and does not harm the plant. Other 'myrmecophilous' (ant-welcoming) plants are *Leconopteris* and *Dischidia*.

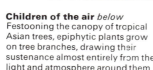

Scale insects
More like a fungal growth than an animal, the insect of the Coccidae family (left) is 'milked' by an ant. The coccid is an adult female, a flattened and degenerate form beneath a waxy protective covering. The males are delicate flying insects. Some species of ant 'milk' the coccid of its waxy secretion as a food. The garden aphids – greenfly and blackfly – are also coccids.

Camponotus compressus   *Aphis gossypii*

Dischidia rafflesiana

Myrmecodia echinata

Lecanopteris carnosa

Milkmaid ant *above and left*
The ant *Camponotus* sp. 'milks' an aphid – by mistake (above). Ants feed each other and confuse the aphid's tail with the head of another ant.

Children of the air *below*
Festooning the canopy of tropical Asian trees, epiphytic plants grow on tree branches, drawing their sustenance almost entirely from the light and atmosphere around them.

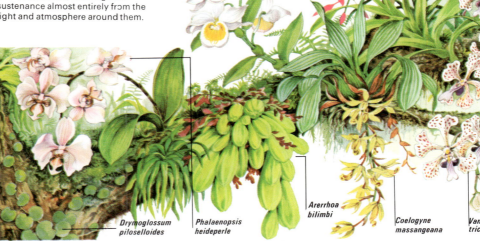

Dendrobium finlayanum

Drymoglossum piloselloides   *Phalaenopsis heideperle*   *Arerrhoa bilimbi*   *Coelogyne massangeana*   *Vanda tricolor*

Acrobats of the Trees

In the stable world of the southeast Asian tropical forest, animals may adapt advantageously to a permanent existence in the forest canopy high above the ground. Unlike the deciduous forests typical of many temperate regions the tropical forest supplies a constant food source in the crown of the trees. Although there may be seasonal fluctuations in the availability of plant species, so many sorts grow in the forest – producing new 'crops' at different times of the year to each other – that there is rarely a total lack of buds, flowers, fruits or leaves.

Over millions of years species of animal have evolved in the tropical forest as specialist climbers and fliers passing all their lives in the canopy, and specialist feeders – always eating fruits, for instance, and perhaps fruits only from a limited range of plant species. Specialization of this kind is not possible in the forests of temperate regions where purely arboreal animals are at a disadvantage in winter months and where a specialist fruit eater would find food only during a few months of the year.

The continuous growing season of the tropical forest produces far greater quantities of plant material than the temperate, and the resident animal population is correspondingly higher, but with many 'specialists' present the numbers of individual species are often quite low. There is intense competition for food supplies and although most types of food are constantly available there are peaks and troughs of abundance, particularly of insects.

Climbing animals that have evolved gliding mechanisms are particularly characteristic of the Oriental jungles which have probably been a stable habitat for a longer period than either the Amazon or the Congo forests. In the great age of reptiles, pterodactyls dominated the air but modern reptiles are not noted for their flying abilities. Yet three types in southern Asia have evolved gliding mechanisms – a snake, an agamid lizard and a gecko.

There are gliding frogs, too. Bats are a widespread group of flying mammals and a host of them dwell in the Asian tropical forests. Many are insectivores exploiting the abundance of insects at all levels of the forest; others are fruit eaters relying on the year-round presence of their food. A unique gliding mammal is the colugo (above right) which is found only in the forests of southeast Asia and is not clearly related to any other mammal. There is a great variety of flying squirrels, but like the snakes, lizards, frogs and colugo they are not true fliers with sustained powers of flight. The considerable distances they can glide, however, are of great use when they are pursued by predators.

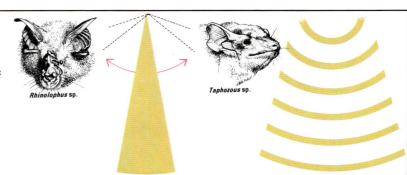

The bat's 'radar'
The demands of highspeed navigation and pursuit of insect food has evolved in the bat, one of the wonders of nature—a system of echolocation far more efficient than the radar of man. On the wing the bat emits signals less than 1/10,000th of a second long, picking up the echo of the signal from its target. The horseshoe bat *Rhinolophus* sp. controls its signal in a sharp beam while sweeping its head. *Rousettus* sp., like most bats, emits a wide, fixed beam.

Rhinolophus sp.

Taphozous sp.

Airborne animals
The freedom of birds to forage and to flee the predator of the rain forest canopy is shared in part by some of southeast Asia's small reptiles, squirrels and frogs. These small vertebrates are not true fliers but have evolved gliding techniques and adaptations to move from tree to tree and to the ground. A gecko, *Ptychozoon* sp. has developed wide flaps of skin on both sides of its abdomen, webbed limbs and toes and a flattened tail to control flight through a 45° descent. An agamid lizard, *Draco* sp. has evolved from a simple green tree lizard into a creature with broad membrane wings, as lovely as a giant butterfly. The coloration of *Draco* varies from species to species but the most brilliantly marked is orange with black spots. The flying squirrel *Aeromys* sp. is mainly nocturnal and uses the gliding membranes between its limbs to help it forage for fruits and nuts in the treetops. The flying frog *Rhacophorus* sp. 'planes' by means of webs between its toes.

Winged fingers *left*
The gliding frog *Rhacophorus nigropalmatus* glides through the trees of Malaysia.

Courtship *above*
Draco volans, the airborne agamid, displays its wings for courtship purposes.

Accomplished
The gliding lemur or colugo (above) is the most skillful glider. (right) The gliding gecko *Ptychozoon* at rest.

Normal

In flight

The gliding snake *Chrysopelea pelias* launches itself into space, controlling its fall by concaving its ventral surface.

Oriental jungles are one of the three great strongholds of the mammalian order Primates, the order to which man himself belongs. The order is typified by grasping hands, large brains, short noses, forwardly-directed eyes and flattened, digital nails. The other two primate **centres** are to be found in the tropical forests of Africa and South America.

Although Asia has fewer species (about 40) than Africa or South America, its species belong to a wider range of distinctive groups. For instance, on the jungle-clad island of Borneo live a loris (family Lorisidae), a tarsier (Tarsiidae), two macaque species (Cercopithecidae, subfamily Cercopithecinae), the proboscis monkey and three langurs (another sub-family of the Cercopithecidae), a gibbon (Hylobatidae) and the orangutan (Pongidae). Tree shrews also occur there, a family of insectivorous and mostly day-active animals which have sometimes been considered as primates. It is now generally agreed that they are not primates but relatives of the African elephant shrews – though to the zoologist they bear resemblances to some of the earliest primates of 70 million years ago.

Primates are typically animals of the warm forests and although some Asian forms inhabit open woodland, human habitation and cool montane forest, the group is predominantly one of tropical rain forest. While their overall habitat is similar they display a great variety of form, **behaviour,** social organization and ecology. These are the results of the evolutionary development of their several lineages over millions of years – and of the adaptation of the surviving forms to the forest conditions which exist today.

Macaque (5) and langur (6)
Through the trees and on the ground the langur walks and runs with a quadrupedal movement. From one tree-top to another, it leaps with a strong propulsive push-off by its hind limbs and may cover distances of up to 40 feet (10m). The species of macaque are rather more terrestrial and move quadrupedally but they are known to climb trees and cliffs in search of food and shelter.

Gibbon (1) and orangutan (2)
The gibbon brachiates, or uses its arms to swing through the branches. The orangutan moves cautiously, walking on treelimbs. It brachiates mainly when it is young.

Loris (3) and tarsier (4)
Using a slow, deliberate movement the loris works its way through the trees, spiralling to avoid projecting branches. It will hang by its feet to collect food. The tarsier leaps energetically in a vertical position, often turning through 180° to land hands and feet first in a neighbouring tree.

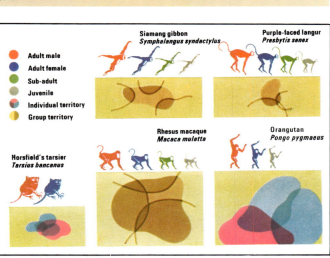

Nocturnal tarsier
The illustration (below) shows the huge eye sockets in the skull of the tarsier, *Tarsius* sp. The eyes of the tarsier are acutely adapted to night vision, and are positioned for maximum range.

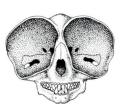

Juvenile

Sub-adult male

Adult male

Faces of the growing orangutan
The huge cheek pads of a mature male orangutan *Pongo pygmaeus* are not known to have any function but are probably 'impression' ornaments. Illustrated are stages of growth.

Social groupings
The tarsier and the orangutan are relatively solitary animals. The territory of the males in each species overlaps those of a few females. The tarsier marks out its territory by urinating on favourite perches. The small social group of the gibbon is in contrast with the macaque's where up to 50 individuals live as one big family. The males impose discipline on the group while the females rear the young and look after them after weaning. This continues the bonds of kinship within the macaque family group.

- Adult male
- Adult female
- Sub-adult
- Juvenile
- Individual territory
- Group territory

Siamang gibbon
Symphalangus syndactylus

Purple-faced langur
Presbytis senex

Horsfield's tarsier
Tarsius bancanus

Rhesus macaque
Macaca mulatta

Orangutan
Pongo pygmaeus

Mangroves: The Moving Forests

Mangrove swamps flourish, a half-world between sea and shore, on sheltered tropical coastlines in many parts of the world. The tangled, stiltlike roots of the mangrove trees and shrubs trap debris brought down by the rivers and retain other detritus washed in by the tide. The enriched mud produced by these ingredients provides a home and food for a characteristic and populous fauna.

The swamp, or mangal, usually shows a clear zonation for the conditions endured by plants at the lower edge of the tide (which floods them daily) different from those farther inland, which are only flooded by a handful of exceptional tides each year. In southeast Asia there are commonly six horizontal zones, each characterized by particular mangrove tree species or group of species.

The main requirement of a mangrove plant is a tolerance to flooding of its root system by sea water. Individual species vary in their acceptance of salt water and some occur only in the upper reaches of estuaries where there is a high admixture of fresh water. The highly specialized root systems are shallow and widespread for most of the oxygen and vital mineral salts are concentrated in the upper layers of mud. Even then, oxygen supplies are inadequate and many mangroves such as *Sonneratia* have developed pneumatophores, 'breathing' projections of the roots which protrude above the surface of the mud. *Sonneratia* is characteristic of the wetter regions of the mangrove where the roots are flooded with the advance of each high tide.

The mangal often adjoins lowland rain forest in the Orient and the two zones share many faunal elements. Animals common on shores where no mangrove occurs may also be found in this muddy forest, but several species are typical mangrove dwellers and are uncommon elsewhere. Most have a marine rather than a terrestrial ancestry and their adaptation to a life half in water and half on land is an indication that the mangal may well have been one of the habitats where evolution from sea dweller to land animal took place.

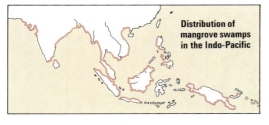

Distribution of mangrove swamps in the Indo-Pacific

Banded sea snake
Laticauda colubrina

Wagler's pit viper
Trimeresurus wagleri

Mangrove snake
Boiga dendrophila

Dog-headed water snake
Cerberus rhynchops

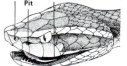

Mangrove snakes *left*
Mangroves provide a meeting place for arboreal snakes and those which have adopted an aquatic way of life. Wagler's pit viper is sluggish when compared with the bird-eating *Boiga*. The dog-headed water snake hunts fish and pursues crabs into their burrows. The pit viper head (below) shows the heat sensory pit between nostril and eye with which it is able to detect its prey.

Nostril Pit Moveable fang (folded back)

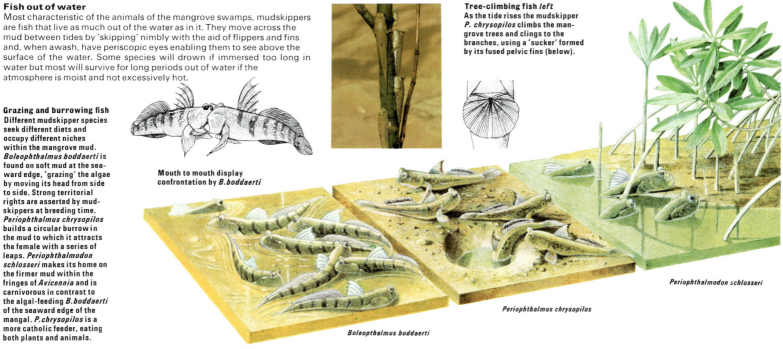

Fish out of water
Most characteristic of the animals of the mangrove swamps, mudskippers are fish that live as much out of the water as in it. They move across the mud between tides by 'skipping' nimbly with the aid of flippers and fins and, when awash, have periscopic eyes enabling them to see above the surface of the water. Some species will drown if immersed too long in water but most will survive for long periods out of water if the atmosphere is moist and not excessively hot.

Grazing and burrowing fish
Different mudskipper species seek different diets and occupy different niches within the mangrove mud. *Boleophthalmus boddaerti* is found on soft mud at the seaward edge, 'grazing' the algae by moving its head from side to side. Strong territorial rights are asserted by mudskippers at breeding time. *Periophthalmus chrysopilos* builds a circular burrow in the mud to which it attracts the female with a series of leaps. *Periophthalmodon schlosseri* makes its home on the firmer mud within the fringes of *Avicennia* and is carnivorous in contrast to the algal-feeding *B.boddaerti* of the seaward edge of the mangal. *P.chrysopilos* is a more catholic feeder, eating both plants and animals.

Mouth to mouth display confrontation by *B.boddaerti*

Tree-climbing fish *left*
As the tide rises the mudskipper *P. chrysopilos* climbs the mangrove trees and clings to the branches, using a 'sucker' formed by its fused pelvic fins (below).

Boleopthalmus boddaerti

Periophthalmus chrysopilos

Periophthalmodon schlosseri

March of the mangroves

Moving forever seaward, the mangrove forests claim new territory for the coastline. The protruding roots of *Sonneratia* retain the soft mud just above the level of low water. Then come species of *Rhizophora* to consolidate the gains, their roots like the flying buttresses of some vegetable cathedral. Finally *Bruguiera* a genus that tolerates infrequent doses of salt water at high spring tides, marks the beginning of permanently reclaimed land.

1 *Sonneratia* zone
  S. griffithii S. alba

2 *Rhizophora* zone
  R. mucronata, R. aspiculata

3 *Bruguiera* zone
  B. parliflora, B. gymnorniza
  B. cylindrica, B. sexangula

4 *Nypa* palms

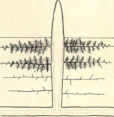

Sonneratia *above*
Pioneer mangrove *Sonneratia griffithii* survives frequent flooding of salt water. Its regiments of air-absorbing pneumatophores (left) form thickets through which it is difficult to walk. (Below) new lateral roots are formed.

Rhizophora *above*
Seeds of the Rhizophora mangrove germinate before they leave the parent plant and thus are ready to take root and become established before the tide can wash them away. The characteristic roots of *Rhizophora* (right) act as props to the trunk of the tree and form a mesh which helps to retain the tide-borne mud. The aerial roots help also to obtain oxygen for the tree.

Bruguiera *above*
Contrasting with the branch-like roots of *Rhizophora* and the protruding pneumatophores of *Sonneratia* is the knee-like structure of the root system of *Bruguiera*, which is found farther from the sea than the other two mangroves.

Birds of the mangrove

Apart from an occasional groan and a snap of its mandibles the painted stork *Ibis leucocephalus* (above) is a silent bird, moving quietly about the mangrove swamp. Another angler of the swamps, the chestnut collared kingfisher (right) is one of a number of the species of the genus *Halcyon* ranging the coast and inland waters of tropical Asia.

Archerfish *Toxotes jaculatrix*

Proboscis monkey
Nasalis larvatus

Dusky langur
Presbytis obscurus

Silvered langur
Presbytis cristatus

Mangrove monkeys *left*

Few monkeys are natives of or frequent the mangal but the mangroves of Borneo are the home of the grotesque and amiable proboscis monkey *Nasalis larvatus*. S.E. Asian langurs such as the silvered langur *Presbytis cristatus* and dusky langur *P. obscurus* feed like *Nasalis* on the mature leaves of the swamp plants.

An adept swimmer *left*
Tracts of water limit the movements of most monkeys but not the proboscis monkey, which will dive into wide rivers and swim across easily. This habit offers excellent opportunities for its one enemy, the crocodile.

Survivor *right*
Top and underside views of the king crab *Carcinoscorpius*. Beneath its carapace it is not a crab at all but an ancient species of spider.

King crab
Carcinoscorpius sp

Dorsal surface

Ventral surface

Shellfish eater *below*
The crab-eating macaque *Macaca uris* spends much of its time in tidal shallows, seeking out crabs and mollusks.

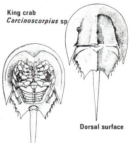

Marksman fish *above*

High and dry on a leaf above water an insect is not safe

from the archer fish which brings it down with a jet of water squirted from its mouth.

Crab-eating frog *left*

Widely distributed throughout the islands of southeast Asia *Rana cancrivora* is a frog which tolerates the partially salty waters of tidal rivers and mangrove. It will enter the sea and eat crabs; onshore its diet consists of scorpions and other insects.

Exhibitionist
Almost all claw and very little else the male fiddler crab genus *Uca* uses its huge cheliped, or claw (which is as big and heavy as the rest of it) mostly for propaganda purposes—to attract a mate or to threaten a rival, but only rarely to fight. The huge and evil-looking weapon does very little damage.

Sideways signalling of *Uca lactea*

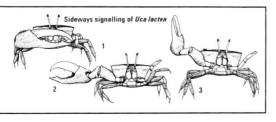

Sundaland: Stepping Stones to Australia

In the history of animals on earth, countless species have appeared, invaded new areas and then, faced with competition from other species, their range has withered and they have become extinct. Some species adapted to a habitat of limited geographical range and never spread very widely; others have thrived in a great variety of diverse environments.

Such adaptable forms may spread across several continents but in millions of years, geological and climatic changes lead to the isolation of some populations. Islands form where a continuous land mass once stood, mountains rise and deserts advance. The isolated populations diverge as they adapt to local conditions and new species are born. Later, unrelated species – perhaps more efficient at exploiting a food source, or escaping predators – appear and in the face of these new pressures, many of the original species become extinct, leaving only a few in existence.

Two examples of spread and incipient speciation to be found in eastern and southern Asia are the tiger *Panthera tigris* and one of its main prey, the wild pig *Sus scrofa*. The tiger probably originated in eastern Siberia at some time during the last million years and spread to form seven different races, west to the Caspian Sea and south and east to the Indian subcontinent, Java and Bali.

The most northern, and the largest, of the tigers is the Manchurian or Siberian tiger; the most southern race, of the island of Bali, is the smallest and darkest. Man, the tiger's only real enemy, has proved deadly and the greatest of all cats is now rare. The Bali race may be extinct and the neighbouring Javan tiger, too has almost vanished.

The wild pig, quarry of the tiger throughout its range, has fared a little better. Wiped out in many parts of Europe it is still common in much of southern Asia and occurs also in North Africa. Southern Asia is also the home of several relics whose ancestors must have had a much wider distribution. The Malay tapir is typical for its nearest relatives are in the Americas.

The rhinoceroses, an antique group, roamed Europe, Asia, Africa and North America millions of years ago but the existing five species, three of them in southern Asia, are becoming increasingly rare.

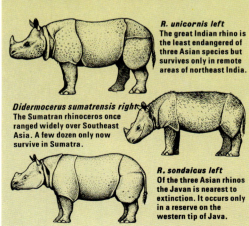

The vulnerable giant *above*
An inhabitant of Asia for more than 50 million years, the rhinoceros faces extinction. Man is destroying its habitat and killing it for the supposedly magic properties of its horn.

R. unicornis left
The great Indian rhino is the least endangered of three Asian species but survives only in remote areas of northeast India.

Didermocerus sumatrensis right
The Sumatran rhinoceros once ranged widely over Southeast Asia. A few dozen only now survive in Sumatra.

R. sondaicus left
Of the three Asian rhinos the Javan is nearest to extinction. It occurs only in a reserve on the western tip of Java.

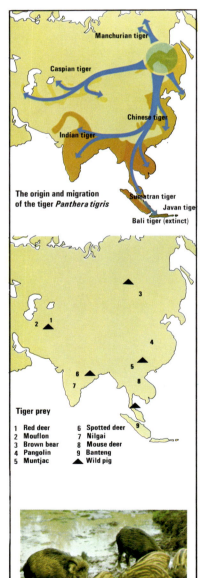

The origin and migration of the tiger *Panthera tigris*

Manchurian tiger
Caspian tiger
Chinese tiger
Indian tiger
Sumatran tiger
Javan tiger
Bali tiger (extinct)

Tiger prey

1 Red deer
2 Mouflon
3 Brown bear
4 Pangolin
5 Muntjac
6 Spotted deer
7 Nilgai
8 Mouse deer
9 Banteng
▲ Wild pig

Dangerous dish
The wild pig *Sus scrofa* is probably the most common item in the diet of tigers. Cornered, it is dangerous and has even killed the tiger.

Racial markings of the tiger
The seven races of tiger (some are shown below) are distinguished by coats of different lengths and markings and by size. The Manchurian tiger reaches 13ft (4m).

Manchurian tiger
Panthera tigris altaica

Sumatran tiger
Panthera tigris sumatrae

Albino Indian tiger
Panthera tigris tigris

Indian tiger
Panthera tigris tigris

Caspian tiger
Panthera tigris virgata

Shifts in the distribution of land and sea on the surface of the earth, the retreat of one, the advance of the other, have been fundamental to the spread and extinction of species of land animals. In the contact zone between the Orient and Australasia a complex inter-action has been in progress for millions of years. Australia and New Guinea, part of the same continental land mass with only a shallow sea separating them, have come close to the tip of the Eurasian plate. This tip is Sundaland, another island area of shallow seas. Where the Asian and Australian plates grind together is an area of frequent earthquakes and eruptions, which have thrown up volcanic islands such as Celebes.

Flying animals, birds, bats and insects, have long exploited the narrowing gap between the areas, and there has been some 'island hopping' by drifting on debris, and swimming. New Guinea has been invaded by Asian species. Some Australasian examples have gone the other way, but the still considerable sea barriers have held the movement of land animals in check. Zoological demarcation lines have been drawn to mark the supposed boundaries of Asia and Australasia – 'Wallace's Line' for the eastern limits of Asian fauna: 'Weber's Line' for the truly Australasian fauna. Between the two is the area of faunal mixing.

The Celebes macaque
An emigrant to the faunal 'no-man's land' between Asia and Australia during the Pleistocene the Celebes macaque *Macaca maurus* probably shares the same ancestors as the pigtailed and crab-eating macaques of nearby Borneo.

Insular variations *above*
Celebes, an island created by volcanic forces, was empty of competition when *M. maurus* arrived. It was able to spread and develop distinctive local forms throughout the 'fingers' of the island. The external features of the Celebesian species of *Macaca* are differentiated more than other macaques. Most striking are the variations of the posterior callosities. Illustration (left centre) shows tumescent *M. maurus*

1 *M. tonkeana*
2 *M. hecki*
3 *M. nigrescens*
4 *M. maurus*
5 *M. nigra*
6 *M. ochreata*
7 *M. brunnescens*

The Greater Sunda Islands, Sumatra, Borneo and Java, were once linked to continental Asia by the Sunda shelf, until the melting of the glaciers caused the sea level to rise. Similarly New Guinea was joined to Australia by the Sahul shelf. Between the two regions is an unstable area of active volcanos where new islands were thrust up.

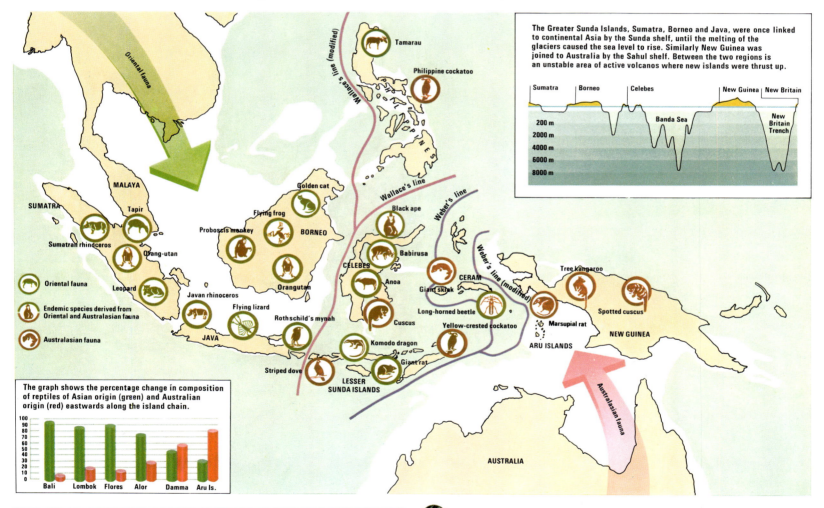

The graph shows the percentage change in composition of reptiles of Asian origin (green) and Australian origin (red) eastwards along the island chain.

Oriental fauna

Endemic species derived from Oriental and Australasian fauna

Australasian fauna

Land bridge links *right*
The frogs of the Philippines demonstrate the appearance and disappearance, over the ages, of land bridges linking the complex of shallow-sea islands which mark the southeastern edge of Asia. Once there were no frogs in the Philippines: now they have a complement of Bornean origin (Palawan has 15 species, Mindanao 16 species, Luzon seven species) most of which will have used 'bridges' which no longer exist. A few may have travelled with man, hitching a lift on his boats

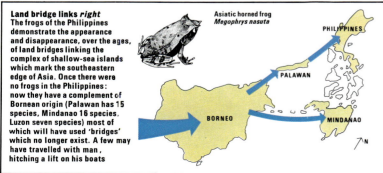

Asiatic horned frog
Megophrys nasuta

Uninhibited fliers
Sea barriers do not inhibit the movement of birds and flying insects. The white-breasted cuckoo shrike *Cora-cina pectoralis* (right) is of a family ranging from Africa through Asia to Australia.

Australia and New Zealand
THE AUSTRALASIAN REALM

Australia and New Zealand

Isolated, geographically, from the rest of the world for at least 50 million years, Australia is the flattest of continents. Just over half its area is more than 1,000 feet (304 metres) above sea-level and this, mostly, is in an arc of mountains reaching from northern Queensland south to the Bass Strait and beyond into Tasmania. To the west of the mountains is the greater part of the continent and those regions that characterize it best; the deserts of sand, stone and clay. At first forbidding and inhospitable, these deserts are friendless only to modern man for they were the arena where nature best demonstrated the effects of a long, predation-free isolation on life forms which have no counterpart in other continents – except, vestigially, in South America to which it may once have been joined as part of a great, southern continent. These life forms were the marsupials, the 'pouched' animals, which radiated into almost as wide a range of forms and niches as those occupied by their more advanced placental counterparts in the rest of the world; and the even stranger monotremes, a breakaway group tracing its ancestry back to that moment in time when the early reptilians were diverging into primitive mammals. Across 1,000 miles of sea from this ancient landmass, the twin islands of New Zealand were developing another distinct theatre of evolution of plants and helpless, peaceful animals – including the reptile relic of a species which vanished elsewhere more than 135 million years ago – unprepared for the invasion of man.

Grey kangaroo in arid scrubland, Eastern Australia

Key to panorama

1 Koala	16 Great grey kangaroo	31 Rainbow lorikeet
2 Sulphur-crested cockatoo	17 Emu	32 Frilled lizard
3 Galah	18 Northern native cat	33 Giant stick insect
4 Cockatiel	19 Brolga crane	34 Little quail
5 Budgerigar	20 Bearded dragon	35 Agile wallaby
6 Kookaburra	21 Red tailed cockatoo	36 Cicada
7 Crimson winged parrots	22 Wedge tailed eagle	37 Marsupial mouse
8 Lace monitor	23 Termite mound	38 Carpet python
9 King brown snake	24 Sand monitor	39 Checkered swallowtail
10 Tawny frogmouth	25 Echidna	40 Jerboa marsupial mouse
11 Sugar glider	26 Rainbow bee eater	41 Death adder
12 Black kite	27 Hairy nosed wombat	42 Holly cross toad
13 Dingo	28 Rufous rat kangaroo	43 Common Australian crow butterfly
14 Wallaroo	29 Turquoise grass parrot	
15 Great red kangaroo	30 Long nosed bandicoot	

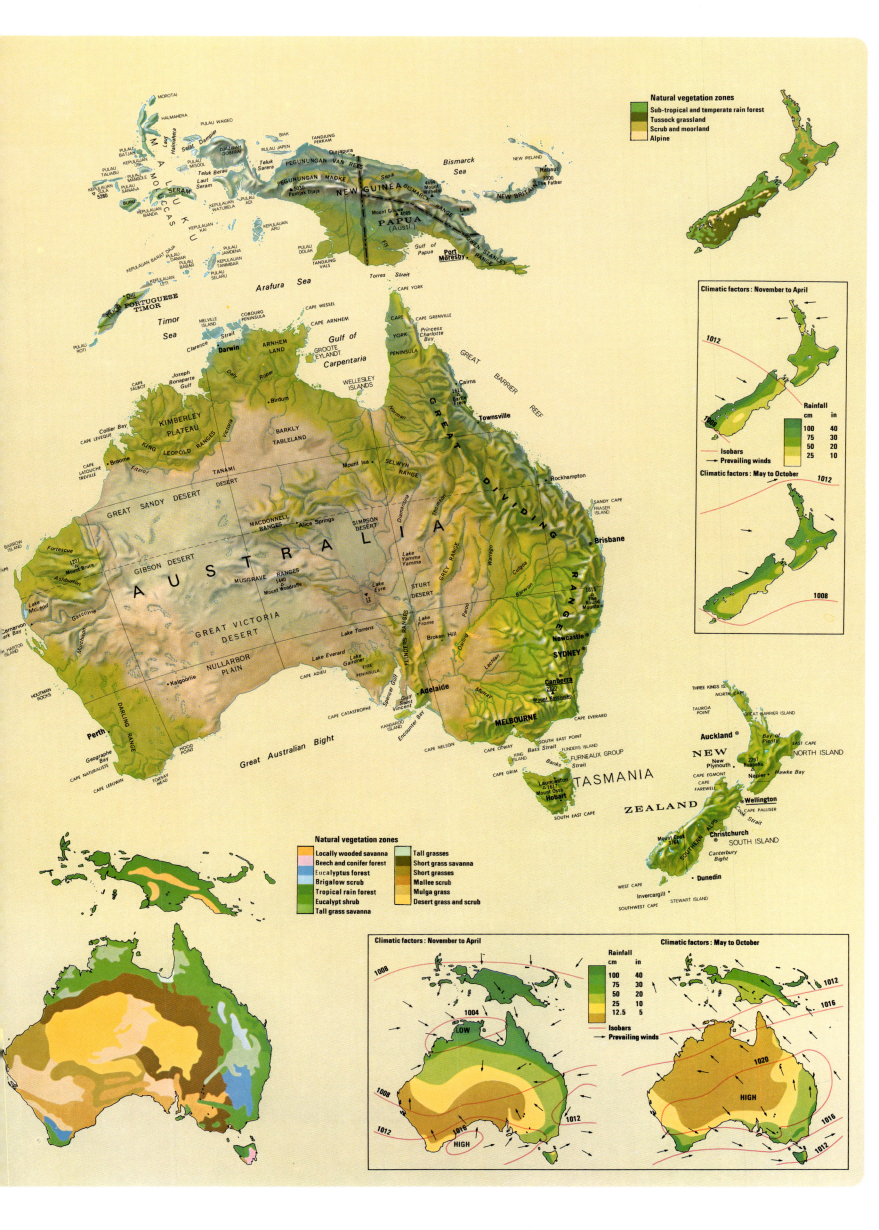

Natural vegetation zones
- Sub-tropical and temperate rain forest
- Tussock grassland
- Scrub and moorland
- Alpine

MOLUCCAS
MOROTAI
HALMAHERA
PULAU WAIGEO
Laut Halmahera
PULAU BATJAN
KEPULAUAN BATJAN
Selat Dampier
DJAZIRAH DOBERAI
PULAU JAPEN
BIAK
TANDJUNG PERKAM
NEW IRELAND
PULAU TALIABU
KEPULAUAN SANANA
PULAU MANGOLE
Teluk Berau
Teluk Sarera
PEGUNUNGAN VAN REES
Djajapura
Sepik
Bismarck Sea
Rabaul
The Father
PULAU MISOOL
PULAU ADI
PEGUNUNGAN MAOKE
NEW GUINEA
BISMARCK RANGE
Mount Wilhelm 4693
NEW BRITAIN
BURU
SERAM
Laut Seram
KEPULAUAN WATUBELA
Puntjak Djaja 5030
Mount Giluwe 4269
Lae
5280
KEPULAUAN KAI
KEPULAUAN BANDA
KEPULAUAN ARU
PAPUA (Austl.)
OWEN STANLEY RANGE
KEPULAUAN BARAT DAJA
PULAU DAMAR
PULAU JAMDENA
PULAU TANIMBAR
PULAU DOLAK
TANDJUNG VALS
Fly
Gulf of Papua
Port Moresby
KEPULAUAN BABAR
KEPULAUAN LETI
PULAU SELARU
PULAU ROTI
PORTUGUESE TIMOR
Dili
Arafura Sea
Torres Strait
CAPE YORK

Timor Sea

Climatic factors : November to April
1012
1008
Rainfall
cm   in
100   40
75   30
50   20
25   10
— Isobars
→ Prevailing winds

Climatic factors : May to October
1012
1008

CAPE WESSEL
MELVILLE ISLAND
COBOURG PENINSULA
CAPE ARNHEM
CAPE YORK
CAPE GRENVILLE
Princess Charlotte Bay
YORK PENINSULA
GREAT BARRIER REEF
Darwin
Clarence Strait
GROOTE EYLANDT
ARNHEM LAND
Gulf of Carpentaria
WELLESLEY ISLANDS
Cairns
Bartle Frere 1611
Daly
Roper
Birdum
Norman
Townsville
CAPE TALBOT
Joseph Bonaparte Gulf
Collier Bay
KIMBERLEY PLATEAU
Victoria
BARKLY TABLELAND
Mount Isa
SELWYN RANGE
CAPE LEVEQUE
KING LEOPOLD RANGES
Rockhampton
Broome
Fitzroy
TANAMI DESERT
GREAT DIVIDING RANGE
CAPE LATOUCHE TREVILLE
GREAT SANDY DESERT
SANDY CAPE
FRASER ISLAND
BARROW ISLAND
Fortescue
MACDONNELL RANGES
Alice Springs
SIMPSON DESERT
Diamantina
Mount Bruce 1227
Ashburton
GIBSON DESERT
A U S T R A L I A
Lake Yamma Yamma
Brisbane
CAPE
Gascoyne
MUSGRAVE RANGES 1440
Mount Woodroffe 12
Lake Eyre
STURT DESERT
GREY RANGE
1615 The Mount Kosciusko
Lake McLeod
Murchison
GREAT VICTORIA DESERT
Lake Frome
Paroo
Warrego
Culgoa
Barwon
Carnarvon Shark Bay
DIK HARTOG ISLAND
Lake Torrens
FLINDERS RANGES
Broken Hill
Darling
Lachlan
Newcastle
HOUTMAN ROCKS
Kalgoorlie
NULLARBOR PLAIN
Lake Everard
Lake Gairdner
EYRE PENINSULA
Murray
SYDNEY
Canberra 2253
Mount Kosciusko
DARLING RANGE
CAPE ADIEU
Adelaide
MELBOURNE
CAPE EVERARD
Perth
Geographe Bay
Spencer Gulf
Gulf Saint Vincent
CAPE CATASTROPHE
KANGAROO ISLAND
Encounter Bay
CAPE NELSON
SOUTH EAST POINT
FLINDERS ISLAND
FURNEAUX GROUP
CAPE NATURALISTE
CAPE LEEUWIN
TORBAY HEAD
HOOD POINT
Great Australian Bight
CAPE OTWAY
KING ISLAND
Bass Strait
Banks Strait
TASMANIA
CAPE GRIM
Launceston 1611 Mount Ossa
Hobart
SOUTH EAST CAPE

NEW ZEALAND
THREE KINGS IS.
NORTH CAPE
TAUROA POINT
GREAT BARRIER ISLAND
Auckland
Bay of Plenty
EAST CAPE
NORTH ISLAND
New Plymouth
Ruapehu 2797
Napier
Hawke Bay
CAPE EGMONT
CAPE FAREWELL
Wellington
CAPE PALLISER
Cook Strait
Mount Cook 3764
SOUTHERN ALPS
Christchurch
SOUTH ISLAND
Canterbury Bight
WEST CAPE
Dunedin
Invercargill
STEWART ISLAND
SOUTHWEST CAPE

Natural vegetation zones
- Locally wooded savanna
- Beech and conifer forest
- Eucalyptus forest
- Brigalow scrub
- Tropical rain forest
- Eucalypt shrub
- Tall grass savanna
- Tall grasses
- Short grass savanna
- Short grasses
- Mallee scrub
- Mulga grass
- Desert grass and scrub

Climatic factors : November to April
1008
1004
LOW
1008
1012
1016
HIGH
Rainfall
cm   in
100   40
75   30
50   20
25   10
12.5 5
— Isobars
→ Prevailing winds

Climatic factors : May to October
1012
1016
1020
HIGH
1016
1012

Marsupials: Masters of Adaptation

When a plant or animal group breaks into a new environment it escapes from the pressures of competition for food and the way of life in its old environment. The breakthrough can be geographical, in the case of invasion of a new land area, or anatomical where the perfection of some new structure allows a new way of life; for example, wings. In each case the group shows a rapid increase in the number of species. When this occurs a whole new range of types appear.

This pattern of evolution is called adaptive radiation and is demonstrated by the marsupial fauna of Australia. During the early Mesozoic (150–200 million) years ago, the mammal group evolved, although where is not clear. The great southern continent broke up about this time and it is thought that the marsupials spread from South America to Australia by passing through Antarctica, which was not then the icy continent it is today. The three continents have separated over the past 100 million years and Australia and New Guinea have since been moving north towards the Equator and southeast Asia.

No eutherian, or placental, mammals seem to have passed into Australia by the same route as the marsupials, which were left, unhindered by competition, to adapt and to radiate throughout a whole range of ways of life and ecological niches. Some plants seem also to have seized their opportunities in Australia. The eucalypts and acacias (although found not only in Australia) have radiated to give all types of tree and shrub and each has about 400 species living from the treeline in the Australian Alps to the driest part of the central desert. Both are adapted to resist fire, a common feature of an arid environment. It would seem that both groups entered the continent early in its development, either before the evolution of, or isolated from, the advanced flowering plants which dominate the rest of the earth.

Among the vertebrates, each class has undergone an adaptive radiation as it has developed the key anatomical features which separate it from its ancestors. Jaws, independence from water, development of a warm body temperature and internal gestation are some of the advances made by the vertebrates and within the classes, families and genera, similar evolutionary patterns have taken place on a smaller scale.

Similarities between marsupial and placental . . .

In the absence of competition from placental animals the marsupials have diverged into every ecological niche. The requirements of the anteater, for example, have resulted in its development of powerful digging claws, long snout, narrow tongue and dense fur for protection against ant bites. But the same demands apply to both the marsupial and placental versions with the result that there is a remarkable resemblance between the two groups wherever they are found, for they share the same way of life. The marsupial fauna of Australia includes examples which in many ways are almost identical to non-marsupial forms: dog-like *Thylacinus*, cat-like *Dasyurus*, mole-like *Notorcytes*, shrew-like *Antechinus*, among others.

Mole Eurasia

Dormouse Africa

Tamandua South America

Long nosed bandicoot

Numbat

Marsupial mole

Pigfooted bandicoot

Mongoose Africa

Tasmanian devil

Rabbit eared bandicoot

Hand

Tiger cat

Feet

Crested-tailed marsupial mouse

Tasmanian wolf

Fat tailed marsupial mouse

Terrestrial
Arboreal
Herbivorous
Subterranean
Insectivorous
Carnivorous

The platypus – an echo of prehistory

The duckbilled platypus has characteristics of both reptiles and mammals and echoes a time, perhaps 150 million years ago, when certain lines of reptile began to evolve into mammals – the synapsids. The drawing (below) compares shoulder bones and reproductive organs of the platypus with past and present reptiles.

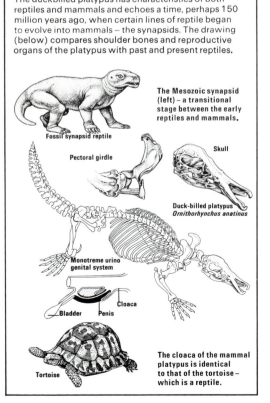

Fossil synapsid reptile

The Mesozoic synapsid (left) – a transitional stage between the early reptiles and mammals.

Pectoral girdle

Skull

Duck-billed platypus *Ornithorhynchus anatinus*

Monotreme urino genital system

Bladder Cloaca Penis

Tortoise

The cloaca of the mammal platypus is identical to that of the tortoise – which is a reptile.

Marsupial and monotreme

Two endemic animals of Australia are the rat kangaroo *Aepyprymnus rufescens* (left) and echidna *Tachyglossus aculeatus* (below). one of the most primitive mammals

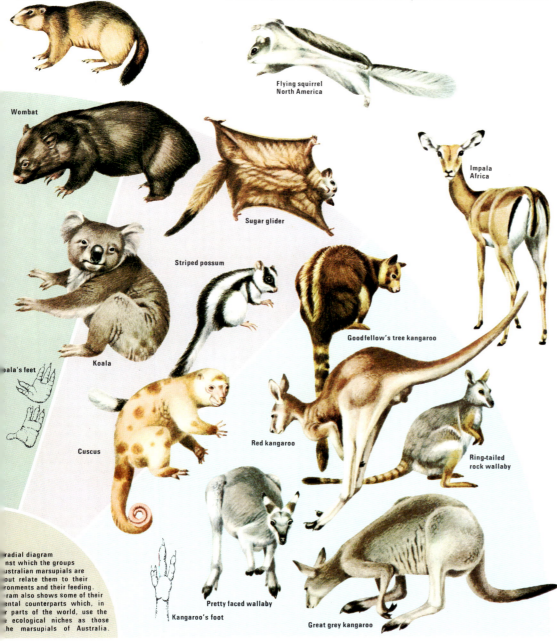

. . . and the differences

The grassland herbivores in continents other than Australia are made up largely of grazing placentals which seek their safety in numbers and in their ability to escape rapidly from predators; for example the antelopes and zebras of the African savanna. The llamas and vicuñas of South America behave similarly – and so do the red and grey kangaroos of Australia, except that the Australian marsupials have an entirely different form of locomotion. Another contrast, among the arboreal herbivores, is provided by the Australian possums and the gliders, which are the marsupial equivalents of the squirrels, the marmosets and the monkeys in other regions. Outside Australasia, marsupials are limited to the Americas.

Woodchuck or Marmot North America

Flying squirrel North America

Wombat

Impala Africa

Sugar glider

Koala

Striped possum

Koala's feet

Cuscus

Goodfellow's tree kangaroo

Red kangaroo

Ring-tailed rock wallaby

Pretty faced wallaby

Kangaroo's foot

Great grey kangaroo

radial diagram nst which the groups ustralian marsupials are out relate them to their ronments and their feeding. am also shows some of their ental counterparts which, in r parts of the world, use the ecological niches as those he marsupials of Australia.

Invasion and isolation

Vegetational cover dictates the spread and in some cases the isolation of invading species. Australia's main zones of entry have been through the plant-rich northern zone the Torresian invasion, and through the temperate forest cover of southwest and southeast Australia, known as the Bassian invasion.

Torresian region

Eyrean region

Bassian region

The nature and density of plant cover determines the distribution of mammals. The Eyrean region – the great Australian desert – has acted as an overall barrier, but at one time was less extensive.

O. unguifera

O. fraenata

O. lunata

E. caudata

Nail-tail wallabies Onychogalea sp.

E. macrura

The nail-tail wallabies have become three distinct species, having followed vegetational cover which was once continuous and is now broken – isolating them to develop separately (left).

Pygmy phalangers Eudromica Cercartetus

C. n. concinnus

C. n. nanus E. lepida

The pygmy phalangers invaded from the north. After spreading widely in eastern Australia they became isolated in five species and found only in rain forest areas (right).

Mouse and possum

Similar in size and shape to the common mouse, the marsupial mouse *Antechinus flavipes* (above) feeds on a cicada. It is an efficient killer of mice and large insects. Leadbeater's possum *Gymnobelideus leadbeateri* (right) is one of Australia's rarer animals. It clings to the branches of forest trees, using its wide and spatulate fingers and toes. It relies on these pads, rather than claws, for climbing the branches.

Non-marsupial rats, bats, mice – and dog

Overshadowed by the continent's unique range of marsupials which radiated, unhindered, into many forms over countless centuries, Australia's placental animals (some are shown on this page), are comparatively new arrivals and will not have changed much since they first came to the continent.

Water rat *above*
The water rat *Hydromys chrysogaster* lives in river bank burrows and eats crustaceans, frogs, fish and birds' eggs.

Delicate mouse *below*
Small pebbles are placed around its nest to catch the dew, by the delicate mouse *Leggadina delicatula*.

The stick rat below *Leporillus conditor* constructs complicated nests of sticks to breed, and for defensive purposes.

The dingo *below right*
Australia's largest carnivore, the dingo *Canis dingo* was probably introduced by early man.

Flying fox *below*
Bananas form a popular part of the diet of the flying fox, or fruit bat *Pteropus poliocephalus*.

Tropical Queensland and New Guinea

A narrow, shallow channel, the Torres Strait, separates the mainland of Australia from New Guinea, an ancient continental island which, next to Greenland, is the largest in the world. There are vegetational and faunal affinities between New Guinea and the northeastern coastal areas of Australia. Time and again in prehistory they were joined. Those neighbouring areas apart, no greater contrast could exist than between the vast, flat desert regions of the island continent and the mist-clad montane forests that cover most of New Guinea.

The island of New Guinea is nearly 1,500 miles (2,200km) long and is part of the Australian geological 'raft'; that is to say, it has been moving northward over ages of time toward the southeastern fringes of Asia. Echidna, tree kangaroos, cuscuses, Taipan snakes, cassowaries, birds of paradise and their relatives the bowerbirds, are found on either side of the Torres Strait.

Numerous birds have made the island-hopping transition from southeast Asia, and New Guinea is particularly rich in avian species. Of more than 900 species to be found in the Australia-New Guinea region, slightly more than half are to be found in New Guinea, although Australia is geographically ten times its size. Rich though the island is, however, there is an absence of some major groups of birds found in other tropical forests of the world. Trogons, for example, are missing, as are woodpeckers, whose role in New Guinea is taken by the small, stiff-tailed parrots which are found nowhere else. Notable among the mammal absentees are the monkeys. Their niche is occupied by the much older, prehensile-tailed arboreal phalangers.

A backbone of mountain ridges, concealing forest and grassland valleys not penetrated until the advent of the airplane, reaches above 16,000 feet (5,000m), affording an alpine contrast with the dripping montane and lowland rainforests which are the island's predominant cover. Some upland valleys, unknown to the outside world until recently, are the home of primitive peoples' whose simple way of life is now under a fatal pressure.

Relict plant and fruit trees

The landmass of New Guinea – which has undergone climatic change in recent times (see diagram right) – shows the typical gradations of vegetation, from the nival (permanent snow) tundra, subalpine and montane forest, to lowland rainforest. Relict plants abound, including *Araucaria cunninghamii, Phyllocladus hypophylla* and *Drymys winteri*. The lowland forests are rich in fruit-bearing trees ; coconuts fringe the beaches, bananas and pawpaw form dense groves with the nipa palm and breadfruit. Habitats thus range from the sparse and cold to the lush and humid.

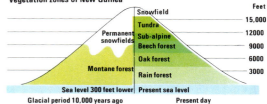

Vegetation zones of New Guinea

		Feet
	Snowfield	15,000
Permanent snowfields	Tundra	
	Sub-alpine	12000
	Beech forest	9000
	Oak forest	6000
Montane forest	Rain forest	3000
Sea level 300 feet lower	Present sea level	

Glacial period 10,000 years ago   Present day

Pioneer plant *below*
The pandanus palm is a pioneer plant, growing in deep sand or rocky crevices, throughout the west Pacific islands.

Palm seed eater *below*
The great palm cockatoo *Probosciger aterrimus* feeds on pandanus palm seeds splitting them delicately in two.

Dangerous giant *right*
The giant, flightless and sometimes dangerous Cassowary *Casuarius casuarius* also feeds on New Guinea pandanus.

Phyllocladus hypophylla

Araucaria cunninghamii

Drymys winteri

Coconut palm
Cocos nucifera

Nipa palm
Nipa fruticans

Areca palm
Areca catechu

Papaya
Carica papaya

Banana
Musa sapientum

Bread fruit
Artocarpus incisa

Bowenia spectabilis

The crows of heaven

Across the water barriers of prehistory a drab, crowlike bird made its way from Asia to New Guinea. In its new, isolated home, it founded a family which has evolved into one of nature's most spectacular wonders, the Paradisaeidae, or birds of paradise. Although four species are to be found in the northern forests of Australia, New Guinea is their true home. Some, like the magnificent and the Wilson's birds of paradise, are widespread over the drier lowlands of the island; the dramatic twelve-wired bird of paradise frequents mangroves. Others, like the sickle-bills and the King of Saxony's bird of paradise, are found in mountain forests. Their incredible display techniques, three of which are shown (below), are explained biologically as elaborate recognition marks between species well known for their polygamous and promiscuous habits.

Birds of Paradise distribution

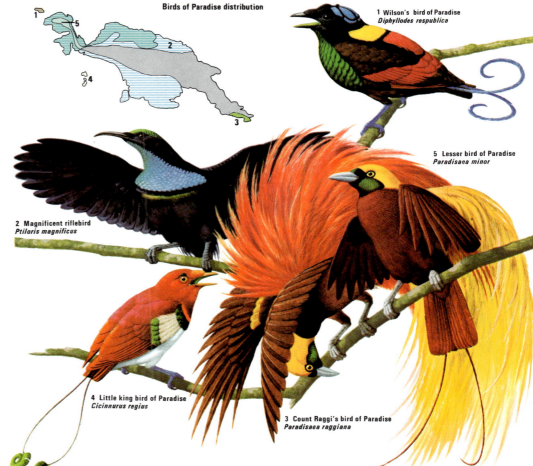

1 Wilson's bird of Paradise
Diphyllodes republica

5 Lesser bird of Paradise
Paradisaea minor

2 Magnificent riflebird
Ptiloris magnificus

4 Little king bird of Paradise
Cicinnurus regius

3 Count Raggi's bird of Paradise
Paradisaea raggiana

Sicklebill
Epimachus fastosus

Blue bird of Paradise
Paradisaea rudolphi

Lesser superb bird of Paradise
Lophorina superba

Arboreal phalangers

The cuscus *Phalanger maculatus* (left) and the sugar glider *Petaurus breviceps* (below) are found either side of the Torres Strait.

Orientated nest *above right*
The termite *Amitermes meridionalis* builds a mound, flat side north-south, to produce cool conditions during heat of the day.

Breeding prolifically – to survive

Hunted by man for its flesh, its eggs and young an easy meal for land and marine predators, the green turtle *Chelonia mydas* breeds prolifically. The female hauls ashore after dark to lay its eggs above the tide line before returning to mate again with the male offshore. Female turtle breeding sequence (right).

Young turtle fanciers *right*
As the young green turtles head for the sea they provide easy pickings for the goanna monitor lizards *Varanus* sp. and the predatory Dominican gull, *Larus dominicanus*.

Dominican gull
Larus dominicanus

Sand goanna
Varanus sp.

A female heads for sea after laying the first batch of eggs.

A nest hole up to three feet deep is excavated in the sand.

Up to seven batches of 100 eggs may be laid during one season.

After hatching, the young turtles work together to reach the surface.

By instinct the young turtles head straight for the sea.

Once in the sea many young fall prey to predatory fishes.

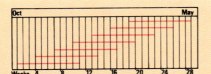

139

Outback: The Arid Interior

Most of Australia is arid. Sparse, desert-like land covers more than two-thirds of the continent, but very little of it is true, or totally lifeless desert. The principal factors which have been instrumental in creating this vast, arid 'outback' are the Great Dividing Range of mountains in the eastern part of the continent - and the cold sea currents which wash the western shore of Australia.

The eastern mountains play their part by forcing the moist, southeasterly trade winds from the Pacific to shed their contents on the eastern seaboard so that the wind flowing on beyond the mountains has no moisture left. The westerly winds which approach the continent from the southern Indian Ocean are chilled by cold currents flowing up from the subpolar waters and thus, in turn, carry no moisture.

Of all continents (with the exception of Antarctica) Australia receives the least average amount of rainfall each year. It is most abundant in the temperate southeast, but very little of the desert as a whole receives less than five inches (12.7 cm) annually. The most northerly of the desert areas may receive as much as 25 inches (63.5 cm).

Arid Australia is made up of five different types of desert - sand, stony, mountain, shield and clay plains. The accompanying map describes the distribution of these regions which blanket the whole of the centre of the continent. Each is the creation of the climate which, by means of the atmospheric forces of wind, rain, frost and temperature changes, has weathered the upper layers of the earth's crust.

Desert types

- Stony desert
- Sand desert
- Mountain desert
- Shield desert
- Claypan desert

Distribution of desert regions in Australia (above). All five of the principal land forms in the continent have a widespread 'discontinuous' coverage. Much coastline is desert-free.

Venomous snakes *left*
The mulga snake *Pseudechis australis* is one of Australia's profuse Elapids, or front fanged snakes. More than 70 species of this highly venomous group exist there, more than in any other continent. The heart of the Australian landmass (below) near Alice Springs.

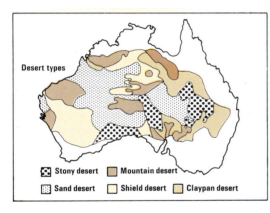

Sand desert

Stony desert

Mountain desert

Shield desert

Claypan desert

Sand deserts of Australia consist largely of parallel ridges running with the prevailing winds. Desert oak *Casuarina decaisnea* (1) and mulga *Acacia aneura* (2) grow in the inter-ridge corridors and cane grass *Zyglochloa paradoxa* (3) binds the ridge caps together. Most widespread of all plants is Spinifex grass *Triodia pungens* (4).

Residual mountain ranges harbor small pockets of water-dependent vegetation. Beside the deep gorge pools grow the plants *Livistona mariae* (5), and nearby the white ghost gums *Eucalyptus papuana* (6), unchanged since earliest times, with *Macrozamia macdonnelli* (8). The tea tree *Melaleuca glomerata* (7) and salt bush *Atriplex* (9) grow close to clay plain salt pans.

Sturt's desert pea *Clianthus formosus* (10) mulla mulla *Trichinium* sp. (11) and parakeelya *Calandrinia* (12) grow on the clay plains.

Animals are far more common in desert areas than they seem, because they are mostly of nocturnal habit. The period just after dark and just before dawn are the times of maximum activity. During the cold of the night and the heat of the day they retreat to underground burrows to escape extremes of temperature.

Most desert vertebrates can survive on little or no drinking water since they are adapted to obtain and retain water from food and from the digestion of fats. Kangaroos, like desert ungulates, recycle nitrogen compounds (rather than excreting them in urine), preventing the wastage of water in removing toxic metabolic nitrogen compounds as non-desert animals must do. Smaller vertebrates may avoid the extreme summer temperatures by aestivating – the summer equivalent of the hibernation adopted by Arctic vertebrates.

The need to range widely for food and the impoverished nature of the vegetational cover provide the reason why most Australian animals move rapidly. Not only kangaroos but some smaller vertebrates such as rodents and lizards, have developed long hind limbs and stabilizing tails for rapid, bipedal movement. Many of the smaller animals harvest and store food against times of drought and – because a lack of cover stresses the importance of sight and sound for protection – acute vision and enlarged ears, as in the rabbit-eared bandicoot, are commonplace. Adaptive coloration is one of the most important survival factors in any region that lacks shelter. In general all desert animals, with few exceptions, are marked to blend with their habitual surroundings.

Airborne predators
The grey goshawk *Falco hypoleucos* (right) and the peregrine falcon *Falco peregrinus* (below) prey on other desert birds, small marsupials and reptiles. As raptors they do not need to drink water, gaining it from the bodies of their victims. The peregrine is the world's widest-ranging diurnal land bird, present with little variation in behaviour or appearance from the Arctic to the far southern hemisphere.

The phascogale *right*
Both prey of hawks and, in turn, predator of insects, birds, rodents and lizards, Swainson's phascogale *Antechinus swainsonii* is a brush-tailed marsupial. Phascogales of one species or another are found throughout the Australian continent.

Spiral nest *right*
The desert scorpion *Urodacus yaschenkoi* digs a spiral burrow in the sand to a depth of about 3ft (1m), with the base of the nest in permanently moist sand, where it remains during the heat of the day. At night it catches insects at its 'front door'.

Dual-purpose tail *above*
The tail of the rat kangaroo *Bettongia* sp. has a dual adaptation. It stores fat against adverse conditions and is also prehensile, for carrying nesting material.

All four limbs used in pursuit of prey by marsupial mouse *Antechinomys*.

Placental rodent *Notomys* leaps elegantly, using hind limbs.

Brief lives *right*
The three Australian crustacea dwell in freshwater desert pools, living their lives out between the brief rainfalls and the evaporation of the water. Their eggs, in contrast, survive high, dry temperatures, often for years. The catholic frog *Notaden bennetti* (far right) emerges from the soil after heavy showers.

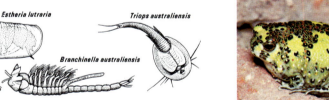

Geckos, skinks and legless lizards
Australia's huge deserts are rich in their number and variety of lizards, the animal group which has made the most successful adjustment to existence in arid conditions. Bizarre geckos, velvety skinks and the confusing legless lizards (which look more like snakes) are not often seen despite their numbers for most only emerge to feed nocturnally.

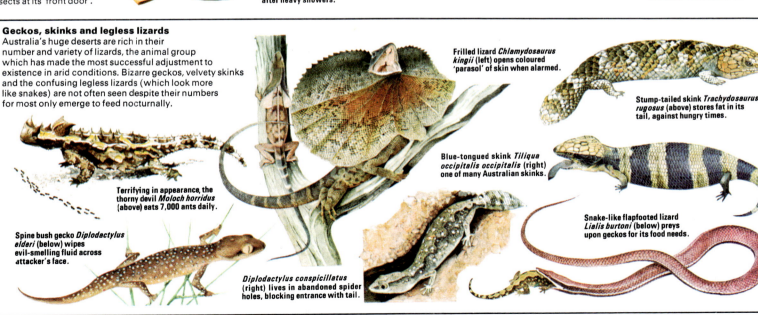

Frilled lizard *Chlamydosaurus kingii* (left) opens coloured 'parasol' of skin when alarmed.

Stump-tailed skink *Trachydosaurus rugosus* (above) stores fat in its tail, against hungry times.

Blue-tongued skink *Tiliqua occipitalis occipitalis* (right) one of many Australian skinks.

Snake-like flapfooted lizard *Lialis burtoni* (below) preys upon geckos for its food needs.

Terrifying in appearance, the thorny devil *Moloch horridus* (above) eats 7,000 ants daily.

Spine bush gecko *Diplodactylus elderi* (below) wipes evil-smelling fluid across attacker's face.

Diplodactylus conspicillatus (right) lives in abandoned spider holes, blocking entrance with tail.

Courtship and Reproduction

The courtship behaviour of the bowerbirds of Australia and New Guinea is at once remarkable and attractive. The elaborate activities indulged in by the males at breeding time range from the conventional nest-building behaviour of the catbird to that of the satin bowerbird, which builds a walled enclosure festooned with brightly-coloured objects of all kinds.

Favourite colours are blues and reds and pieces of plastic, broken glass, cigarette packets and even note-paper with blue writing have been put to use. Another species prefers white bones, stones and shiny nails and has been known to steal cutlery and car keys. Yet another has been seen to shred a twig and, using it like a brush, has coated the interior of the bower with saliva and coloured soil, to give it a painted appearance.

Once a mate has been attracted, the decorating stops and the female is left to get on with the mundane task of building the actual nest of twigs. There are a number of mud nest builders among Australian species, including the magpie lark and the white-winged chough. Other birds collect spider webs and weave the threads into a tough but flexible hanging nest, disguised with leaves and twigs. Most birds nest in hollow trees, as the common eucalypts have a tendency to become hollow, through termite attack.

The bowerbirds
The regent bowerbird *Sericulus chrysocephalus* (right) lives in the dense jungles of Queensland and New Guinea. The female is much less conspicuous than the male – a survival factor which protects her and her young from predators at breeding time. The satin bowerbird *Ptilonorhynchus violaceus* (below) paints its bower with a mixture of saliva and earth using a frayed twig as a brush – a rare example of tool use by a bird.

Building the bower *below*
Clearing an area about three feet (1m) across the male satin bowerbird begins the construction of his tempting grotto on a mat of grass and twigs. Into this he inserts interlocking upright sticks to form a short tunnel, and 'paints' the inner wall. Brightly coloured objects are placed at the tunnel entrance.

Building groups
Bowerbirds are grouped into four classes, according to their type of bower – the stage makers, the maypole builders, the avenue builders (like the satin bowerbird) and those – the primitive catbirds, so called for their mewing cries – that build no bowers at all.

Courtship display *left*
When a female comes to call the male bowerbird attends her during her inspection of his handiwork and then displays with ritual movements, including wingspreading. If his overtures are successful the female sits on the floor of the bower. In courtship, bowerbirds are considered, evolutionarily, to be highly developed.

A practical nest *right*
Sexual union takes place in the bower if the courtship has been successful. Once the female is fertile she leaves the bower and constructs a simple but practical nest. Two eggs are laid and incubated by the female. She also tends the chicks until they are able to fend for themselves.

Newton's bowerbird
Prionodura newtoniana

Orange-crested gardener
Amblyornis subalaris

Macgregor's bowerbird
Amblyornis macgregoriae

Instinctive temperature control
The mallee fowl *Leipoa ocellata* is an 'incubator' bird. It does not hatch out its eggs by normal means but places them in a laboriously-prepared mound of rotting vegetation and sand, depending on the heat of decomposition and the sun to hatch them. The initial hole is made by pairs after the first autumn rains, and filled with damp leaves and other organic matter. This is covered by layers of heat-insulating earth as, with a remarkable instinct, the male maintains the nest temperature at around 34°C.

Tending the incubator
The hen begins laying in early spring at the rate of one egg about every six days, over a period of eight months. Through-out this time the male mallee fowl opens and closes the mound, applying its innate knowledge to control the temperature. During the heat of the summer the male strips the top-soil during the cool early hours to allow the heat of decomposition to escape. The cool earth is piled back during the course of the day to close in the heat of decomposition by nightfall. In the cool months of winter the process is reversed, as the diagram below demonstrates.

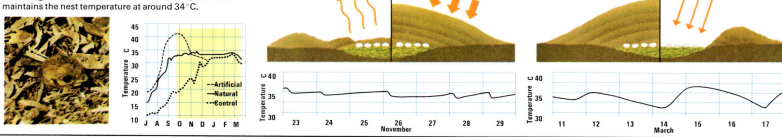

Australia's long history of geographic isolation – for at least 50 million years – has given protection to a number of primitive forms of which perhaps the most remarkable are the monotremes, the platypus and the echidna – egg laying mammals that have the reproductive system of a reptile. They are the last survivors of a Mesozoic group which were in process of evolving from reptiles into what are now known as mammals.

During the same period there evolved the most characteristic of all Australian animals, the kangaroo, a marsupial. Like 'conventional' mammals, the marsupial fertilizes and initially develops its young internally but at an early stage the young leaves the reproductive tract and migrates to a pouch where it attaches firmly to a nipple and continues to develop there. In some desert marsupials, notably the red kangaroo, the mother mates again immediately after the birth of the young, but the development of the embryo in the reproductive tract is held stationary until the young in the pouch requires to suckle less from the mother. As soon as the suckling stimulus declines, either by the young becoming independent or by death, the development of the embryo starts again and a new individual will be born about three weeks later.

Contrasts in reproductive systems

The primitive urogenital system of the egg-laying monotremes are contrasted (below) with the increasingly complex reproductive organs of marsupial and placental mammals.

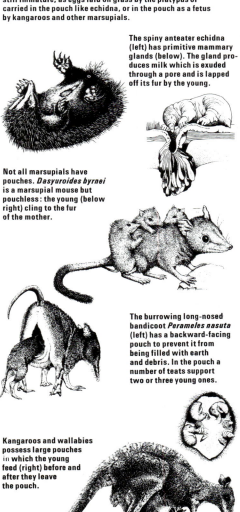

Monotreme

Marsupial

Placental

a Kidneys
b Ureters
c Ovary
d Uterus
e Urinogenital sinus
f Cloaca
g Fallopian tube

h Lateral vagina
j Median vagina
k Bladder
l Vagina
m Urethra
n Anal canal

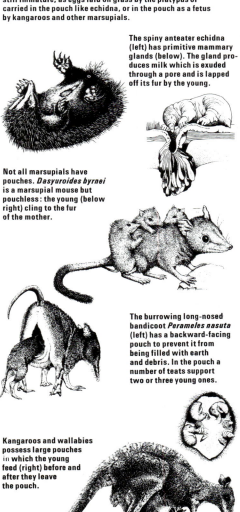

Birth among pouched mammals
Eutherian, or placental mammals—of which man is one—give birth to their young after a prolonged gestation so that the offspring are well developed when born. With monotremes and marsupials the young leave the reproductive tract while still immature, as eggs laid on grass by the platypus or carried in the pouch like echidna, or in the pouch as a fetus by kangaroos and other marsupials.

The spiny anteater echidna (left) has primitive mammary glands (below). The gland produces milk which is exuded through a pore and is lapped off its fur by the young.

Not all marsupials have pouches. *Dasyuroides byrnei* is a marsupial mouse but pouchless: the young (below right) cling to the fur of the mother.

The burrowing long-nosed bandicoot *Perameles nasuta* (left) has a backward-facing pouch to prevent it from being filled with earth and debris. In the pouch a number of teats support two or three young ones.

Kangaroos and wallabies possess large pouches in which the young feed (right) before and after they leave the pouch.

Joey comes home
Long after the young kangaroo, or joey, has grown too large to re-enter its mother's pouch it will return to feed and the mother often supports both a young kangaroo on foot and an immature sibling in the pouch. The picture is of a pretty faced wallaby.

1 Red kangaroo, displaying male, with female.

2 Precopulation posture; the gestation period lasts 33 days.

3 Birth position

4 Two days after birth, second mating occurs: 5 young attached to teat.

6 Suckling of first 'joey' lessens and the second blastocyst develops.

8 First young suckling from outside; developing young attached to different teat.

7 Second birth occurs 7 months after first

Red kangaroo breeding
Reproduction in the red kangaroo *Megaleia ruffa* (sequence left) in common with some but not all desert marsupials, is complex in that the female can support a dormant blastocyst in her uterus, a suckling in her pouch, and another suckling 'joey' on foot.

Embryo kangaroo (top) soon makes its way into its mother's pouch (centre) and attaches itself to one of her teats (above)

The frog that chooses a flooded nest
The frog *Limnodynastes dorsalis* constructs a burrow in the bank of a slow-moving stream. When the burrow partially fills with water, the female deposits her egg mass in the chamber.

Burrowing frog
Limnodynastes dorsalis

143

The Luxuriant Quarter

Cut off from Australia's dominating dry, rocky and sandy desert by the natural barriers of the hilly Pilbara region and the Nullarbor plain, the southwestern corner of the continent is a biologically isolated region. It is the home of an extraordinarily rich collection of plants (some 6,000 species), most of which are found nowhere else.

There is a resident population of animals also not to be found anywhere else. Equally striking is the fact that many animals common to the east of the continent have failed to penetrate the region, among them the kookaburra, the koala and many of the smaller passerines. The eastern species which have managed to invade have developed into a number of local variants or races. One explanation for this isolation and variety is that at one time much of the southern part of the continent had a wetter climate and that the common birds and mammals now split into two populations were found all along the southern rim of the landmass. With the change to a drier climate and the rise of the Nullarbor plain many species were separated into two isolated populations

Thirty-seven of the 54 species of *Banksia*, a flowering tree, are found in southwest Australia. With the eucalypts and the *Grevillea* group, they provide a rich resource for pollen and nectar-eating animals. Small phalangers and many parrots live on the nectar and a number of bats have taken to the diet. The Porongorup range south of Perth is covered in forest of a spectacular eucalypt, the karri, which grows densely and to a very great height. In drier areas the *Hakea* group, represented by 71 of the 103 known species, is dominant. This group has waxy flowers and produces nectar to attract pollinators.

Rainfall is confined to the winter months and it has been noted that most of the bird species nest in the winter and early spring. Some species breed regardless of the time of year – so long as it has been wet enough. One unique bird – thought to have been extinct – is the noisy scrub bird, a primitive, almost flightless passerine found in dense scrub alongside streams on the south coast.

The offshore islands have provided for many marsupials a refuge from the predation of introduced carnivores and from habitat destruction. The quokka, on Rottnest Island, is an example.

With an abundance of plants which need to have their seeds fertilized by pollen from another plant, many southwestern Australia vertebrates carry out this function. Their tongues are usually long and thin so that they can be pushed into the flower to pick up nectar, or are brush-tipped to sweep up pollen. Thus they feed, and provide a service to the plants that give them sustenance.

Parched home
Home of the quokka, Rottnest Island off the west coast of Australia, is covered with a variety of low-growing scrubs.

There is no standing fresh water but the quokka has adapted to utilize brackish water to help it make up its mineral and water needs.

Living mainly on Rottnest island the Quokka, *Setonix brachyurus*, uses brackish water to supplement its diet. Its digestive system resembles a ruminant's, using bacteria to digest cellulose.

Location map of Rottnest Is.

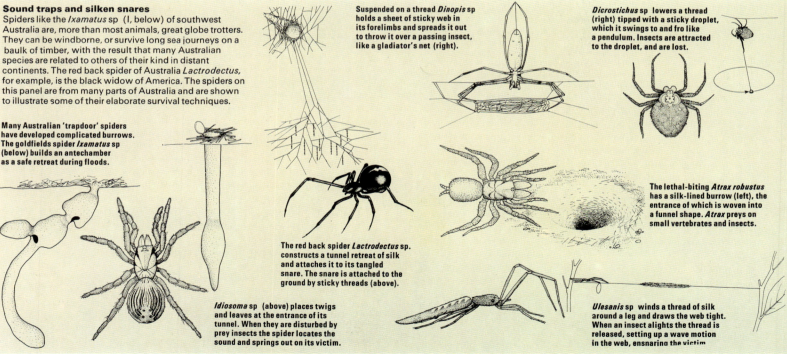

Sound traps and silken snares
Spiders like the *Ixamatus* sp (I, below) of southwest Australia are, more than most animals, great globe trotters. They can be windborne, or survive long sea journeys on a baulk of timber, with the result that many Australian species are related to others of their kind in distant continents. The red back spider of Australia *Lactrodectus*, for example, is the black widow of America. The spiders on this panel are from many parts of Australia and are shown to illustrate some of their elaborate survival techniques.

Many Australian 'trapdoor' spiders have developed complicated burrows. The goldfields spider *Ixamatus* sp (below) builds an antechamber as a safe retreat during floods.

Suspended on a thread *Dinopis* sp holds a sheet of sticky web in its forelimbs and spreads it out to throw it over a passing insect, like a gladiator's net (right).

Dicrostichus sp lowers a thread (right) tipped with a sticky droplet, which it swings to and fro like a pendulum. Insects are attracted to the droplet, and are lost.

The red back spider *Lactrodectus* sp. constructs a tunnel retreat of silk and attaches it to its tangled snare. The snare is attached to the ground by sticky threads (above).

The lethal-biting *Atrax robustus* has a silk-lined burrow (left), the entrance of which is woven into a funnel shape. *Atrax* preys on small vertebrates and insects.

Idiosoma sp (above) places twigs and leaves at the entrance of its tunnel. When they are disturbed by prey insects the spider locates the sound and springs out on its victim.

Ulesanis sp winds a thread of silk around a leg and draws the web tight. When an insect alights the thread is released, setting up a wave motion in the web, ensnaring the victim

A fly forced to fertilize a flower
Guided by the sepals of the orchid *Pterostylas barbata* a small fly, *Mycomyia*, alights on the flower's hairy labellum (1). The labellum jerks upright, throwing the fly into the base of the flower. Now trapped by a bearded 'gate' (2) the fly is forced to pass the flower's stigma to escape and any pollen on its back is deposited. On its way out it also brushes the pollen sac and collects more grains to take on to another orchid. *Mycomyia* fly (right).

Subterranean flower
Burrowing insects are thought to fertilize the orchid *Rhizanthella* sp. (below). It flowers just beneath the soil surface near rotting tree roots, with the fungus *Aspergilla* sp. Its tiny clusters of flowers are contained within a modified leaf structure.

Cowslip orchid *below*
One of the world's 17,000 species of orchid, but terrestrial rather than epiphytic, the cowslip orchid grows in sheltered places.

Goat orchid *above*
The humid forests of southwest Australia boast many orchids, among them the goat orchid *Diuris maculata*, one of many terrestrial forms.

Plants trade food for service
Pollen-rich plants and pollen- and nectar-feeding animals have evolved a close interdependence in the southwest. The trees provide a rich food resource for many species of insect, bird and mammal – and these, by way of payment, provide transport of the pollen from one plant to its fellow, thus ensuring the survival of the plant species. Some of the plants use the simple lure of an attractive flower, or a rich scent, to tempt the pollinator; others, such as the orchid *Pterostylus* and the trigger plant *Stylidium* (see this page) have evolved a form of behaviour to ensure that the pollen is taken away. Shown (below) are some of the birds and mammals which play a vital role in fertilizing the banksia and gum flower.

Honey-eating adaptations
With narrow nose and long tongue the honey possum *Tarsipes spenceriae* seeks nectar among banksia flowers. Pollen adheres to its fur and may be carried to a female plant.

Oesophagus and duodenum entrances of honey-eating birds are close together. Nectar, needing little breakdown, goes straight to small intestine. Solids go to stomach for complete digestion.

Tongues of brush-tongued parrots soak up nectar and catch up pollen which is carried to another plant.

1 Scrub (Mulga *Acacia aneura*)

2 Dry *Eucalyptus* forest

100 mi

3 Salmon gum (*Eucalyptus salmonophloia*)

4 Wet *Eucalyptus* forest (jarrah *Eucalyptus marginata*)

5 Mallee (open *Eucalyptus* scrub)

6 Karri forest (*Eucalyptus diversicolor*)

Prevailing winds

Oceanic currents

With an average rainfall of 30-40ins (75-100cm) southwest Australia supports an abundant and diverse flora. It is separated from the rest of Australia by a 10ins (25cm) rainfall belt.

Common plants
Golden kangaroo paw *Anigosanthos* sp. (above) blooms in the Australian midsummer on coastal plains. The grass tree *Xanthorrhea* sp. (below) has a wider distribution.

Rich forest growth
An equable climate with high rainfall have created the species-rich forests of southwest Australia. Constant dampness aids growth of mosses and ferns.

Trigger plant *left*
If a bee disturbs the flower of *Stylidium* sp. the plant's male anther bends to coat the bee in pollen. The pollen is thus transferred to another flower.

Red-capped parrot *Purpureicephalus spurius*

Marri gum *Eucalyptus calophylla*

Oesophagus

Duodenum

Gizzard

Honey possum *Tarsipes speaceriae*

Banksia hookeriana

New Holland honeyeater *Phylidonyris novae hollandiae*

Dormouse possum *Cercartetus concinnus*

Banksia attenuata

Banksia coccinea

Banksia ashbyii

Purple-crowned parakeet *Glossopsitta porphyrocephala*

145

The Temperate Southeast

Southeastern Australia is the most temperate region of the continent and the area where man has had the greatest impact. It has, typically, a narrow coastal plain covered in dense eucalypt forest with heaths on some of the more exposed areas, where the dominant plants are the spiny *Hakea* species. On the slopes of the Great Dividing Range, which rises to 7,000 feet (2,100m), there is a wet eucalypt forest with an impressive growth of tree ferns and bryophytes in damp gullies.

In New South Wales the Great Dividing Range is made of a hard sandstone which rises nearly 1,000 feet (300m) sheer from the coastal plain. The escarpment is etched deeply with canyons and caves. The top, relatively flat and forming tablelands, is covered with an open, dry forest of the savanna type. On the higher slopes of the Snowy Mountains – the highest part of the Range, dense forests of snow gums give way at high altitudes to alpine meadows found only there and in some parts of Tasmania. The Snowy Mountains are the source of the Murray and Murrumbidgee Rivers which flow westward to the sea at Spencer Gulf. The coastal rivers, by contrast, are many but quite small. West from the ranges the climate becomes drier and the vegetation changes from dry eucalypt to the mallee and spinifex of the desert areas.

The island of Tasmania, to the south, is separated from Australia by the Bass Strait zone, a boundary sufficiently wide for wildlife populations to have become isolated and evolve into separate species. Tasmania has a far cooler and wetter climate. Its animals are diverse and many of the marsupial groups are found there.

The forests of the slopes and highlands are the habitat of the arboreal phalangers, opossums and gliders, as well as the koala, wombat, and several of the larger wallabies. The rivers of the southeast are the home of the platypus, the peculiar mammal found only in the Australian region. It is one of the only two living examples of the Montremata which lay eggs in the reptile mode of reproduction but produce milk to suckle their young, in the mammalian manner. Rare mammals such as the Tasmanian devil, *Sarcophilus*, survive and until the 1930s the Tasmanian wolf *Thylacinus*, a dog-like predator, was fairly common but may now be extinct.

Gum *above* **and beech**
A characteristic tree of southeast Australia the gum *Eucalyptus* sp. protrudes from the winter snows of the Great Dividing Range. Much of Tasmania is clad in dense stands of *Nothofagus* beech (right). High rainfall and fertile soil produce jungle conditions.

Vegetation cover
The slopes of the Great Dividing Range of mountains in southeast Australia show vegetation zonation and contrasts between the drier western slopes and the moister east, facing the Pacific.

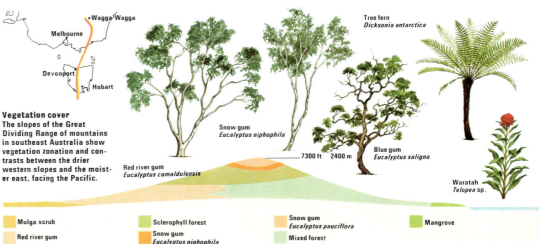

Tree fern
Dicksonia antarctica

Snow gum
Eucalyptus niphophila

7300 ft   2400 m

Blue gum
Eucalyptus saligna

Red river gum
Eucalyptus camaldulensis

Waratah
Telopea sp.

Mulga scrub	Sclerophyll forest	Snow gum *Eucalyptus pauciflora*	Mangrove
Red river gum	Snow gum *Eucalyptus niphophila*	Mixed forest	

Link with a lost continent
Evidence that Australasia and South America were once linked by land as part of a great southern continent is provided by the Nothofagus beech. It grows in southeast Australia Tasmania and South America, and traces indicate that it once grew in the Antarctic. Koala *Phascolarctos cinereus* (below) is bearlike, but not a bear.

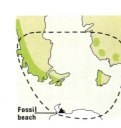

Fossil beach

Gaudy mime *above*
The forests of southeast Australia are the home of the largest of perching birds, the lyre bird *Menura novaehollandiae.* The male builds a mound of soil as a 'stage' where it shows off the remarkable tail from which it takes its name. It is also a fine mimic, imitating other birds, the rustle of the wind and even human voices – but its own song is loud and tuneless. The undramatic female (right) lays a single egg.

Moss-dwelling frog *below*
The corroboree frog *Pseudophryne corroboree is* at home in cold, damp moss at high altitudes in the Australian Alps. Any accumulation of water in the moss is sufficient for its tadpoles to hatch out and metamorphose.

Survivors from prehistory *below*
Koonunga cursor (restricted shoreline, Victoria) and *Anaspides tasmaniae* (small mountain lakes in Tasmania) are two relict invertebrates.

Koonunga cursor

Anaspides tasmaniae

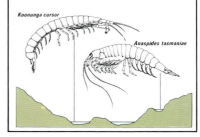

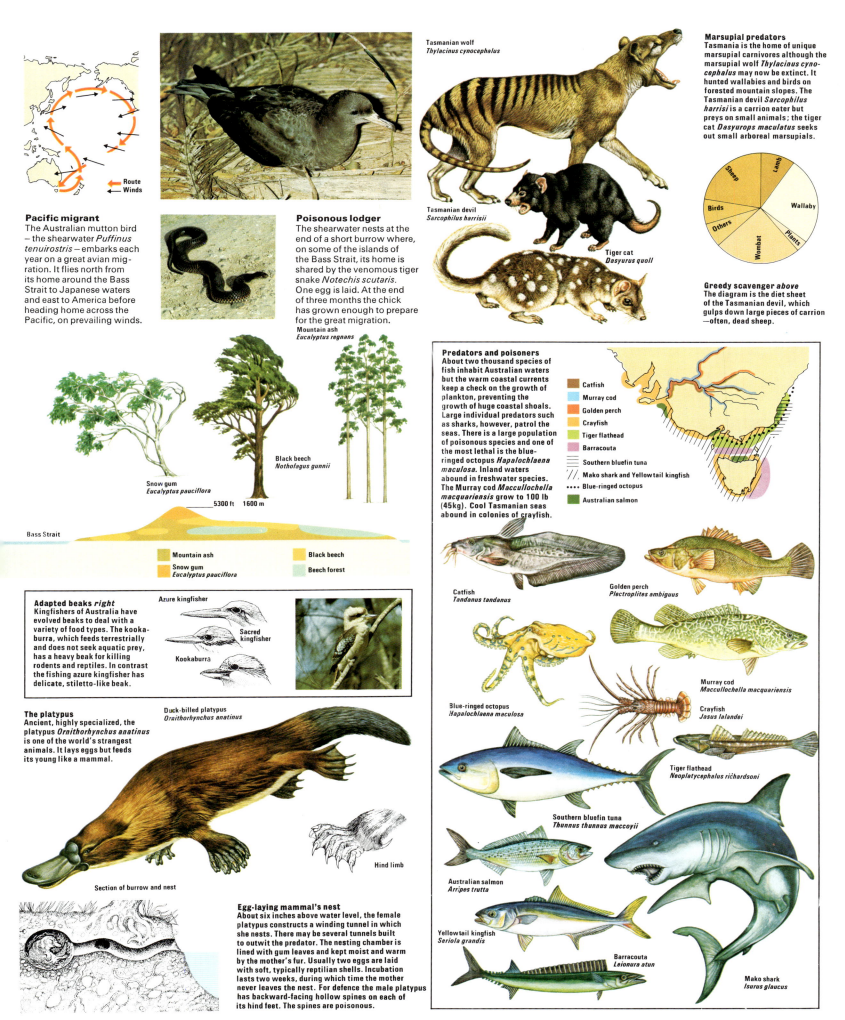

Pacific migrant
The Australian mutton bird – the shearwater *Puffinus tenuirostris* – embarks each year on a great avian migration. It flies north from its home around the Bass Strait to Japanese waters and east to America before heading home across the Pacific, on prevailing winds.

Route
Winds

Poisonous lodger
The shearwater nests at the end of a short burrow where, on some of the islands of the Bass Strait, its home is shared by the venomous tiger snake *Notechis scutaris*. One egg is laid. At the end of three months the chick has grown enough to prepare for the great migration.

Tasmanian wolf
Thylacinus cynocephalus

Tasmanian devil
Sarcophilus harrisii

Tiger cat
Dasyurus quoll

Marsupial predators
Tasmania is the home of unique marsupial carnivores although the marsupial wolf *Thylacinus cynocephalus* may now be extinct. It hunted wallabies and birds on forested mountain slopes. The Tasmanian devil *Sarcophilus harrisii* is a carrion eater but preys on small animals; the tiger cat *Dasyurops maculatus* seeks out small arboreal marsupials.

Sheep
Lamb
Birds
Wallaby
Others
Wombat
Plants

Greedy scavenger *above*
The diagram is the diet sheet of the Tasmanian devil, which gulps down large pieces of carrion —often, dead sheep.

Mountain ash
Eucalyptus regnans

Black beech
Nothofagus gunnii

Snow gum
Eucalyptus pauciflora

5300 ft   1600 m

Bass Strait

Mountain ash
Snow gum
Eucalyptus pauciflora
Black beech
Beech forest

Predators and poisoners
About two thousand species of fish inhabit Australian waters but the warm coastal currents keep a check on the growth of plankton, preventing the growth of huge coastal shoals. Large individual predators such as sharks, however, patrol the seas. There is a large population of poisonous species and one of the most lethal is the blue-ringed octopus *Hapalochlaena maculosa*. Inland waters abound in freshwater species. The Murray cod *Maccullochella macquariensis* grow to 100 lb (45kg). Cool Tasmanian seas abound in colonies of crayfish.

Catfish
Murray cod
Golden perch
Crayfish
Tiger flathead
Barracouta
Southern bluefin tuna
Mako shark and Yellowtail kingfish
Blue-ringed octopus
Australian salmon

Catfish
Tandanus tandanus

Golden perch
Plectroplites ambiguus

Blue-ringed octopus
Hapalochlaena maculosa

Murray cod
Maccullochella macquariensis

Crayfish
Jasus lalandei

Tiger flathead
Neoplatycephalus richardsoni

Southern bluefin tuna
Thunnus thunnus maccoyii

Australian salmon
Arripes trutta

Yellowtail kingfish
Seriola grandis

Barracouta
Leionura atun

Mako shark
Isurus glaucus

Adapted beaks *right*
Kingfishers of Australia have evolved beaks to deal with a variety of food types. The kookaburra, which feeds terrestrially and does not seek aquatic prey, has a heavy beak for killing rodents and reptiles. In contrast the fishing azure kingfisher has delicate, stiletto-like beak.

Azure kingfisher
Sacred kingfisher
Kookaburra

The platypus
Ancient, highly specialized, the platypus *Ornithorhynchus anatinus* is one of the world's strangest animals. It lays eggs but feeds its young like a mammal.

Duck-billed platypus
Oraithorhynchus anatinus

Hind limb

Section of burrow and nest

Egg-laying mammal's nest
About six inches above water level, the female platypus constructs a winding tunnel in which she nests. There may be several tunnels built to outwit the predator. The nesting chamber is lined with gum leaves and kept moist and warm by the mother's fur. Usually two eggs are laid with soft, typically reptilian shells. Incubation lasts two weeks, during which time the mother never leaves the nest. For defence the male platypus has backward-facing hollow spines on each of its hind feet. The spines are poisonous.

Flightless Birds and Living Fossils

Almost all land forms and environments are to be found in New Zealand, an oceanic group consisting of two large islands, North and South, and a number of smaller ones. The group lies more than 1,000 miles (1,600 km) east of Australia across a prevailing west-east airstream which gives it an oceanic climate with frequent 'fronts' and rapidly changing weather. Most of the currents playing on the coasts are cold, coming north and west from the southern ocean, but there are warmer currents to the north.

North Island is dominated by active volcanoes, Ruapehu and Ngauruhoe, on a plateau in the centre of the island. The largest lake, Taupo, was created by volcanic forces thousands of years ago. The plateau forests and those of the slopes are mainly podocarps with *Nothofagus* to the south. In contrast the South Island consists of a backbone range of mountains, the Southern Alps, with well-developed glaciers and fiords. On the western slopes, lush forests of *Nothofagus* and podocarp provide for New Zealand's unique flightless birds, the weka and the kiwi. To the east, great grasslands and some forest were once the home of the huge grazing birds, the now-extinct moas.

There are no mammals native to New Zealand, apart from two rare bat species, because the islands probably became isolated about 190 million years ago before mammals developed into the important group they now are; but there are a number of relic species, notably the tuatara and the tailed frog *Leiopelma*.

Australia has had little influence on the wild life of New Zealand: the main route of invasion by the few land animals which successfully made the crossing to the islands seems to have been from the north, through New Caledonia and Lord Howe Island. Some groups may have moved north, as – for example – both islands have native podocarp species. One, the Norfolk Island pine, has been taken all over the world by man.

The outlying islands to the south and west of New Zealand, the Chathams and the Auckland Islands, are the home of a selection of animals which have succeeded in crossing the ocean and show the adaptive features of colonizers living on small oceanic islands.

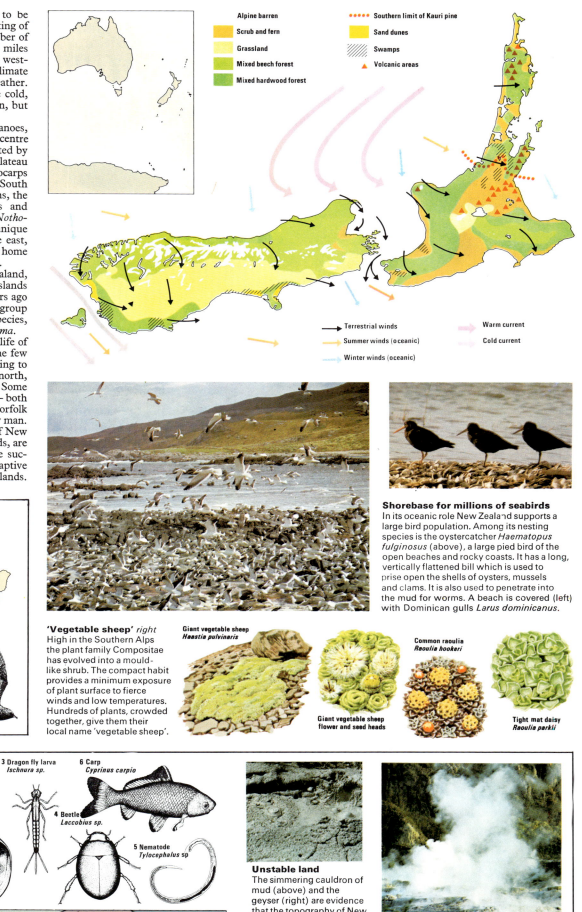

Legend:
- Alpine barren
- Scrub and fern
- Grassland
- Mixed beech forest
- Mixed hardwood forest
- Southern limit of Kauri pine
- Sand dunes
- Swamps
- Volcanic areas

- Terrestrial winds
- Summer winds (oceanic)
- Winter winds (oceanic)
- Warm current
- Cold current

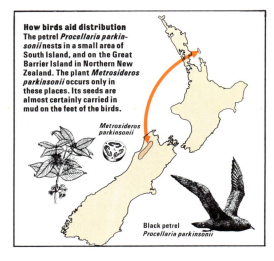

How birds aid distribution
The petrel *Procellaria parkinsonii* nests in a small area of South Island, and on the Great Barrier Island in Northern New Zealand. The plant *Metrosideros parkinsonii* occurs only in these places. Its seeds are almost certainly carried in mud on the feet of the birds.

Metrosideros parkinsonii

Black petrel
Procellaria parkinsonii

Shorebase for millions of seabirds
In its oceanic role New Zealand supports a large bird population. Among its nesting species is the oystercatcher *Haematopus fulginosus* (above), a large pied bird of the open beaches and rocky coasts. It has a long, vertically flattened bill which is used to prise open the shells of oysters, mussels and clams. It is also used to penetrate into the mud for worms. A beach is covered (left) with Dominican gulls *Larus dominicanus*.

'Vegetable sheep' *right*
High in the Southern Alps the plant family Compositae has evolved into a mould-like shrub. The compact habit provides a minimum exposure of plant surface to fierce winds and low temperatures. Hundreds of plants, crowded together, give them their local name 'vegetable sheep'.

Giant vegetable sheep
Haastia pulvinaris

Giant vegetable sheep
flower and seed heads

Common raoulia
Raoulia hookeri

Tight mat daisy
Raoulia parkii

Life where it shouldn't exist
Fed by bubbling geysers, mountain streams boil through the volcanic regions of New Zealand. But despite the heat and the high chemical content of the streams, life adapts to conditions almost inhospitable enough to preclude any form of existence.

1 Rotifer
2 Water snail *Lymnaea tomentosa*
3 Dragon fly larva *Ischnura sp.*
4 Beetle *Laccobius sp.*
5 Nematode *Tylocephalus sp*
6 Carp *Cyprinus carpio*

20°C to 30°C
30°C to 35°C
35°C to 45°C
45°C to 80°C

Unstable land
The simmering cauldron of mud (above) and the geyser (right) are evidence that the topography of New Zealand is not yet stable. Among plants, only highly-tolerant blue-green algae is able to survive in the immediate vicinity of the bubbling hot springs.

Flightless crickets
The ancestors of the weta crickets of New Zealand may once have flown but the amiable habitat of the islands enabled them to shed their wings and become flightless like many of the islands' birds. Wetas have developed specialized structures, some to live in caves, others in trees or at ground level.

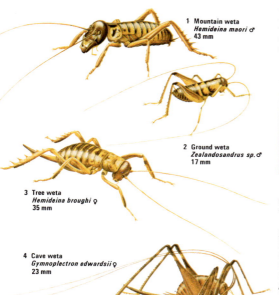

1 Mountain weta
Hemideina maori ♂
43 mm

2 Ground weta
Zealandosandrus sp. ♂
17 mm

3 Tree weta
Hemideina broughi ♀
35 mm

4 Cave weta
Gymnoplectron edwardsii ♀
23 mm

The vanished birds of New Zealand
The abundance of flightless birds – next to its lack of native mammals – is the best-known feature of the fauna of New Zealand. The facts are closely related because it was probably an absence of predators that first enabled the primitive ancestors of the flightless birds to come down from the trees and exploit the grasslands. There – until the arrival of man – a whole family of grazing birds evolved, the largest of which was *Dinornis maximus*, a moa which grew to a height of 15 feet (4.5 m). The smallest moa was *Anomalopteryx parva* which, like its giant relative, has vanished. Clumsy, without the power of flight and unused to any form of predator they had little hope of survival once man and other animals arrived. New Zealand also had the only flightless perching bird, the Stephens Island wren, discovered when a lighthouse keeper's cat brought it in. The cat went on to exterminate the whole population.

1 *Anomalopteryx*
2 Cassowary
   Casuarius casuarius
3 Emu
   Dromiceius casuarius
4 African ostrich
   Struthio camelus
5 Moa skeleton
6 Moa
   Dinornis maximus

Wings – for balance only
The weka *Gallirallus* sp. (above) is one of New Zealand's many flightless birds, although it has well-developed wings which it uses for balance. The gaily marked swamphen *Porphyrio porphyrio* (right), almost flightless, feeds in water shallows.

Spectacular display of lights lures insects to death
A cold and fatal light attracts many small insects to their doom on the ceilings of some New Zealand caves. The rocks sparkle with the light of thousands of glowworms (below); the fine threads of glowing droplets suspended from their lair act as a bait for the glowworms' prey.

The deadly glowworms (above) are the larvae of the fungus gnat *Arachnocampa luminosa* (right) which lives for only a few days. The luminescence, in the adults as well as the larvae, is produced by the chemical luciferin which is oxidized within special cells.

Fungus gnat
Arachnocampa luminosa

The last survivor
The kiwi *Apteryx australis* (above) is the last surviving member of the archaic family of moas. It has rudimentary wings and its body is covered with long, hairlike feathers. A parrot oddity, the kea *Nestor notabilis* (right) has a brush tongue to obtain nectar but it will also eat meat.

Primitive frog keeps its tail
Found only in two districts of New Zealand the frog *Leiopelma* is among the world's most primitive. Vestigial tail muscles remain in the frog after it has become adult.

Leiopelma lays its eggs in moist conditions under stones, The young frog develops from the tadpole stage inside the egg and hatches out by thrashing its muscular tail.

Ancient beak-head *right*
The tuatara *Sphenodon punctatus* is a relic of a group of ancient reptiles, the beak-heads, which flourished at the beginning of the Age of Reptiles, upwards of 150 million years ago. Among its characteristics is the absence of any copulatory organ in the male. Breeding is a slow process, in keeping with its metabolic rate, which is the lowest on record. Eggs are laid eight months after the sperms have entered the female's body and the young hatch out 12-15 months later. The tuatara has 'pseudoteeth' (a serrated jawbone) and feeds on insects, worms, lizard, or nestling petrels.

Tuatara eats petrel *left*
The ancient tuatara is happy to make its home in the tunnels of burrow-nesting birds such as the shearwater. The relationship is generally amicable but temptation will sometimes overcome the reptile and it will eat a young nestling to supplement its diet. The tuatara lives to a ripe old age, even in captivity.

The Northern Ice Cap

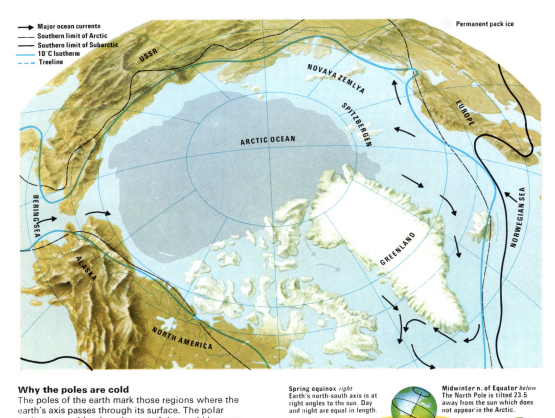

Legend:
- → Major ocean currents
- ···· Southern limit of Arctic
- — Southern limit of Subarctic
- — 10°C Isotherm
- --- Treeline

Permanent pack ice

USSR · NOVAYA ZEMLYA · SPITZBERGEN · EUROPE · ARCTIC OCEAN · NORWEGIAN SEA · BERING SEA · ALASKA · GREENLAND · NORTH AMERICA

The Arctic region is an ice-covered ocean basin, rimmed by the northern edges of North America and, Eurasia and the ice-capped islands of Greenland and the Canadian archipelago. Its southern boundary on land is the tree line which coincides roughly with the 10°C summer isotherm: the Arctic is the region where trees do not grow and mean July air temperatures do not rise above 10°C. Within this boundary lies tundra – low standing communities of grasses, sedge, shrubs, mosses and lichens growing on 'permafrost' soils which are frozen solid for most of the year and thaw only at the surface for a brief growing period each summer. At the tree line tundra becomes taiga or forest tundra, a narrow zone where stunted, wind-crippled trees struggle for a foothold among the waterlogged grasslands.

The marine Arctic can be defined by the same summer isotherm but oceanographers prefer a marine boundary. For them, the Arctic extends only to the limit of the layer of cold, dilute surface waters which are – biologically – poor. Covered permanently with drifting pack ice it receives very little penetrating sunlight even in summer and remains cold and relatively desolate throughout the year. Subarctic waters – zones of mixing between Arctic and Pacific or Atlantic waters – and coastal waters of the Arctic basin are warmer, richer in dissolved nutrients and covered only by broken, dispersed pack ice in summer. They support a host of plant and animal forms ranging in size from microscopic diatoms of the phytoplankton (floating plant life) at the base of the ecological pyramid, to walruses and whales.

Why the poles are cold

The poles of the earth mark those regions where the earth's axis passes through its surface. The polar regions are colder than the rest of the world because they receive less energy from the sun. The received warmth is proportional to the angle at which the rays strike the surface, and at the poles they glance tangentially. The cold is intensified because the poles are ice-covered 'mirrors', reflecting back into space the greater part of the solar energy. The diagram (right) shows the earth's seasonal 'tilt'.

Spring equinox *right*
Earth's north-south axis is at right angles to the sun. Day and night are equal in length.

Midwinter n. of Equator *below*
The North Pole is tilted 23.5 away from the sun which does not appear in the Arctic.

Midsummer n. of Equator *above*
North Pole tilts 23.5 towards the sun which remains above the horizon for 24 hours a day.

Autumn equinox *left*
Once again the earth's axis is at right angles to the sun. Days and nights of equal length.

Angmagssalik — Temperature in °C / Rainfall in inches — J F M A M J J A S O N D

Verkhoyansk — Temperature in °C / Rainfall in inches — J F M A M J J A S O N D

The drifters *below*

Plankton, the drifting, microscopic organisms in the sea's surface waters were first named in the 19th century to distinguish them from the nekton, or swimming organisms, and the benthos, the name given to the other major group, the sea bed forms.

Phytoplankton, tiny, drifting plant life, is the most fundamental sea food and the primary converter of the sun's energy into food.

Zooplankton, a wide variety of minute animal forms, feeds on phytoplankton and in turn provides food for higher animal species.

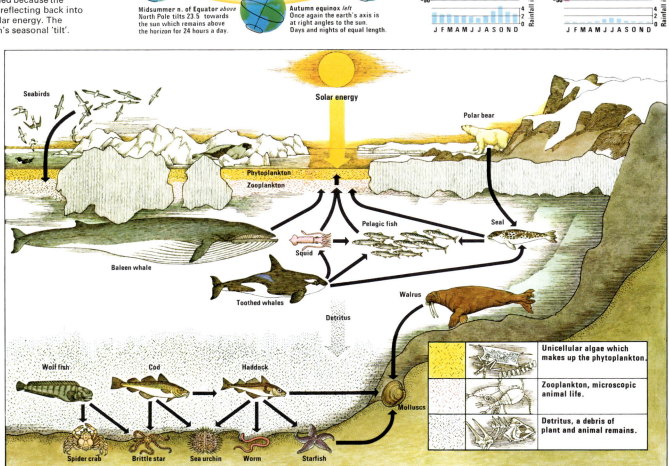

Seabirds · Solar energy · Polar bear · Phytoplankton · Zooplankton · Pelagic fish · Seal · Squid · Baleen whale · Toothed whales · Detritus · Walrus · Wolf fish · Cod · Haddock · Molluscs · Spider crab · Brittle star · Sea urchin · Worm · Starfish

- Unicellular algae which makes up the phytoplankton.
- Zooplankton, microscopic animal life.
- Detritus, a debris of plant and animal remains.

Squid
Ommastrephes sp

Prosperity of life in the seas of the world depends upon the great pastures of phytoplankton a sort of marine 'savanna', with algae taking the place of grass. Minute animals, the zooplankton, which graze on these pastures, provide food for pelagic or surface-living fishes and birds. The sun is the motor which starts up the Arctic chain of life, breaking up the ice and penetrating deep into the water. Even in the depths its benefits are felt as debris from activity near the surface rains down to feed creatures which dwell on the bottom.

Productivity in the Arctic ocean is highest in summer when the days are long and the sun is highest in the sky. Light penetrates deep in the water and the diatoms and other surface living plants multiply rapidly. The energy they trap by photosynthesis is the mainspring of life in the sea. Hosts of minute drifting animals, the zooplankton, migrate to surface waters in spring to browse on the phytoplankton. Zooplankton includes crustaceans, jellyfish, arrow worms, surface living polychaets and larval forms of starfishes, sea urchins and many bottom living fish.

Some planktonic animals live on the diatoms; others are carnivorous and feed on each other. All grow fat and are in turn eaten by fishes, seals, birds and other predators. Fishes are eaten by seals; both fishes and seals are taken by killer whales. Squid, which live in mid-water and at the surface, feed on fish and plankton and are eaten by sperm whales, other toothed whales and seals. Debris from all these animals, together with moribund and dead plankton, rains constantly down upon the sea bed where it feeds masses of clams, corals, sponges, sea anemones and other detritus collectors. They in turn are browsed upon by deep-sea fishes and such specialised feeders as narwhals and walruses, who swim down to the sea bed to eat clams.

At the end of the summer the sun disappears, ice forms on the water and the remaining light is reflected away. Photosynthesis stops, food becomes scarce at the surface and the zooplankton sinks to spend the winter in deep water. Birds, seals and whales migrate south, to seek food in warmer parts of the ocean.

Deadly digger
Hunting across the Arctic ice raft the polar bear picks up the scent of a seal pup hidden beneath the surface. The bear drives its powerful forelimbs through the crust for its victim.

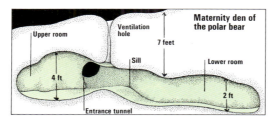

Maternity den of the polar bear

Upper room — Ventilation hole — 7 feet — Sill — Lower room — 4 ft — 2 ft — Entrance tunnel

Solitary wanderer
The polar bear *Thalarctos maritimus* is a solitary animal except during the first two years of life when the cubs are with their mother (above). Pregnant females and some other adults hole up in ice caves (left and right) during the worst of the winter months.

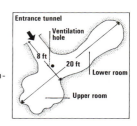

Entrance tunnel — Ventilation hole — 8 ft — 20 ft — Lower room — Upper room

Maritime mammals
The pinnipeds—or fin-footed animals—are a distinct mammalian order which includes true seals, fur seals sea lions and walruses. They are thought to have descended from land animals over many millions of years to become true creatures of the sea with finely streamlined bodies and all four limbs modified into flippers. The true seals (some are illustrated below) are the best adapted for swimming. Their hind flippers are useless on land to which all pinnipeds must return to give birth to their young, and to moult.

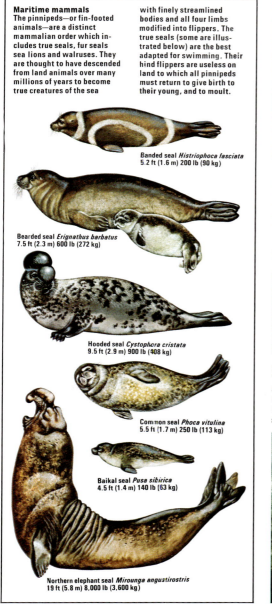

Banded seal *Histriophoca fasciata*
5.2 ft (1.6 m) 200 lb (90 kg)

Bearded seal *Erignathus barbatus*
7.5 ft (2.3 m) 600 lb (272 kg)

Hooded seal *Cystophora cristata*
9.5 ft (2.9 m) 900 lb (408 kg)

Common seal *Phoca vitulina*
5.5 ft (1.7 m) 250 lb (113 kg)

Baikal seal *Pusa sibirica*
4.5 ft (1.4 m) 140 lb (63 kg)

Northern elephant seal *Mirounga angustirostris*
19 ft (5.8 m) 8,000 lb (3,600 kg)

Burrowing seabird *right*
One of the endemic species of northern Atlantic waters the puffin *Fratercula arctica* nests in burrows it makes.

Colonial nesters
The shag *Phalacrocorax aristotelis* (above) and the kittiwake *Rissa tridactyla* (below) compete for nesting sites on northern cliffs.

Adapted egg *left*
The single egg laid by the common guillemot *Uria aalge* is acutely pear-shaped, a form which prevents it rolling from the bare rock ledge where it has been laid. The guillemot (murre in North America) fishes for its food in the cold northern waters of the Atlantic and Pacific.

Deep sea diver *above*
On rocks inaccessible to man the gannet *Sula bassana* nests in huge colonies. Gannets are dramatic fishermen, diving from great heights to plunge deeply in search of fish. A network of air sacs beneath the skin (like the pelican's, a distant relative) gives them great buoyancy and they bob to the surface in seconds.

Courtship in a crowded colony
The crowded gannetries where it lives ashore have bred in the gannet *Sula bassana* an aggressive and turbulent attitude towards its neighbours—and a ritualized courtship display in which each stance has a precise meaning.

Bowing display

Chick soliciting food

Mutual fencing display

Sky-pointing display

Migrants of the Barren Lands

The Arctic is a new kind of environment in the recent history of the world. Since the age of birds, mammals and flowering plants began, only in the last two or three million years have icecaps covered the ends of the earth, causing long, bitterly cold winters and short cold summers in high latitudes. Few kinds of plant or animal have yet had time to adapt to polar living in the new, recently-exposed areas left by retreating ice. Polar land plants are often alpine plants which have found themselves at home at sea level on the tundra. Terrestrial animals show few physical adaptations for polar life; they survive only if an earlier way of life pre-adapted them to polar existence.

The coldest areas by far are the Subarctic heartlands of Canada and Siberia, where mean winter temperatures reach −30°C and lower. Winters last for eight or nine months of the year. Many plants and animals avoid these extremes of cold. Aquatic forms winter as seeds, eggs, or other resting stages in the unfrozen mud of deep ponds. Small land plants and animals survive under the snow which blankets them and allows them to be warmed by the remnant of summer heat in the earth's surface. Perennial plants like creeping Arctic willows, grasses and close-growing mosses and lichens survive only where snow-drifts cover the ground during the coldest spells. Insects remain dormant in the earth or pass the winter safely as resistant eggs or pupae. Mice, lemmings and voles of the tundra burrow at ground level beneath the snow, maintaining their high body temperature and activity levels by feeding on last season's crop of hay and seeds. Arctic hares and larger herbivorous mammals live actively at the surface throughout winter, travelling widely in search of food. Hares live in groups which seek high ground where the snow is thin and vegetation abundant. Musk oxen travel together in small family herds, huddling together in the coldest weather under a cloud of their own water vapour which shields them from the sky. Large enough to carry huge reserves of fat, they lose weight steadily throughout the winter and fatten up again when the new vegetation appears in the spring. Matted, windproof fur over a foot (30cm) long keeps them warm and dry.

Foxes, weasels and other carnivores hunt through the cold months. All wear thick winter fur which helps reduce heat losses and maintain a layer of fat under their skin as a food store and insulation. Some hide away food in summer, seeking it out in the lean period before spring. Brown, grizzly and polar bears sleep in winter, emerging periodically to feed, for winters are too long and too cold for complete hibernation to be a success.

Wolf
Canis lupus

Tundra herds and predators
A scattered herd of barren-ground caribou (top) makes its way across the thaw water of melted snow during the Arctic summer. Its moves are always watched carefully by the grey or timber wolf *Canis lupus* (above) which hunts down the young and sick stragglers. The musk oxen *Ovibos moschatus* (left) form themselves into a defensive group which wolves will not attack. (Right) Siberian tundra in summer.

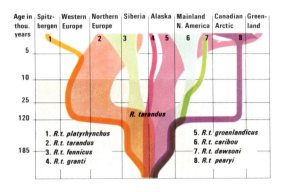

Age in thou. years	Spitz-bergen	Western Europe	Northern Europe	Siberia	Alaska	Mainland N. America	Canadian Arctic	Green-land
	1	2	3	4	5	6	7	8
5								
10								
25								
120			*R. tarandus*					
185								

1. *R.t. platyrhynchus*
2. *R.t. tarandus*
3. *R.t. fennicus*
4. *R.t. granti*

5. *R.t. groenlandicus*
6. *R.t. caribou*
7. *R.t. dawsoni*
8. *R.t pearyi*

Reindeer *Rangifer tarandus* figures in the earliest history of man, as part of his cave drawings, more than 25,000 years ago. By that time *Rangifer* had long since spread from its probable place of origin in northeastern Siberia to the forest edges and plains of the world's Arctic zones.

Old and New World deer
To the left of the centre-fold the moose, caribou and wapiti are the North American cousins of the elk, reindeer and red deer of northern Eurasia, on the right. The dominant animals are caribou in the New World and reindeer in the Old. Together they represent a single species.

Food in the freezer *above*
Reindeer moss *Cladonia rangiferina*, one of the staple foods of reindeer and caribou, is really a lichen — fungus and algae in symbiosis.
The deer scrape and shovel through the snow with their broad hooves to reach the matted carpet of lichen 'stored' beneath for them.

Wapiti *Cervus canadensis*
Known as the elk in North America; second only to the moose in size. Counterpart of Eurasian red deer.

Moose *Alces alces*
Largest of the northern deer, widely distributed through Arctic forests of North America.

They stay for the winter
The tundra in summer provides support for 100 species of birds. Only a few, among them those illustrated here, are hardy enough to stay for the winter.

Raven
Corvus corax

Peregrine falcon
Falco peregrinus

Gyr falcon
Falco rusticolus

Rock ptarmigan
Lagopus mutus

Snowy owl
Nyctea scandiaca

Redpoll
Carduelis flammea

Expert fishermen
Despite a reputation for ferocity the brown bears of northern Canada and Alaska are normally mild-mannered and tend to be vegetarian. They will take small mammals when chance offers and they are expert fishermen, like *Ursus horribilis* (above).

'Polygon' tundra *above*
The characteristic 'Polygons' of the tundra are formed by alternate freezing and thawing of sub surface water.

Caribou *Rangifer tarandus*
North American counterpart of Eurasian reindeer, ranges tundra in summer, winters in forests.

Elk *Alces alces*
Eurasian equivalent of North American moose, differing only in its range.

Reindeer *Rangifer tarandus*
Domesticated caribou of northern Europe and Asia, live sheltered life in care of nomadic herdsmen.

Red deer *Cervus elaphus*
Widespread in temperate Europe, Asia Minor and Caucasus to the Caspian. Introduced Australia, New Zealand.

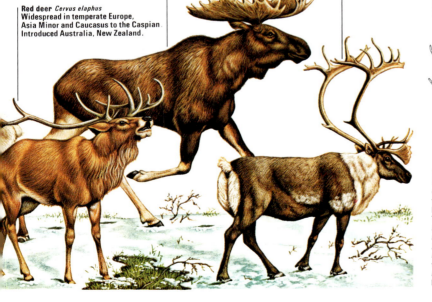

6th year

5th year

4th year

3rd year

2nd year

1st year

Red Deer antler growth *above*
From bottom to top, the series of antlers show the increasing tines, or prongs, on antlers between one and six years. The antlers are shed each autumn then begin to grow again in the following spring. At first they are 'in velvet' and bleed if damaged. Later in the year the velvet falls away and the antlers become hard before being shed again.

Sub-zero survival adaptations
Polar mammals and birds maintain body temperature by efficient insulation. Dense fur or feathers provide most of the insulation of land animals : marine mammals lay down thick subdermal fat instead. The thick winter fur of Arctic wolves, foxes, caribou and other larger mammals helps them to keep warm without additional expenditure of energy. Smaller mammals (anything smaller than an Arctic hare) cannot grow fur long enough to protect them from the rigorous cold and spend the winter in the shelter of burrows.

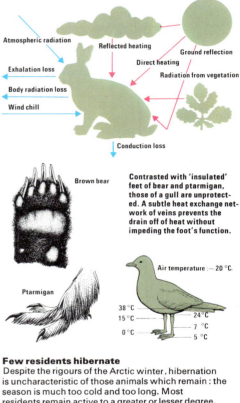

Atmospheric radiation

Reflected heating

Ground reflection

Direct heating

Radiation from vegetation

Exhalation loss

Body radiation loss

Wind chill

Conduction loss

Brown bear

Ptarmigan

Contrasted with 'insulated' feet of bear and ptarmigan, those of a gull are unprotected. A subtle heat exchange network of veins prevents the drain off of heat without impeding the foot's function.

Air temperature : — 20 °C.

38 °C   24 °C
15 °C   7 °C
0 °C   5 °C

Few residents hibernate
Despite the rigours of the Arctic winter, hibernation is uncharacteristic of those animals which remain : the season is much too cold and too long. Most residents remain active to a greater or lesser degree. An exception is the Arctic ground squirrel (below).

Citellus undulatus, the Arctic ground squirrel, lives in the far north of the American continent, on well-drained slopes. It survives its long hibernation within an insulated burrow at a very low metabolic rate, just sufficient to maintain its body temperature above freezing point. Its summer is spent getting over or preparing for hibernation.

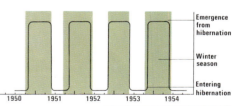

Emergence from hibernation

Winter season

Entering hibernation

1950   1951   1952   1953   1954

Active beneath snow
Shrews, lemmings and voles do not hibernate but remain active under the snow. It is important for the temperature to remain below zero : thawing snow will soak the animals and they will die of cold.

Tundra Summer

Though Arctic winters are cold the brief summers are warm and relatively comfortable. Snow disappears in May or June at many points along the Arctic coast, the ground thaws quickly and air temperatures rise to 7°C or more by midsummer. Only the heart of the pack ice and the high, ice-clad interior of Greenland remain below freezing point in summer. On well-drained tundra, organic soils absorb the sun's rays and warm thoroughly. Perennial herbs burst into activity as the days lengthen, carpeting the tundra with green in spring, a wealth of flowers in summer, and berries and seeds during the brief days of autumn.

As lakes thaw and streams quicken insects in their thousands emerge from winter dormancy. Springtails, beetles, mites and spiders scurry over the black soil; moths, butterflies and bumblebees seek nectar among the flowers and blowflies hover and swarm over the corpses of winter. Mosquito, midge and blackfly larvae fatten among the algae in ponds and lakes, emerging between June and August in swarms which rise like a dark mist over the tundra.

In summer the Arctic draws many millions of migrant birds and tens of thousands of mammals from the crowded temperate regions of the earth. The tundra wetlands, with their rich flush of new vegetation, attract ducks, geese and swans from America, Europe and Asia. The myriads of insect larvae are food for waders which fly in from wintering quarters along temperate coasts and settle to breed on the lush tundra grasslands. Voles and lemmings, with unstable populations which periodically 'explode', attract predatory owls and skuas from the south. Pipits and wagtails fly in to catch insects among the soil and vegetation; songbirds, including wheatear, redwings, fieldfares and yellowhammers, feed on insects, seeds and berries, and horned larks and sand martins swoop among the clouds of airborne insects. The small migrants attract merlins and falcons who follow them north and catch them on the wing. Of the hundred or more species which nest on the tundra in summer, all but five or six are migrants.

Caribou and reindeer migrate annually from forest to tundra to feed on lichens and grasses newly exposed by the melting snow. Barren-ground caribou of the Canadian tundra winter in north central Canada, moving northward in April with their newly-born calves. From May onward they feed voraciously, growing their antlers as they spread north, and fattening visibly from day to day. In August the antlers harden and mating occurs in September as the herds move south again. By October the caribou are back in the warmth and shelter of the forest.

Moss and lichen *above*
Sphagnum moss springs to life as the melting snow exposes it to the rays of the Arctic sun. *Cladonia,* a lichen (below), makes its home in the bark and crevices of a weather-beaten tree trunk.

Carpet vegetation
Protected from the deep cold of the long Arctic winter night by a thick overlay of snow, plants such as these provide forage locally for tiny animals which remain active in their snow tunnels. When summer comes the flowering carpet of vegetation becomes a subtropical habitat for myriads of insects.

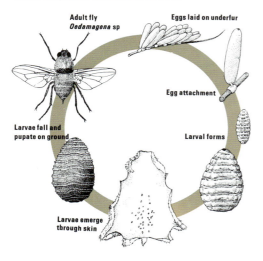

Ground Ivy
Linnaea borealis

Wood cranesbill
Geranium silvaticum

Purple saxifrage
Saxifraga oppositifolia

Clubmoss
Lycopodium sp.

Flies and parasites
In the swampy stands of meltwater, or thawed snow, plants proliferate and provide a temperate habitat for insects which make life miserable for man but provide ample food for migrant birds. Insects, too, are an irritant for caribou and reindeer, which are parasitized by the warble fly. This fly lays its eggs in the underside fur of the deer. The larvae burrow into the skin and live in the deer's flesh, emerging as maggots through its back before falling to the ground, pupating and taking to the wing again (see diagram below).

Adult fly
Oedamagena sp

Eggs laid on underfur

Egg attachment

Larvae fall and pupate on ground

Larval forms

Larvae emerge through skin

Bog meadow
Beneath the ephemeral blooms of an Arctic summer (above), the unchanging 'permafrost' or perpetually frozen sub-soil (below) prevents water draining away. Pools are formed in which insects breed profusely during the few weeks of the Arctic summer.

Summer

Winter

1 metre   Waterlogged

Permafrost

Frozen ground

Magnet for birds
Swarming over the tundra pools, mosquitoes, caddis flies and others provide rich food sources for birds, their larvae food for ducks and waders.

Caddis fly
Apatania zouella

Dragonfly
Agrion splendens

Mosquito
Aedes impiger

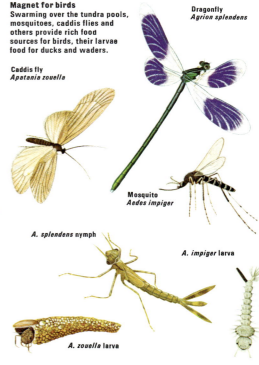

A. splendens nymph

A. impiger larva

A. zouella larva

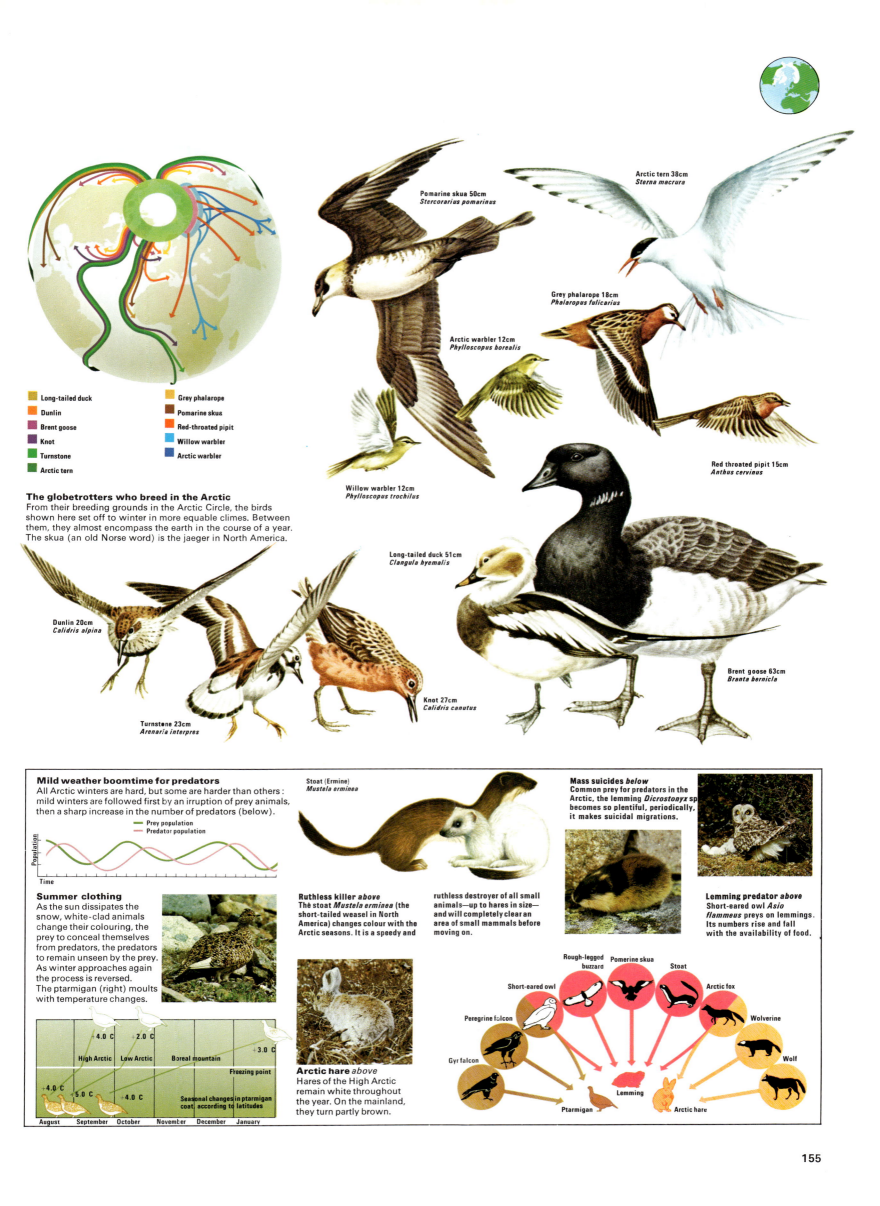

Pomarine skua 50cm
Stercorarius pomarinus

Arctic tern 38cm
Sterna macrura

Grey phalarope 18cm
Phalaropus fulicarius

Arctic warbler 12cm
Phylloscopus borealis

Red throated pipit 15cm
Anthus cervinus

Willow warbler 12cm
Phylloscopus trochilus

Long-tailed duck 51cm
Clangula hyemalis

Brent goose 63cm
Branta bernicla

Dunlin 20cm
Calidris alpina

Turnstone 23cm
Arenaria interpres

Knot 27cm
Calidris canutus

Legend
- Long-tailed duck
- Dunlin
- Brent goose
- Knot
- Turnstone
- Arctic tern
- Grey phalarope
- Pomarine skua
- Red-throated pipit
- Willow warbler
- Arctic warbler

The globetrotters who breed in the Arctic

From their breeding grounds in the Arctic Circle, the birds shown here set off to winter in more equable climes. Between them, they almost encompass the earth in the course of a year. The skua (an old Norse word) is the jaeger in North America.

Mild weather boomtime for predators

All Arctic winters are hard, but some are harder than others : mild winters are followed first by an irruption of prey animals, then a sharp increase in the number of predators (below).

- Prey population
- Predator population

Population

Time

Stoat (Ermine)
Mustela erminea

Mass suicides *below*
Common prey for predators in the Arctic, the lemming *Dicrostonyx* sp becomes so plentiful, periodically, it makes suicidal migrations.

Summer clothing

As the sun dissipates the snow, white-clad animals change their colouring, the prey to conceal themselves from predators, the predators to remain unseen by the prey. As winter approaches again the process is reversed. The ptarmigan (right) moults with temperature changes.

Ruthless killer *above*
The stoat *Mustela erminea* (the short-tailed weasel in North America) changes colour with the Arctic seasons. It is a speedy and ruthless destroyer of all small animals—up to hares in size— and will completely clear an area of small mammals before moving on.

Lemming predator *above*
Short-eared owl *Asio flammeus* preys on lemmings. Its numbers rise and fall with the availability of food.

	+4.0 C	+2.0 C			+3.0 C
	High Arctic	Low Arctic	Boreal mountain		
				Freezing point	
+4.0 C	+5.0 C	+4.0 C	Seasonal changes in ptarmigan coat, according to latitudes		
August	September	October	November	December	January

Arctic hare *above*
Hares of the High Arctic remain white throughout the year. On the mainland, they turn partly brown.

Rough-legged buzzard
Pomerine skua
Short-eared owl
Stoat
Arctic fox
Peregrine falcon
Wolverine
Gyr falcon
Wolf
Lemming
Ptarmigan
Arctic hare

155

The Frozen Desert

Antarctica is the world's most desolate continent. Over two-thirds of its surface consists of ice, nearly two miles (3km) thick in places, more than 8,000 feet (2,500m) above sea level. All but five per cent of the ice in the world is concentrated in Antarctica and the lowest temperature on earth – minus 88.3°C – was encountered there by a Russian expedition.

It is a mountainous continent. One great range forms the spine of the Antarctic Peninsula jutting northward towards South America – of which, geologically, it is a continuation. Others cross the continent from the Weddell to the Ross Sea.

Explorers have described the blizzards sweeping across the arid and bleak desert which is Antarctica. Most of the snow is actually drift blowing from one place to another. The annual snowfall inland rarely exceeds the equivalent of 10-15cm of water. Much of it evaporates and among the Victoria Land mountains there are dry, snow-free valleys that, like hot deserts, have salt crusts and crystal growths on the soil surface.

Along the coasts of the island-continent the influence of the sea – relatively warm around freezing point – keeps temperatures higher and moisture-laden winds bring more snow, or even summer rains, on the northernmost islands and coasts of the Antarctic Peninsula. Here, there is much snow-free moist ground in summer and many small lakes whose surfaces thaw for a month or two. These regions are relatively rich in land plants and animals, and in seals and seabirds supported by a wealth of marine food.

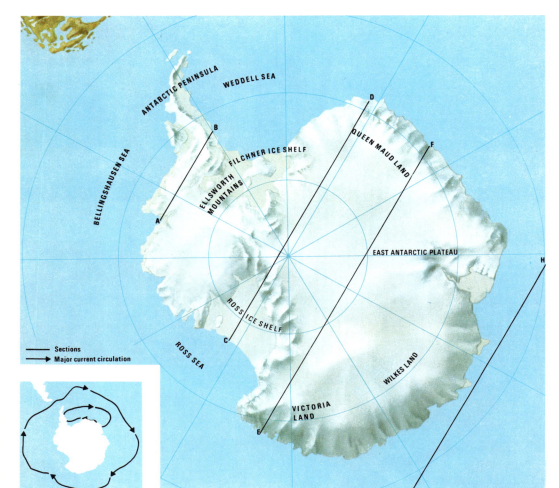

Sections

Major current circulation

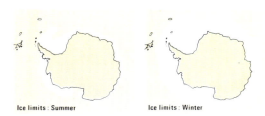

Ice limits : Summer   Ice limits : Winter

Great island beneath the snow *above and below*
For more than four million years the great island-continent of Antarctica has been covered with an ice cap which, in places, is more than two miles thick.

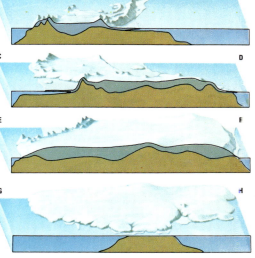

Chilling the sea *above*
Pouring through the ranges of Antarctica, ice spills into the sea, forming icebergs, feeding ice shelves and cooling the waters. In winter vast areas of sea freeze over : in summer this ice breaks up and shrinks.
Summer : South Georgia (right).

Old shorelines ring a shrinking lake in a Victoria Land dry valley.

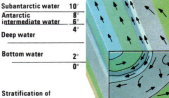

Subantarctic water	10°
Antarctic intermediate water	8°
	6°
Deep water	4°
Bottom water	2°
	0°

Stratification of ocean waters adjoining antarctic continent.

Life in the Antarctic is chiefly limited by the lack of moisture and warmth. Water is released when snow melts, but where the soil is permeable, seeps rapidly out of reach. The ground is warmed by the sun – continuously above the horizon for many summer weeks – and on clear days, when the air temperature is around zero °C, soil and moss can reach as much as 15°C, providing ideal conditions for plant growth and the activity of soil animals. When the sun is hidden, or in winter darkness, temperatures plummet. Life for the cold-blooded invertebrates and lower plants of Antarctica goes by fits and starts, with spurts of activity in the sporadic warm spells.

Even in the richest habitats the vegetation is patchy. In the continental interior lichens are the commonest plants, growing as tufts and encrustations on the rocks. Antarctica has some 400 species all told.

Near the coast, about 70 species of moss and 15 species of liverworts form deep carpets, building up peat banks more than a metre thick. On the islands around the tip of the Antarctic Peninsula grow the region's only two higher plants – a grass, *Deschampsia antarctica* and a cushion plant, *Colobanthus quitensis*.

Animal life, too, is richest in the Peninsula and islands, where there are two species of midge – the largest true land animals of the region. The small lakes have felts of moss and alga on the rocks and a fauna of small Crustacea, the largest a brine shrimp about half an inch long. In soil and moss the commonest animals are springtails, mites and nematode worms, all under a quarter of an inch long.

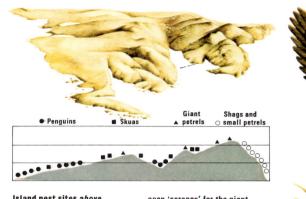

Island nest sites *above*
A typical Antarctic island will provide a range of nesting zones for a variety of birds; shelving, water's edge sites for penguins; open 'scrapes' for the giant petrel and the great skua, and ledges on precipitous rock faces for the blue-eyed shag and small petrels.

Blue-eyed shag
Phalacrocorax atriceps

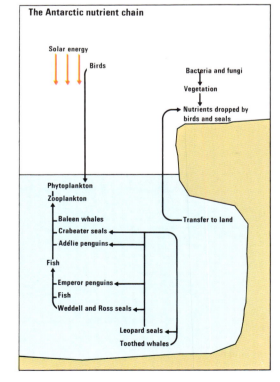

Great skua
Catharacta skua

Skua robs its neighbours
The piratical great skua preys on the eggs and chicks of other birds; a colony of 2,000 pairs of Adélie penguins will have 20 pairs of great skuas nesting on its fringes, ready to pounce on the unattended egg or chick. The great skua preys also on petrel colonies.

Giant petrel
Macronectes giganteus

Adélie penguin
Pygoscelis adeliae

Antarctic plant life
The two species of higher plants native to Antarctica, *Colobanthus quitensis* and *Deschampsia antarctica* (below) occur only in the Peninsula sector of the continental mainland and in Subantarctic islands. Both plants thrive in mean summer temperatures near 0°C.

Bird of two summers
The Arctic tern *Sterna macrura* breeds in the far north during the brief Arctic summer. It then migrates to the southern hemisphere and Antarctic waters, enjoying two summers every year and more daylight in its lifetime than any other animal.

Fringe of a cold desert
Vegetation has little more than a toehold in Antarctica. Only in the ice-free areas and coastal strips (amounting to about four per cent of the continent) is there any plant life, most of it lichen in the dry and exposed places and moss where the niches are moister and milder. The moss *Brachythecium* sp. (left) coats rocks beside runnels of water. The tiny buttercup (right) grows in 'meadows' on Subantarctic islands like South Georgia (above).

The Antarctic nutrient chain

Solar energy

Birds

Bacteria and fungi

Vegetation

Nutrients dropped by birds and seals

Phytoplankton
Zooplankton

Baleen whales

Crabeater seals

Adélie penguins

Transfer to land

Fish

Emperor penguins

Fish

Weddell and Ross seals

Leopard seals

Toothed whales

Warm niche in a cold world
In a cushion of turf intermittent spells of warming sunshine (see diagram below) allow bursts of activity for the continent's largest terrestrial animal forms—mites, midges, springtails and other insects. Three of the more common are shown (right): a springtail *Cryptopygus antarcticus* (top) and mites *Alaskozetes antarcticus* and *Tydeus tilbrooki*.

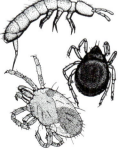

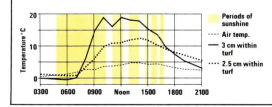

Periods of sunshine	
--- Air temp.	
— 3 cm within turf	
···· 2.5 cm within turf	

Temperature °C
20
10
0
0300 0600 0900 Noon 1500 1800 2100

Mite populations *above*
Antarctic species are few but populations often numerous, locally. The picture shows an aggregation of *Alaskozetes* sp. mites on the alga *Prasiola* sp.

● Penguins   ■ Skuas   ▲ Giant petrels   ○ Shags and small petrels

Life in the Pack Ice

The Antarctic coastal zone is renowned for its vast colonies of penguins and seals and the Antarctic ocean for its whales. Today the Southern Ocean is the scene of a fast-expanding fishery and it has been estimated that over 45 million tons of 'krill', a shrimplike Crustacean three centimetres long and abundant in the surface waters, could be caught annually. This would almost double world fishery landings. The contrast between desert land and teeming ocean is the most dramatic feature of Antarctic life.

It happens because the upwelling of water around the continent brings a continual supply of the salts essential for plant growth into the surface layers where, in summer, there is abundant light. The result is a summer bloom of plant plankton – tiny, one-celled algae – which in turn provides abundant food for krill and other small animals. The Antarctic seas are productive and support a 'standing crop' of life four to seven times as great as many tropical oceans. This life sustains the populations of seals and whales, penguins and petrels.

There are four truly Antarctic seals, each with characteristic breeding habits and foods. They are perfectly adapted to life in the cold seas. Even in freezing water, the temperature 40 millimetres beneath the skin remains constant at 35°C. Weddell seals can dive to 300 metres and stay submerged for an hour. Their blood has five times the oxygen-carrying capacity of human blood and the seal has twice as much blood per unit of bodyweight. During diving, a further remarkable adaptation comes into play: the heart slows and the circulation is cut off from less important tissues so that brain, liver, kidney and womb remain well supplied with blood.

High population turnover
The true seals of the Antarctic are very much larger than their counterparts in the Arctic, but live shorter lives – potentially, about 20 years. Females attain puberty at about three years – in half the time of a northern seal – but the death rate is also higher, producing a more rapid population turnover. Breeding cycle (below).

1 Mating
2 Implantation
3 Full term
4 Birth
5 Lactation

Distribution of Antarctic seals

Ross seal
● *Ommatophoca rossi*
Crabeater seal
Lobodon carcinophagus
Weddell seal
Leptonychotes weddelli
Leopard seal
Hydrurga leptonyx

The endemic seals
Antarctic seals are found in all seas around the continent but each species has a distinct ecological niche and there is thus little competition between them. The four principal species are the Weddell seal *Leptonychotes weddelli* (above, pup and cow); the crabeater seal *Lobodon carcinophagus* (right, with a drawing of its teeth); the ferocious leopard seal *Hydrurga leptonyx* (below); and the Ross seal *Ommatophoca rossi* (above right).

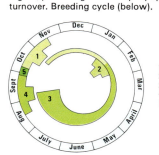

Ross seal
Ommatophoca rossi

Crabeater seal
Lobodon carcinophagus

Penguin hunter
In summer, leopard seals often patrol offshore from penguin colonies, awaiting a favourite dish, the Adélie penguin. They also eat fish, squid and sometimes the pups of other seal species. As if aware of this threat to its existence an Adélie penguin often appears reluctant to be the first of its group to enter the water.

Leopard seal
Hydrurga leptonyx

Adélie penguin
Pygoscelis adeliae

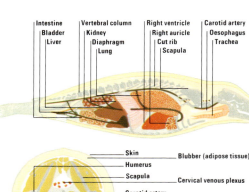

Intestine	Vertebral column	Right ventricle	Carotid artery
Bladder	Kidney	Right auricle	Oesophagus
Liver	Diaphragm	Cut rib	Trachea
	Lung	Scapula	

Skin
Humerus
Scapula
Carotid artery
Spinal cord
Trachea
Sternum

Blubber (adipose tissue)
Cervical venous plexus
Vertebral centrum
Oesophagus

Purposeful packaging left
The sleek, streamlined form of the seal encloses a 'power pack' which has evolved to meet survival requirements in a habitat as harsh as any on earth – the waters around and beneath the ice shelves fringing Antarctica.
A unique swimming talent and an ability to dive deeply are the result of steady anatomical and physiological adaptations; the insulating blubber layer which keeps out the cold also acts as a food reserve particularly during the pupping season. Reproductive modifications ensure that the young are born at optimum survival time.

Long before the Antarctic ice cap formed, the clownish penguin family evolved in the cool seas of the southern hemisphere. They are birds which have long lost the power of flight and have become adapted for a life of swimming and diving by their streamlined form, insulation of close-set feathers over fatty blubber and the conversion of their wings into flippers which are used for swimming in a manner similar to a bird's use of its wings.

Such adaptations fitted the penguins to survive in a cooling Antarctic which continued to provide abundant sea food and safe breeding and moulting grounds ashore. Today, five kinds of penguin inhabit the true Antarctic zone and many more live in Sub-antarctic and temperate regions, ranging north to the Equator at the Galapagos Islands.

Generally, the smallest and least well-insulated species, like the fairy and the little blue penguins of Australasia, live farthest north, while the biggest and the best insulated, the emperor, is southernmost, but there is no exact rule.

All penguins spend most of their lives at sea, coming ashore to breed and moult. Despite the apparent chaos of thousands of identical birds in a penguin colony, the same pairs commonly re-form, at the same nesting site, each year.

Distribution of penguins

Giant penguin ancestor

5 Feet
4
3
2
1

Miocene penguin
Emperor
Adélie
Blue

King
Aptenodytes patagonica
35 lb 94 cm

Chinstrap
Pygoscelis antarctica
10 lb 68 cm

Adélie
Pygoscelis adeliae
11 lb 71 cm

Emperor
Aptenodytes forsteri
65 lb 114 cm

Southern Gentoo
Pygoscelis papua ellsworthii
12 lb 71 cm

Royal
Eudyptes schlegeli
10 lb 61 cm

Erect-crested
Eudyptes atratus
8 lb 66 cm

Magellanic
Spheniscus magellanicus
11 lb 71 cm

Macaroni
Eudyptes chrysolophus
9 lb 71 cm

Rockhopper
Eudyptes crestatus
6 lb 56 cm

Snares Islands
Eudyptes robustus
7 lb 53 cm

Yellow-eyed
Megadyptes antipodes
12 lb 66 cm

Southern Blue
Eudyptula minor minor
2 lb 41 cm

Galapagos
Spheniscus mendiculus
5 lb 53 cm

Peruvian
Spheniscus humboldti
9 lb 66 cm

Jackass
Spheniscus demersus
6 lb 71 cm

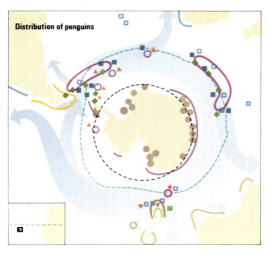

At the nesting site
The busy 'market-place' scene of King penguins (left) at their nesting site and (right) Macaroni penguins at theirs. The drawing (below) shows an incubating Emperor penguin.

Outside temperature
−30 C to −50 C

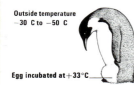

Egg incubated at +33°C

Walking and 'tobogganing'
Most human of all penguins in its gait the Adélie 'toboggans' readily, using flippers and feet, as fast as a sprinting man.

Walking

Running

Tobogganing

Movement in water and coming ashore

'Porpoising' into shore the Adélie pops out of the water, up to heights of six ft, to land on its feet or flat on its stomach.

The penguin's lungs are protected from increased pressure by a series of air sacs which are compressed as the bird dives in search of food.

air sacs

Faithful pairs occupy same nest sites
The breeding season among Adélie penguins begins in September/October (the Antarctic spring) when the birds return to their rookeries and occupy the nest sites. Although they may be covered in snow the same nest sites are habitually used by the same pair of mating birds who may have travelled over 200 miles (300km) of rough sea ice to reach them. Two eggs – sometimes three – are laid and hatch out after about 35 days. After nine weeks, chicks make for the sea.

Breeding behaviour key
1 Male brings stone for nest and for female's acceptance.
2 Fight between nesting bird and unestablished wanderer.
3 Ecstatic display between two birds at nest site.
4 Creche of chick penguins during partly-fledged stage.
5 Parent regurgitates food into gaping throat of chick.

The Albatross Latitudes

The Antarctic subpolar zone is almost entirely oceanic. Only a few, widely-scattered and mostly volcanic islands break the surface to provide habitats for land animals and plants, and seabirds and seals. These remote islands are difficult for land organisms to colonize and their floras and faunas are poor in species, although richer than the Antarctic mainland.

The southern frontier of the Subantarctic is often set at the Antarctic convergence, where cold polar currents meet and sink beneath warmer waters. The islands are treeless and green with coastal tussock grasslands, and the lower ground inland bears heathland and bogs. There are insects and a few true land birds, but seals and seabirds dominate the region as they do the high polar zone.

Elephant and fur seals, which only penetrate the northern fringes of the Antarctic zone, are widespread and abundant. The elephant seal is the world's largest, full size bulls reaching 18 feet (six metres) in length and three tons in weight. In the breeding colonies 'beachmaster' bulls herd together small harems of cows, their roaring challenges to rivals resonating through their inflated trunks, or proboscences. When two bulls fight, they rear up and slash at each other's necks with open mouths and short, powerful tusks.

Fur seals – almost exterminated by sealers a century ago, but now abundant again – are also colonial, polygamous and bellicose, but here each bull defends an area of beach rather than a harem, and the same is true among the sea lions (three bulls and families, right) that also occur in the Subantarctic.

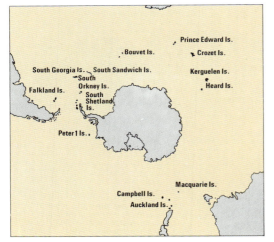

Otariids and Phocids
Otariid seals are a compromise, anatomically, between terrestrial and aquatic modes of life. The other major group of seals, the true seals or Phocids, have become adapted to exploit far more of the polar seas. A fur seal *Arctocephalus* sp. is illustrated below.

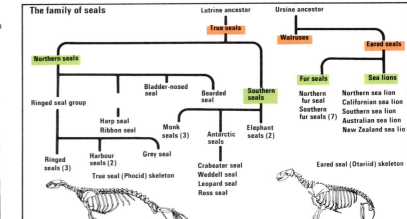

The albatross is the distinctive and characteristic seabird of the subpolar waters of Antarctica even though it ranges north into temperate and even tropical seas. The greatest of all is the wanderer, whose 12-foot (3.6 metres) wingspan is the largest of any sea bird. Smaller species like the black-browed, grey-headed or yellow-nosed, called 'mollymawks' by sailors, or the two sooty albatrosses with their eerie calls and unrivalled mastery of soaring flight, reach a wingspan of about eight feet (2.5 metres).

All albatrosses build nest mounds of earth and grass, generally on windy slopes, for the birds are built like high-performance sailplanes and need a fresh wind or downhill run – better still, both – to take off easily. The wanderers have a spectacular courtship display involving a weird variety of braying and bubbling calls, and postures that include the full spreading of the wings. They breed only in alternate years because the whole cycle, from the arrival of the parents to the departure of the chick, may take as much as 380 days: smaller mollymawks may, however, nest every year.

At sea, the albatrosses are unmistakable by their soaring flight, skimming downwind into the trough of the seas, turning and rising sharply into the wind, and circling ships with hardly a wingbeat. They have enchanted mariners since ships first sailed the 'albatross latitudes'.

If unforgettable, the albatrosses are far from being the only Subantarctic seabirds. Petrels, penguins, prions, gulls, shags, terns and skuas breed in great numbers on the southern islands, alongside a few land birds.

Home of the albatross
To the northern tip of South Georgia Island (above) thousands of albatrosses return each year to breed. Both parents take part in the incubation of the single egg which hatches after about 70 days. Eating regurgitated fish the chick grows quickly until it is about three months old when it is left unguarded and fed more erratically. (Left) a young grey-headed albatross *Diomedea chrysostoma*.

Diomedea and *Phoebetria*
Heads and beaks of seven of the 13 species of albatross. They occur as two genera, Diomedea the larger, and Phoebetria with only two species.

Sooty albatross
Phoebetria fusca

Light-mantled albatross
Phoebetria palpebrata

Shy albatross
Diomedea cauta

Yellow-nosed albatross
Diomedea chlororhynchos

Bullers albatross
Diomedea bulleri

Wandering albatross
Diomedea exulans

Black-browed albatross
Diomedea melanophris

The family of seals

			Lutrine ancestor		Ursine ancestor	
			True seals		Walruses	Eared seals
Northern seals					Fur seals	Sea lions
		Bladder-nosed seal	Bearded seal	Southern seals	Northern fur seal	Northern sea lion / Californian sea lion
Ringed seal group					Southern fur seals (7)	Southern sea lion / Australian sea lion / New Zealand sea lio
	Harp seal / Ribbon seal	Monk seals (3)		Elephant seals (2)		
Ringed seals (3)	Harbour seals (2)	Grey seal	Antarctic seals			
	True seal (Phocid) skeleton		Crabeater seal / Weddell seal / Leopard seal / Ross seal		Eared seal (Otariid) skeleton	

Breeding among elephant seals

Male elephant seals are old enough to dominate a harem and rookery (the breeding territory) at an age of six years. The female carries her embryonic young for about six months before she comes ashore to give birth some time in September or October. Mating occurs a month later before the population disperses to the sea for a brief period of heavy feeding. The females return to shore to moult in January. Since copulation the blastocyst has remained free in the female's uterus. After the moult it implants in the uterine wall and gestation begins.

Confrontation
The scars on the head and neck of an old bull elephant seal testify to the ferocity of the fighting which takes place between males at breeding time. The deep wounds are caused by the huge canine teeth with which it rips at its adversary. Although scarring is heaviest on the bull's head and shoulders the whole body is often marked.

Symbol of maturity
A mature male elephant seal *Mirounga leonina* (above) splashes contentedly in a mud wallow surrounded by seeding tussock grass. The symbol of its maturity is an 'inflatable' nose or proboscis which takes a number of years to develop. Out of season the proboscis is low and flattened, but during the mating season it erects impressively as the diagram (left) shows. In old bulls it is often severely lacerated in fights.

3 year old

6 year old

8 year old Harem bull

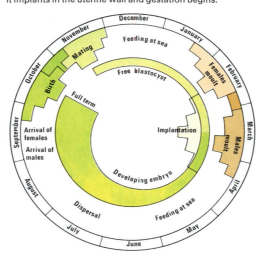

December
November
January
Mating
Feeding at sea
October
February
Birth
Females moult
Free blastocyst
September
Full term
Males moult
March
Arrival of females
Implantation
Arrival of males
April
August
Developing embryo
Dispersal
Feeding at sea
July
June
May

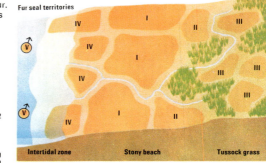

Waterproof underfur
The pelage, or coat, of fur seals *Arctocephalus gazella* (left) is the most luxuriant of all seals. Long guard hairs overlay a secondary layer of finely curled hairs which in turn protect a dense underfur. A secretion of sweat and oils waterproofs this underfur which never becomes wet while the seal is swimming.

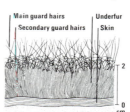

Main guard hairs · Underfur
Secondary guard hairs · Skin

2
0 cm

Knock-out contest for breeding sites
Bull fur seals fight fiercely to establish breeding territories, the strongest gaining the choice sites on the beach. 'Runners-up' pup farther from the sea, with the 'also-rans' at the water's edge or in the inland tussock grass. Those unable to win territory cruise off shore.

Fur seal territories

IV · I · II · III
V
IV · I
IV · III · III
V
IV · I · II · III

Intertidal zone · Stony beach · Tussock grass

The perfect flier
The most efficient flier of all birds, the albatross lets the wind do its work. On outstretched, motionless wings it speeds downwind in a shallow dive until, in the turbulent air above the wave tops, it banks sharply and begins its climb upwind. Now the momentum of its dive carries it along – still on motionless wings.

Altitude metres · Wind speed m.p.h.
18 · 40
Wind direction
15 · 39
65
12 · 38
75 · 65 · 75
9 · 36
Speed of flight m.p.h.
3 · 32
0 · 20 · 68 · 46 · 68
True direction of flight

The albatross latitudes
The west wind drift through the albatross latitudes of the southern hemisphere is the motive power for bird wanderings. Some birds spend the winter 8,000 miles from their nesting sites.

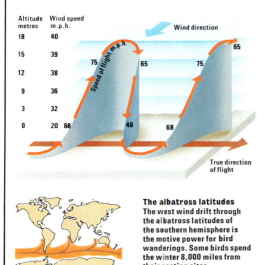

Grey-headed albatross

'Tapping' for its food
A young albatross grows quickly on fish and other sea animals regurgitated from its parents' stomachs and at three months may weigh as much as an adult. The chick taps the beak of its parent (left) an action which probably stimulates the stomach muscles of the parent, forcing it to bring the food up into its mouth for transfer to the fledgling. Older chicks are left unattended for great lengths of time while the parents wander thousands of miles in search of food, which is taken from the surface of the sea.

Courtship, copulation
At the onset of the breeding season albatrosses perform elaborate displays of bill clapping, bowing and neck waving. 'Sky pointing' involves the spreading of wings. Courtship ends when the female is subdued by the male's advances. Copulation follows, the male seizing his mate's neck with his beak.

Courtship dance of the Wandering albatross *Diomedea exulans*

Nursery of Life on Earth

Viewed from far out in space, the earth is a blue planet, with oceans and seas covering more than 70 per cent of its surface. The presence of these great quantities of water, most of it aggregated into the oceans on the surface of the globe, has determined the course of evolution of all living organisms.

In their constant processes of formation and destruction the six major structural plates of the earth's crust have caused the continents to wander and have formed the major features of the sea bed – the almost unfathomable abysses, the arcs of islands thrown up by vulcanism.

The oceans are largely cold dark places, and it is only in the upper few hundred metres that sunlight penetrates significantly and the water warmed by its energy. Below these upper layers and often separated from them by a sharp layer where temperatures drop very sharply, the oceans extend to average depths of about 13,000 feet (4,000 metres) – and more than twice that depth in the trenches where there is virtually complete darkness. Although ocean water is not uniformly saline, almost everywhere there is enough oxygen to support life.

The seas and oceans are a restless world. The upper, warm water, to a depth of a few hundred feet, is blown along by the prevailing winds of the planet. Together with the motion imparted by the rotation of the earth, the drag of the winds produce the major shallow current systems of the oceans. Below the surface layers, density differences between water masses produce great, slow currents as dense water slides below lighter. Both the surface, wind-driven currents and the subsurface density currents transport enormous quantities of water over great distances.

The current systems largely determine the richness or poverty of marine life. Life forms occur throughout the oceans below the tropics to below the polar ice cap and from the sunlit waters to the great deeps. Where two currents, or a current and a land mass, interact, so as to draw deep water to the surface, carrying fresh nutrients for plant growth into the lighted zone, animal and plant life burgeons.

Undersea landscape *left*
Beneath the oceans covering the greater part of the earth's surface lies a landscape more diverse and spectacular than anywhere on dry land. Submerged continental fringes cover millions of square miles sloping down to the abyssal plains two and a half miles (4km) below sea level. The central volcanic ridges form an oceanic mountain range running almost unbrokenly for 40,000 miles through the centres of the world's great oceans. They represent the constant replacement of the earth's crust by upward movement from its mantle below.

Stranded guyot *above*
Rising from an arid plain inland from the Red Sea, Mount Asmara was formed beneath the sea which eroded the volcanic top of the mountain into a shallow saucer. This is the classic shape of a guyot, or undersea island.

| Continental shelf | Guyot | Mid-ocean ridge | Trench |

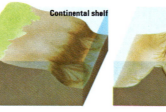

Distribution and abundance of zooplankton

Milligrams of plankton per cubic metre of sea water

- More than 500
- 201-500
- 51-200
- Less than 50

→ Cold currents
→ Warm currents

Oceanic salinity *right*
The main oceanic currents are shown (left). The waters are a solution of inorganic compounds with a suspension of solid matter, mainly organic. In a kilogram of seawater, 965 gm. is water, the remainder dissolved salts, mainly sodium chloride—common salt. Salinity is great near the Equator, or in enclosed seas.

Composition of seawater

a Calcium 1.5%
b Potassium 1.5%
c Magnesium 3.7%
d Sulphates 7.7%
e Sodium 30.6%
f Chlorine 55.0%

965 gm water
35 gm dissolved salts

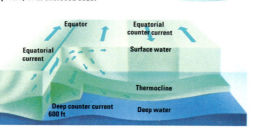

Equator
Equatorial counter current
Equatorial current
Surface water
Thermocline
Deep counter current 600 ft
Deep water

Pacific circulation *left*
The circulation system of the eastern equatorial Pacific Ocean, and the interaction of the various currents is caused by surface winds and the variation of pressures in the deeps. Between the surface waters and the deep layers, the thermocline is a sharp discontinuity barrier where temperatures drop acutely.

Life probably originated in the oceans. Certainly the fossil record in the sedimentary rocks shows that most of the major forms of life evolved there. The concentration and reaction of elements and compounds within the shallow layers of tropical seas is one of the more likely sites to have been proposed for the early evolution of the biochemical precursors of organized life.

The earliest assemblages of fossil animals of which we have examples – from the Cambrian period – consist of marine animals. They are the medusae and arthropods which had already, by that time, passed through a long and complex evolutionary process to arrive at forms remarkably like some of those still living in the oceans today.

From these beginnings, invertebrate life in the oceans evolved into a series of groups, each having a fundamentally different form, and differing from each other basically in the means by which feeding, reproduction and survival were solved – and only a few having lived elsewhere than in the oceans or brackish coastal waters. It is mainly the insects, the spiders and the higher vertebrates that have evolved on land, leaving their origins behind in the ocean.

The fossil record shows how some of the major groups of animals that evolved in the sea persisted for long periods, and then died out. It is only as fossils that they are known. It shows also how almost all groups have slowly and continuously evolved in response to changing environmental conditions while retaining their fundamental plan, or bodily form.

Fossil gallery
Portrait of a fish that lived a hundred million years ago, the fossil of *Dapedium politum* (above) is found in sedimentary rocks throughout Europe. Its scales were much heavier than those of modern fish. The fossil sea lily (left), (an echinoderm), is imprinted in coral. Both the sea lily and coral were abundant and widespread, but corals are found today only in warm tropical seas.

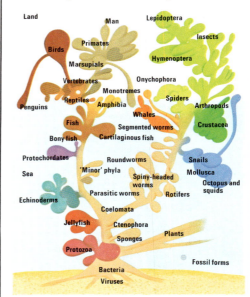

The origins of life
The phylogeny, or evolutionary pedigree, of life on earth, in diagrammatic form (below) shows the probable order of evolution of all life forms. The sea is still home for the greatest number of living creatures.

Urchins and ammonites
The fossil remains of the sea urchin *Phymosoma koenigii* (above) are often found in flint rocks. Like the ammonite molluscs (right) of the class Cephalopoda (which includes the octopus), *Phymosoma* died out during the Cretaceous, more than 70 million years ago.

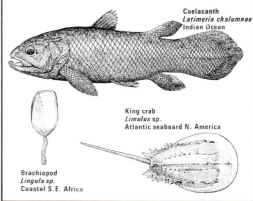

The three remnant species (below) closely resemble their fossil forms. The most remarkable is the king crab — it has not changed in 150 million years.

Coelacanth
Latimeria chalumnae
Indian Ocean

King crab
Limulus sp.
Atlantic seaboard N. America

Brachiopod
Lingula sp.
Coastal S.E. Africa

Return to the sea
All land animals evolved from marine forms and became adapted to a life out of water. Those illustrated here followed this pattern – then reversed it, to re-enter the sea, either to live permanently, or just to feed. Each has adapted in physiology or behaviour to survive.

Galápagos habitat of marine iguana.

A one-time land insect *Halobates* sp. now spends all its life at sea.

Above, vestigial pelvic girdle of humpback whale.

Whales have evolved from a group of mammals that returned to the sea 70 million years ago

Like all penguins the chinstrap *Pygoscelis antarctica* uses its wings to swim rapidly

Marine iguana *Amblyrhynchus cristatus* breeds ashore but feeds on submerged algae.

Sea otter *Enhydra lutris* eats crustaceans, crushing shells with stones, or in strong teeth.

Flattened tail of sea snake *Aipysurus laevis* aids its swimming. Lays eggs on reefs.

163

Living Pastures of the Sea

Marine animals live according to the same fundamental principles as life on land. All life in the oceans is based upon a food supply generated by plant growth, fuelled by energy from the sun and building with the same basic elements – carbon (from carbon dioxide), nitrogen (from ammonia, nitrites or nitrates) and hydrogen. The plants are grazed down by herbivores, as on land, and these in turn serve as food for a series of carnivores.

There is one great difference between life ashore and at sea; almost all oceanic plant life occurs as single cells or simple chains of cells visible only microscopically, so that food of the herbivorous animals must painstakingly be strained from the water in which it is suspended before it can be consumed. Only along the margins of the oceans, attached to the shoreline and just below it, are there large plants in any way comparable to those ashore; but while this large vegetation produces important food for a numerous and varied fauna it is relatively unimportant in the economy of the oceans as a whole. These macroscopic plants reach their greatest development in the beds of giant kelp lying in the mid-latitudes of American coastal waters.

The production of phytoplankton – the free-floating single plant cells – is not uniform over all the oceans: as on land, there are apparently deserts where plant life is sparse and, in contrast, places where it is so abundant that the water is opaque and green or brown in colour. Since plant life requires sunlight and nutrient salts, phytoplankton is produced only in the first few hundred feet or so below the surface, to a depth at which sufficient sunlight penetrates – and most abundantly where nutrient-rich water wells up from below, into the lighted zone.

The need to strain food from water has given rise to a wonderful diversity of filtering mechanisms in almost all groups of marine invertebrates both among those of the plankton which drift passively with their phytoplankton pastures, and also among the animals which live buried in or upon the floor of the ocean at depths at which the phytoplankton occurs.

An undersea pyramid of life
The lumpsucker *Cyclopterus* devours a dozen *Beroe*, the large comb jelly. To reach its size *Beroe* will have eaten 3,500 smaller comb jellies, *Bolinopsis*. These, in turn, will have fed upon 100,000 copepods – and the copepods will have grazed untold millions of phytoplankton.

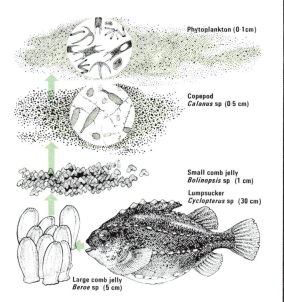

Phytoplankton (0·1 cm)

Copepod
Calanus sp (0·5 cm)

Small comb jelly
Bolinopsis sp (1 cm)

Lumpsucker
Cyclopterus sp (30 cm)

Large comb jelly
Beroe sp (5 cm)

Vertical migrations *right*
Planktonic animals migrate to and from the surface as the density of light changes during the day. Such migrations mean that plankton – which cannot travel far of its own volition – gains transport to new pastures in the faster surface currents.

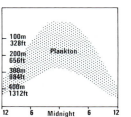

100m 328ft
200m 656ft
300m 984ft
400m 1312ft

Plankton

12 6 Midnight 6 12

Components of pasture
Plankton consists mainly of unicellular diatoms (far right). As in higher forms, these manufacture food substances from the light energy in the upper layers of the sea and are eaten by the zooplankton – the animal component of plankton. Photo shows zooplankton.

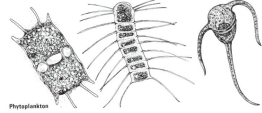

Phytoplankton

The living pastures *below*
The natural destiny of more than 90 per cent of all sea creatures is to be swallowed by other animals. Part of this incalculable living pasture is composed of minute larval forms. Most are mobile in contrast to the more sluggish adult forms; many achieve their movement by the use of tiny, hair-like processes called cilia, which beat rhythmically for propulsion. The ascidian tadpole, a larval form of sea squirt, contains a rod-like structure which suggests that an animal similar to it may have given rise to the higher vertebrates. The jellyfish shows two distinct phases; a fixed polyp form like a sea anemone which then separates into tiny, saucer-like jellyfish swimming free.

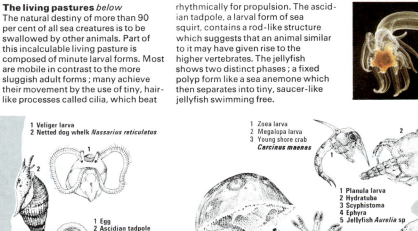

1 Veliger larva
2 Netted dog whelk *Nassarius reticulatus*

1 Egg
2 Ascidian tadpole
3 Ascidian tadpole settling
4 Adult sea squirt *Clavelina* sp

1 Bipinnaria larva
2 Starfish *Asterias* sp

1 Ophiopluteus larva
2 Brittle star *Ophiothrix* sp

1 Zoea larva
2 Megalopa larva
3 Young shore crab
Carcinus maenas

1 Planula larva
2 Hydratuba
3 Scyphistoma
4 Ephyra
5 Jellyfish *Aurelia* sp

1 Auricularia larva
2 Sea cucumber *Holothuria* sp

1 Echinopluteus larva
2 Sea urchin
Echinus sp

Feeding and movement among invertebrates

Among the complex forms of ocean life the sea gooseberry has tentacles to catch its prey. The copepod *Calanus* uses filter feeding, food being trapped by hairs in the mouth processes. *Oikopleura* filters food through tubes and 'windows'.

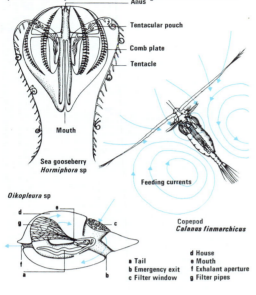

Sea gooseberry
Hormiphora sp

- Anus
- Tentacular pouch
- Comb plate
- Tentacle
- Mouth

Feeding currents

Oikopleura sp

- a Tail
- b Emergency exit
- c Filter window
- d House
- e Mouth
- f Exhalant aperture
- g Filter pipes

Copepod
Calanus finmarchicus

Stingers of the surface waters

The simple arrangement of the Portuguese man of war *Physalia* and the purple sail fish *Velella* sp. (below) shows the development of their specialized cells for reproduction, locomotion, feeding and defence. Surface winds propel them through the warm ocean currents.

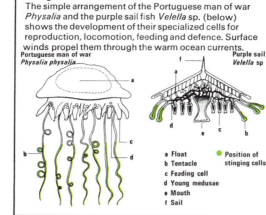

Portuguese man of war
Physalia physalia

Purple sail
Velella sp

- a Float
- b Tentacle
- c Feeding cell
- d Young medusae
- e Mouth
- f Sail
- ● Position of stinging cells

Velella (left). The nematocysts, or stinging cells (below), are characteristic of the Hydrozoa. The Portuguese man of war can kill and eat prey up to the size of a large mackerel.

Discharged

Undischarged

- a Trigger
- b Barbs
- c Lid
- d Filament

The 'flying' gasteropod
Limacina retroversa

Pause

Rising through the water

Sinking

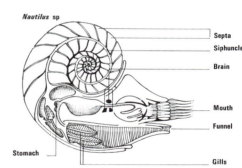

Sea slugs

The tropical sea slug (right) is a mollusc that has lost its shell. Many sea slugs are gaudily marked like terrestrial caterpillars, and fill a similar niche by browsing on sea weed. *Doris* (below) is an Atlantic species.

- Position of mouth on ventral surface
- Tentacle
- Heart
- Anus
- Gill

Sea slug
Doris sp

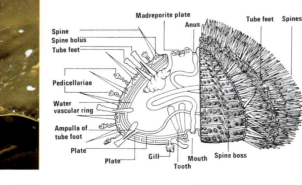

'Satellite' snail *below*
Opening its vanes like a research satellite the sea snail *Limacina retroversa* flaps along slowly.

Nautilus sp

- Septa
- Siphuncle
- Brain
- Mouth
- Funnel
- Gills
- Stomach

Echinoderms – the spiny invertebrates

The characteristic form of the sea urchin of the class Echinoidea is that of a starfish, with its arms drawn together above its centre. The cross-sections (below) show the position of the spines and the tube feet.

- Madreporite plate
- Anus
- Tube feet
- Spines
- Spine
- Spine bolus
- Tube feet
- Pedicellariae
- Water vascular ring
- Ampulla of tube foot
- Plate
- Plate
- Gill
- Mouth
- Tooth
- Spine boss

Mollusc relatives *above*
The octopus (top) is a large-brained, intelligent mollusc. The nautilus (above) crawls and swims like an octopus.

Not a flower . . . *below*
The peacock worm uses its characteristic branchia, or tentacles, to trap food passing through them.

Tube-footed urchin
Close-up view (right) of the tube feet of a sea urchin. The feet are capped in suction pads pressurised by a sac, the ampulla, to enable the echinoderm to make its way across rocks, where it scrapes off vegetation to feed upon.

Starfish *right*
A perfect example of the symmetry of the echinoderms is provided by the star-fish. Starfish are commonly predators on molluscs, prising open the shells with the tube feet, used in sequence until the mollusc tires and gives way.

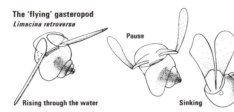

Silver Shoals and Lone Hunters

The number and diversity of fish make them by far the most successful of the lower vertebrates. They provide an excellent example of how evolution has enabled a great variety of form and function to be built up upon a single, fundamental body plan. Whether a fish is eel-like, or is as bizarre as a seahorse, it shares great similiarities of development, basic anatomy and physiology with all other fishes.

The basic fish-plan has only a small number of fundamental variations, and only two of these are important in the fish fauna of today – the Chondrichthyes (sharks, rays, dogfish, among others) with cartilaginous skeletons, thorn-like scales, and their method of solving the problem of living in a salty medium; and the Teleostei, the more familiar forms with shiny scales, bony skeletons and often airbladders to adjust their buoyancy.

Once their basic advance in bodily organization had been achieved, fishes evolved into a great and diverse assembly of animals which, at the present day, form many of the primary and most of the secondary carnivores in the ocean – that is, those species which feed directly, or at one remove, upon the herbivores, which are mostly invertebrates.

Fishes live in all parts of the oceans, down to the dark and cold of the greatest depths. The species of the shallow, lighted zones frequently form great shoals, like herrings and sardines; some, like the tuna, make long, even transoceanic migrations. The problems of life in the great depths have resulted in the evolution of many beautiful and curious species, including those with luminous organs.

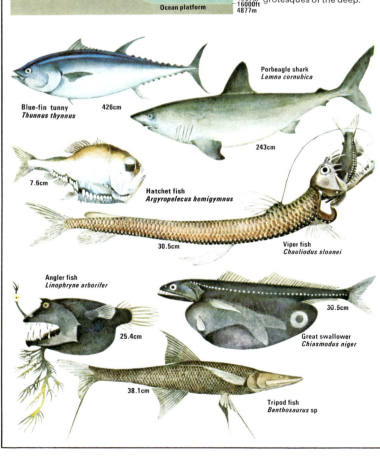

Niches for fishes
The layers of the ocean (left) from the translucent surface waters through the twilight zone to the depths of eternal gloom provide a range of habitats to which the ocean's wealth of species has become adapted. The 'conventional' configurations of the tuna and the shark, which live in the upper layers are in marked contrast to the grotesques of the deep.

Safety in numbers *above*
The shoal is almost a single unit, gaining protection for the individual by its sheer numbers.

Light organs *below*
The glowing hatchet fish *Argyropelecus* sp. lives — with most luminescent fish — in the middle waters.

Migrating elvers *above*
Born as eggs in the Sargasso sea, elvers — young eels — migrate to coastal waters and river mouths.

Littoral zone | Shallow water zone | Deep water zone

Continental shelf

Euphotic zone — SL
— 600ft 183m
— 2000ft 610m

Bathyal zone — 4000ft 1219m
— 6000ft 1829m

Continental slope

Abyssal pelagic zone — 8000ft 2438m
— 10000ft 3048m
— 12000ft 3658m
— 14000ft 4267m

Ocean platform — 16000ft 4877m

Blue-fin tunny
Thunnus thynnus 426cm

Porbeagle shark
Lamna cornubica

243cm

7.6cm

Hatchet fish
Argyropelecus hemigymnus

30.5cm

Viper fish
Chauliodus sloanei

Angler fish
Linophryne arborifer

30.5cm

25.4cm

Great swallower
Chiasmodus niger

38.1cm

Tripod fish
Benthosaurus sp

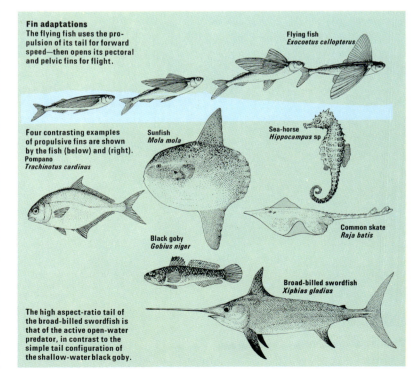

Fin adaptations
The flying fish uses the propulsion of its tail for forward speed—then opens its pectoral and pelvic fins for flight.

Flying fish
Exocoetus callopterus

Four contrasting examples of propulsive fins are shown by the fish (below) and (right).
Pompano
Trachinotus cardinus

Sunfish
Mola mola

Sea-horse
Hippocampus sp

Black goby
Gobius niger

Common skate
Raja batis

Broad-billed swordfish
Xiphias gladius

The high aspect-ratio tail of the broad-billed swordfish is that of the active open-water predator, in contrast to the simple tail configuration of the shallow-water black goby.

Like most marine invertebrates, many species of oceanic fish ensure proper dissemination of their species to all suitable habitats during their larval stages – the first few days or weeks, of life. Typically, marine fish shed their eggs and sperm so that fertilization occurs in the water, and outside the bodies of both parents. This apparently haphazard event is in fact remarkably efficient and is made possible by complex behavior patterns that ensure the event is properly coordinated.

Although fertilization itself is almost always totally effective, most larvae do not survive their larval life and fewer than one per cent metamorphose into juvenile fish. In species such as the cod and its relatives, each female releases several hundred thousand eggs at each spawning. These prolific fish are at one end of the spawning spectrum; at the other extreme, some species release fewer, larger eggs that are cared for parentally, sometimes (as in the catfish) in the mouth, or in a ventral pouch of a seahorse.

Compared with their helpless, drifting larvae, adult fish can accept only a much lower individual rate of mortality to ensure the survival of sufficient numbers to maintain healthy populations. To this end, a great range of defensive mechanisms has evolved. They range from the subtle camouflage of the silvery, midwater fish which merge into their background, to the striking, warning color patterns of some reef fish which bear poisonous spines, and similar weapons. Among the most lethally toxic of all is the stonefish *Synanceja horrida* which is almost impossible to detect, resembling a clump of mud or debris.

The herring, its spawning and food
From birth to adulthood the herring passes through a series of stages illustrated (below). The herring is a prolific breeder, laying 100,000 eggs at a spawning, on the sea bed. Few survive, for bottom-feeding fish like the haddock gorge themselves on the unprotected eggs. The youngsters that escape these pressures face other threats later; the predatory sea gooseberry *Pleurobrachia* sp. may eat five of them at a time. The juvenile herring or whitebait itself feeds first on phytoplankton, and later on a variety of invertebrates as it joins the great shoals swimming through northern waters.

The life cycle of the English herring
➡ Buchan stock
➡ Dogger Bank stock
1 Movement of whitebait
2 Movement of adults
3 Spawning grounds
4 Movements of larvae

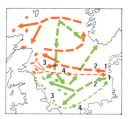

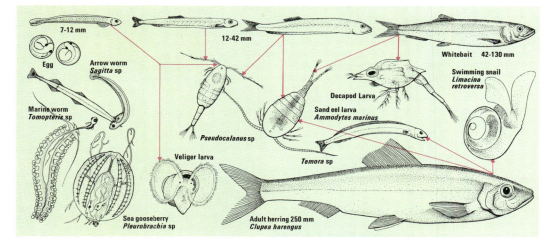

Protective egg capsule
The 'mermaid's purse' is the protective egg capsule of the nursehound *Scyliorhinus stellaris*.

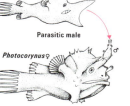

Sexual dimorphism
Male and female angler fish are linked at larval stage – and stay that way. Female reaches 3ft, male 6in.

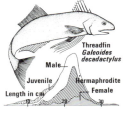

Eggs of sea bass
The transparent eggs of the sea bass *Dicentrarchus labrax*, are laid in May and June in inland waters.

Sex-change fish
Seventy-five per cent of this West African Polynemid go through sex change, the rest develop normally.

Octopus eggs
The octopus lays its gelatinous egg capsules in clusters in the crevices of rocks.

Making for the surface
Young seahorses emerging from male's pouch make for surface to swallow air to fill their swim bladders.

Attack and defence in the ocean
The armory of aggression and defence possessed by many fishes and other animals ranges from motionless camouflage to gaudy threat; the whiplash sting of rays, the slashing teeth of sharks. The scorpionid fish (below) combines camouflage with a potent sting; in contrast, the turkey fish (photo far right), a member of the same poisonous family, has warning colours and configuration.

'Chameleon' plaice *right*
In no way dangerous, the plaice *Pleuronectes platessa* lives unnoticed on shallow, sandy bottoms. It is able, chameleon-like, to change its colour to match its surroundings by means of chromatophore cells and reflecting cells.

Savage antagonists
Its name a synonym for predatory behaviour the shark (above) has serried rows of teeth in each jaw. Rear and side views of the jaw are shown (right). Almost as savage the moray eel (jaw below right) has knife-like, canine teeth. The jaw (below) is that of the sea snake whose fangs are like those of the cobra, but reduced.

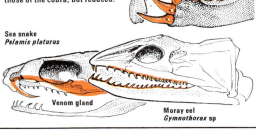

Jaws of sand shark
Carcharias taurus
Teeth

Sea snake
Pelamis platurus
Venom gland

Moray eel
Gymnothorax sp

Sting in the tail-and elsewhere
The venom apparatus of the stingray (below left) is an integral part of its tail. The star-gazer (right), a bottom-dweller, has lethal poison spines behind its pectoral fins.

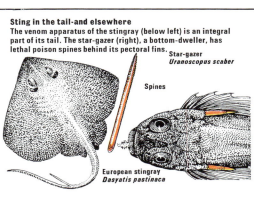

Star-gazer
Uranoscopus scaber
Spines
European stingray
Dasyatis pastinaca

Corals: Architects of the Reef

The coral reef is a living graveyard where in numbers beyond comprehension the polyps, or coral animals, live out their lives on the bones of their predecessors. They are architect, builder and raw material of the reef where, as nowhere else in the oceans, there is a fantastic diversity of colour, form and life.

Reef-forming corals depend for their existence on their ability to extract calcium carbonate from sea-water and use it to lay down millions of calcareous skeletons. Piled one above the other and fused into a mass, they form the limestone rock on which the living plants and animals of the reef grow. In some reefs the depth of limestone rock which has been produced measures many hundreds of feet. It has been calculated that the greatest of all coral growths, the Great Barrier Reef, more than 1,000 miles (1,600 km) long off the east coast of Australia, could provide enough limestone to build eight million replicas of Egypt's largest pyramid.

The reef began its life forming on a rocky outcrop in shallow water. The sea deepened during the evolution of the continents, but not so rapidly that the reef was unable to grow sufficiently fast to 'keep its head above water.' The animals and plants which form the reefs grow only in warm seas where winter temperatures never fall below 18°C and where the water is clear and free from riverborne silts. Few grow at any depth; most species require strong sunlight for growth.

Within the tissues of many species of reef-building corals there occur multitudes of minute, individual plant cells which live in association with their hosts and within the stony skeletons of the coral animals there dwell great quantities of thread-like green algae. These animal and plant associations are the key to the great productivity and diversity of coral reefs, extending to such strange creatures as the giant clam *Tridacna* which gapes its two huge shells to expose colourful pads of plant-cell bearing tissue. Tiny, one-cell plants live symbiotically with the clam, providing it with oxygen and food substances by means of photosynthesis.

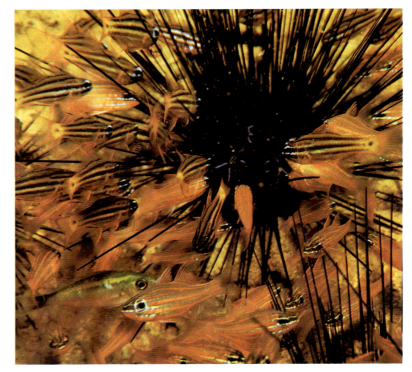

The cleaner fish
An abundance of brightly-coloured fish inhabits the waters of the coral reef. The imperial angel fish *Pomacanthus imperator* (below) is groomed of parasites around its mouth and gills by *Labroides* sp. Other species seek the services of this tiny cleaner.

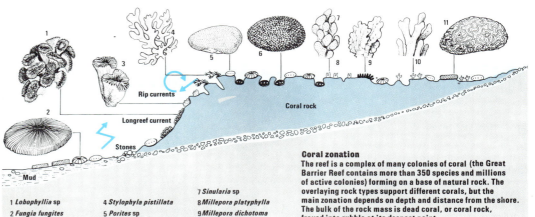

1 *Lobophyllia* sp
2 *Fungia fungites*
3 *Gyrosmilia* sp
4 *Stylophyla pistillata*
5 *Porites* sp
6 *Tubipora musica*
7 *Sinularia* sp
8 *Millepora platyphylla*
9 *Millepora dichotoma*
10 *Platygyra* sp

Coral zonation
The reef is a complex of many colonies of coral (the Great Barrier Reef contains more than 350 species and millions of active colonies) forming on a base of natural rock. The overlaying rock types support different corals, but the main zonation depends on depth and distance from the shore. The bulk of the rock mass is dead coral, or coral rock, frayed into rubble at its deepest point.

Soft and hard coral
The feeding tentacles of soft coral (above) paralyze the minute prey on which it lives. Soft coral contributes little to reef structure; this is the work of hard coral (right). One of the most dangerous of venomous fishes is the stone fish, shown (below).

The complex community
Coral reefs and lagoons contain the most complex and highly organized community of living creatures in the sea, due principally to the high rate of nutrient turnover in the environment. Many corals live in close interdependence with algae, which give out oxygen from photosynthesis and in return are supplied with carbon dioxide. The reefs also supply algae with the important nutrients — phosphates and nitrates — for their healthy growth. It has been calculated that there are more than 3,000 species of animals living in the Great Barrier Reef. Jellyfish and sea anemones — members of the same group as the corals — abound; the fish are brightly coloured, but so are the invertebrate shrimps, crabs, starfish and slugs. The most formidable of the reef's predators is an invertebrate — the octopus, which may reach a span of 30 feet (9m) from tip to tip of its tentacles.

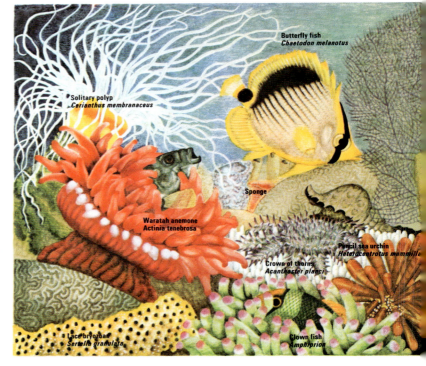

Butterfly fish
Chaetodon melanotus

Solitary polyp
Cerianthus membranaceus

Sponge

Waratah anemone
Actinia tenebrosa

Pencil sea urchin
Heterocentrotus mammillatus

Crown of thorns
Acanthaster planci

Lace brvozoan
Sertella granulata

Clown fish
Amphiprion

The reef wrecker
Predator of coral animals, the crown of thorns starfish *Acanthaster planci* spells doom to the reef structure.

The crown of thorns star-fish, a 'reef eater', feeds on the coral, leaving only the chalky skeleton. After reaching epidemic proportions off Australia, the starfish has spread through the reefs of New Guinea, Indonesia and the islands of the Pacific.

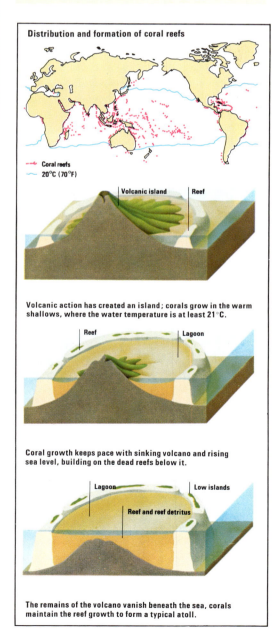

Distribution and formation of coral reefs

Coral reefs
20°C (70°F)

Volcanic island — Reef

Volcanic action has created an island; corals grow in the warm shallows, where the water temperature is at least 21°C.

Reef — Lagoon

Coral growth keeps pace with sinking volcano and rising sea level, building on the dead reefs below it.

Lagoon — Low islands
Reef and reef detritus

The remains of the volcano vanish beneath the sea, corals maintain the reef growth to form a typical atoll.

The Wind-borne Colonists

The sea presents a formidable barrier to terrestrial organisms yet these are present on remote oceanic islands that were once the lifeless products of volcanic action. Eruptions and explosions such as that at Krakatau in historical times have enabled science to observe the process of colonization – or recolonization – as in a test tube.

Dispersal of organisms to such islands may occur by one of three main agencies; by wind, or sea, or on animals. Most biologists believe that wind dispersal is the most important agency. Numerous small animals and plants have been found in the so-called 'aerial plankton' many thousands of feet above the surface of the earth.

Drifting on ocean currents is a means of dispersal of importance to a number of species of plants, and animals such as rats, lizards and snakes are carried to islands on rafts of hurricane-ripped vegetation. Transportation on, or in, animals is yet another means of dispersal. Birds often carry seeds in their intestines and seeds, snails and insects among their feathers.

The colonization of an island is, to a large extent, due to chance. If an island is seen as a dart board and the organisms as randomly thrown darts, it is apparent that the chances of an island being hit, or reached by an organism, depend on the age and size of the island as well as on its distance from the homes of its potential colonists.

Colonization is not a simple matter of reaching an island. It involves the establishment of a balanced population, and this occurs only if sufficient numbers of a species arrive to permit a population to thrive and if suitable habitats are present. A predatory species will only colonize an island if suitable prey species are already present.

The first colonists of islands are generally weedy plant species and omnivorous animals. The plants create a new range of habitats and opportunities to allow other plants and animals to establish themselves and in this way the flora and the fauna of the island begin to diversify.

The range of species on an island depends on a diversity of available habitats and where the number of species is large, competition breaks out. Some species adapt to exploit new niches, but others less able to adapt become extinct, until a dynamic equilibrium of life comes into being.

Lava pioneers *above*
The pioneers of the barren lava flows on volcanic islands are often cacti, snakes and other reptiles.

Waiting for the soil *below*
Plant colonization is a gradual, patchy process, depending on the production of fertile soil.

After complete disaster, life springs up again
The nuclear explosions of man pale into insignificance beside the volcanic explosion which destroyed the island of Krakatau in 1883. The island itself almost vanished beneath the waves and life was apparently wiped out on what was left of Krakatau and its neighbours. Catastrophic though the effect had been, on living forms, within months a tiny spider had parachuted in on its windborne silken thread. It probably starved to death—but within 14 years, 132 species of insects and birds were found there, with 61 plant species.

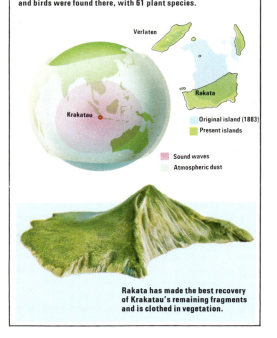

Verlaten

Rakata

Krakatau

Original island (1883)
Present islands

Sound waves
Atmospheric dust

Rakata has made the best recovery of Krakatau's remaining fragments and is clothed in vegetation.

Destruction and creation of islands
The volcanic Westmann Islands, off Iceland (below), turned on their animal and plant colonizers in 1973; Surtsey (bottom) had created a new island habitat ten years before.

The first colonizers *below*
Within 20 years of its creation the first migrant species have established on the new island.

Ferns 13
Flowering plants
Total plant species 35
Grasses and sedges 16
64

Calophyllum inophyllum

Emerald dove
Chalcophaps indica

Wedelia biflora

Beetle
Colasposoma metallicum

Ant
Brachyponera luteipes

Pennisetum macrostachyum

Acrostichum aureum

Eupteris aquilina

Scorpion
Thelyphonus caudatus

Lizard
Varanus salvator

Hawaii – fertilized by the winds

In mid-Pacific, the Hawaiian Islands are one of the most isolated groups in the world: yet they have been colonized by birds of American affinity, and by plants and insects mainly Oriental in origin. Prevailing winds and—importantly—hurricanes have probably provided the vehicle for these huge, oversea journeys.

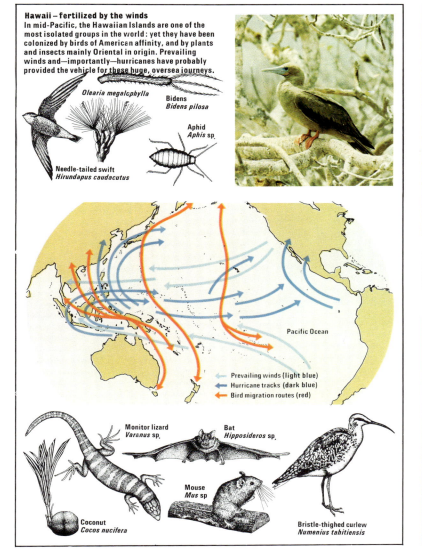

Olearia megalophylla

Bidens
Bidens pilosa

Aphid *Aphis* sp.

Needle-tailed swift
Hirundapus caudacutus

Pacific Ocean

→ Prevailing winds (light blue)
→ Hurricane tracks (dark blue)
→ Bird migration routes (red)

Monitor lizard
Varanus sp.

Bat
Hipposideros sp.

Mouse
Mus sp.

Coconut
Cocos nucifera

Bristle-thighed curlew
Numenius tahitiensis

Plant communities *above* Monocotyledons – coconut palms and grasses – number only a few species but establish a stable vegetational cover. Flowering plants, including cacti (below), are abundant.

Vegetation cover *above* Time, weathering and plant growth between them create a topsoil in which the dominant plant cover establishes itself. Cacti (above) adapt supremely to the least hospitable surfaces; grass takes root on the gentler slopes with palms and flowering plants.

A stability is reached

After 40 years the new habitat assumes a stability and a greater balance among its animal and plant species. The first mammals, including ubiquitous rats, gain a foothold.

Ferns 35
Conifers
Grasses and palms 42
Total plant species 184
Flowering plants 106

Morinda citrifolia

Nicobar pigeon
Caloenas nicobarica

Hibiscus papilionaceus

*Commoniora
Aegithina tiphia*

Coconut
Cocos nucifera

Spinifex sp.

Snail
Kaliella indifferens

Rat
Rattus jaloreisis

Nephrolepis exaltata

Bug
Cyclopelta obscura

Crocodile
Crocodilus porosus

A community established

At the end of a century, plant cover is widespread. The established animal community will be fewer in species than total arrivals, for some will not have survived.

Ferns 52
Conifers
Grasses and palms 64
Total plant species 271
Flowering plants 153

Fig
Ficus hispida

Flowers
Thespesia populnee

Coconut
Cocos nucifera

Owl
Otus bakkamoena

Fruit bat
Rousettus amplexicaudatus

Pandanus tectorius

Orchid
Phajus tankcarvilliae

Fern
Polypodium sinuosum

Python reticulatus

Butterfly
Lampides boeticus

Earth's Living Laboratories

Ideal laboratory conditions are those of isolation and constant environmental values. In the world of nature these conditions are found in an oceanic island group such as the Galapagos or the Hawaiian, whose geography is one of clear separation by distance from environmental influences and where the climate is both benevolent and stable.

In habitats such as these the forces of evolutionary change are seen most clearly. Since Darwin first visited the Galapagos, many oceanic groups have been studied intensively, each one adding its piece to a still admittedly incomplete, jigsaw of knowledge.

In the volcanic Galapagos and Hawaiian groups, animal and plant life have been established long enough to have evolved a stability common to endemic species. An example is provided by the development in each group of the Compositae. On Hawaii they are tall, elegant silverwoods and greenwoods. In the Galapagos, they form dense stands or are small, stunted shrubs growing on low lava flows.

Birds particularly display unique characteristics after long periods of isolation and the finches of the Galapgos (see below) are a famous example. The honeycreepers of Hawaii demonstrate a similar lesson; a lack of competition has enabled both species to radiate into niches that might otherwise have been filled by a variety of birds and animals.

These amiable Gardens of Eden, free from competitive influxes and free, too, from the worst effects of predation, have seen the evolution of creatures of remarkable design, particularly in the Galapagos. The mechanisms of an ideal life are, however, those which suffer most when invasion – as of man, domestic animals and rats – does come about. The laboratory conditions break down, and the dangerous dimension of competitive survival is added to the lives of once unthreatened species.

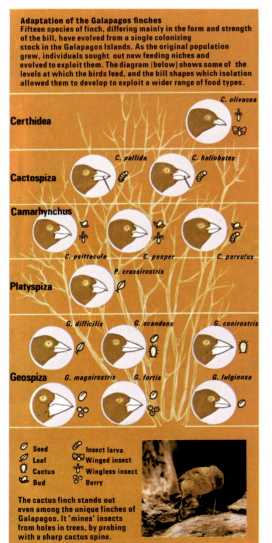

Adaptation of the Galapagos finches
Fifteen species of finch, differing mainly in the form and strength of the bill, have evolved from a single colonizing stock in the Galapagos Islands. As the original population grew, individuals sought out new feeding niches and evolved to exploit them. The diagram (below) shows some of the levels at which the birds feed, and the bill shapes which isolation allowed them to develop to exploit a wider range of food types.

Certhidea — C. olivacea

Cactospiza — C. pallida, C. heliobates

Camarhynchus — C. psittacula, C. pauper, C. parvulus

Platyspiza — P. crassirostris

Geospiza — G. difficilis, G. scandens, G. conirostris, G. magnirostris, G. fortis, G. fuliginosa

Key: Seed, Leaf, Cactus, Bud, Insect larva, Winged insect, Wingless insect, Berry

The cactus finch stands out even among the unique finches of Galapagos. It 'mines' insects from holes in trees, by probing with a sharp cactus spine.

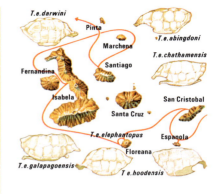

Changing shapes of carapace
Galàpagos tortoises differ from each other, from island to island in the group, in the shapes of their carapaces; 'saddleback' in the northern islands, dome-shaped elsewhere.

Reptile combatants
The massive male land iguanas *Conolophus sub-cristatus* of the Galapagos fight ferociously during the mating season. The fight is begun by an intruder; the defending iguana first bobs his head in warning and if this is not successful bites at the head of the intruder with his well-developed teeth. After the first wound has been inflicted one of the combatants backs off. As with most wild species fights to the death are rare.

Flightless birds *above*
A graceful and competent swimmer, the cormorant *Nannopterum harrisi* has found the predation-free Galapagos a safe place to be, and has lost the power of flight. It uses its ragged, poorly-feathered wings for sheltering its young on the barren lava nest sites.

Marine iguana *left*
A life spent in the narrow zone on either side of the tideline is the lot of the only marine iguana, *Amblyrhynchus cristatus*. At first light it emerges from its crevice home in the Galapagos, to spend the day in the sea, feeding on the sea weed coating the rocks below the waterline. For all its gross appearance the marine iguana swims well. The red crab *Grapsus grapsus* (below) shares its habitat on the rocky shore.

Opportunities for honeycreepers

The honeycreepers of Hawaii surpass even the finches of the Galapagos in diversity, probably because a wider range of niches was open to the early colonists. The thick and heavy bills of some are the result of a need to crack open tough seeds and nuts, or to eat fleshy fruits in the manner of parrots; others have the typical slender bills of the nectar feeders to probe deep into flowers; another digs deep into tree crevices in search of grubs.

Fruit
Freycinetia sp.

Ohiolehua tree
Metrosideros sp.

Laysan finch
Psittacirostra cantans

Iiwi
Vestaria coccinea

Cyanerpes cyaneus

Morning glory
Ipomea sp.

Clytarlus modestus

Plagithymus vitticolis

Plagithymus finschi

Crested honeyeater
Palmeria dolei

Apapane
Himatione sanguinea

Clytarlus pennatus

Seed *Broussaisia* sp.

Snail vales

Five valleys in the Pacific island of Oahu have enabled the snail Achatinella to diverge into five separate species each having distinct markings.

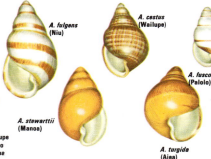

OAHU

Niu
Wailupe
Palolo
Manoa
Aiea

A. fulgens (Niu)

A. cestus (Wailupe)

A. fuscobasis (Palolo)

A. stewartii (Manoa)

A. turgida (Aiea)

Oceanic birds

Hawaii and Galapagos provide nesting sites for strongly-built oceanic birds like the boobies (left) and the piratical frigate bird *Fregata minor* (below). During courtship the male frigate bird inflates a huge, brilliant red sac beneath its bill.

Successful colonists

The Compositae family of plants are adaptable colonists, successfully adjusting to a range of niches in oceanic islands, as pioneers on low lava flows, in dense forest stands, or in clumps in higher ground situations.

Scalesia incisa
15ft (4.5m) Galapagos

Scalesia pedunculata
20ft (6.0m) Galapagos

Argyroxyphium sandwichense
11ft (3.3m) Hawaii

Argyroxyphium virescens
8ft (2.4m) Hawaii

Dubautia plantaginea
13ft (3.9m) Hawaii

Scalesia affinis
4ft (1.2m) Galapagos

Evolution Unchecked

In the isolated environment provided by oceanic islands, many life forms are offered opportunities to establish new ways of life. Some fail to secure a foothold but others, more successful, are often able to shed attributes that were once necessary for survival; and some, to develop characteristics that were always present, but kept in check, in their original environments.

Extremes of size are free to evolve in these sanctuaries. On the small Indonesian island of Komodo a monitor lizard has grown to Wellsian proportions – the Komodo dragon *Varanus komodoensis*. The giant tortoises of the Galapagos and Aldabra live to greater ages than any other living creature. In contrast, among the unique lemurs of Madagascar is the smallest primate, the mouse lemur *Microcebus* spp., only about six inches in length. Another oddity among island primates is the proboscis monkey of Borneo, the male of which has evolved a huge nose with which it 'honks' a warning to its fellows.

Some evolutionary changes bring about a total commitment to the new island habitat. The lacewing insects of Hawaii have developed wings too heavy to fly with, and are thus unable to leave. The wings of some birds dwindled to uselessness, as in the kiwi of New Zealand, the Aldabra rail and the now-extinct dodo of Mauritius. An inability to fly, and an island-induced fearlessness, made the dodo an easy prey for the first predator it met – man.

Species of plants which have long since vanished from their mainland habitats continue to flourish in the undisturbed environments of oceanic islands, and often achieve great size. The giant cactuses (prickly pear) growing in the Galapagos islands reach heights of 30 feet (10m) and more. In Australia a grass Xanthorrhea takes on a tree form 20 feet (4.6m) tall.

To the unique plant and animals residents of the islands are added the flocks of visiting birds, using them as staging posts on their long oceanic migrations, or to breed and sometimes settle. The albatrosses of the northern latitudes provide an example of the way in which islands provide new bases far from the range of the species as a whole.

Most but certainly not all of the extinct or endangered species of birds and mammals – in historical times – were and are inhabitants of islands where the impact of man has been sudden, rather than gradual.

Aldabra freaks
The Aldabra white-throated rail *Dryolimnas cuvieri aldabranus* (right) has lost the power of flight. It often walks – slowly – behind the giant tortoise *Testudo gigantea* (below), feeding on invertebrates disturbed by the giant. The same bird on Madagascar flies easily.

Aldabra islet
Startled noddy terns rise up from a weird lagoon islet in Aldabra, an oceanic island north of Madagascar with 80,000 giant tortoises.

Dodo and solitaire
Flightless, tame and quite unable to cope with man and his animal attendants the dodo *Raphus cucullatus* and the solitaire *Pezophaps solitarius* of Mauritius and other Indian Ocean islands are now only memories.

Mauritius dodo
Raphus cucullatus

Rodriguez solitaire
Pezophaps solitarius

Specialized crabs
A strange inhabitant of Indo-Pacific islands, the robber crab *Birgus latro* (right) is an adept climber of trees, particularly the coconut palm, where it feeds on old and broken fruit. The mangrove crab *Seylla serrata* (below) is more of an opportunist, taking a variety of foods, from carrion to living creatures as it moves through the mangrove. *S. serrata* is able to swim, defending itself by burrowing into mud.

Madagascan malachite kingfisher
Alcedo cristata vintsioides

Smallest kingfisher
The Madagascar kingfisher *Alcedo cristata vintsioides* is closely related to the African malachite kingfisher and is the smallest of all kingfishers.

Philippines

Aldabra

Madagascar

Rodriguez

Mauritius

Reunion

Krakatau

Komodo

Celebes

Australia

INDIAN OCEAN

5

Laysan albatross
Diomedea immutabilis

Escaped albatross
The Laysan albatross *Diomedea immutabilis* (above) is one of three species which 'broke out' from the albatross latitudes of the southern hemisphere, through the Doldrums, to breed north of the Equator. It nests on a number of mid-Pacific islands and has a flight range from California to China. Other northern albatrosses are the black-footed, and Steller's, a once-threatened species now thriving.

Reptile rover
The boa constrictor *Constrictor constrictor* is found throughout tropical South America, but has successfully colonized the West Indies. It may have migrated to the Antilles by rafting on dislodged vegetation.

Island magic
Islands have a magic of their own, imparted not only by their remoteness but by the colour given to them by both plants and animals. The brilliant yellow flowering spikes of *Agave* sp. (left) are commonly seen in the West Indies and there is no more glorious bird than the scarlet ibis *Eudocimus ruber* (below) which ranges into the Antilles and beyond from South America.

Hawaiian Hawk
Buteo solitarius

Hawaiian hawk *(above)*
A bird of prey, the Hawaiian hawk *Buteo solitarius* nests high in island's forest trees.

Loss of flight as a protection
After colonizing Hawaii, some lacewing insects (below) grew heavier wings and lost the power of flight. This was a subtle form of protection – for the wind which ferried them in could no longer blow them away.

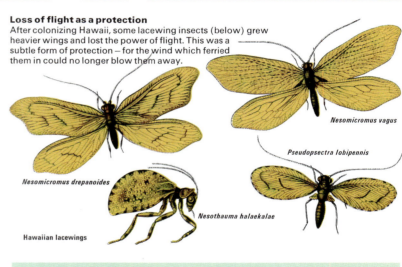

Nesomicromus vagus

Pseudopsectra lobipennis

Nesomicromus drepanoides

Nesothauma halaekalae

Hawaiian lacewings

Pig-like oddity
The strange, pig-like babirusa *Babyrousa babyrussa* has a pair of tusks which grow from its lower jaw and pierce its upper lip.

Babirusa
Babyrousa babyrussa

Relics of the ancient world
Plant species, which have long since vanished from mainland landscapes which they once ruled, continue to thrive in the context of remote islands.

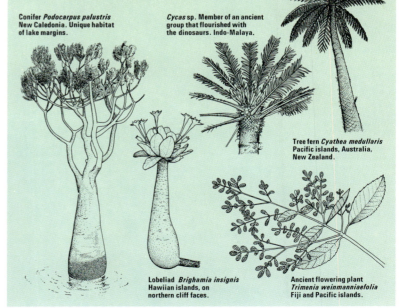

Conifer *Podocarpus palustris* New Caledonia. Unique habitat of lake margins.

Cycas sp. Member of an ancient group that flourished with the dinosaurs. Indo-Malaya.

Tree fern *Cyathea medullaris* Pacific islands, Australia, New Zealand.

Lobeliad *Brighamia insignis* Hawiian islands, on northern cliff faces.

Ancient flowering plant *Trimenia weinmanniaefolia* Fiji and Pacific islands.

Widespread monitors
The monitor lizard *Varanus griseus* is a member of a widespread Old World family. Species of monitor occur in the African savanna, through southern Asia and Polynesia to Australia. Their geographical range is matched by their variety of sizes :
At one end of the scale the huge Komodo dragon (see page 183) and at the other, the short-tailed monitor of Australia (20cm).

(see page 183)

A Question of Balance

While early man was a simple hunter-gatherer, killing only to subsist and supplementing his diet with readily available fruits and leaves, his position in the interlocking web of nature was that of just another warmth-loving mammal. A developing intelligence, the acquisition of tools and simple weapons probably took him no further than that of first among equals: rather, they compensated him for the lack of agility and strength possessed by his prey, and his competitors. As his killing techniques improved, the animals among whom he lived became warier, and more difficult to hunt down. Here was a reason – probably among many other pressures – for migrating.

His first simple steps in animal husbandry as a nomad herdsman saved him the trouble of pursuit for it gave him readily available supplies of food. He was able to migrate out across drier lands and unconsciously to cause man's first degradation of his environment. The nomad herds grazed down the surface covering of plants and the structure of the soil deteriorated to desert conditions.

Man's first attempts at settled agriculture are thought to have begun about 8,000 BC, in the 'fertile crescent' of the Middle East. From this epoch, one of the most important milestones in the development of modern civilization, the first towns and cities were to grow and the great Mediterranean cultures were to spring. They were also the first steps toward the modern environmental 'crisis' for the effect of agriculture is to remake the landscape, one in which there is no room for the larger forms of wild life. For example, the decline and extinction of the Asiatic lion in southeast Europe and the Near East will have begun, imperceptibly, at that time.

In global terms, the first few thousand years of modern man made no more than superficial, and highly localized, marks on the landscape and its life. Only in the last few hundred years, since the Age of Discovery, has he carried the problems of his new way of life, and the paraphernalia of his civilization, into the realms of wild life in all parts of the world. And his paraphernalia has included the firearm which has added new dimensions to his ability to slaughter for fun and for profit. Even in less dramatic ways, his presence either by accident or design has had its influence on the landscape and its life, as examples on the opposite page show.

Early artists and the animals they drew
Balanced on the prow of his canoe an Egyptian wildfowler of the 18th Dynasty (1,570-332 BC) hunts through the papyrus reed beds of the Nile. A member of a settled and highly advanced society he may have been hunting to supplement his diet, or purely for sport – then, as in later times, the prerogative of the rich. A more fundamental, even mystical appreciation of his fellow creatures is conveyed in the cave painting of a European bison by Palaeolithic man, a simple hunter whose society nevertheless included accomplished artists.

Mesolithic man (11,000 years ago) was a hunter as his forebears had been, but possessed more efficient tools and weapons.

The secrets of crop growing from seed and animal husbandry were found by New Stone Age man, about 8,000 years ago.

Waterside forest homes
Lake and riverside settlements – offering alternative food sources – were established by early man. In contrast the African pygmies, or Twides (right) are completely adapted to life in the deep forest. Where others would have difficulty in moving about, the pygmy will almost glide, aided by his small size, light weight – on average half that of a European – and highly flexible joints.

Unchanged life *above*
At one with his surroundings, a South American Indian fishes the waters of his native Mato Grosso.

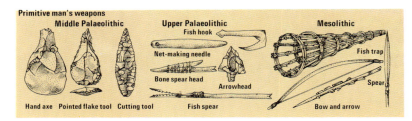

Primitive man's weapons

Middle Palaeolithic	Upper Palaeolithic	Mesolithic
	Fish hook	
	Net-making needle	Fish trap
	Bone spear head	
	Arrowhead	Spear
Hand axe Pointed flake tool Cutting tool	Fish spear	Bow and arrow

The road of *Homo sapiens*

Man has followed many paths since his origins, two million years ago, in the tropics of the Old World, where there are abundant signs of his ancestry. At first he was no more successful than other species until those qualities that set him apart — speech, the power of reason, the use of tools — carried him away on his own evolutionary road. And, perhaps to escape some local pressure or threat or out of instinctive curiosity, he migrated. Since then, he has not stopped moving.

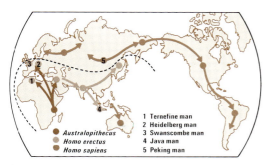

1 Ternefine man
2 Heidelberg man
3 Swanscombe man
4 Java man
5 Peking man

Australopithecus
Homo erectus
Homo sapiens

Tho first migrations

The map (above) shows stages in the prehistoric dispersion of mankind outward from Africa; the tentative movements of *Australopith-* *ecus*, the further steps of *Homo erectus* and the global range of modern man, *Homo sapiens*. Land bridges no longer in existence will have aided their movements.

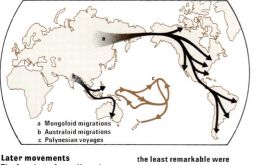

a Mongoloid migrations
b Australoid migrations
c Polynesian voyages

Later movements

The Americas, Australia and the numerous islands of the Pacific Ocean were the last lands to gain their own, indigenous populations. Not the least remarkable were the great oceanic voyages which were to populate Polynesian islands, movements whose origins and motivations still remain obscure.

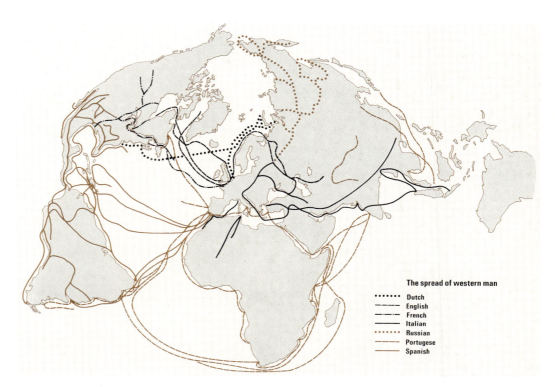

The spread of western man

..... Dutch
--- English
-·-·- French
— Italian
····· Russian
— Portugese
— Spanish

The great journeys *above*

Western man's great exploratory journeys in search of wealth beyond the seas were at first in response to economic pressures; to find new routes to the Indies, the spice islands whose products had become essential to his way of life, Tatar irruptions and Turkish wars had blocked older land routes to the east, but square-rigged ships designed to use the trade winds enabled navigators to encircle the globe.

Fatal impact *left*

The impact of European sailors on island life forms was severe; species which had known neither predator nor competition were helpless or fatally naive in their contact with man, his dogs and cats — and that other great seafarer, the rat. On Mauritius (left) the strange, flightless dodo was a typical victim. Many other species provided easy pickings for sailors ashore to re-victual their ships.

Threat of the 'exotics'

By accident or design, man has been responsible for the introduction to new habitats of many species that have found their new homes entirely to their liking — often with disastrous results for the indigenous wild life and the new habitats as a whole. Both plant and animal 'exotics' (introduced species) have been involved in this involuntary colonization of new environments, far from their native homes.

Extinct rails of the Pacific

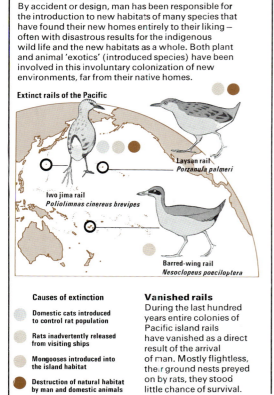

Laysan rail
Porzanula palmeri

Iwo jima rail
Poliolimnas cinereus brevipes

Barred-wing rail
Nesoclopeus poeciloptera

Causes of extinction

○ Domestic cats introduced to control rat population

○ Rats inadvertently released from visiting ships

○ Mongooses introduced into the island habitat

● Destruction of natural habitat by man and domestic animals

Vanished rails

During the last hundred years entire colonies of Pacific island rails have vanished as a direct result of the arrival of man. Mostly flightless, their ground nests preyed on by rats, they stood little chance of survival.

Rabbit problem, Eastern Australia

Old world rabbit
Oryctolagus cuniculus

▭ Introduction Victoria 1859 distribution 70 miles per year
● First site successful virus release 1949
▢ Extent of Myxomatosis virus

Plague of rabbits *above*

Rabbits first arrived in Australia with the convict ships. They became a pest in Tasmania, then spread like a forest fire on the mainland. A virus myxamatosis, introduced in 1948, reduced the population of many millions to a small fraction.

Larva *Cactoblastis cactorum*

Prickly pear *Opuntia inermis*

Adult *C. cactorum*

Mosquito *Anopheles sp*

A natural control *above, left*

First welcome, then an unwelcome migrant the prickly pear was taken to Australia for ornamental reasons. It then spread, destroying millions of acres of pasture. A natural control, the moth *Cactoblastis* spp.—its larva feeds on the prickly pear tissue—was introduced, bringing it to heel.

Unwelcome travellers

The American oyster *Crassostrea virginica* was used to replenish British stocks but brought with it the slipper limpet *Crepidula fornicata* and oyster drill *Urosalpinx cinerea*. Both became serious pests on oyster farms and *Crepidula* spread to the farms of mainland Europe.

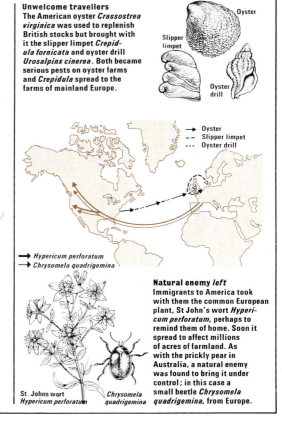

Oyster
Slipper limpet
Oyster drill

→ Oyster
-- Slipper limpet
···· Oyster drill

→ *Hypericum perforatum*
→ *Chrysomela quadrigemina*

St. Johns wort *Hypericum perforatum*

Chrysomela quadrigemina

Natural enemy *left*

Immigrants to America took with them the common European plant, St John's wort *Hypericum perforatum*, perhaps to remind them of home. Soon it spread to affect millions of acres of farmland. As with the prickly pear in Australia, a natural enemy was found to bring it under control; in this case a small beetle *Chrysomela quadrigemina*, from Europe.

The Imprint of Man

Modern civilization is the creation of settled, agricultural man and its future is as firmly in his hands as was its birth and growth. In the developed countries of the world, the empirical methods of his ancestors have been changed by the application of scientific principles to his work; in the underdeveloped countries, techniques continue to be used that would have been recognizable to the first farmers of the 'fertile crescent' of the Near East.

So productive are the modern methods of farming that, despite the stunning growth in the world's population, the overall harvest remains well in excess of the world's needs; but so patchy and scattered (in a global sense) is the use of up-to-date skills, two-thirds of the population remains underfed.

The problems of distribution and starvation are not unique to the latter part of the 20th Century, nor to the underdeveloped nations. The drift from the land which accompanied the Industrial Revolution in Britain brought to prosperous mid-Victorian Britain the real prospect of starvation to the masses of people huddled in the grimy streets of mill towns.

Technology came to their aid. Across the world in the southern continents of America and Australia, the plains were burgeoning with livestock which, until that time, could not have survived the long, hot journey through the tropics to the markets of Europe. The introduction of refrigeration and refrigerated ships was the solution, a cool technology which also provides a 'cushion' against shortage (during wars and other emergencies) by enabling perishable foodstuffs to be stored.

The use of refrigeration to these ends is no part of farming; rather, of distribution and storage, but these are vital to those stages of the harvest between culling and consumption. In recent centuries science has turned its attention to the improvement of domestic animal and plant stock, to produce more hardy and more fruitful species; tailoring them to new habitats, increasing their resistance to diseases that once attacked to destroy the livelihoods and lives of communities. Agriculture will continue to remain man's dominating consideration, if he is to survive.

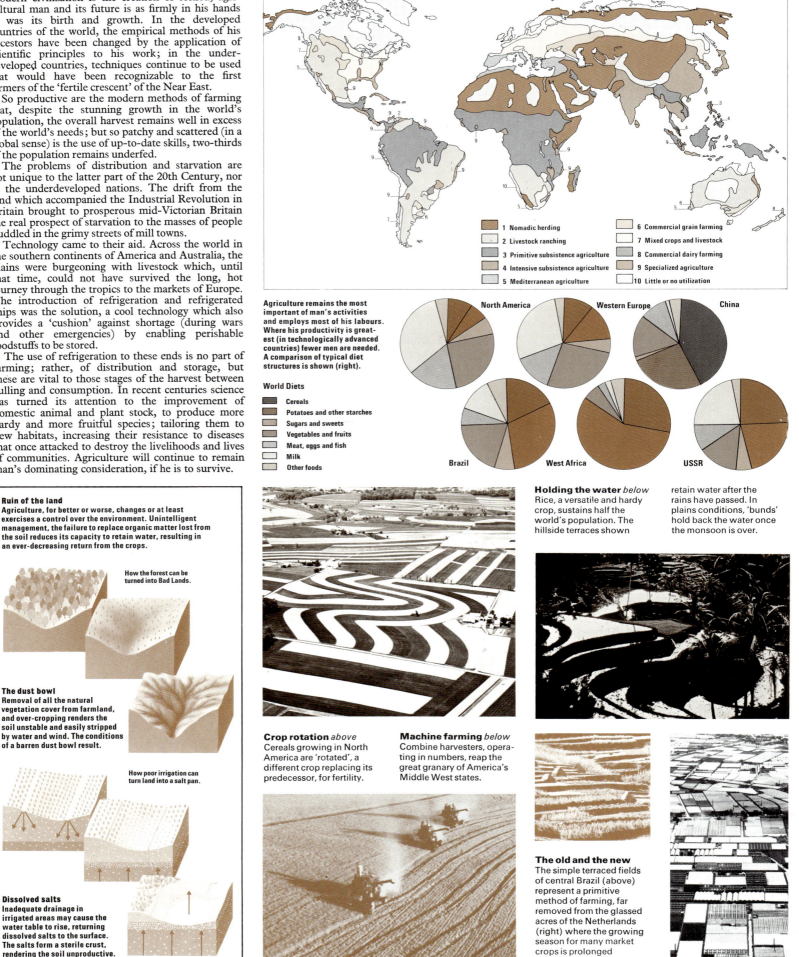

1 Nomadic herding	6 Commercial grain farming
2 Livestock ranching	7 Mixed crops and livestock
3 Primitive subsistence agriculture	8 Commercial dairy farming
4 Intensive subsistence agriculture	9 Specialized agriculture
5 Mediterranean agriculture	10 Little or no utilization

Agriculture remains the most important of man's activities and employs most of his labours. Where his productivity is greatest (in technologically advanced countries) fewer men are needed. A comparison of typical diet structures is shown (right).

North America   Western Europe   China

Brazil   West Africa   USSR

World Diets
- Cereals
- Potatoes and other starches
- Sugars and sweets
- Vegetables and fruits
- Meat, eggs and fish
- Milk
- Other foods

Ruin of the land
Agriculture, for better or worse, changes or at least exercises a control over the environment. Unintelligent management, the failure to replace organic matter lost from the soil reduces its capacity to retain water, resulting in an ever-decreasing return from the crops.

How the forest can be turned into Bad Lands.

The dust bowl
Removal of all the natural vegetation cover from farmland, and over-cropping renders the soil unstable and easily stripped by water and wind. The conditions of a barren dust bowl result.

How poor irrigation can turn land into a salt pan.

Dissolved salts
Inadequate drainage in irrigated areas may cause the water table to rise, returning dissolved salts to the surface. The salts form a sterile crust, rendering the soil unproductive.

Crop rotation *above*
Cereals growing in North America are 'rotated', a different crop replacing its predecessor, for fertility.

Machine farming *below*
Combine harvesters, operating in numbers, reap the great granary of America's Middle West states.

Holding the water *below*
Rice, a versatile and hardy crop, sustains half the world's population. The hillside terraces shown retain water after the rains have passed. In plains conditions, 'bunds' hold back the water once the monsoon is over.

The old and the new
The simple terraced fields of central Brazil (above) represent a primitive method of farming, far removed from the glassed acres of the Netherlands (right) where the growing season for many market crops is prolonged artificially.

Breeding and movement of livestock

The application of scientific knowledge to farming has enabled the farmer to breed animals to meet his special needs and adapted to environments far from their native homes. As most of the settlers who migrated to the distant continents were European, the domestic stock populations in America and Australia are largely of European stock. Friesian, Hereford cattle, landrace pigs, Suffolk and Merino sheep have bred happily in their new homes — and now return to their original homes as meat in refrigerated ships, or as wool and hide for the industries of the Old World.

————————	Merino sheep
– – – – – –	Suffolk sheep
— · · — · ·	European cattle
· · · · · · · ·	Brahman cattle

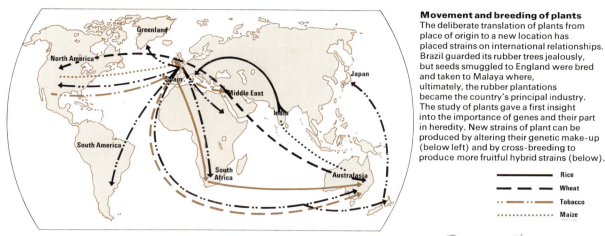

Movement and breeding of plants

The deliberate translation of plants from place of origin to a new location has placed strains on international relationships. Brazil guarded its rubber trees jealously, but seeds smuggled to England were bred and taken to Malaya where, ultimately, the rubber plantations became the country's principal industry. The study of plants gave a first insight into the importance of genes and their part in heredity. New strains of plant can be produced by altering their genetic make-up (below left) and by cross-breeding to produce more fruitful hybrid strains (below).

————————	Rice
– – – – – –	Wheat
· — · — · —	Tobacco
· · · · · · · ·	Maize

Improved domestic animals have been produced by selecting, from original wild stock, those with the desired characteristics, then controlling breeding to emphasize these features. Interbreeding of selected animals can be carried out to suit isolated environments, like the Australian Illawara shorthorn. Breeding bulls are used to maintain the 'pools' of desirable genes.

Texas Longhorn

Brahman

Charolais

Highland

Hereford

Ankole

Jersey

Irradiation of the durum wheat seeds (below) resulted in a mutant variety—shorter and sturdier and able to stand up to rain and wind which flattened the standard variety.

Durum wheat (Cappelli variety) tends to lodge in soil treated with fertilizers

Natural   Fertilized

Stronger mutant strain

Cappelli seeds subjected to radiation

Cross-breeding of two already crossed corn seeds produces a new, larger variety (above).

Crossbred strain

Irrigation

Early farm technology; the bullock walks his endless path around the paddle to irrigate an Indian farmer's fields in the old manner (right). A modern technique in countries where there is an ample supply of water, is the use of pressurised pipes (below) to spray the crops.

African stockman *above*
A pastoral scene in Kenya; a stockman watches over his Boran cattle.

British stockyard *below*
Cattle pens, with Friesian dairy cattle in foreground, on market day in England.

A family concern *below*
In societies based on agriculture, the whole family tends the crops.

The draught animal *above*
Man's first ally in agriculture, the draught animal, has been almost entirely replaced by the tractor in developed countries. But in the greatest number of agricultural communities, it still provides the muscle.

179

The Impact of Industry

Industrial man is probably as old as the discovery that one member of a social group was better at making spear heads than he was at spearing game, an archetypal craftsman who applied simple thought, rather than instinct and strength.

The establishment of settled societies gave an impetus to his numbers as the demands for more specializations grew, but such industry as there was remained at cottage level. The greater number of people were engaged in husbandry, even until recent times in the now-developed nations.

The balance remains heavily tilted towards agriculture in the underdeveloped countries; industrial man and the effect he has had upon his environment are phenomena of the 'western world' and where its culture has been most influential.

The industrial society as considered on this page is the product of one of man's great forward surges – what is now known as the Industrial Revolution. Although straws of thought had been in the wind for centuries before, the revolution dates from the 18th century, and is generally placed in Britain. Manufacturing industries sprang up, at first to make cloth, then to make the machinery that made the cloth. The drift to the towns began and soon those engaged in the 'dark satanic mills' outnumbered those in farming.

The effect of this great change on the environment was overwhelming; some now say catastrophic, but the considerations of man's environmental needs were not foremost in the minds of the new industrialists, caught up in the momentum of trade and invention.

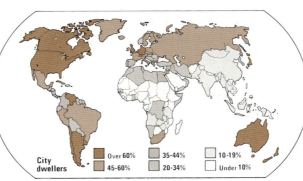

Room for all
The population of the world grows at an accelerating rate as fertility increases and science defeats disease. Yet there is room and enough for all; the entire population of the world could stand, shoulder to shoulder, in Baltimore County, Md.

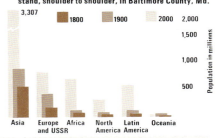

3,307

1800   1900   2000

2,000
1,500
1,000
500

Population in millions

Asia   Europe and USSR   Africa   North America   Latin America   Oceania

City dwellers
Over 60%   35-44%   10-19%
45-60%   20-34%   Under 10%

Industrial moth
The peppered moth *Biston betularia* exists in two varieties, one a pale grey and white version, the other black, or blackish. The colour of the first, once an effective camouflage, gave it away where it lived in industrial neighbourhoods and fumes and soot fallout darkened the woodlands and hedgerows. Its numbers decreased sharply while those of the darker version, now less easily spotted by the predator, increased in numbers in industrial areas.

Peppered moth
Biston betularia

Light form

Melanic form

Rape of the land
Industrial growth, to which western society is seemingly committed to survive, has little respect for the environment. The road, once a simple track for the movement of man and his goods is now a concrete serpent, crushing the older, smaller communities and feeding the industrial conurbations (top). The open-pit mine in South West Africa (above) is an example of wasteful land use; the quarry (right) is in process of reclamation.

Landscape surgery
Open-pit mining carried out regardless of the nature of the land will scar it permanently – yet it remains an economic method of winning minerals from the soil. Modern techniques make the scar a temporary one, by stockpiling first the topsoil, then the undersoil. As the seam is worked the soil is replaced progressively and within a few years agriculture can begin again on the land which has been reclaimed.

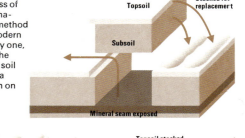

Topsoil
Stacked for replacement
Subsoil
Mineral seam exposed

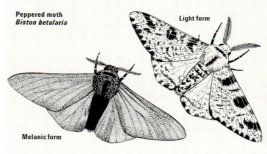

Mineral extracted
Topsoil replaced
Topsoil stacked
Direction of progress
Subsoil infill
Direct infill

Overkill
Chemically-dressed seeds and pesticides used indiscriminately – and with little real knowledge of their long-term effects – cause the decline, often the death, of creatures with whom man has no quarrel. The diagrams in this panel describe some of these 'chains of doom'.

Persistent pesticides

DDT

Dieldrin

Endosulfan

Heptachlor

Slow poison
A pigeon eats treated grain, and dies. A badger eats the grain, and the pigeon, and also dies. Small birds, which have fed on treated seeds or insect survivors of the spray, are killed by hawks. Chemicals build up in the hawks, upsetting their metabolism. Result : failure to breed.

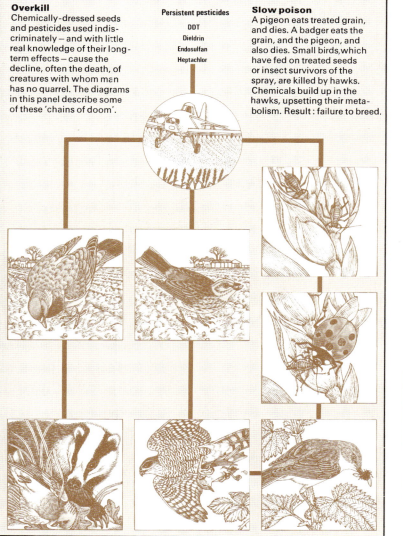

Major oil routes

The dwindling resource
The fuel of modern industry is oil. In the hundred years after the first well was drilled in 1859, world output rose to more than 1,000 million tons annually and has continued to rise even more rapidly since then. New oil fields have been constantly discovered but estimated reserves are declining. The world's oil shipping routes (left).

The great bulk of the world's oil is moved from field to refinery and market by sea in tankers many times larger, in tonnage, than the greatest passenger liners. In their wake they bring the hazard of spillage through collision or sinking, and pollution of the sea and beaches. The effect of one such disaster is shown (right) and below (right). In the picture (below) an oil slick is broken up with a detergent spray which, to some degree, also damages marine and shoreline habitats.

Industrial pollution of rivers
Rivers provide a cheap and easy outlet for industrial wastes and a source of coolant for nuclear and conventional power plants. The result has been the death of all aquatic life in the rank and poisoned waters.

1 The village creates slight local pollution which is quickly oxidized. River life does not suffer.

2 A small town creates a depression of oxygen supplies. The river may recover to support life downstream.

3 Pollution from heavy industry may quickly render the river sterile as ecological cycles fail.

Too much salmon
Medieval London apprentices protested at the amount of fresh salmon they had to eat. It was caught leaping the weir beneath London Bridge. Pollution has long since driven away the salmon and other fish. But life is returning to the Thames as control measures take effect.

North America *above*
Detergent effluent and chemical wastes pour into this Minnesota river.

Europe *right*
Steam rises from the River Trent, England, as hot water pours from a cooling plant.

Changing Role of the Zoo

Zoos, once the plaything of kings and rich men, became popular in 19th century cities when new species of animal were being discovered at an ever-increasing rate by colonial explorers. Like the traditional circus and fairground, zoos were regarded solely as a form of light family entertainment, and little understanding was given to the needs of the animal. But a few, run by zoological societies and a handful of enlightened private owners, began to apply scientific principles to the study of their collections, and they started to create artificial environments more closely related to their animals' natural habitats.

Fortunately times have changed since the days of the menagerie. While many bad zoos and parks still exist today, great advances have been made in the field of animal management which makes the poorly-run zoo even more inexcusable than in the past. Knowledge of animal diets, medical care, breeding biology and display techniques have improved tremendously. Such steps forward have resulted in better health, longer life and improved breeding results for many species. The best zoos today are self-sufficient as their animals breed and replace each other, making inroads into the wild populations unnecessary. Another bonus is that much greater attention is now being paid to the design of cages. One no longer thinks in terms of the naked cage with bars but of the environment with plants, trees and companions. Given the opportunity to behave naturally, zoo animals are happier and far more interesting to watch than the individual pacing back and forth.

The modern zoo's code is 'Conservation, education, research and entertainment'. Its role in conservation is particularly important. Human demands for more agricultural land is infringing on the world's last wild places – and wild animals are disappearing in many parts of the world as a result. Certain species have a chance of being saved from extinction through captive breeding, and some have been saved already.

Responsible zoos also realize that their role in education is unique. Wildlife lecture programmes and films are some of the many services that zoos should offer along with detailed labels and information about each animal. For most city dwellers their only contact with wildlife is through a zoo and, therefore, this vital link with nature in the form of a repository of living creatures is as beneficial to man as it is to the health and future of the wild species.

Enlightened zoo management
The San Diego Wild Animal Park provides a fine example of enlightened wildlife management. Habitats have been created like those the animals will have enjoyed in their natural environments – in sharp contrast to the traditional, confined cage of the prowling leopard (above).

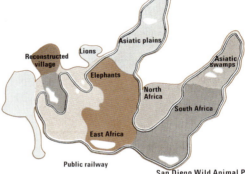

Fundamental research
In the near-ideal conditions created in modern zoo parks it becomes possible to provide not only a natural spectacle that is both entertaining and informative, but to carry out fundamental research from which the species will benefit: not only those that are on show, but also those that remain in their wild habitats. Information that may be gained at close quarters is fed back to observers in the field.

San Diego Wild Animal Park
Reconstructed village · Lions · Asiatic plains · Elephants · Asiatic swamps · North Africa · South Africa · East Africa · Public railway

The waste of the world's wildlife
Twenty-seven million fish, 500,000 reptiles and amphibians, 200,000 birds and 74,000 mammals (mostly primates for laboratories) are imported each year into the United States alone; a horrifying consumption, mostly for the pet trade and research. The figures are a mere fraction of the number of imported hides and animal products like whale and kangaroo meat for pet foods. The diagram (below) shows how the diminishing population of gorillas is squandered for marginal returns.

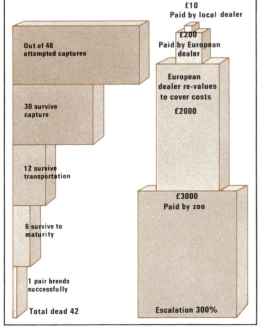

Out of 48 attempted captures
30 survive capture
12 survive transportation
6 survive to maturity
1 pair breeds successfully
Total dead 42

£10 Paid by local dealer
£200 Paid by European dealer
European dealer re-values to cover costs £2000
£3000 Paid by zoo
Escalation 300%

Co-operating with man
Loquacious, endearing and highly intelligent, dolphins in captivity prove to be the most co-operative of wild species for research. Even their fiercer relative, the killer whale (left), has displayed an amiable disposition when studied closely. Not until World War II was science able to prove that members of the whale family were able to group, navigate and communicate by sound signals. In marine zoo conditions they have been known to transmit signals by means of whistles and clicks to others from whom they had been separated. Both baleen and toothed whales can signal.

To the rescue of survivors

Zoos and parks have played an important role in saving certain species which were on the brink of extinction in the wild. By organizing long-term breeding programmes and initiating stud books which trace the ancestry of each animal, some conservation-conscious zoos have virtually saved species like Père David's deer, the Przewalski horse, Néné goose, European bison and Swinhoe pheasant. Successes such as these are merely a start, as more and more species become endangered. Some are notoriously difficult to breed in captivity, some have never been bred at all in a zoo. In their struggle to keep certain species from disappearing once and for all, zoologists are posed questions to which they have yet to find answers. Do captive animals retain their wild genetic diversity ; will they domesticate ultimately ; do traits appear which would be weeded out by natural selection in the wild ?

Saved from extinction
Once reduced to about 50 in number in Hawaii and Maui (the Sandwich Islands) the Nene goose *Branta sandvicensis* was saved from extinction by breeding at the British Slimbridge Wildfowl Trust. There, more than 800 were reared, many of them to be released anew in the Hawaiian islands. The European bison *Bison bonasus* (left) once extinct in the wild, has been bred in numbers from zoo stock.

Mouse deer *right*
Shy and retiring, the mouse deer, or Chevrotain *Tragulus napu* was unhappy in a large zoo cage. It was then discovered (at the New York Bronx Zoo) that the tiny deer was far happier, and bred regularly, in cages no larger than a rabbit hutch. Przewalski's horse *Equus przewalski* (below) now exists in the wild in small numbers in southwest Mongolia. The only surviving wild horse, it has been bred successfully in zoos and parks.

Fennec fox
Fennecus zerda

Fooling the fennec *left*
Nocturnal fennec foxes of the Sahara seldom bred in captivity until it was discovered at London Zoo that, by altering the day length – by lights, humidity and temperature, the fox can be 'tricked' into believing that the seasons are changing as in Africa. It then breeds.

Hitches and hazards in zoo breeding
Some animals – lions, baboons, fallow deer – are as easy to breed in captivity as others – gorillas, rhinoceroses and cranes, among others – are not. Some animals may need more room than most zoos can afford ; the behaviour and dietary requirements of others may never have been studied sufficiently. Sometimes a zoo thinks it is providing an ideal environment when, from the animal's point of view, it is all wrong. Pairs of rare animals are often incompatible, moping or fighting until separated.

Douc langur
Pygathrix nemaeus

Doomed monkey
The last wild herds of European bison (see this page) in the Caucasus and Poland were killed off in World War One. A similar fate approaches the Douc langur *Pygathrix nemaeus* (left), victim of the war in Vietnam. A shy, fragile monkey, it has a special stomach to cope with its fibrous diet of leaves – in an area of southeast Asia that has seen huge defoliation and destruction of its habitat. Its chances of survival are far lower than those of the bison, for it seldom thrives in captivity.

Rare eagle, rare civet
Zoos have placed a ban on the purchase of monkey-eating eagles, of which only a handful survive on two islands in the Philippines. The future of the bird is grim for captive monkey-eating eagles have never bred. A rare zoo specimen is shown (right). The otter civet *Cynogale bennetti* (below), the only member of its family to develop an aquatic form, was reduced in its southeast Asia habitat by the invasion of true otters. Its chances of survival are slim for it has never bred in captivity.

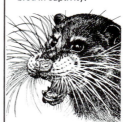

Threatened 'dragon'
Like the monkey-eating eagle, the Komodo dragon has been placed on the proscribed list by zoos. Few of these 'dragons'—the largest living lizards, growing up to 12 feet (3.6m) in length on the island of Komodo—are held in captivity and they have never bred in zoos outside the Far East.

Man the Protector

In the last 500 years one in every hundred of the world's higher animals has become extinct and the shadows are closing around several more. Extinction is a 'biological reality' for no species has yet existed for more than a few million years without evolving into something different, or dying out completely. But the reasons for present-day rarity are overwhelmingly those created by man. Perhaps a quarter of the species of animals which have become extinct in recent centuries has done so for natural, evolutionary reasons. The remainder have vanished probably as a result, either direct or indirect, of man's actions.

Hunting and habitat destruction stand out as the dominant causes. The subsistence hunting of early man, and as pursued still by the remoter peoples, offered no great threat to the wild life forms, but hunting, backed by modern techniques for commercial gain, is altogether different (though fundamentally the purpose – killing to obtain animal products for human use – remains the same). The result is once-prolific species brought to the portals of extinction, and in some cases through them.

Conservation legislation in the form of international agreements, and local licensing to prevent 'overkill' has had notable successes and some species thrive once more that were thought to be beyond saving. More ominous, because it is the more difficult to control, is habitat destruction brought about by the needs of a swelling population (the clearance of virgin forest areas, among other areas) or the demand of modern industry for the exploitation of mineral resources such as oil. In an increasing number of countries, only the 'last ditch' of the national park (a man-created defense against his own depredations) remains to harbour the few survivors of a once-abundant species.

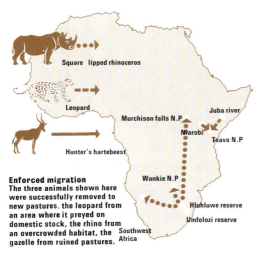

Rescue operation
The construction of the Kariba dam (right) on the River Zambezi flooded thousands of square miles of land and dispossessed the animal population. A rescue operation was mounted to save the wild life. Herds of antelopes and other animals trapped on diminishing islands were herded into the water and forced to swim to higher ground. Others which could not swim were doped and rafted to safety (above).

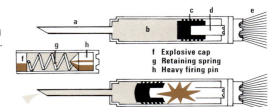

Enforced migration
The three animals shown here were successfully removed to new pastures, the leopard from an area where it preyed on domestic stock, the rhino from an overcrowded habitat, the gazelle from ruined pastures.

Square lipped rhinoceros
Leopard
Juba river
Murchison falls N.P
Nairobi
Tsavo N.P
Hunter's hartebeest
Wankie N.P
Hluhluwe reserve
Umfolozi reserve
Southwest Africa

Drugged to safety
Relocation of animal stocks – either as an emergency measure in situations where a habitat is destroyed (the Kariba dam) or as a long-term programme to reestablish balanced communities – have been helped by the use of modern anaesthetizing drugs.

These are fired in 'flying syringes' (right) which incapacitate animals like the rhinoceros, which would otherwise be unmanageable. In this way many species of animal can be moved from degraded habitats to surroundings which will continue to support them. Examples shown (left).

a Hollow needle
b Tranquilizing drug
c Rubber plunger
d Firing charge
e Coloured tailpiece

f Explosive cap
g Retaining spring
h Heavy firing pin

Victim of the poacher *below*
Snared by a crude wire loop, an elephant lies dead, its tusks coveted by ivory poachers. Native Africans have always trapped and killed animals to support themselves and their families, but the most threatening inroads on game stocks are made by ruthless poaching for financial gain.

Illegal hunting
Game poachers in Tanzania (above) examine their victim, a wildebeest. The stockpile of tusks (left) represent the haul of elephant poachers. Illegal hunting has been stepped up as a result of the mobility provided by trucks and the increased firepower of modern weapons. An African national park anti-poaching patrol sets out (right).

Coming of the oil man

The balance of life in the Arctic — until recent times a secure, if finely adjusted, ecosystem — now comes under the threat of industrial man, particularly the oil man. His vehicle tracks scar the surface irreparably (see below) and impassable pipelines four feet (1.2m) in diameter may bar the migratory routes of the tundra caribou. Crude townships spring up and the way of life of the Eskimo comes under pressure which threated his extinction.

1 Alaskan pipeline

- ▨ Oilfields
- --- Proposed pipeline
- — Roads
- ⊶ Railways
- — Existing
- --- Proposed

2 Trans-Amazonica highway

Permanent tracks *above*
Thrusting into the heart of the tundra, heavy machinery carves out a route for a new oil pipeline.

One vehicle and the havoc one journey can make. In three months its track has become a gully 10 ft (3m) deep and 30 ft (9m) wide as surface meltwater drains into it, causing a flash flood.

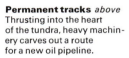

Animal barrier *below*
The cleared area of a jungle highway acts as a formidable barrier to the movement of forest species.

Scientist pioneers
Driving like a lance into the heartlands of Amazonia a great new transcontinental highway opens up the world's last great forest wilderness. Scientists move ahead of the roadmakers in an effort to lessen the impact of modern society on plants, animals and men living in a hitherto undisturbed environment. The impact is none the less savage for the road will provide opportunities for commercial exploitation.

Profit from protection
Protection and sensible culling of wildlife stocks, in contrast to profligate slaughter, enables species to thrive healthily and provide food stocks. The saiga, once almost extinct in Russia, now breeds again in controlled conditions. The eland — a native of the African savanna — is now bred in the United States for its meat, as is the hippopotamus in a Uganda game park. The Thais farm the once-threatened Siamese crocodile for its skin, at once ruining the market for poachers.

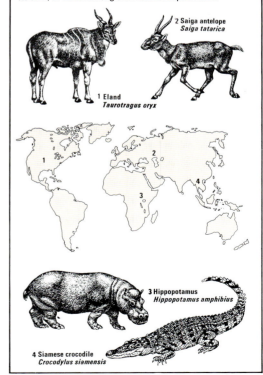

2 Saiga antelope
Saiga tatarica

1 Eland
Taurotragus oryx

3 Hippopotamus
Hippopotamus amphibius

4 Siamese crocodile
Crocodylus siamensis

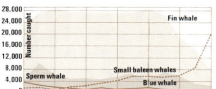

New targets for the whaler's gun
As stocks of the giant blue whale have dropped to near-extinction hunters have switched their attentions to the less-economical but still numerous small whales, like the sei.

Fallen giant
The blue whale, the largest animal ever known, has been brought almost to extinction by whalers, but it is now protected. It is a member of the genus *Balaenoptera*, the baleen whales which range in size from 30ft(9m) to 100ft (30m). Properly managed, they are a valuable resource but — ironically — much whale meat has found its way to the pet food industry.

The Endangered Species 1

Success in evolution is measured in terms of survival, failure by extinction. The extinction of organic life has thus been an integral part of evolutionary development since the beginnings of life on earth. Successful forms have survived; the failures have faded into oblivion. This is the harsh law by which organic life over long periods of time has been enriched.

As this proceeding is both natural and inevitable, one may wonder why there should be concern at the animal extinctions taking place in the world today. The quintessence of evolution is the continual enrichment and diversification of organic life. Evolutionary extinction, as part of this process, is characterized by the emergence of new and more dynamic forms to replace the old. Extinction by man, on the other hand, is the antithesis of this natural process, for it impoverishes organic life and leaves only a void.

Most recent extinctions can be imputed, either directly or indirectly, to man; more specifically to man's demographic and technological expansion. Some species have been wantonly destroyed, often as the result of commercialized exploitation, as with the fur seals and the blue whale.

The majority of recent extinctions, however, are attributable to environmental change arising from alteration and degradation of natural habitats. Pastoral and agricultural expansion and extensive deforestation are the principal causes. These have been accentuated by spreading urbanization and by the phenomenon of unprecedented mobility resulting from the invention of the internal combustion engine; areas which because of their remoteness or inaccessibility were hitherto undisturbed natural sanctuaries have been thrown open to human intrusion. The reduction of the fauna of the Arabian Peninsula by motorized slaughter is a prime example of this trend: convoys of jeeps drive across country in extended formation shooting at every living thing.

Introductions of exotic plants and animals have also contributed to the decline of some species. The effects of introductions are particularly evident among insular floras and faunas which have evolved during long isolation to take advantage of often highly specialized ecological opportunities. Island ecosystems are finely balanced, and their endemic faunas vulnerable to environmental change, to competition from alien animals and to the diseases that frequently accompany them. Flightless and ground-nesting birds, which are frequently found among insular bird faunas, are highly vulnerable to predation by rats, cats, dogs and pigs, as are the eggs and hatchlings of tortoises and turtles; while insular herbivores, such as the giant tortoises of Aldabra and the Galapagos, are unable to withstand the competition of goats.

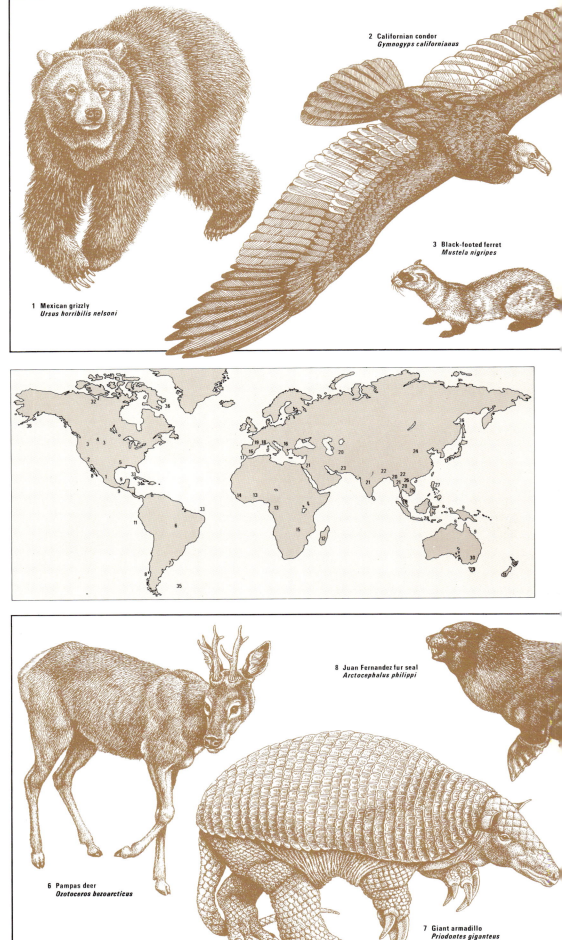

1 Mexican grizzly
Ursus horribilis nelsoni

2 Californian condor
Gymnogyps californianus

3 Black-footed ferret
Mustela nigripes

6 Pampas deer
Ozotoceros bezoarcticus

7 Giant armadillo
Priodontes giganteus

8 Juan Fernandez fur seal
Arctocephalus philippi

Mexican grizzly bear

The Mexican grizzly *Ursus horribilis nelsoni*, the southernmost representative of the grizzly bears, once occupied an extensive range from Arizona and New Mexico to Baja California. By the 1940s, however, it had been exterminated except for a small group living in the mountains about 50 miles north of Chihuahua. Despite formal protection under presidential proclamation, and under the game laws, destruction continued by shooting, trapping and poisoning. The last Mexican grizzlies were believed to have been killed in the early 1960s. In 1969, however, a few were found to have survived on a cattle ranch in the upper Yaqui Basin of Sonora.

California condor

The original range of the California condor extended along the whole of the western side of the Rockies from the Columbia River to Lower California. This inoffensive bird was killed in the mistaken belief that it was a menace to livestock; in fact it is strictly a carrion-eater and thus both harmless and beneficial. Many died as the result of consuming the poisoned carcasses of prairie dogs and *Continued on opposite page*

4 Wood bison
Bison bison

5 American alligator
Alligator mississipiensis

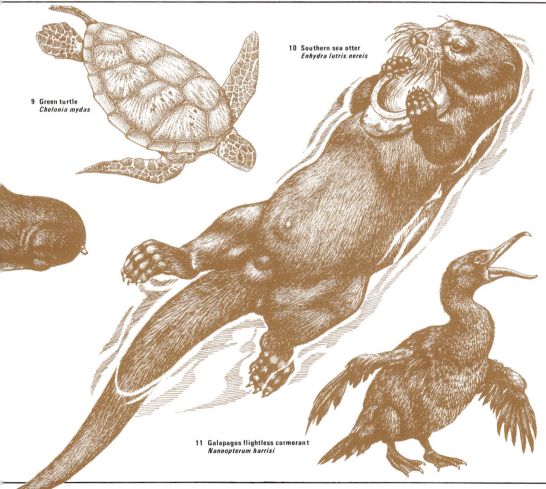

9 Green turtle
Chelonia mydas

10 Southern sea otter
Enhydra lutris nereis

11 Galapagos flightless cormorant
Nannopterum harrisi

other rodents destroyed during intensive rodent control operations. Today, the condor's breeding range is restricted to the mountains northwest of Los Angeles, where the total population numbers no more than about 60.

Black-footed ferret

The black-footed ferret is probably the rarest mammal in the United States. Its range coincides with that of the prairie dog, and it is generally believed that the ferret is dependent on its rodent host both as its principal source of food and for the shelter afforded by its burrows. The widespread destruction of prairie dogs which followed the settlement of the Great Plains, destroyed not only the prairie dog but the ferret also. Very few sightings have been made in recent years.

Wood bison

The immense herds of bison, estimated to have totalled 60,000,000 animals, that once dominated the prairies were almost completely destroyed. By the 1890s, both sub-species – the plains bison *B.b.bison* and the wood bison *B.b.athabascae* – had been reduced to remnants. All that remained of the wood bison was a herd of about 300 animals in the vicinity of Great Slave Lake. The Canadian Government later established the Wood Buffalo National Park in this area to protect the subspecies. In the 1920s, following the introduction of several thousand plains bison into the park, it was assumed that the distinctive wood bison had been bred out of existence. In 1957, however, a pure-bred herd of about 200 wood bison was discovered in a remote part of the park where it had remained isolated.

Mississippi alligator

The American alligator, *Alligator mississipiensis* is estimated to have been reduced by 98 per cent since 1960. Unless the commerce in skins can be regulated by national and international action, the outlook for the crocodilians is bleak.

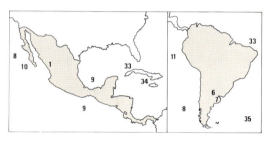

Pampas deer

Before European settlement, the pampas deer *Ozotoceros bezoarticus* was the most abundant deer species on the grasslands of South America. The development of the cattle industry in the latter half of the last century resulted in the introduction of various diseases, such as anthrax and foot-and-mouth, to which the native deer were highly vulnerable. Development of the pampas resulted in the elimination of the clumps of tall pampas grass which afforded cover and fencing hindered movement.

Giant armadillo

The giant armadillo *Priodontes giganteus* is the largest of the living armadillos. Despite its wide range, which covers much of eastern South America and the Peruvian Amazon, this animal is sparsely distributed. It has disappeared from areas which have been taken up for settlement ; deforestation, and the expansion of cultivation and pastoralism represent the principal threats to its survival.

Juan Fernandez fur seal

Until the end of the eighteenth century, all the islands off the Pacific coast of South America were inhabited by immense numbers of fur seals. Their slaughter to meet the demands of the fur trade continued until so few seals remained that the trade was no longer profitable. The endemic fur seal of the Juan Fernendez archipelago was no exception : by the 1890s it was presumed extinct. In 1968 it was found that a small population had survived.

Green turtle

Once common throughout the world's warm oceans, the Green turtle has suffered drastically at the hand of man. The removal of eggs from breeding beaches, and an annual "take" of up to 20,000 adults, have reduced several populations (including the Caribbean) almost to nil. The only remaining large populations exist in Malaysia and the Philippines.

Southern sea otter

Until a century ago, the southern race of the sea otter *Enhydra lutris nereis* was abundant off the coast of California. It was so remorselessly hunted for its valuable pelt, however, that the last one was believed to have been killed in 1911. But in 1938 the animal was rediscovered ; since then it has been stringently protected.

Galapagos flightless cormorant

The world's only flightless cormorant, *Nannopterum harrisi*, is one among half a dozen endemic Galapagos birds currently endangered. It is mainly restricted to the island of Isabela (Albemarle). The colonists hunt this large cormorant for food and collect its eggs.

187

The Endangered Species 2

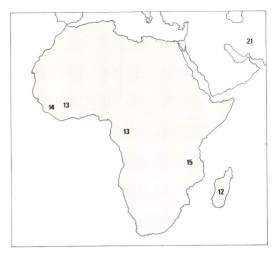

Indri
The indri, largest of the living lemurs and their allies, is confined to parts of the humid coastal rain forest of northeastern Madagascar, where it is very localized. Deforestation, which over much of the country is almost absolute, is the principal reason for the decline of the Malagasy fauna; the arboreal lemurs have been particularly severely affected. The Foret de Masoala was set aside as a reserve in the 1920s, partly to safeguard the indri. In 1964, however, this important reserve was thrown open to commercialized logging.

Bare-headed rock-fowl
The genus *Picathartes* is confined to the rain forests of West Africa. It comprises two species, which differ principally in the skin colour of their bald heads: the white-necked rock-fowl *P. gymnocephalus*, which lives in Sierra Leone, Ghana and Togo; and the grey-necked rock-fowl *P. oreas* from central and southern Cameroon.
Little is known about this rare genus. Its decline is attributable to uncontrolled exploitation for the bird trade and to destruction and degradation of its forested habitat.

Jentink's duiker
Jentink's duiker *Cephalophus jentinki* is a most elusive animal. The three original specimens — all females — were collected in the 1880s. Thereafter, evidence of the existence of this species was limited to occasional skins procured from tribesmen. The skull of an adult male discovered in 1948 was the first evidence of a male. In 1968, however, a living male and two females were secured.

Black lechwe
Excessive commercialized slaughter is responsible for the dramatic decline of the black lechwe *Kobus leche smithemani,* which is confined to Lake Bangweulu, in Zambia. The development of the copper mines provided a ready market for unlimited quantities of game meat, with the result that the black lechwe population fell from several hundred thousand at the turn of the century to about 4,500 in 1966. It was not the only casualty: sitatunga, tsessebe, roan antelope, puku and zebra, all of which were previously common around Lake Bangweulu, were virtually exterminated in this region.

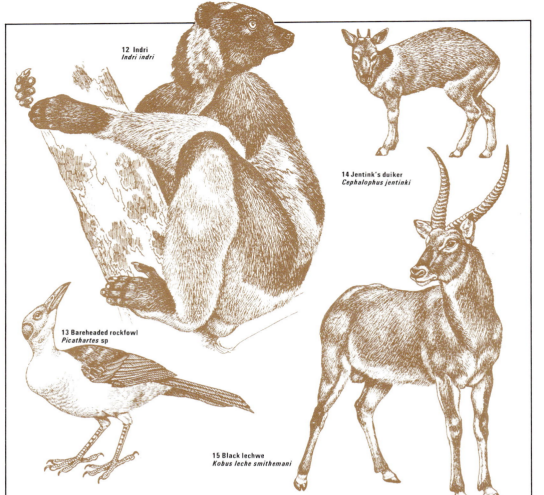

12 Indri
Indri indri

14 Jentink's duiker
Cephalophus jentinki

13 Bareheaded rockfowl
Picathartes sp

15 Black lechwe
Kobus leche smithemani

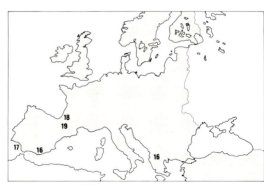

Spanish Imperial Eagle
The western race of the Imperial eagle, once widely distributed across western Europe, is now confined to the Iberian Peninsula. Until recently, the range extended to northeastern Morocco, where occasional sighting reports continued to be made from the High Atlas and other mountainous regions until the 1960s. Destruction by shooting and egg-collecting, in combination with extensive land clearance and habitat modification, are the principal causes of decline. The reproductive rate is moreover low. Even if undisturbed, a breeding pair rears only a single young each year. *Continued on opposite page*

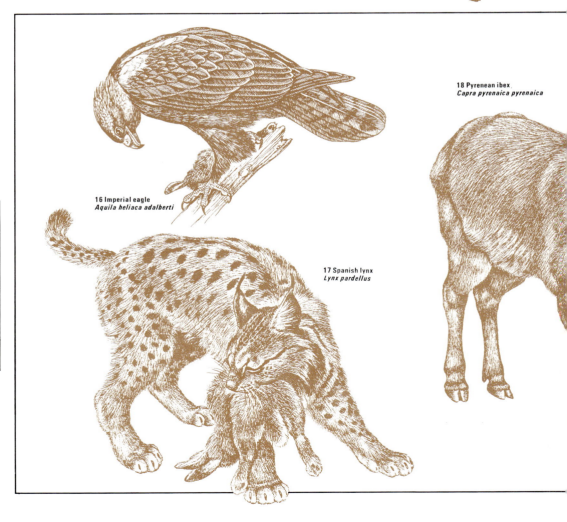

16 Imperial eagle
Aquila heliaca adalberti

17 Spanish lynx
Lynx pardellus

18 Pyrenean ibex
Capra pyrenaica pyrenaica

Spanish lynx

The Spanish lynx is smaller and more prominently marked than its northern congener. At one time it inhabited the greater part of the Iberian Peninsula, but is now known with certainty only from southern Spain where it is restricted to some of the more inaccessible mountainous regions and to the delta of the Guadalquivir where numbers are estimated at a maximum of about 15 pairs. The decline of the Spanish lynx is attributable to the destruction of its natural habitat by extensive deforestation and to remorseless persecution because of its inclination to prey on domestic livestock.

Pyrenean ibex

The Pyrenean race of the ibex, *Capra pyrenaica pyrenaica*, is restricted to a small area around Mount Perdida in the extreme north of Spain's Huasca Province. In the Middle Ages the ibex was abundant on both sides of the Pyrenees. The demand for wild goat meat, which was regarded as a delicacy, led to incessant hunting that increased in intensity as the efficiency of firearms improved. By the beginning of the present century the total population of this race of the ibex had been reduced to about a dozen animals. Despite legal protection introduced in 1959, the number has risen only slightly, to about two dozen.

Pyrenean desman

The Pyrenean desman *Galemys pyrenaicus* is a member of the mole family which has become adapted to an aquatic existence. Its range is restricted to parts of the Pyrenean region, where it inhabits cold, fast-flowing streams, obtaining the aquatic larvae on which it feeds. This is a relict species which has survived unchanged since the Tertiary by virtue of the fact that it occupies a highly specialized ecological niche in which it is largely free from competition and predation. Modification of its aquatic habitat either by pollution or by dams and barrages represents the greatest threat to this species' survival.

Caspian tiger

Land reclamation schemes inevitably have serious repercussions on local fauna. The development of large-scale projects along many of the river valleys in central Russia, for example, has eradicated much riverine vegetation. The dense *tugai* thicket along the banks of the Amu Dar'ya (Oxus) was reputedly the best tiger habitat known. This tiger was of the Caspian race, *Panthera tigris virgata*, whose principal prey species – apart from wild pig, which was to be had in abundance – included the Bactrian wapiti *Cervus elaphus bactrianus*. Both tiger and wapiti have been exterminated throughout their respective ranges, except in the few remaining large patches of *tugai* vegetation in the basin of the upper Amu Dar'ya and Pyandzh rivers on the border between the Soviet Union and Afghanistan.

Asiatic cheetah

The Asiatic cheetah *Acinonyx jubatus venaticus* is far rarer than the African form. Its original range embraced most of the semi-arid country from central India to the Levant and from Russian Turkmenia to northern Africa, where it intergrades with the African race. Occasional sightings are still made in North Africa.

Pygmy hog

This diminutive wild pig is the smallest member of the family Suidae ; a mature boar is no bigger than a hare. The pygmy hog is an inhabitant of the *terai*, the belt of swampland lying at the foot of the Himalayas. After the Second World War, much of the *terai* was drained and cleared for cultivation, grazing and settlement.
Recent reports confirm the continued existence of the animal in parts of Nepal, Assam and Bhutan.

Persian fallow deer

The Persian fallow deer *Dama dama mesopotamica* exemplifies a rare subspecies which could not be accorded adequate protection in its natural habitat, and would certainly have been exterminated if measures had not been taken to establish a captive herd. Between 1953 and 1968, numbers declined from an estimated 100-150 animals to a remnant of no more than 30 in Iran.

Przewalski's horse

Przewalski's horse *Equus przewalskii* is the only surviving species of wild horse. Its original range extended from northern Sinkiang to western Mongolia, but is now reduced to a small area of semi-desert country in southwestern Mongolia on the frontier with China, whence it moves into the Gobi Desert in search of grazing.

20 Caspian tiger
Panthera tigris virgata

21 Cheetah
Acinonyx jubatus venaticus

22 Pygmy hog
Sus salvanius

23 Persian fallow deer
Dama dama mesopotamica

19 Pyrenean desman
Galemys pyrenaicus

24 Przewalski's horse
Equus przewalskii

The Endangered Species 3

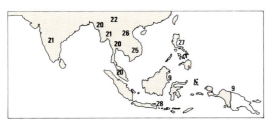

Siamese crocodile
The Siamese crocodile *C. siamensis* is virtually extinct in the wild state, and survives only on a Thai crocodile farm. Even the Nile crocodile *C. niloticus* has undergone a drastic decline within the last two decades.

Monkey-eating eagle
The monkey-eating eagle, one of the largest and most spectacular of Asiatic birds, is endemic to the Philippines, where, with the possible exception of Luzon, it is now confined to the island of Mindoro. Although precise figures are not known, the population is believed to total no more than 40 individual birds. The monkey-eating eagle is an inhabitant of the forest canopy where it preys on small mammals such as flying lemurs and squirrels. Reduction of its natural habitat and uncontrolled shooting, are responsible for its decline.

Douc langur
The douc langur *Pygathrix nemaeus* is an inhabitant of tropical rain forest in Vietnam and Laos; it may also occur in Hainan, although only a solitary specimen has ever been recorded from that island. This large monkey has been little studied and almost nothing is known about it. It must be presumed, however, that its status has been adversely affected by the Vietnam war.

Komodo dragon
The giant monitor *Varanus komodoensis,* usually known as the Komodo dragon, has a very limited distribution on four small islands off the coast of Indonesia. The monitor itself has no natural enemies — not even man. But although it is not hunted by the local people, its numbers are nonetheless governed by human predation on the monitor's own prey species — wild pigs and deer. Protection of prey species is thus the key to conserving the monitor. With this aim in view, the island of Komodo has been declared a strict nature reserve.

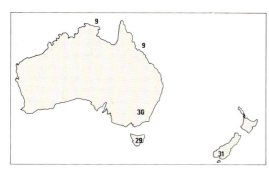

Thylacine
The thylacine, or Tasmanian 'wolf', is the largest of the living carnivorous marsupials. By the time Europeans first settled in Australia, it was already extinct on the mainland, though still common in Tasmania. The development of sheep farming brought the thylacine into sharp conflict with stockowners who regarded it as a threat to their livelihood. A sudden dramatic decline in numbers, which occurred in 1910, is believed to have been caused by disease, possibly distemper, to which the thylacine was highly vulnerable. The surviving remnant took refuge in the rugged, western part of Tasmania, where it was thought to have become extinct during the 1930s. Some may still survive, as tracks have been seen and sightings made.

Kakapo
In the absence of native mammals, New Zealand's bird fauna evolved in a highly distinctive manner, including pronounced flightlessness. The introduction of exotic predators, particularly the rat and the stoat, had calamitous effects on the ground-dwelling birds. The kakapo, or owl parrot, is one of several native bird species to have been endangered in this way. Fewer than 100 birds remain.

White-throated wallaby
The white-throated wallaby *Macropus parma* has an unusual recent history. The clearance of its rain forest habitat in New South Wales for agricultural development resulted in the disappearance of the species and it was presumed extinct. In the 1960s, however, a thriving colony was found living on the New Zealand island of Kawau, descended from animals introduced about 1870.

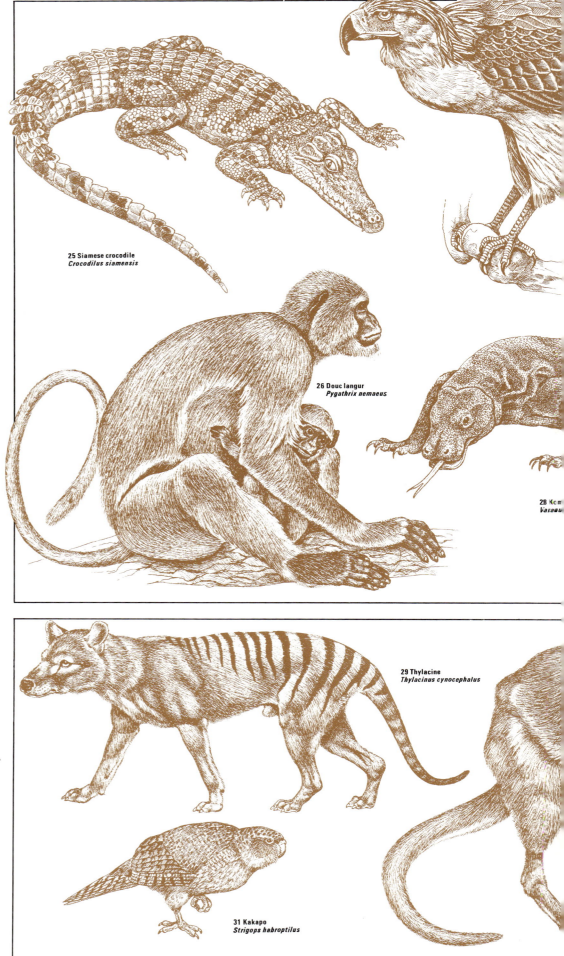

25 Siamese crocodile
Crocodilus siamensis

26 Douc langur
Pygathrix nemaeus

28 Kom
Varanu

29 Thylacine
Thylacinus cynocephalus

31 Kakapo
Strigops habroptilus

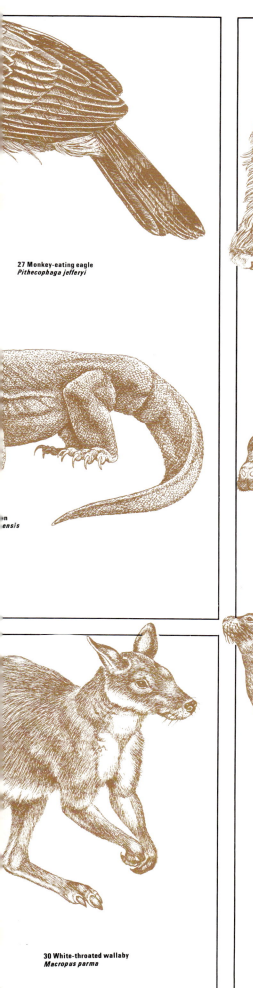

27 Monkey-eating eagle
Pithecophaga jefferyi

ensis

30 White-throated wallaby
Macropus parma

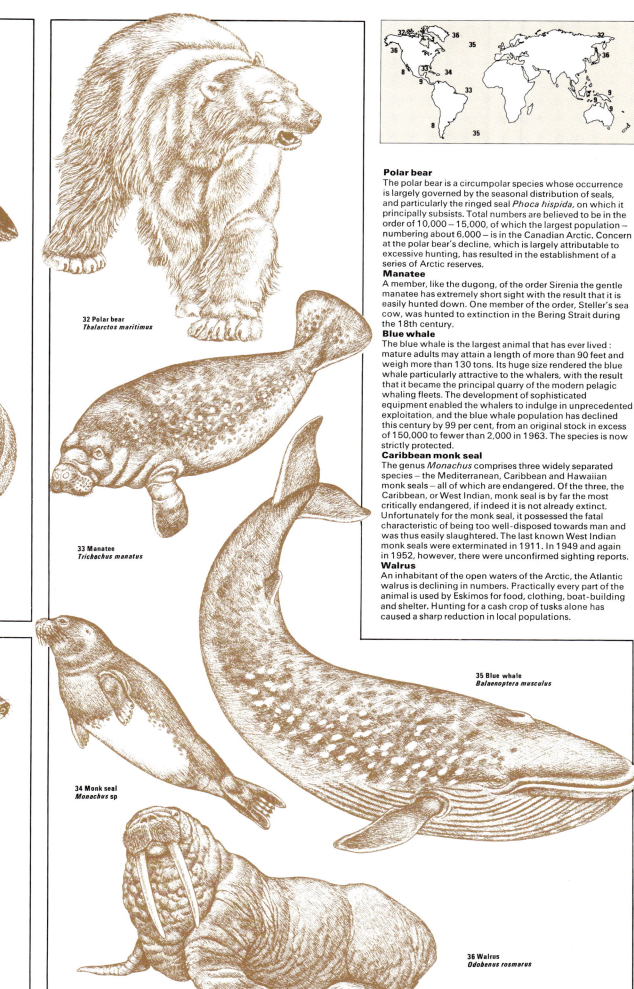

32 Polar bear
Thalarctos maritimus

33 Manatee
Trichechus manatus

34 Monk seal
Monachus sp

35 Blue whale
Balaenoptera musculus

36 Walrus
Odobenus rosmarus

Polar bear

The polar bear is a circumpolar species whose occurrence is largely governed by the seasonal distribution of seals, and particularly the ringed seal *Phoca hispida*, on which it principally subsists. Total numbers are believed to be in the order of 10,000 – 15,000, of which the largest population – numbering about 6,000 – is in the Canadian Arctic. Concern at the polar bear's decline, which is largely attributable to excessive hunting, has resulted in the establishment of a series of Arctic reserves.

Manatee

A member, like the dugong, of the order Sirenia the gentle manatee has extremely short sight with the result that it is easily hunted down. One member of the order, Steller's sea cow, was hunted to extinction in the Bering Strait during the 18th century.

Blue whale

The blue whale is the largest animal that has ever lived : mature adults may attain a length of more than 90 feet and weigh more than 130 tons. Its huge size rendered the blue whale particularly attractive to the whalers, with the result that it became the principal quarry of the modern pelagic whaling fleets. The development of sophisticated equipment enabled the whalers to indulge in unprecedented exploitation, and the blue whale population has declined this century by 99 per cent, from an original stock in excess of 150,000 to fewer than 2,000 in 1963. The species is now strictly protected.

Caribbean monk seal

The genus *Monachus* comprises three widely separated species – the Mediterranean, Caribbean and Hawaiian monk seals – all of which are endangered. Of the three, the Caribbean, or West Indian, monk seal is by far the most critically endangered, if indeed it is not already extinct. Unfortunately for the monk seal, it possessed the fatal characteristic of being too well-disposed towards man and was thus easily slaughtered. The last known West Indian monk seals were exterminated in 1911. In 1949 and again in 1952, however, there were unconfirmed sighting reports.

Walrus

An inhabitant of the open waters of the Arctic, the Atlantic walrus is declining in numbers. Practically every part of the animal is used by Eskimos for food, clothing, boat-building and shelter. Hunting for a cash crop of tusks alone has caused a sharp reduction in local populations.

National Parks and Reserves

The best-known game reserves are those of Africa. The first was Pongola, established after a big-game hunter, Paul Kruger (later President of the Transvaal) noticed a sudden depletion of game. It is an interesting reflection that sportsmen have always been concerned with the survival of their game and by that token of the habitat in which their game abounds. Today the national parks of Africa are plentiful and generally well-managed, because they have become tourist attractions earning valuable revenue for otherwise poor countries.

The modern wildlife park is more than a huge, free-range zoo. Its management has to recognize that man himself has always played a predatory role and that where protection is absolute, some species over-proliferate, particularly those free from natural predation, like hippopotamuses and elephants. Hippopotamuses in the Queen Elizabeth National Park, Uganda, became so numerous that they destroyed their own grazing and also that of buffalo and kob.

Elephants are among the most destructive of feeders, uprooting trees and bushes and destroying the food stocks of other browsers. Their numbers have to be kept in check by regular culling, or selective killing, a technique used in many parts of the world where animal numbers exceed the ability of their habitat to support them.

In other parts of the world, reserves have been set up to provide protection of individual species like the rare Javanese rhinoceros. The Chinese have designated the Hsifan Reserve as a protected home for the giant panda. In the foothills of the Himalayas, the Indian government has established the Corbett National Park (named after a famous big-game hunter) to protect the tiger, whose numbers have diminished from 40,000 at the turn of the century to one-twentieth of that number, with total extinction not far away.

The setting aside of reserves and park-lands for the protection of the landscape, and its plants and animals, is as old as princes, who sequestered tracts of countryside to protect their sport. To do so out of concern for the survival of plant and animal species is an idea that is little more than 100 years old. The first national park to be established anywhere in the world was Yellowstone, in the United States, in 1872, and more soon followed in North America. By the turn of the century Australia had followed suit, and Sweden, where the first European park was declared. Today there are thousands throughout the world, thanks largely to the efforts of international organizations such as the World Wildlife Fund and the International Union for the Conservation of Nature.

Mt. Rainier *above*
At the heart of one of North America's national parks, Mt. Rainier is a dormant volcano clad in wild flowers for which it is famous — fawn lily, glacier lily and western pasqueflower. Black bear, bobcat, mule deer, and more than 130 bird species, are found there. The damaged trees in Tsavo National Park, Kenya (left) bear witness to the havoc wrought on vegetation by elephants — if their numbers are not kept under control. At foot of page (far left) La Vanoise National Park in the French Alps harbors chamois, ibex and rare alpine plants.

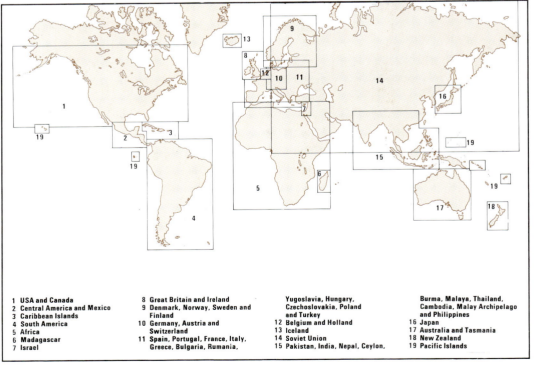

1 USA and Canada	8 Great Britain and Ireland	Yugoslavia, Hungary, Czechoslovakia, Poland and Turkey	Burma, Malaya, Thailand, Cambodia, Malay Archipelago and Philippines
2 Central America and Mexico	9 Denmark, Norway, Sweden and Finland	12 Belgium and Holland	16 Japan
3 Caribbean Islands	10 Germany, Austria and Switzerland	13 Iceland	17 Australia and Tasmania
4 South America	11 Spain, Portugal, France, Italy, Greece, Bulgaria, Rumania,	14 Soviet Union	18 New Zealand
5 Africa		15 Pakistan, India, Nepal, Ceylon,	19 Pacific Islands
6 Madagascar			
7 Israel			

U.S.A.
and Canada

U.S.A. and Canada
1. Yellowstone National Park
2. Grand Teton National Park
3. Glacier National Park
4. Rocky Mountain National Park
5. Theodore Roosevelt National Memorial Park
6. Grand Canyon National Park
7. Zion National Park
8. Bryce Canyon National Park
9. Carlsbad Caverns National Park
10. Big Bend National Park
11. Mesa Verde National Park
12. Yosemite National Park
13. Sequoia-Kings Canyon National Park
14. Olympic National Park
15. Mount Rainier National Park
16. Lassen Volcanic National Park
17. Everglades National Park
18. Great Smoky Mountains National Park
19. Shenandoah National Park
20. Acadia National Park
21. Mammoth Cave National Park

22. Isle Royal National Park
23. Mount McKinley National Park
24. Katmai National Monument
25. Glacier Bay National Monument
26. Death Valley National Monument
27. Joshua Tree National Monument
28. Organ Pipe Cactus National Monument
29. Craters of the Moon National Monument
30. Natural Bridges National Monument
31. Aransas National Wildlife Refuge
32. National Bison Range
33. Aleutian Island National Wildlife Refuge
34. Kenai National Moose Range
35. Desert Game Range
36. Kofa Game Range
37. Cabeza Prieta Game Range
38. Wood Buffalo National Park
39. Jasper National Park
40. Banff National Park
41. Prince Albert National Park
42. Riding Mountain National Park

43. Kootenay National Park
44. Glacier National Park
45. Yoho National Park
46. Cape Breton Highland National Park
47. Waterton Lakes National Park
48. Terra Nova National Park
49. Kejimkujik National Park
50. Mount Revelstoke National Park
51. Fundy National Park
52. Elk Island National Park
53. Prince Edward Island National Park
54. Point Pelee National Park
55. Georgian Bay Island National Park
56. St. Lawrence Island National Park
57. Cypress Hills Provincial Park
58. Dinosaur Provincial Park
59. Algonquin Provincial Park
60. Vérandrye Provincial Park
61. Laurentides Provincial Park
62. Gaspesian Provincial Park
63. Pitts Pond Provincial Park
64. Thelon Game Reserve

North America is particularly rich in national parks and those of the United States alone (280) cover an area greater than that of the Low Countries and Denmark together. Canada has added to its number regularly and its Wood Buffalo Park is the continent's largest.

Central and
South America

Central America, Mexico and Caribbean Islands
1. Barro Colorado Reserve
2. Rio Dulce National Park
3. Santa Rosalia National Park
4. Atitlan National Park
5. La Malinche
6. Iztaccihuatl-Popocatepetl
7. Pico de Orizaba
8. Lagunas de Chacahua
9. Zoquiapan
10. Cofre de Perote
11. Lagunas de Zempoala
12. Desierto de los Leones
13. Insurgente Miguel Hidalgo y Costilla
14. El Chico
15. Desierto del Carmen
16. El Vedado Haina-Duey National Park
17. Armando Bermudez and José del Carmen Ramirez National Parks
18. Capeyal Nature Reserve
19. El Cabo Nature Reserve
20. Jaguani Nature Reserve
21. Cabo Corrientes National Reserve
22. Ciénaga de Zapata National Park

23. Flamencos Reserve
24. Bosque Nacional de Luquillo
25. Derby Island Reserve
26. Virgin Islands National Park
27. Buck Island Reef National Monument
28. Bonaire Flamingo Reserve

South America
1. Nahuel Huapi National Park
2. Los Glaciares National Park
3. Lanin National Park
4. Rio Pilcomayo National Park
5. Los Arerces National Park
6. Perito Francisco P. Moreno National Park
7. Tierra del Fuego National Park
8. Iguazu National Park
9. El Rey National Park
10. Laguna Blanca National Park
11. Laguna Blanca National Park
12. Petrified Forest National Monument
13. Cape Born National Park
14. Nahuebuta National Park
15. Fray Jorge National Park
16. Tolhuaca National Park
17. Mount Sajama National Park
18. Paso del Puerto National Park

19. Cabo Polonia National Park
20. Iguazu National Park
21. Monte Pascoal National Park
22. Brastlia National Park
23. Aparados da Serra National Park
24. Itatiaia National Park
25. Sobretama Biological Reserve
26. Serra dos Orgãos National Park
27. Caparão National Park
28. Sete Cidades National Park
29. Tijuca National Park
30. Jacarepagua Biological Reserve
31. Kaieteur National Park
32. Kaysergebergte Nature Reserve
33. Coppename River Nature Reserve
34. Tafelberg Nature Reserve
35. Wia-Wia Nature Reserve
36. Nature Reserve at mouth of Coppename River
37. Brinckheuvel Nature Reserve
38. Canaima National Park
39. Guatopo National Park
40. Henri Pittier (Rancho Grande) National Park
41. El Avila National Park
42. Yacambu National Park
43. Yurubi National Park

Vast areas of South America are uninhabited and are still inaccessible — vast natural expanses protected by their remoteness. One major park, Iguazu, is shared by Argentina, Brazil and Paraguay. Nahuel Huapi, in the Argentinian Andes, is one of the best-known.

193

National Parks and Reserves

Africa

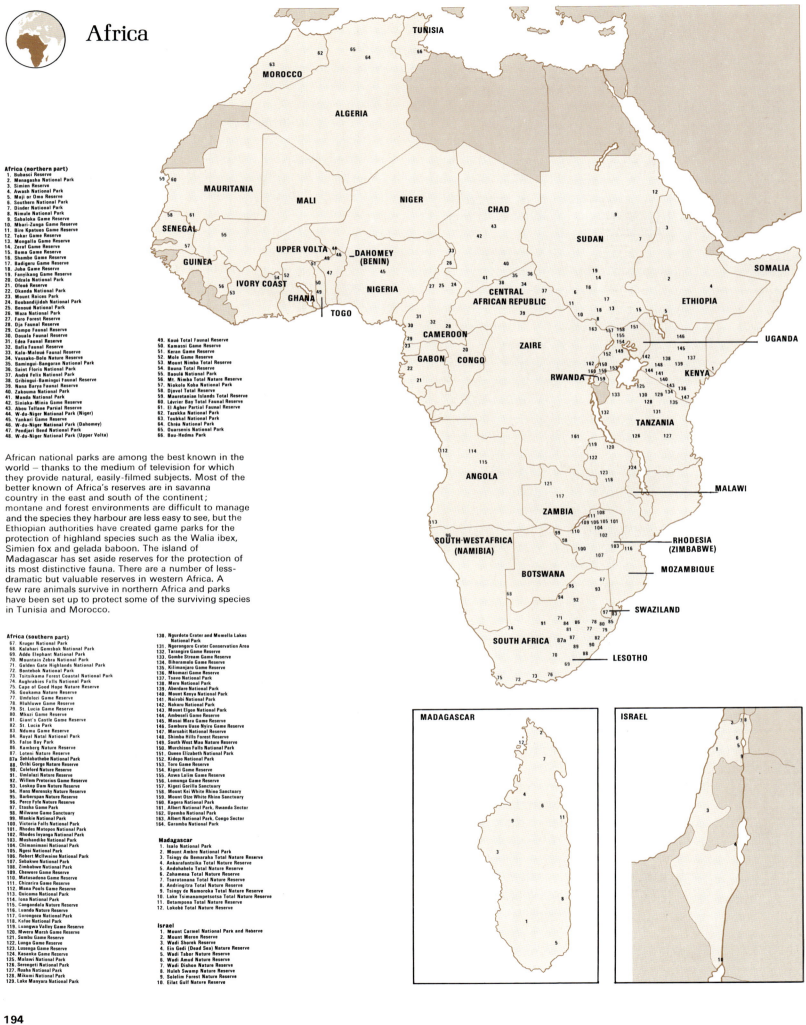

African national parks are among the best known in the world — thanks to the medium of television for which they provide natural, easily-filmed subjects. Most of the better known of Africa's reserves are in savanna country in the east and south of the continent; montane and forest environments are difficult to manage and the species they harbour are less easy to see, but the Ethiopian authorities have created game parks for the protection of highland species such as the Walia ibex, Simien fox and gelada baboon. The island of Madagascar has set aside reserves for the protection of its most distinctive fauna. There are a number of less-dramatic but valuable reserves in western Africa. A few rare animals survive in northern Africa and parks have been set up to protect some of the surviving species in Tunisia and Morocco.

Africa (northern part)
1. Bubasci Reserve
2. Menagasha National Park
3. Simien Reserve
4. Awash National Park
5. Maji or Omo Reserve
6. Southern National Park
7. Dinder National Park
8. Nimule National Park
9. Sabaloka Game Reserve
10. Mbari-Zunga Game Reserve
11. Bire Kpatuos Game Reserve
12. Tokar Game Reserve
13. Mongalla Game Reserve
14. Zeraf Game Reserve
15. Boma Game Reserve
16. Shambe Game Reserve
17. Badigeru Game Reserve
18. Juba Game Reserve
19. Fanyikang Game Reserve
20. Odzala National Park
21. Ofoué Reserve
22. Okanda National Park
23. Mount Raices Reserve
24. Boubandjidah National Park
25. Benoué National Park
26. Waza National Park
27. Faro Forest Reserve
28. Dja Faunal Reserve
29. Campo Faunal Reserve
30. Douala Faunal Reserve
31. Edea Faunal Reserve
32. Bafia Faunal Reserve
33. Kala-Maloué Faunal Reserve
34. Vassako-Bolo Nature Reserve
35. Bamingui-Bangoran National Park
36. Saint Floris National Park
37. André Felix National Park
38. Gribingui-Bamingui Faunal Reserve
39. Nana Barya Faunal Reserve
40. Zakouma National Park
41. Manda National Park
42. Siniaka-Minia Game Reserve
43. Abou Telfane Partial Reserve
44. W-du-Niger National Park (Niger)
45. Yankari Game Reserve
46. W-du-Niger National Park (Dahomey)
47. Pendjari Bend National Park
48. W-du-Niger National Park (Upper Volta)
49. Koué Total Faunal Reserve
50. Kamassi Game Reserve
51. Keran Game Reserve
52. Mole Game Reserve
53. Mount Nimba Total Reserve
54. Bouna Total Reserve
55. Baoulé National Park
56. Mt. Nimba Total Nature Reserve
57. Niokolo Koba National Park
58. Djovol Total Reserve
59. Mauretanian Islands Total Reserve
60. Lévrier Bay Total Faunal Reserve
61. El Agher Partial Faunal Reserve
62. Tazekka National Park
63. Toubkal National Park
64. Chréa National Park
65. Ouarsenis National Park
66. Bou-Hedma Park

Africa (southern part)
67. Kruger National Park
68. Kalahari Gemsbok National Park
69. Addo Elephant National Park
70. Mountain Zebra National Park
71. Golden Gate Highlands National Park
72. Bontebok National Park
73. Tsitsikama Forest Coastal National Park
74. Aughrabies Falls National Park
75. Cape of Good Hope Nature Reserve
76. Goukama Nature Reserve
77. Umfolozi Game Reserve
78. Hluhluwe Game Reserve
79. St. Lucia Game Reserve
80. Mkuzi Game Reserve
81. Giant's Castle Game Reserve
82. St. Lucia Park
83. Ndumu Game Reserve
84. Royal Natal National Park
85. False Bay Park
86. Kamberg Nature Reserve
87. Loteni Nature Reserve
87a. Sehlabathebe National Park
88. Oribi Gorge Nature Reserve
89. Coleford Nature Reserve
90. Umlalazi Nature Reserve
91. Willem Pretorius Game Reserve
92. Loskop Dam Nature Reserve
93. Hans Merensky Nature Reserve
94. Barberspan Nature Reserve
95. Percy Fyfe Nature Reserve
96. Etosha Game Park
97. Milwane Game Sanctuary
98. Wankie National Park
99. Victoria Falls National Park
100. Rhodes Matopos National Park
101. Rhodes Inyanga National Park
102. Mushandike National Park
103. Chimanimani National Park
104. Ngesi National Park
105. Robert McIlwaine National Park
106. Sebakwe National Park
107. Zimbabwe National Park
108. Chewore Game Reserve
109. Matusadona Game Reserve
110. Chizarira Game Reserve
111. Mana Pools Game Reserve
112. Quicama National Park
113. Iona National Park
114. Cangandala Nature Reserve
115. Luando Nature Reserve
116. Gorongoza National Park
117. Kafue National Park
118. Luangwa Valley Game Reserve
119. Mweru Marsh Game Reserve
120. Sumbu Game Reserve
121. Lunga Game Reserve
122. Lusenga Game Reserve
123. Kasanka Game Reserve
124. Malawi National Park
125. Serengeti National Park
126. Ruaha National Park
127. Mikumi National Park
128. Lake Manyara National Park
129.
130. Ngurdoto Crater and Momella Lakes National Park
131. Ngorongoro Crater Conservation Area
132. Tarangire Game Reserve
133. Gombe Stream Game Reserve
134. Biharamulo Game Reserve
135. Kilimanjaro Game Reserve
136. Mkomazi Game Reserve
137. Tsavo National Park
138. Meru National Park
139. Aberdare National Park
140. Mount Kenya National Park
141. Nairobi National Park
142. Nakuru National Park
143. Mount Elgon National Park
144. Amboseli Game Reserve
145. Masai Mara Game Reserve
146. Samburu Uaso Nyiro Game Reserve
147. Marsabit National Reserve
148. Shimba Hills Forest Reserve
149. South West Mau Nature Reserve
150. Murchison Falls National Park
151. Kidepo National Park
152. Toro Game Reserve
153. Kigezi Game Reserve
154. Aswa Lolim Game Reserve
155. Lomunga Game Reserve
156. Kigezi Gorilla Sanctuary
157. Mount Kei White Rhino Sanctuary
158. Mount Otze White Rhino Sanctuary
159.
160. Kagera National Park
161. Albert National Park, Rwanda Sector
162. Upemba National Park
163. Albert National Park, Congo Sector
164. Garamba Park

Madagascar
1. Isalo National Park
2. Mount Ambre National Park
3. Tsingy du Bemaraha Total Nature Reserve
4. Ankarafantsika Total Nature Reserve
5. Andohahelo Total Nature Reserve
6. Zahamena Total Nature Reserve
7. Tsaratanana Total Nature Reserve
8. Andringitra Total Nature Reserve
9. Tsingy de Namoroka Total Nature Reserve
10. Lake Tsimanampetsotsa Total Nature Reserve
11. Betampona Total Nature Reserve
12. Lokobé Total Nature Reserve

Israel
1. Mount Carmel National Park and Reserve
2. Mount Meron Reserve
3. Wadi Shorek Reserve
4. Ein Gedi (Dead Sea) Nature Reserve
5. Wadi Tabor Nature Reserve
6. Wadi Amud Nature Reserve
7. Wadi Dishon Nature Reserve
8. Huleh Swamp Nature Reserve
9. Solelim Forest Nature Reserve
10. Eilat Gulf Nature Reserve

Europe

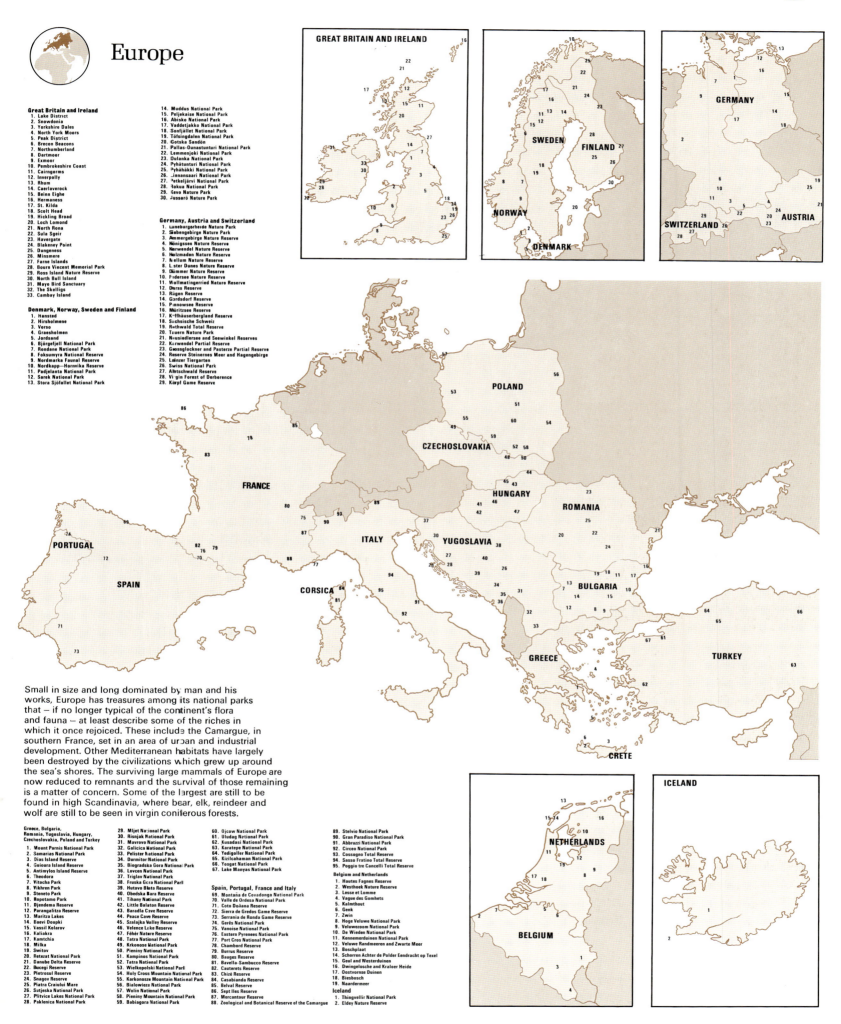

Great Britain and Ireland
1. Lake District
2. Snowdonia
3. Yorkshire Dales
4. North York Moors
5. Peak District
6. Brecon Beacons
7. Northumberland
8. Dartmoor
9. Exmoor
10. Pembrokeshire Coast
11. Cairngorms
12. Inverpolly
13. Rhum
14. Caerlaverock
15. Beinn Eighe
16. Hermaness
17. St. Kilda
18. Scolt Head
19. Hickling Broad
20. Loch Lomond
21. North Rona
22. Sula Sgeir
23. Havergate
24. Blakeney Point
25. Dungeness
26. Minsmere
27. Farne Islands
28. Bourn Vincent Memorial Park
29. Ross Island Nature Reserve
30. North Bull Island
31. Mayo Bird Sanctuary
32. The Skelligs
33. Cambay Island

Denmark, Norway, Sweden and Finland
1. Hansted
2. Hirsholmene
3. Vorso
4. Graesholmen
5. Jordsand
6. Björgefjell National Park
7. Rondane National Park
8. Foksumyra National Reserve
9. Nordmarka Faunal Reserve
10. Nordkapp—Hornvika Reserve
11. Padjelanta National Park
12. Sarek National Park
13. Stora Sjöfallet National Park
14. Muddus National Park
15. Peljekaise National Park
16. Abisko National Park
17. Vaddetjakko National Park
18. Sonfjället National Park
19. Töfsingdalen National Park
20. Gotska Sandön
21. Pallas-Ounastunturi National Park
22. Lemmenjoki National Park
23. Oulanka National Park
24. Pyhätunturi National Park
25. Pyhähäkki National Park
26. Linnansaari National Park
27. Petkeljärvi National Park
28. Rokua National Park
29. Kevo Nature Park
30. Jussarö Nature Park

Germany, Austria and Switzerland
1. Lüneburgerheide Nature Park
2. Siebengebirge Nature Park
3. Ammergebirge Nature Reserve
4. Königssee Nature Reserve
5. Karwendel Nature Reserve
6. Holzmaden Nature Reserve
7. Nellum Nature Reserve
8. Lister Dunes Nature Reserve
9. Dümmer Nature Reserve
10. Federsee Nature Reserve
11. Wollmatingerried Nature Reserve
12. Darss Reserve
13. Rügen Reserve
14. Gardsdorf Reserve
15. Pannowsee Reserve
16. Müritzsee Reserve
17. Kÿffhäuserbergland Reserve
18. Sächsische Schweiz
19. Rothwald Total Reserve
20. Tauern Nature Park
21. Neusiedlersee and Seewinkel Reserves
22. Karwendel Partial Reserve
23. Grossglockner and Pasterze Partial Reserve
24. Reserve Steinernes Meer and Hagengebirge
25. Lainzer Tiergarten
26. Swiss National Park
27. Aletschwald Reserve
28. Virgin Forest of Derborence
29. Kärpf Game Reserve

Small in size and long dominated by man and his works, Europe has treasures among its national parks that — if no longer typical of the continent's flora and fauna — at least describe some of the riches in which it once rejoiced. These include the Camargue, in southern France, set in an area of urban and industrial development. Other Mediterranean habitats have largely been destroyed by the civilizations which grew up around the sea's shores. The surviving large mammals of Europe are now reduced to remnants and the survival of those remaining is a matter of concern. Some of the largest are still to be found in high Scandinavia, where bear, elk, reindeer and wolf are still to be seen in virgin coniferous forests.

Greece, Bulgaria, Romania, Yugoslavia, Hungary, Czechoslovakia, Poland and Turkey
1. Mount Parnis National Park
2. Samarias National Park
3. Dias Island Reserve
4. Goioura Island Reserve
5. Antimylos Island Reserve
6. Theodora
7. Vitocha Park
8. Vikhren Park
9. Steneto Park
10. Ropotamo Park
11. Djendema Reserve
12. Parangalitza Reserve
13. Maritza Lakes
14. Baevi Doupki
15. Vassil Kolarov
16. Kaliakra
17. Kamtchia
18. Milka
19. Switov
20. Retezat National Park
21. Danube Delta Reserve
22. Bucegi Reserve
23. Pietrosul Reserve
24. Snagov Reserve
25. Piatra Craiului Mare
26. Sutjeska National Park
27. Plitvice Lakes National Park
28. Paklenica National Park
29. Mljet National Park
30. Risnjak National Park
31. Mavrovo National Park
32. Galicica National Park
33. Pelister National Park
34. Durmitor National Park
35. Biogradska Gora National Park
36. Lovcen National Park
37. Triglav National Park
38. Fruska Gora National Park
39. Hutovo Blato Reserve
40. Obedska Bara Reserve
41. Tihany National Park
42. Little Balaton Reserve
43. Baradla Cave Reserve
44. Peace Cave Reserve
45. Szalajka Valley Reserve
46. Velence Lake Reserve
47. Fehér Nature Reserve
48. Tatra National Park
49. Krkonose National Park
50. Pieniny National Park
51. Kampinos National Park
52. Tatra National Park
53. Wielkopolski National Park
54. Holy Cross Mountain National Park
55. Karkonosze Mountain National Park
56. Bialowieza National Park
57. Wolin National Park
58. Pieniny Mountain National Park
59. Babiagora National Park
60. Ojcow National Park
61. Uludag National Park
62. Kusadasi National Park
63. Karatepe National Park
64. Yedigoller National Park
65. Kizilcahaman National Park
66. Yozgat National Park
67. Lake Manyas National Park

Spain, Portugal, France and Italy
69. Montaña de Covadonga National Park
70. Valle de Ordesa National Park
71. Coto Doñana Reserve
72. Sierra de Gredos Game Reserve
73. Serrania de Ronda Game Reserve
74. Gerês National Park
75. Vanoise National Park
76. Eastern Pyrenees National Park
77. Port Cros National Park
78. Chambord Reserve
79. Burrus Reserve
80. Bauges Reserve
81. Bavella-Sambucco Reserve
82. Cauterets Reserve
83. Chizé Reserve
84. Casabianda Reserve
85. Belval Reserve
86. Sept Iles Reserve
87. Mercantour Reserve
88. Zoological and Botanical Reserve of the Camargue
89. Stelvio National Park
90. Gran Paradiso National Park
91. Abbruzzi National Park
92. Circeo National Park
93. Cossogno Total Reserve
94. Sasso Fratino Total Reserve
95. Poggio tre Cancelli Total Reserve

Belgium and Netherlands
1. Hautes Fagnes Reserve
2. Westhoek Nature Reserve
3. Lesse et Lomme
4. Vague des Gomhets
5. Kalmthout
6. Genk
7. Zwin
8. Hoge Veluwe National Park
9. Veluwezoom National Park
10. De Wieden National Park
11. Kennemerduinen National Park
12. Veluwe Randmeeren and Zwarte Meer
13. Boschplaat
14. Schorren Achter de Polder Eendracht op Texel
15. Geul and Westerduinen
16. Dwingelosche and Kraloer Heide
17. Oostvorne Duinen
18. Biesbosch
19. Naardermeer

Iceland
1. Thingvellir National Park
2. Eldey Nature Reserve

National Parks and Reserves

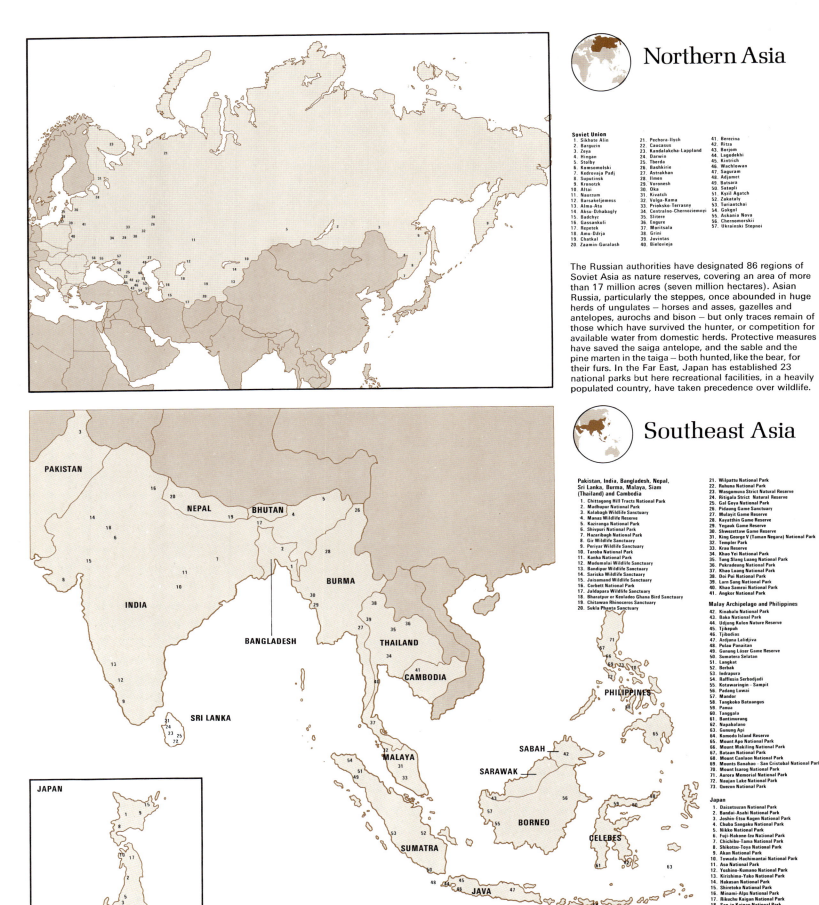

Northern Asia

Soviet Union

1. Sikhote Alin	21. Pechora-Ilych	41. Berezina
2. Barguzin	22. Caucasus	42. Ritza
3. Zeya	23. Kandalakcha-Lappland	43. Borjom
4. Hingan	24. Darwin	44. Lagodekhi
5. Stolby	25. Tberda	45. Kintrich
6. Komsomolski	26. Bashkirie	46. Wachlowan
7. Kedrovaja Padj	27. Astrakhan	47. Saguram
8. Suputinsk	28. Ilmen	48. Adjamet
9. Kronotzk	29. Voronesh	49. Batsara
10. Altai	30. Oka	50. Satapli
11. Naurzum	31. Kivatch	51. Kyzil Agatch
12. Barsakeljemess	32. Volga-Kama	52. Zakataly
13. Alma-Ata	33. Prioksko-Terrasny	53. Turiantchai
14. Aksu-Dzhabagly	34. Centralno-Chernoziemnyi	54. Gokgol
15. Badchyz	35. Slitere	55. Askania Nova
16. Gassankuli	36. Engure	56. Chernomorskii
17. Repetek	37. Moritsala	57. Ukrainski Stepnoi
18. Amu-Dárja	38. Grini	
19. Chatkal	39. Juvintas	
20. Zaamin-Guralash	40. Bielovieja	

The Russian authorities have designated 86 regions of Soviet Asia as nature reserves, covering an area of more than 17 million acres (seven million hectares). Asian Russia, particularly the steppes, once abounded in huge herds of ungulates — horses and asses, gazelles and antelopes, aurochs and bison — but only traces remain of those which have survived the hunter, or competition for available water from domestic herds. Protective measures have saved the saiga antelope, and the sable and the pine marten in the taiga — both hunted, like the bear, for their furs. In the Far East, Japan has established 23 national parks but here recreational facilities, in a heavily populated country, have taken precedence over wildlife.

Southeast Asia

Pakistan, India, Bangladesh, Nepal, Sri Lanka, Burma, Malaya, Siam (Thailand) and Cambodia

1. Chittagong Hill Tracts National Park	21. Wilpattu National Park
2. Madhupur National Park	22. Ruhuna National Park
3. Kalabagh Wildlife Sanctuary	23. Wasgomuva Strict Natural Reserve
4. Manas Wildlife Reserve	24. Ritigala Strict Natural Reserve
5. Kaziranga National Park	25. Gal Goya National Park
6. Shivpuri National Park	26. Pidaung Game Sanctuary
7. Hazaribagh National Park	27. Mulayit Game Reserve
8. Gir Wildlife Sanctuary	28. Kayathtin Game Reserve
9. Periyar Wildlife Sanctuary	29. Yegauk Game Reserve
10. Taroba National Park	30. Shwezettaw Game Reserve
11. Kanha National Park	31. King George V (Taman Negara) National Park
12. Mudumalai Wildlife Sanctuary	32. Templer Park
13. Bandipur Wildlife Sanctuary	33. Krau Reserve
14. Sariska Wildlife Sanctuary	34. Khao Yei National Park
15. Jaisamand Wildlife Sanctuary	35. Tung Slang Luang National Park
16. Corbett National Park	36. Pukradeung National Park
17. Jaldapara Wildlife Sanctuary	37. Khao Luang National Park
18. Bharatpur or Keoladeo Ghana Bird Sanctuary	38. Doi Pui National Park
19. Chitawan Rhinoceros Sanctuary	39. Larn Sang National Park
20. Sukla Phanta Sanctuary	40. Khao Samroi National Park
	41. Angkor National Park

Malay Archipelago and Philippines

42. Kinabalu National Park	
43. Bako National Park	
44. Udjung Kulon Nature Reserve	
45. Tjikepuh	
46. Tjibodias	
47. Ardjuna Lalidjiva	
48. Pulau Panaitan	
49. Gunung Löser Game Reserve	
50. Sumatera Selatan	
51. Langkat	
52. Berbak	
53. Indrapura	
54. Rafflesia Serbodjadi	
55. Kotawaringin – Sampit	
56. Padang Luwai	
57. Mandor	
58. Tangkoko Batuangus	
59. Panua	
60. Tanggala	
61. Bantimurung	
62. Napabalano	
63. Gunung Api	
64. Komodo Island Reserve	
65. Mount Apo National Park	
66. Mount Makiling National Park	
67. Bataan National Park	
68. Mount Canlaon National Park	
69. Mounts Banahao – San Cristobal National Park	
70. Mount Isarog National Park	
71. Aurora Memorial National Park	
72. Naujan Lake National Park	
73. Quezon National Park	

Japan

1. Daisetsuzan National Park
2. Bandai-Asahi National Park
3. Joshin-Etsu Kogen National Park
4. Chuba Sangaku National Park
5. Nikko National Park
6. Fuji-Hakone-Izu National Park
7. Chichibu-Tama National Park
8. Shikotsu-Toya National Park
9. Akan National Park
10. Towada-Hachimantai National Park
11. Aso National Park
12. Yoshino-Kumano National Park
13. Kirishima-Yako National Park
14. Hakusan National Park
15. Shiretoko National Park
16. Minami-Alps National Park
17. Rikuchu Kaigan National Park
18. San-in Kaigan National Park

The burgeoning populations of India and other countries of southeast Asia have placed formidable strains on the indigenous wildlife, but there has been some compensation where religious beliefs have acted as a protection for many species. Reserves set up by colonial governments have been continued and extended by their successors. The forest of Gir, in northwest India, is protected as the last known habitat of the Asiatic lion and a tiger reserve has been set up in northern India.

Australia and New Zealand

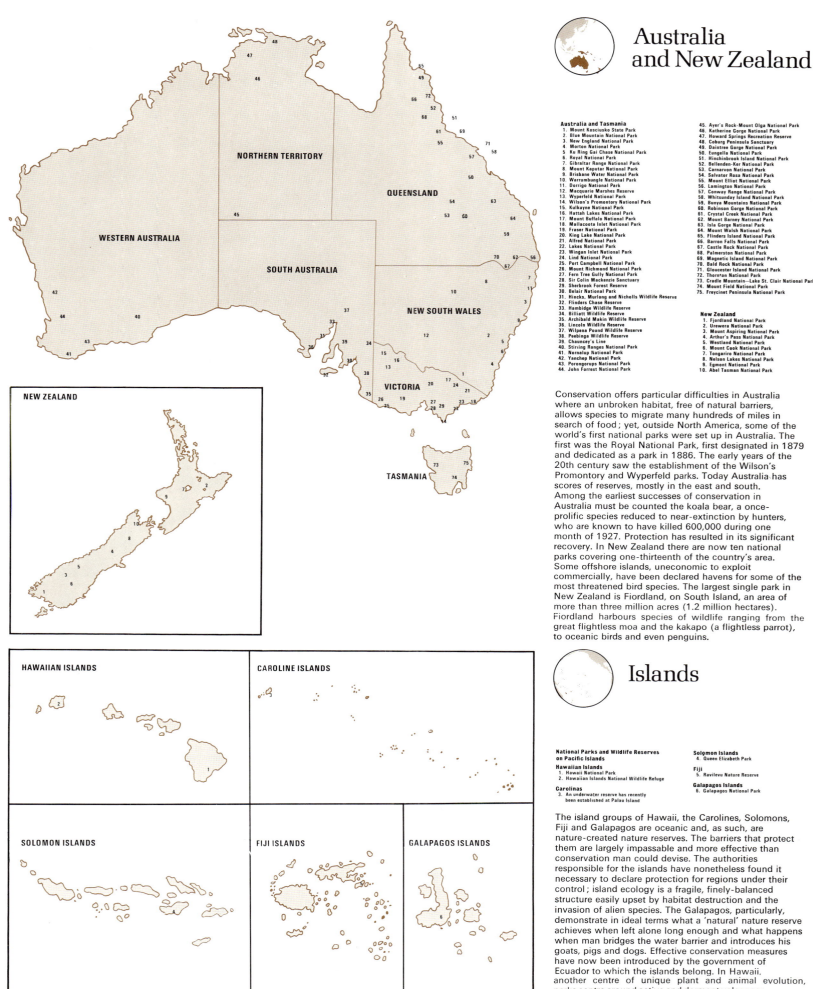

NORTHERN TERRITORY

QUEENSLAND

WESTERN AUSTRALIA

SOUTH AUSTRALIA

NEW SOUTH WALES

VICTORIA

TASMANIA

NEW ZEALAND

Australia and Tasmania
1. Mount Kosciusko State Park
2. Blue Mountain National Park
3. New England National Park
4. Morton National Park
5. Ku Ring Gai Chase National Park
6. Royal National Park
7. Gibraltar Range National Park
8. Mount Kaputar National Park
9. Brisbane Water National Park
10. Warrumbungle National Park
11. Dorrigo National Park
12. Macquarie Marshes Reserve
13. Wyperfeld National Park
14. Wilson's Promontory National Park
15. Kulkuyne National Park
16. Hattah Lakes National Park
17. Mount Buffalo National Park
18. Mallacoota Inlet National Park
19. Fraser National Park
20. King Lake National Park
21. Alfred National Park
22. Lakes National Park
23. Wingan Inlet National Park
24. Lind National Park
25. Port Campbell National Park
26. Mount Richmond National Park
27. Fern Tree Gully National Park
28. Sir Colin Mackenzie Sanctuary
29. Sherbrook Forest Reserve
30. Belair National Park
31. Hincks, Murlong and Nicholls Wildlife Reserve
32. Flinders Chase Reserve
33. Hambidge Wildlife Reserve
34. Billiatt Wildlife Reserve
35. Archibald Makin Wildlife Reserve
36. Lincoln Wildlife Reserve
37. Wilpena Pound Wildlife Reserve
38. Peebinga Wildlife Reserve
39. Chauncey's Line
40. Stirling Ranges National Park
41. Nornalup National Park
42. Yanchep National Park
43. Porongorups National Park
44. John Forrest National Park

45. Ayer's Rock-Mount Olga National Park
46. Katherine Gorge National Park
47. Howard Springs Recreation Reserve
48. Coburg Peninsula Sanctuary
49. Daintree Gorge National Park
50. Eungella National Park
51. Hinchinbrook Island National Park
52. Bellenden-Ker National Park
53. Carnarvon National Park
54. Salvator Rosa National Park
55. Mount Elliot National Park
56. Lamington National Park
57. Conway Range National Park
58. Whitsunday Island National Park
59. Bunya Mountains National Park
60. Robinson Gorge National Park
61. Crystal Creek National Park
62. Mount Barney National Park
63. Isla Gorge National Park
64. Mount Walsh National Park
65. Flinders Island National Park
66. Barron Falls National Park
67. Castle Rock National Park
68. Palmerston National Park
69. Magnetic Island National Park
70. Bald Rock National Park
71. Gloucester Island National Park
72. Thornton National Park
73. Cradle Mountain—Lake St. Clair National Park
74. Mount Field National Park
75. Freycinet Peninsula National Park

New Zealand
1. Fjordland National Park
2. Urewera National Park
3. Mount Aspiring National Park
4. Arthur's Pass National Park
5. Westland National Park
6. Mount Cook National Park
7. Tongariro National Park
8. Nelson Lakes National Park
9. Egmont National Park
10. Abel Tasman National Park

Conservation offers particular difficulties in Australia where an unbroken habitat, free of natural barriers, allows species to migrate many hundreds of miles in search of food; yet, outside North America, some of the world's first national parks were set up in Australia. The first was the Royal National Park, first designated in 1879 and dedicated as a park in 1886. The early years of the 20th century saw the establishment of the Wilson's Promontory and Wyperfeld parks. Today Australia has scores of reserves, mostly in the east and south. Among the earliest successes of conservation in Australia must be counted the koala bear, a once-prolific species reduced to near-extinction by hunters, who are known to have killed 600,000 during one month of 1927. Protection has resulted in its significant recovery. In New Zealand there are now ten national parks covering one-thirteenth of the country's area. Some offshore islands, uneconomic to exploit commercially, have been declared havens for some of the most threatened bird species. The largest single park in New Zealand is Fiordland, on South Island, an area of more than three million acres (1.2 million hectares). Fiordland harbours species of wildlife ranging from the great flightless moa and the kakapo (a flightless parrot), to oceanic birds and even penguins.

Islands

HAWAIIAN ISLANDS

CAROLINE ISLANDS

SOLOMON ISLANDS

FIJI ISLANDS

GALAPAGOS ISLANDS

National Parks and Wildlife Reserves on Pacific Islands
Hawaiian Islands
1. Hawaii National Park
2. Hawaiian Islands National Wildlife Refuge

Carolinas
3. An underwater reserve has recently been established at Palau Island

Solomon Islands
4. Queen Elizabeth Park

Fiji
5. Ravilevu Nature Reserve

Galapagos Islands
6. Galapagos National Park

The island groups of Hawaii, the Carolines, Solomons, Fiji and Galapagos are oceanic and, as such, are nature-created nature reserves. The barriers that protect them are largely impassable and more effective than conservation man could devise. The authorities responsible for the islands have nonetheless found it necessary to declare protection for regions under their control; island ecology is a fragile, finely-balanced structure easily upset by habitat destruction and the invasion of alien species. The Galapagos, particularly, demonstrate in ideal terms what a 'natural' nature reserve achieves when left alone long enough and what happens when man bridges the water barrier and introduces his goats, pigs and dogs. Effective conservation measures have now been introduced by the government of Ecuador to which the islands belong. In Hawaii, another centre of unique plant and animal evolution, parks centre around active and dormant volcanoes.

Index

Note

Figures in italic type (*57*) refer to the written text

Figures in roman type (57) refer to photographs or to material in the captions to the photographs

Figures in bold type (**57**) refer to illustrations other than photographs or to material in the captions to the illustrations

Index

Index

Index

Glossary

Aestivation Dormancy during summer months (or other dry season). Applied to both animals and plants.

Alluvium Solid material *eg* sand, silt, gravel, deposited by rivers.

Amphibian Of the class Amphibia. Vertebrates typically aquatic and gill-breathing in larval stage and air breathing in adult form *eg* frogs, salamanders.

Angiosperm Class of flowering plant. The *ovule* (unfertilized seed) is contained within a *cavity* or *ovary*. After fertilization the *ovary* develops with a *fruit* containing the seeds.

Bayou American; an area of swamp or marsh adjacent to, or forming an offshoot of, a lake or river.

Biome A major ecological community comprising animals and plants and covering a large area *eg* Savanna, Temperate forest, Tundra.

Boreal The northern regions *eg* Boreal forest.

Carnivore Flesh eating animal. More specifically, a member of the mammal order Carnivora.

Climax Plant community which has evolved to reach its most stable composition. A condition of equilibrium under prevailing environmental conditions.

Clone A community of identical organisms all having derived asexually from a single parent.

Deciduous Term applied to plants which shed their leaves during part of the annual cycle.

Detritus Organic debris derived from the decomposition of animal and plant matter.

Dimorphism The existence of two morphologically different forms of the same organism.

Ecology The study of relationships within animal and plant communities and between the community and the physical environment.

Ecosystem A biological community existing within and interacting with, a physical environment, *eg* a forest, a lake.

Endemic Confined to a particular geographical area or region. Typical of that region.

Ephiphyte A plant which lives attached to another plant for support. Not parasitic; the epiphyte derives nutrients from the atmosphere and from accumulated detritus.

Fauna The animal population of a given area.

Flora The plant population of a given area.

Gestation Period of development between fertilization and birth in a viviparous animal.

Gymnosperm Primitive class of plant in which the *ovules* are carried unprotected on the surface *eg* conifers.

Halophyte Plant which has a high tolerance of saline soils. Typical vegetation of salt-marsh and estuaries.

Herbivore Plant-eating animal.

Hibernation Winter dormancy occurring in temperate and polar animals, particularly reptiles and amphibians. Metabolism slows down and, in mammals, temperature falls to that of the surroundings.

Humus Decomposed animal and plant material forming the organic component of soil.

Indigenous Plant or animal native to a particular area *ie* not introduced.

Insectivorous Insect eating.

Invertebrate Having no backbone *eg* snails, starfish, insects, sponges. One of the two major divisions of the Animal Kingdom *cf* Vertebrates.

Macroscopic Visible to the naked eye.

Mandible The lower jaw in vertebrates or one of the pair of mouth parts in insects.

Maxilla The bones of the upper jaw, carrying the teeth in vertebrates. One of the pair of mouth parts in insects.

Metabolism General term for the chemical processes occurring within a living organism *eg* conversion of food into energy.

Parasite An organism which lives on, or within, another *host* organism from which it derives its nutrient requirements.

Pelagic Inhabiting the upper masses of an aquatic environment.

Photosynthesis The creation of organic compounds and oxygen from water and carbon dioxide by means of light energy absorbed by chlorophyll in green plants.

Prehensile Having the ability to grasp

Spore Single or multi-celled reproductive body which is expelled from the parent body and develops into an adult.

Succulent A xerophytic plant capable of storing moisture within the tissues; often has thick fleshy leaves.

Symbiosis Two unrelated organisms living in a close mutually advantageous, relationship *eg* food, protection.

Viviparous Giving birth to live young.

Xerophyte Broad group of plants able to withstand extreme arid conditions either by storage of water *see* *succulents*, or by recovery from partial desiccation *eg* desert shrubs.

Key to birds of the Amazon
Illustration on page 49

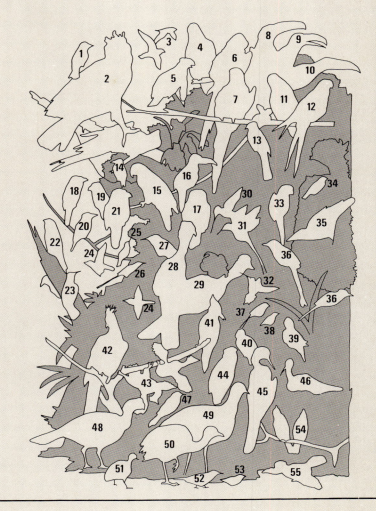

1. Blue cotinga
2. Harpy eagle
3. Swifts
4. Blue and yellow macaw
5. Ornate umbrella bird
6. Hyacinthine macaw
7. Scarlet macaw
8. Toco toucan
9. Sulphur-breasted toucan
10. Cuvier's toucan
11. Channel-billed toucan
12. Swallow-tailed kite
13. Bar-tailed trogon
14. Bellbird
15. Amazon parrot
16. Green aracari
17. Spectacled owl
18. Striolated puffbird
19. Toucan barbet
20. White-necked puffbird
21. White-eared puffbird
22. Pottoo
23. Barred woodcreeper
24. Great kiskadee
25. White-throated jacamar
26. Paradise jacamar
27. Great jacamar
28. Piping guan
29. Spix's guan
30. Sword-billed hummingbird
31. Topaz hummingbird
32. Sooty-capped hermit hummingbird
33. Golden conure
34. Scarlet tanager
35. Chestnut-headed oropendola
36. Motmots
37. Blue-backed manakin
38. Gould's manakin
39. Amazon kingfisher
40. Ruddy quail dove
41. Chestnut woodpecker
42. Hoatzin
43. Young hoatzin
44. Collared forest falcon
45. Anhinga
46. Sunbittern
47. Nunbird
48. Great razor-billed curassow
49. Horned screamer
50. White-winged trumpeter
51. Variegated tinamou
52. Striated earth creeper
53. Black-bellied gnat-eater
54. Cock-of-the-rock females
55. Cock-of-the-rock male

Acknowledgments

A great many individuals and institutions have given invaluable help and advice during the preparation of the Atlas of World Wildlife. The publishers wish to extend their thanks to them all, and in particular to the following:

General acknowledgments

Dr. J. Rzoska, International Biological Programme. Donald Jay, Centre for Overseas Pest Research. Nigel Bonner, Lowestoft Seals Research Unit. The Trustees of the British Museum (Natural History) and in particular the Departments and Libraries of Botany, Entomology, Reptiles, Mammals, Birds, Fish, Arachnids, Crustacea. The Zoological Society of London, in particular Mr. R. Fish, librarian. Dr. Barbara Weir, Wellcome Institute of Comparative Physiology. Dr. B. Hamilton, Imperial College Field Station. Philip Wayre, Ornamental Pheasant Trust. Dr. I. W. Whimster, St. Thomas's Hospital. Mr. H. C. Gilson and Dr. G. Fryer, Freshwater Biological Association, Windermere. Dr. Wood, Biology Department, New University of Ulster. Institute of Biology. Royal Entomological Society. Nature Conservancy. The Wellcome Medical Museum. The Fauna Preservation Society. The British Trust for Ornithology. The Royal Society for the Protection of Birds. Dr. Kalkmann, Rijksherbarium, Leiden, Holland. Miss Kabuye, East Africa Herbarium, Kenya. Mr. L. Brown, Karen, Kenya. Mr. R. L. Hughes, University of Reading. Prof. A. N. Duckham, Department of Geography, University of Reading. Ian Player, Natal Parks Board, Pietermaritzburg, S. Africa. David Shelldrick, Tsavo National Park, Kenya. The Embassies and Cultural Offices of Australia, New Zealand, Canada, Japan, South Africa, Malagasi, U.A.R., U.S.A., U.S.S.R., Netherlands, India, Pakistan, Finland, Denmark. The National Library of Science and Invention. Westminster Library. Camden Library. The Entomological Research Institute, Ottawa, Canada. Librairie Hachette, Paris. Museum of South Australia. The Liverpool Museum, in particular Dr. John Gray and Mr. G. Hancock. Mr. D. M. Boston and staff of the Horniman Museum. Dr. D. P. Wilson. Dr. M. Fogden. Dr. Zimmerman. Mr. R. Croll, Scientific Liaison Officer, Australia House. Dr. Tazieff, Centre National de la Recherche Scientifique, Paris. Commonwealth Institute of Entomology. Commonwealth Institute of Animal Breeding and Genetics. Natural Environmental Research Council. Animal Virus Research Institute. Institute of Geological Sciences, London. Royal Geographical Society. Prof. Allan Keast, Queens University, Ontario, Canada. Mr. E. S. Brown. Miss L. Nappe. Institute for Ocean and Mountain Studies, Nevada, U.S.A., J. Louveaux, L'Institut de la Recherche Agronomique, Paris. National Geographical Society. Anglo-Chilean Society. Slimbridge Wildfowl Trust. Marine Biological Association of the United Kingdom. Food and Agriculture Organization (U.N.). Survival Service Commission, International Union for the Conservation of Nature. Geological Survey and Museum. Harvard Centre for Population Studies, U.S.A. Laboratory of Molecular Evolution, Miami, Florida. H. Kacher, Max Planck Institute, Seewiesen, Germany. Dr. M. P. Harris. Dr. G. W. Potts. Mr. A. Johnson, Camargue Biological Research Station, France. Greenwich Maritime Museum. The National Trust. National Coal Board. Royal Botanic Gardens, Kew. Whipsnade Zoo. The London Zoo. British Veterinary Association. C.S.I.R.O., Canberra, Australia. Prof. P. M. Sheppard, University of Liverpool. Grahame Dangerfield, Wildlife Breeding Centre. National Institute of Oceanography. Smithsonian Institution, Washington. Dr. D. J. Shorthouse, Canberra College, Australia. Scott Polar Research Institute, Cambridge. British Antarctic Survey. Dr. Kostermann, Botanic Gardens, Bogor, Indonesia. World Wildlife Fund, Morges, Switzerland. Jersey Wildlife Preservation Trust.

Special acknowledgments

Weidenfeld & Nicolson Ltd. for seaweeds diagram (p. 36) and lumpsucker food diagram (p. 164) *after* Kai Olsen, in Gunnar Thorson *Life in the Sea*, (World University Library, 1971).

The Controller, Her Majesty's Stationery Office and the Hydrographer of the Navy, for permission to use B.A. Chart No. 1323 as base for Chincha Islands map (p. 56.)

Evans Bros. Ltd. (London) for permission to reproduce the compilations of National Parks and Reserves from *Man and Wildlife* by Dr. C. A. W. Guggisberg. (pp 192–197.)

Index prepared by Brenda Hall M.A. Registered indexer of the Society of Indexers.

Illustrators

Key maps throughout by Susan Casebourne and Jonathan Gill Skelton. Page symbols by Jim Bulman and Richard Lewis. Camera-ready copy by Trevor Gordon Giles/ Planned Artwork. Illustrators are credited by descending order of the base line of each illustration. Where two or more illustrations lie on the same base line credits read left to right. Illustrator's agents are credited as follows:–

Artist Partners/AP; Creative Presentation/CP; Freelance Presentation/FP; Garden Studios/GS; Linden Artists/LA; John Martin Artists/JMA; N.E. Middleton/NEM: Tudor Art/TA.

10–11 Bryon Harvey **12–13** Bryon Harvey **14–15** Richard Lewis (globes), Richard Orr/LA **16** Richard Lewis **17** John Davis **18–19** Peter Barrett/AP **20–21** Rand McNally and Co. (relief map), Richard Lewis **22** Roy Flooks, Nicholas Hall, John Davis, Nicholas Hall **23** Nicholas Hall, John Davis, Nicholas Hall **24** David Baxter/GS, John Barber/TA **25** John Davis, John Rignall/ LA, Michael Woods **26** Joyce Tuhill **27** Joyce Tuhill, Richard Orr/LA (line illustrations) **28** Vana Haggerty, Richard Orr/LA **29** Richard Orr/LA, Vana Haggerty, Vana Haggerty, John Davis, Vana Haggerty, Edward Wade **30** John Davis, John Davis, Harry Titcombe, John Barber/ TA **31** Peter Hayman (birds) and Chris Woolmer, Michael Woods, John Barber/TA **32** Michael Woods (line illustrations), David Baxter/GS **33** John Davis, Edward Wade, Edward Wade, Michael Woods, Edward Wade **34** John Davis (diagrams), Edward Wade, John Rignall/ LA **35** Hatton, Tony Swift **36** Roy Flooks, Roy Flooks, Bryon Harvey **37** John Davis, Vana Haggerty, Michael Woods **38–39** Peter Barrett/AP **40–41** Rand McNally and Co. (relief map), Richard Lewis **42–43** Diagram (map), Charles Pickard/CP, John Davis (diagrams) **44** Richard Lewis (map) and Sean Milne/GS, Robert Jefferson/NEM, Sean Milne/GS, Malcolm McGregor **45** Michael Woods, Edward Wade, Edward Wade, Richard Lewis, John Rignall/LA **46** Richard Lewis, Edward Wade, Malcolm McGregor **47** David Nockels, Harry Titcombe, Edward Wade, Richard Lewis **48** Richard Orr/LA **49** Ken Lilly, John Davis **50** Richard Lewis, John Barber/TA **51** Anthony Maynard, Brian Hargreaves, Brian Hargreaves **52** Richard Orr/LA, Harry Titcombe **53** Sean Milne/GS, John Rignall/ LA, Richard Orr/LA, Richard Orr/LA **54** Richard Lewis (diagram) and Edward Wade **55** Jonathan Gill Skelton, Malcolm McGregor, John Barber/TA, Vana Haggerty, Anthony Maynard **56** Ron Hayward Associates, Sean Milne/GS (line drawings), John Davis **57** Malcolm McGregor, Malcolm McGregor, Richard Lewis, Ian Garrard/LA, Malcolm McGregor, John Davis, Edward Wade **58–59** Peter Barrett/AP **60–61** Rand McNally and Co. (relief map), Richard Lewis **62** Vana Haggerty (line drawings) and John Bavosi, Richard Lewis, Ian Garrard/ LA, Richard Lewis **63** Peter Barrett/AP **64** Colin Rose, Harry Titcombe **65** Harry Titcombe, Ken Farrell/JMA, Vana Haggerty **66** Mike Ricketts, Richard Orr/LA, Ken Farrell/JMA **68** Colin Rose, Charles Pickard/CP, Richard Lewis **69** David Nockels, Charles Pickard/CP **70** Nicholas Hall, Malcolm McGregor **71** John Bavosi, John Norris Wood, John Rignall/LA **72** Mike Ricketts, Peter Barrett/ AP **73** Chris Howell Jones/FP **74** Colin Rose, Richard Lewis **75** Anthony Maynard, Ken Farrell/JMA, David Cook, Anthony Maynard, Colin Rose **76** Richard Lewis, Anthony Maynard **77** Richard Lewis, Jim Bulman, John Barber/TA, Edward Wade **78** Edward Wade, Diagram **79** Ian Garrard/LA, Ian Garrard/LA, Anthony Maynard **80** David Cook and John Davis **81** Peter Hayman, Jonathan Gill Skelton, Harry Titcombe, Harry Titcombe, Edward Wade **82** John Davis, Peter Barrett/AP, Sean Milne/GS, Michael Woods **83** Sean Milne/GS, Edward Wade **84–85** Peter Barrett/AP **86–87** Rand McNally and Co. (relief map), Richard Lewis **88** Richard Lewis (map and diagrams) and Harry Titcombe, Richard Orr/LA **89** Richard Lewis **90** Richard Lewis, John Barber/TA, John Barber/TA, Tony Swift **91** John Davis, Patrick Cox/ GS **92** Richard Lewis (key maps), Bryon Harvey, Richard Orr/LA, Joyce Tuhill, John Rignall/LA **93** Richard Lewis (key maps), Richard Orr/LA, Joyce Tuhill, Richard Lewis, Joyce Tuhill, Richard Orr/LA **94** Sheridon Davies, Richard Lewis, Sheridon Davies, Bryon Harvey, Bryon Harvey **95** Richard Lewis, John Barber/TA, John Barber/TA, John Barber/TA, Sheridon Davies **96** John Davis (diagrams) and Joyce Tuhill, Richard Lewington/GS **97** Joyce Tuhill and John Davis (diagrams), Michael Woods, Edward Wade **98** Richard Lewis, Richard Orr/LA, Tony Swift **99** Richard Orr/LA, John Davis (panel) **100** Nicholas Hall **101** Sheridon Davies (line drawings), Bryon Harvey, Edward Wade, Richard Lewis **102–103** Peter Barrett/AP **104–105** Rand McNally and Co. (relief map), Richard Lewis, John Davis, Michael Woods **107** Michael Woods, John Davis, Richard Orr/LA, Bryon Harvey **108** Edward Wade, John Davis **109** Michael Woods, John Davis, Michael Woods (line drawings) and Richard Lewis, Richard Lewis, John Barber/TA **110** John Davis (diagrams), Sheridon Davies, Nicholas Hall **111** John Davis, David Thorpe, John Rignall/LA **112** John Davis (diagrams), Michael Woods, Bryon Harvey **113** Centrum Graphics, Michael Woods, Joyce Tuhill, John Davis, Joyce Tuhill **114** Joyce Tuhill, Richard Lewis, Nicholas Hall **115** Ron Hayward Associates (map), Joyce Tuhill, David Nockels, David Thorpe, Edward Wade **116–117** Peter Barrett/AP **118–119** Rand McNally and Co. (relief map), Richard Lewis **120** John Davis, Richard Lewis, John Davis, Richard Orr/LA **121** John Barber/TA, Sean Milne/GS, Michael Woods, Edward Wade **122** Richard Lewis, Malcolm McGregor, Charles Pickard/CP **123** Malcolm McGregor, Richard Orr/LA, John Rignall/LA, Michael Woods **124** Patrick Cox/GS, Michael Woods, David Baxter/GS (plants) and Richard Lewis **125** Patrick Cox/GS, Michael Woods, Sean Milne/GS, Ian Garrard/LA, Ian Garrard/LA **126** Michael Woods, Sean Milne/GS, Edward Wade **127** Richard Orr/LA (line drawings), John Davis **128** Edward Wade **129** Michael Woods (line drawings) and Richard Lewis, Richard Lewis, Michael Woods, Edward Wade, Richard Orr/LA, Michael Woods **130** Richard Lewis, Michael Woods, Charles Pickard/CP **131** Richard Lewis, John Barber/TA, John Davis, Edward Wade (line drawing) and Richard Lewis, Richard Lewington/GS **132–133** Peter Barrett/AP **134–135** Rand McNally and Co. (relief map), Richard Lewis **136** John Davis (diagram) and Peter Barrett/AP, Richard Orr/LA **137** John Davis, Nicholas Hall **138** Richard Lewis, Sean Milne/GS, Edward Wade **139** John Davis, John Rignall/ LA, John Davis, Susan Casebourne (chart), Michael Woods **140** Ron Hayward Associates, Edward Wade **141** John Davis, John Davis, Richard Lewis, Michael Woods, Edward Wade **142** Nicholas Hall, Nicholas Hall, Richard Lewis **143** Richard Lewis, Nicholas Hall (panel), Richard Orr/LA, Richard Orr/LA, Michael Woods **144** Richard Orr/LA, Michael Woods **145** Richard Lewington/GS, Richard Lewis, Sean Milne/GS (line drawings), John Rignall/LA **146** Richard Lewis (map and diagram) and Ian Garrard/LA, Richard Lewis, Roger Lincoln **147** Richard Lewis, Richard Orr/LA, Richard Lewis, Sean Milne/GS, John Barber/TA, David Baxter/GS **148** Richard Lewis, Nicholas Hall, Ian Garrard/LA, Nicholas Hall **149** John Davis (diagrams), Richard Lewington/GS, (colour illustrations), Nicholas Hall (line drawings) **150** Diagram, Richard Lewis, Harry Titcombe, Harry Titcombe **151** Harry Titcombe (line drawings), John Barber/TA, Peter Barrett/AP **152** Richard Orr/LA, Richard Lewis (diagrams), Richard Orr/LA **153** John Rignall/LA, Richard Lewis, Richard Orr/LA, Nicholas Hall (panel) **154** Patrick Cox/GS, Edward Wade, Richard Lewis, Richard Lewington/GS **155** Richard Lewis, Peter Barrett/AP, John Davis, Jane Neville, John Davis, John Davis **156** Richard Lewis, Diagram, John Davis, Diagram **157** Ron Hayward Associates, John Rignall/LA, Edward Wade, Richard Lewis, Michael Woods, Susan Casebourne **158** Richard Lewis, Richard Lewis, John Barber/TA, John Barber/TA, John Davis **159** John Davis, John Davis (diagram) and John Barber/TA, Michael Woods (line drawings) **160** Alan Iselin, John Rignall/LA **161** Nicholas Hall, Richard Lewis, Nicholas Hall, Nicholas Hall, Richard Lewis, Sean Milne/ GS, Richard Lewis, Sean Milne/GS **162** Diagram, Richard Lewis, Bryon Harvey, Richard Lewis, Bryon Harvey **163** Bryon Harvey, Dave Carl Forbes, John Barber **164** Dave Carl Forbes **165** Sheridon Davies (line drawings), John Davis **166** Richard Lewis, Edward Wade, Dave Carl Forbes **167** Michael Woods, Dave Carl Forbes (panel) **168** Dave Carl Forbes, Jill Norman **169** Richard Lewis **170** Richard Lewis, Ron Hayward Associates, Bryon Harvey **171** Nicholas Hall (line drawings) and Richard Lewis **172** John Davis, Nicholas Hall, John Davis **173** John Barber/TA, David Thorpe, Edward Wade **174** Richard Orr/LA, Richard Lewis (globes), David Thorpe **175** Joyce Tuhill, Richard Orr/LA, Michael Woods, Richard Lewington/GS, Richard Orr/LA, Michael Woods **176** Peter Barrett/AP, Sheridon Davies **177** Centrum Graphics, Diagram, Centrum Graphics, John Davis (diagram), John Barber/TA (line drawings) **178** Diagram, Diagram, Richard Lewis **179** Centrum Graphics, Harry Titcombe, Edward Wade **180** Centrum Graphics, Michael Woods, Richard Lewis **181** Harry Titcombe, John Davis **182** John Davis **183** Richard Orr/LA, Michael Woods, Richard Orr/LA, Michael Woods **184** Jim Bulman **185** Centrum Graphics, Richard Lewis, Centrum Graphics, Richard Orr/LA **186–191** Richard Orr/LA (line drawings), Susan Casebourne (maps) **192–197** maps by Susan Casebourne and Colin Rose **198–202** Richard Orr/LA.

Photographers

Photographers are credited by descending order of the base line of each photograph. Where two or more photographs lie on the same base line credits read left to right. Photographers agents and other sources are credited as follows :–

Animal Photography/AP ; Ardea Photographics/A ; Associated Freelance Artists/AFA ; Australian News & Information Bureau/ANIB ; Canada Wide/CW ; Bruce Coleman Ltd/BC ; Colorific/C ; Colour Library International/CLI ; Susan Griggs/SG ; Institute of Geological Sciences/IGS ; Jacana/J ; Keystone/K ; Frank W. Lane/FL ; Magnum/M ; Natural History Photographic Agency/NHPA ; Natural Science Photos/NSP ; New Zealand National Publicity/NZ ; Okapia/O ; Oxford Scientific Films/OSF ; Photo Aquatics/PA ; Pictor/P ; Picturepoint/Pp ; Paul Popper Ltd/PP ; Rapho Guillumette/RG ; Royal Geographical Society/RGS ; Seaphot/S ; Spectrum/SP ; WeHa Photo/WH ; World Wildlife Fund/WWF ; Diana Wylie/DW ; Zoological Society/ZS.

1 H.D. Dossenbach **2–3** A. Woo fitt/SG **4–5** H.D. Dossenbach/NSP **6–7** A. Woolfitt/SG **8–9** A.G. Leutscher/NSP **16** N.R. Lightfoot, D. Freeman/NSP, M.P.L. Fogden **17** N.R. Lightfoot, T. Willock/A, M & R Borland/BC, W.H. Stribling **20** J.A. Kraulis/CW **22** J.A. Kraulis/CW, Castleton Enterprises, W.H. Stribling, J. Van Wormer/BC, R. Allin/BC, D. Robinson/BC **23** W.H.Stribling, W.H. Stribling, N.R. Lightfoot, K, K **24** C.J. Ott/BC, L.L. Rue/BC, OSF, N.R. Lightfoot, M. Weave-/SG **25** K. Fink/A, E.T. Jones/A, L.L. Rue/BC, J.A. Kraulis/CW, Reflejo/SG **26** J. Van Wormer/BC, T. Willock/A, T. Willock/A, E. Park/BC, K. Fink/A **27** J. Simon/BC, J. Van Wormer/BC, J. Simon/BC, J. Van Wormer/BC, J. Simon/BC, N.R. Lightfoot **28** J. Tallon/NHPA, N.A.M. Verbeek, B. Coleman/BC **29** T. Willock/A, A. Woolfitt/SG, P.J.K. Burton/NSP H.L. Rivarola/BC, CLI, R. Allin/BC, J. Tallon/NHPA, K. Fink/A **30** W.H. Stribling, W.H. Stribling, J. Simon/BC, F. Bruemmer, D. Dickins **31** R Allin/BC, D. Robinson/BC, W.H. Stribling, L.L. Rue/BC, T. Willock/A, N.R. Lightfoot, N.R. Lightfoot **32** K. Fink/A, R. Kinne/BC, H. Albrecht/BC, N.R. Lightfoot, E. Burgess/A, P **33** S.C. Bisserot/BC, C.J. Ott/BC, E. Burgess/A, J. Van Wormer/BC, D. Holyoak/NSP, C.J. Ott/BC, C.J. Ott/BC **34** J.S. Wightman/A, P, D. Burgess/A, J. Norris Wood **35** J. Norris Wood, N.R. Lightfoot, J. Norris Wood, J. Norris Wood **36** J. Tallon/NHPA, J. Burton/BC **37** F. Bruemmer, H.D. Dossenbach/NSP, R.T. Peterson/BC, F. Bruemmer **40** M. Freeman/NSP **44** FL, D. Robinson/BC, C.A. Walker/NSP **45** J. Vasserot/J, P. Morris, C.A. Walker/NSP **46** D. Botting **47** T. Mcrrison/K, H.D. Dossenbach, F. Erize **48** B. Hamilton/RGS, O, F. Erize, F. Erize **50** P.H. Ward/NSP **51** O, P.H. Ward/NSP, P.H. Ward/NSP **52** F. Erize, B. Coleman/BC, F Erize **53** F. Erize, F. Erize, F. Erize, H.D. Dossenbach, F. Erize, F. Erize, K. Williams **54** C. Capa/M **55** H.D. Dossenbach, C. Waterson, F. Erize **56** H.D. Dossenbach, F. Erize/BC, K. Fink/A **57** H.D. Dossenbach, T. Morrison/K, H.D. Dossenbach **60** I. Bennett/NSP **62** K. Dowson/NSP **63** A. Bannister/NHPA, G. Cubitt, CLI, R.M. Bloomfield/A, G. Dangerfield **64** G. Dangerfield, G. Dangerfield, H.D. Dossenbach, L.J. Parker **65** K, PP, P. Morris, L. Norström **66** S.A. Thompson/AP, H. Munzig/SG, H. Munzig/SG **67** H.D. Dossenbach, H.D. Dossenbach, H.D. Dossenbach, A. Bannister/NHPA **69** H. Albrecht/BC, H. Albrecht/BC, O **70** P.H. Ward/NSP, M.P.L. Fogden, O, M.P.L. Fogden **71** PP, P.H. Ward/NSP, P.H. Ward/NSP, A. Bannister/NHPA **72** S. Trevor/BC **73** J. Raines **74** A. Christiansen, J. Raines, A. Christiansen **75** L.H. Brown, L.E. Perkins, CLI **76** G. Rodger/M **77** A. Bannister/NHPA, Standard Oil Co. (N.J.), J. Burton/BC **78** A. Bannister/NHPA **79** E.L. Button, A. Bannister/NHPA, G.L. Maclean, G. Newlands/NSP, A. Bannister/NHPA, G. Newlands/NSP **80** Pp **81** G. Dangerfield, P. Morris, B. Nievergelt, H.D. Dossenbach, P. Morris, M.P. Price **83** G. Cubitt, G. Cubitt, R. Zanatta/AFA **86** W.S. Paton **89** R.K. Murton/BC, M. Berger/WH, P, H. Reinhard/BC **90** WH, M. Berger/WH **91** R. Fletcher/NSP, U. Berggren, WH, T. Suominen, R. Fletcher/NSP **92** WH, A.J. Sutcliffe/NSP **93** W.S. Paton, R. Bille/NHPA, T. Suominen, J. Fernandez/B. Coleman, P **94** A.C. Waltham, D.C. Williamson, S.C. Bisserot/BC **95** FL, R. Kinne/BC, J. Burton/BC **96** P, OSF, H. Angel **97** U. Berggren, A. Christiansen, G. Kinns/NSP **98** G.A. Matthews/NSP, A. Christiansen, I. Trap Lind **99** WH, E. Ashpole, WH, R. Bille/NHPA, WH **100** H. Angel, W.S. Paton, H. Angel, K.J.V. Carlson **101** H. Angel, S.C. Bisserot/BC, J, P. Scoones/S, D.P. Wilson, H. Angel, H. Angel **104** T. Suominen **106** D. Botting, A. Christiansen, D. Botting, T. Suominen **107** A. Christiansen **108** Novosti, A. Christiansen, M.D. England/A, WH **109** F. Vollmar/WWF, Milwaukee/J, Bannikov/O **110** RG, A.G. Bannikov, A.G. Bannikov, Petocz/WWF, E. Hosking, K.H. Hyatt/NSP, T. Suominen **113** Visage/J, F. Vollmar/WWF, Schraml/J, G. Kinns/AFA, E.H. Rao/NHPA, B. Coleman/BC **114** A. Christiansen/FL **115** Schraml/J, K. Takano/BC, F. Vollmar/WWF, I. Neufeldt/A, I. Neufeldt/A **118** E.H. Rao/NHPA **120** J. Simon/BC **121** M.D. England/A, P. Jackson/BC, P. Pfeffer, M.D. England/A, E.H. Rao/NHPA, S. Dalton **122** G.A.C. Herklots, K. Fink/A **123** E. Hosking, P. Pfeffer **124** M.P.L. Fogden, M.P.L. Fogden, P. Pfeffer **125** M.P.L. Fogden, M.P.L. Fogden, M.P.L. Fogden, M.P.L. Fogden, P. I. Polunin/NHPA, A.S. Cheke, PP **126** PP, P. Pfeffer, K. Bong Heang, I. Polunin/NHPA, P. Pfeffer **127** P. Pfeffer **128** P. Morris, NHPA, F.G.H. Allen, P. Pfeffer, W.S. Chin & O.T. Kwee/I. Polunin/NHPA **129** P. Pfeffer, E. Hosking, E.H. Rao/NHPA, P. Pfeffer **130** E.H. Rao/NHPA, P. Jackson/BC, H. Reinhard/BC, Van Kooles/J, E.H. Rao/NHPA **134** D. Baglin/NHPA **136** F. Erize, C. Frith/NSP **137** S & K. Breeden, G. Pizzey/BC **138** Montage E. Lindgren, A. Eddy/NSP, I. Polunin/NHPA **139** E. Lindgren, G. Pizzey/BC, D. Baglin/NHPA, H.A.E. Lucas/SP, R. Taylor/A **140** E. Ashpole, S & K Breeden, G. Chapman **141** S & K. Breeden, ANIB, H & J. Beste/A, A.G. Wells, D.J. Shorthouse, S & K. Breeden **142** C. Frith/NSP, S & K. Breeden, N. Chaffer, O **143** F. Erize, F. Erize, H & J. Beste/A **144** E. Ashpole, J.A. Grant/NSP **145** T. Newbery, B. Smith, V. Serventy/BC, SP, G. Chapman, ANIB, SP **146** S & K. Breeden, PP, N. Chaffer, S & K. Breeden, F. Erize, N. Chaffer **147** N. Chaffer, F. Erize, N. Chaffer **148** A. Gray/NSP, M.F. Soper, G. Chance, Pp **149** M.F. Soper, H. Beste/A, NZ, NZ, M.F. Soper, M.F. Soper, M.F. Soper/BC, G.J.H. Moon/FL **150** D.P. Wilson, D.P. Wilson **151** T. Larsen/WWF, J.J.M. Flegg, F. Bruemmer, J.J.M. Flegg, J. Good/NHPA, H.D. Dossenbach **152** C.J. Ott/BC, B. Hawkes/NHPA, F. Bruemmer **153** D. Robinson/BC, T. Callaghan, D. Botting, C.J. Ott/BC **154** C.J.Ott/BC, P, B. Hawkes/NHPA **155** K.J.V. Carlson, A. Christiansen, W.H. Stribling, C.J. Ott/BC **156** W. Taylor, R.I. Lewis Smith **157** B. Hawkes/NHPA, D.W.H. Walton, R.I. Lewis Smith, R.I. Lewis Smith, O.H.S. Darling **158** R.I. Lewis Smith, W. Taylor, W. Taylor **159** R.I. Lewis Smith, W.N. Bonner, R.I. Lewis Smith **160** F. Erize/BC, R.M. Laws, V.W. Spaull, R.I. Lewis Smith **161** M.F. Soper, D.W.H. Walton, R.M. Laws, W.L.N. Tickell, W.L.N. Tickell **162** OSF, H. Tazieff **163** IGS **164** D.P. Wilson, Carre/J, D.P. Wilson **165** D.P. Wilson, D.P. Wilson, A. Bannister/NHPA, OSF, H. Angel, P, OSF, PP **166** J, J. Burton/BC, J. Fraser/S **167** D.P. Wilson, D.P. Wilson, J. Lewis/FL, Sundance/J, P. Morris, H. Angel, P **168** P, A. Power/BC, PA, V. Taylor/A, V. Taylor/A, A. Power/BC **169** A. Power/BC **170** H.D. Dossenbach, S.A. Thompson/AP, E. Hosking, Solarfilma, Solarfilma **171** E. Hosking, A. Hutson/NSP, H. Angel, S.A. Thompson/AP **172** H.D. Dossenbach, J & D. Bartlett/BC, A. Warren/A, H.D. Dossenbach, S.A. Thompson/AP, J & D. Bartlett/BC **173** R. Zanatta/AFA, H.D. Dossenbach, J & D Bartlett **174** A. Hutson/NSP, A.W. Diamond, A. Hutson/NSP, P. Johnson/NHPA, A. Hutson/NSP **175** H.D. Dossenbach, H. Schultz/BC, S & K. Breeden **176** S. Gooders/A, J. Moss/C, Pp, T. Carr/C **177** S. Gooders/A **178** Pp, Pp, A. Woolfitt **179** J. Moss/C, Sp, Pp, J. Moss/C, Pp, SP **180** B.L. Sage/NSP, K, H. Frawley/NSP **181** L.R. Beynon, Daily Telegraph, B.L. Sage/NSP, Pp, Pp, R.S. Scorer/DW **182** M. Lyster/ZS, N. Duplaix-Hall, N. Duplaix-Hall, N. Duplaix-Hall **183** N. Duplaix-Hall, M. Lyster/ZS, N. Duplaix-Hall, M. Lyster/ZS **184** T. Spencer/C, T. Carr/C, T. Spencer/C, T. Carr/C, D. Shelldrick, D. Shelldrick, M. Boulton/BC **185** D. Botting, B.L. Sage, B.L. Sage, D. Botting, D. Botting, S. Brown/NSP, S. Brown/NSP **192** J. Van Wormer/BC, D, Freeman/NSP, S. Gooders/A

Sources of reference

A vast number of books, journals and scientific papers have been referred to during the preparation of the Atlas of World Wildlife. The publishers wish to express their thanks to the authors and in particular to the following :

Books

Abercrombie M., Hickman C.J., Johnson M.L., (1972) *A Dictionary of Biology* Penguin. Allen G.M., *The Mammals of China and Mongolia, Natural History of Central China, Vol. II* (1938-40) American Museum of Natural History, New York. Allen G.M., (1939) *Bats* Harvard University Press, Cambridge, Mass., USA. Allen G.M. *Extinct and Vanishing Mammals of the Western Hemisphere with the Marine Species of all the Oceans* Spec. Publ. Amer. Int. Wildlife Protection No. 11. Allen G.M., (1939) *A Checklist of African Mammals* Bull. Mus. Comp. Zool. Harv. 83 :1–763. American Museum of Natural History (1970) *Field Studies in Natural History* Van Nostrand. Ansell W.F.H., (1960) *Mammals of Northern Rhodesia* Lusaka, Zambia. Arnold A.F., (1968) *The Sea-Beach at Ebb-Tide* Dover Publications Inc., New York. Arthur A.F., (1968) *Survival, Man and his Environment* English University Press. Asdell S.A. (1946) *Patterns of Mammalian Reproduction* Constable. Austin O., (1961) *Birds of the World* Hamlyn. Axelrod H., & Vorderwinkler W., (1968) *Encyclopaedia of Tropical Fishes.*

Backhouse K.M., (1969) *Seals* Arthur Barker Limited, London. Bailey V., (1971) *Mammals of the Southeastern United States* Dover Publications Inc., New York. Bakker E.S., (1971) *An Island Called California* Berkley University Press, California. Borradaile L.A., Potts F.A., Eastham L.E.S., and Saunders J.T., (1963) *The Invertebrata* Cambridge University Press, Cambridge. Barret J., and Younge C.M., (1958) *Collins Pocket Guide to the Seashore* Collins. Barrington E.J.W., (1967) *Invertebrate Structure and Function* Nelson. Bates M., (1964) *The Land and Wildlife of South America* Life Nature Library, Time Inc., New York. Beamish T., (1970) *Aldabra Alone* G. Allen & Unwin, London. Bell R.H.V., (1971) *A Grazing Ecosystem in the Serengeti* Scientific American 225(1) :86–93. Bellairs A., (1970) *The Life of Reptiles* Weidenfeld & Nicolson, London. Bere R M., (1962) *The Wild Mammals of Uganda and neighbouring regions of East Africa* Longmans, London. Berg L.S., (1950) *Natural Regions of the U.S.S.R.* The Macmillan Co., New York Houghton Mifflin, Boston. Bergamini D., (1964) *The Land and Wildlife of Australia* Life Nature Library, Time Inc., New York. Berry J.B., (1966) *Western Forest Trees* General Publishing Company, Toronto. Bertin L., (1967) *Larousse Encyclopaedia of Animal Life* Hamlyn Publishing Ltd, London. Bigalke R.C., (1958) *On the present status of ungulate mammals in South West Africa* Mamalia 22(3) :478–497. Bond J., (1971) *Birds of the West Indies* Collins. Borradale L.A., Potts F.A., Eastham L.E.S., & Saunders, (1963) *The Invertebrata* Cambridge University Press. Bourliere F., (1964) *The Land and Wildlife of Eurasia* Life Nature Library, Time Inc., New York. Bridges E.M., (1970) *World Sails* Cambridge University Press. Brocklehurst H.C., (1931) *Game Animals of the Sudan, their Habits and Distribution* Gurney & Jackson, London. Brown L., (1965) *Africa: A Natural History* Hamish Hamilton, London. Brown L.H., (1965) *Ethiopian Episode* Country Life, London. Brown L.H., and Amadon D., (1968) *Eagles, Hawks and Falcons of the World* Country Life, London. Bucherl W., & Buckley E., (1971) *Venomous Animals and Their Venoms Vol. 3 Venomous Invertebrates.* Academic Press, New York. Buechner H.K., (1960) *The Bighorn Sheep in the Unites States, its past, present and future* Wildlife Monogr. No. 4 :1–174. Burt W.H., (Ed) (1971) *Antarctic Pinnipedia* Antarctic Research Series vol. 18. American Geophysical Union of the National Academy of Sciences – National Research Council. Burton M., (1962) *Dictionary of the World's Mammals* Museum Press Ltd, London. Burton M., (1962) *Systematic Dictionary of the Mammals of the World* Museum Press. Burton M., & Burton R., (Ed) *Wildlife Encyclopaedia* B.P.C. London. Bustard R., (1970) *Australian Lizards* Collins, Sydney.

Cabrera A., (1957–61) *Catalogo de los maniferous de America del sur* 2 vols. Buenos Aires. Caldwell L.K., (1972) *In Defense of Earth: international protection of the biosphere* Indiana University Press. Carlquist S., (1965) *Island Life* Natural History Press, New York. Carpenter C.R., (1938) *A Survey of Wild Life Conditions in Atjeh, North Sumatra, with special reference to the Orang-Utan* Netherlands Committee for International Nature Protection, Amsterdam Communication No. 12. Carr A., (1957) *The Turtle: a natural history of sea turtles* Cassell, London. Carter G.F., (1964) *Man and the Land* Holt Rinehart & Winston, New York. Carter T.D., Hill J.E., and Tate G.H.H., (1945) *Mammals of the Pacific World* MacMillan Company, New York. Carthy J.D., (1965) *Animal Behaviour* Aldus Books, London. Chandler A.C., & Read C.P., (1961) *Introduction to Parasitology* John Wiley, New York. Chasen F.N., (1940) *A Handlist of Malaysian Mammals* Bull. Raffles Mus. No. 15. Child J., (1969) *Australian Alpine Life* Lansdown Press, Melbourne. Clegg J., (1963) *Pond and Stream Life* Blandford Press. Cloudsley-Thompson J.L., *The Zoology of Tropical Africa* Weidenfeld & Nicholson. Cole S., (1965) *Races of Man* British Museum, London. Cole S., (1965) *Mato Grosso* George Rainbird. Comber L.C., *Biology of the Modern World* Thames & Hudson. Conant R., (1958) *A Field Guide to Reptiles and Amphibians* Houghton Mifflin, Boston. Coon C.S., (1966) *The Living Races of Man* Jonathan Cape, London. Cott H.B., (1961) *Scientific results of an inquiry into the ecology and economic status of the Nile Crocodile* (*Crocodilus niloticus*) *in Uganda and Northern Rhodesia* Trans. Zool. Soc. London 29. Crandall L.S., (1964) *The Management of Wild Mammals in Captivity* University of Chicago Press. Critchlow K., (1972) *Into the Hidden Environment* George Phillips, London.

Darling F.F., (1960) *An Ecological Reconnaissance of the Mara Plains in Kenya Colony*. The Wildlife Society, Wildlife Monogr. No. 5. Darling F.F., (1960) *Wild Life in an African Territory* Oxford University Press, London. Darling F.F., (1970) *Wilderness and Plenty* The Reith Lectures 1969. British Broadcasting Corporation, London. Darling F.F., and Milton J.P. (Eds) (1966) *Future Environments of North America: Transformation of a continent* The Natural History Press, Garden City, New York. Darling F.F., & Boyd J.M., (1969) *The Highlands and Islands* Collins, London. Darlington P.J., (1957) *Zoogeography: The geographical distribution of animals* John Wiley & Sons Inc. New York. Davey K., (1969) *Australian Desert Life* Lansdown Press, Melbourne. Davis D.D., (1964) *The Giant Panda, a morphological study of evolutionary mechanisms* Fieldians : Zoology Memoirs 3 :1–339. Deacon G.E.R., (1962) *Oceans* Paul Hamlyn. Decary R., (1950) *La Fauna Malgache. Son role dans les croyances et les usages indigenes* Payot, Paris. Dekeysem P.L., (1955) *Les mammiferos de l'Afrique Noire Francaise* Dakar IFAN Initiations Africaines No. 1 IFAN. Dennis A., (1964) *Cats of the World* Constable & Co. Dennler de la Tour G., (1954) *The Vicuna* Oryn 2(6) :347–352. Dorst J., (1970) *Before Nature Dies* Collins, London. Dorst J., & Dandelot P., (1970) *A Field Guide to the Larger Mammals of Africa* Collins, London. Dorst J., (1967) *South America and Central America: a natural history* Hamish Hamilton, London. *The World of Nature Series* Doubleday & Co., New York. Duckham A.N., & Masefield G.B., (1970) *Farming Systems of the World* Chatto & Winders, London. Dupuy A., (1967) *Repartition actuelle des especes menacees de l'Algerie* Bull.Soc.Sci.nat.phys.Maroc. 47(3 & 4) :355–386.

Edberg R., (1969) *On the Shred of a Cloud* University of Alabama Press. Eibl-Eibesfeldt I., (1960) *Galapagos. Die Arche Noahs im Pazific* Piper Verlag, München. Eisenberg J.F., & Gould E., (1970) *The Tenrecs: a study in mammalian behavior and evolution* Smithsonian Contributions to Zoology No. 27, Washington. Ellerman J.R., and Morrison-Scott T.C.S., (1951) *Checklist of Palearctic and Indian Mammals* (1758–1946) British Museum (Natural History), London. Ellerman J.R., Morrison-Scott T.C.S., and Hayman R.W., (1953) *Southern African Mammals* (1758–1951) : a reclassification British Museum (Natural History), London. Ellis E.A., (1965) *The Broads* Collins. Elton C., (1942) *Voles, Mice and Lemmings* Clarendon Press, Oxford. Elton C.S., (1958) *The Ecology of Invasions by Animals and Plants* Methuen, London. Esau K., (1955) *Plant Anatomy* Wiley International Edition, New York. Everett H., (1970) *Living Trees of the World* Thames & Hudson.

Falla R.A., Sibson R.B., & Turbott E.G., (1966) *A Field Guide to the Birds of New Zealand* Collins, London. Fittkau E.J., (Eds) (1969) *Biogeography and Ecology in South America* 2 vols. W. Junk, The Hague. Fisher, J., Simon N., & Vincent J., (1969) *The Red Book: Wildlife in Danger* Collins, London. Fitzsimons V., (1963) *The Namib Wild Life* 17 (3) :215–227. Flerov K.K., (1960) *Fauna of USSR – Mammals* – Vol. 1 No. 2 : *Musk deer and deer* Moscow, Academy of Sciences of the USSR Institute of Zoology, N.S.55, 1952. English edition by the Israel Program for Scientific Translations, published for the National Science Foundation and Smithsonian Institution. Fowells H.A., (1965) *Silvics of Forest trees of the United States* US Department of Agriculture, Washington DC. Frith H.J., & Calaby J.H., (1969) *Kangaroos* Hurst, London and Cheshire, Melbourne. Funaioli U., & Simonetta A.M., (1966) *The mammalian fauna of the Somali Republic: status and conservation problems.* Monitore zool. ital. 74 (Suppl.) :285–347.

Garretson M.S., (1938) *The American Bison* New York Zoological Society, New York. Gee E.P., (1964) *The Wild Life of India* Collins, London. Geist V., (1971) *Mountain Sheep: a study in behavior and evolution* University of Chicago Press. Gillet H., (1965) L'oryx algazelle et l'Addax au Tchad *Terre et la Vie* 112(3) :257–272. Gilliard E.T., (1969) *Birds of Paradise and Bower Birds* Weidenfeld & Nicolson, London. Douglas J., (1952) *Tropical Fish* Paul Hamlyn, London. Gould J., (1933) *The Mammals of Australia* Taylor & Francis, London. Gould J., & Rutgers A., (1967) *Birds of Australia* Methuen. Grandidier G., & Petit G., (1932) *Zoologie de Madagascar* Societe d-Editions Geographiques, Maritimes et Coloniales, Paris. Greenway J.C., (1958) *Extinct and Vanishing Birds of the World* Spec. Publ. Amer. Comm. Int. Wildlife Protection No. 13. Greenwood P.H., (1963) *A History of Fishes* Ernest Benn Ltd. Grimwood I.R., (1960) *Notes on the Distribution and Status of some Peruvian Mammals* Spec. Publ. Amer. Comm. Int. Wildlife Protection No. 21. Groves C.P., (1970) *Gorillas* Arthur Barker Ltd. Guggisberg C.C.W., (1970) *Man and Wildlife* Evans Brothers. Guggisberg C.A.W., (1972) *Crocodiles: their natural history, folklore and conservation* David & Charles, Newton Abbot. Guggisberg C.A.W., (1961) *Simba* Howard Timmins, Cape Town. Guiler E.R., (1960) *Marsupials of Tasmania* Tasmanian Museum and Art Galery. Hobart.

Hachisuka M., (1953) *The Dodo and Kindred Birds, or the Extinct Birds of the Mascarene Islands* H.F. & G. Witherby, London. Halstead B.W., (1959) *Dangerous Marine Animals* Cornell Maritime Press, Maryland. Hardin G., (Introduced) (1968) *39 Steps to Biology* Scientific American, California. Hardy A., (1956) *The Open Sea: The World of Plankton* Collins, London. Harris C.J., (1968) *Otters: A Study of the Recent Lutrinae* The World Naturalist Series, Weidenfeld & Nicolson, London. Harrisson B., (1962) *Orang-utan* Collins, London. Harrison D.L., (1968) *The Mammals of Arabia* Ernest Benn, London. Harrison M.L., (1969–71) *The Life of Mammals* 2 vols. Weidenfeld & Nicolson, London. Harrison Matthews L., (Ed) (1970) *The Whale* Allen & Unwin, London. Harthoorn A.M., (1970) *The Flying Syringe* Geoffrey Bles, London. Hatt R.T., (1959) *The Mammals of Iraq* Misc. Publ. Mus. Zool. Univ. Mich. No. 106. Hedberg I., & Hedberg O., (Eds) (1968) *Conservation of Vegetation South of the Sahara* Acta Phytogeographica Suecica 54, Stockholm. Heinzel H., Fitter R., Parslow J., (1972) *The Birds of Britain and Europe* Collins, London. Hershkovitz P., (1966) *Catalog of Living Whales* Smithsonian Institution, Bulletin 24b. Hickey J.J., (Ed) (1969) *Peregrine Falcon Populations – their Biology and Decline* University of Wisconsin Press. Hill W.C.O., (1953–62) *Primates: comparative anatomy and taxonomy* 5 vols. Edinburgh University Press. Higgins L.G., & Riley N.D., (1970) *Field Guide to the Butterflies of Britain and Europe.* Holcik J., & Mihalik J., (1970) *Freshwater Fishes* Spring Books, London. Holdgate M.W., (1970) *Antarctic Ecology* Academic Press, London & New York. Holmes A., (1944) *Principles of Physical Geology* Nelson, London. Hoogerwerf A., (1970) *Udjung Kulon: the land of the last Javan Rhinoceros.* Howse P.E., (1970) *Termites* Hutchinson, London. Huxley A., (1967) *Mountain Flowers* Blandford Press, London. Huxley J. et al (1963) *The Conservation of Nature and Natural Resources in Ethiopia* Unesco, Paris.

Ingle R., (1969) *A guide to the seashore* Hamlyn, London. Ingold C.T., (1961) *The Biology of Fungi* Hutchinson, London. Iredale T., & Troughton E. le G., (1934) *A check-list of the mammals recorded from Australia* Mem. Aust. Mus. 6 :1–122. I.U.C.N., (1966) *Red Data Books* Vol 1–5 Lausanne, Switzerland.

Jaeger E.C., (1957) *The North American Deserts* Stanford University Press. Jaeger E., (1961) *Desert Wildlife* Stanford University Press, California. Jenkins A.C., (1970) *Wildlife in Danger* Methuen & Co. Ltd., London. Johnson A.W., (1965) *The Birds of Chile and Adjacent Regions of Argentina, Bolivia and Peru* Buenos Aires 2 vols. Jolly A., (1966) *Lemur Behavior: a Madagascar field study* University of Chicago Press. Keast A., (1966) *Australia and the Pacific Islands: a natural history* Hamish Hamilton, London, Keble M.W., (1965) *The Concise British Flora in Colour* George Rainbird Ltd. Kenyon K.W., (1969) *The Sea Otter in the Eastern Pacific Ocean* North American Fauna No. 68 Bureau of Sport Fisheries and Wildlife, Washington. Keradec Y., (1971) *The Sea* Editions Minerva, Geneva. Kies C.H.M.H., (1936) *Nature Protection in the Netherlands Indies* Spec. Publ. Amer. Comm. Int. Wildlife Protection No. 8. King J.E., (1964) *Seals of the World* British Museum. Koford C.B., (1957) *The Vicuna and the puna* Ecol. Monogr. 27 :153–219. Kozhov M., (1963) *Lake Baikal and its Life* W. Junk, The Hague. Krisna K., & Weesner F.M., (1970) *Biology of Termites* Academic Press. Kuroda N., (1939) *Distribution of mammals in the Japanese Empire* J. Mammal 20(1) :37–50.

Lack D., (1971) *Ecological Isolation in Birds* Blackwell. Lack D., (1954) *The Natural Regulation of Animal Numbers* Clarendon Press, Oxford. Lamb E. & B., (1969) *Pocket Encyclopaedia of Cacti* Blandford. Laurie A., (1972) *The Living Oceans* Aldus Books. Laurie E.M.O. & Hill J.E., (1954) *List of Land Mammals of New Guinea, Celebes and Adjacent Islands* (1758–1952) British Museum (Natural History), London. Lawick-Goodall J. van, (1971) *In the Shadow of Man* Collins. Lay D.M., (1967) *A Study of the Mammals of Iran resulting from the Street Expedition of* 1962–63 Fieldiana : Zoology. Leopold A.S. (1959) *Wildlife of Mexico: the game birds and mammals* University of California Press, Berkeley. Leopold A.S. & Darling F.F., (1953) *Wildlife in Alaska: an ecological reconnaissance* Ronald Press, New York. Lewis J.R., (1964) *The Ecology of Rocky Shores* The English Universities Press Ltd. Littlewood C. & Ovenden D.W., (1969) *The World's Vanishing Animals* W. Foulshame & Co Ltd. Lockley R.M., (1970) *Man Against Nature* Andre Deutsch, London. Lorenz K., (1966) *On Aggression* Methuen, London. Luther H., & Rzoska J., (1971) *I.B.P. Handbook No. 21 Project Aqua* Blackwell Scientific Publications. Lydekker R., (1926) *The game animals of India, Burma, Malaya and Tibet* Rowland Ward, London, 2nd Edition. Lyneborg L.,(1971) *Mammals in Colour* Blandford Press.

Mcgraw-Hill, (1967) *Our Living World of Nature* Mcgraw-Hill, New York. Mackintosh N.A., (1946) *The Natural History of Whalebone Whales* Biol. Rev. 21(2) :60–74. Mandahl-Barth G., (1966) *Woodland Life* Blandford Press. Mani M.S., (1962) *Introduction to High Altitude Entomology* Methuen & Co Ltd. Matthews G.V.T., (1955) *Bird Navigation* Cambridge University Press. Matthews L.H., (1971) *The Life of Mammals Vol. II* Weidenfeld & Nicolson. Mazak V., (1965) *Der Tiger, Panthera tigris Linnaeus, 1758.* Die Neue Brehm-Bücherei, Heft 356. Mech L.D., (1970) *The Wolf: the ecology and behaviour of an endangered species* Published for the American Museum of Natural History, The Natural History Press, Garden City. Medway, Lord (1965)

continued on page 208